IFIP – The International Federation for Information Processing

IFIP was founded in 1960 under the auspices of UNESCO, following the First World Computer Congress held in Paris the previous year. An umbrella organization for societies working in information processing, IFIP's aim is two-fold: to support information processing within its member countries and to encourage technology transfer to developing nations. As its mission statement clearly states,

> *IFIP's mission is to be the leading, truly international, apolitical organization which encourages and assists in the development, exploitation and application of information technology for the benefit of all people.*

IFIP is a non-profitmaking organization, run almost solely by 2500 volunteers. It operates through a number of technical committees, which organize events and publications. IFIP's events range from an international congress to local seminars, but the most important are:

- The IFIP World Computer Congress, held every second year;
- Open conferences;
- Working conferences.

The flagship event is the IFIP World Computer Congress, at which both invited and contributed papers are presented. Contributed papers are rigorously refereed and the rejection rate is high.

As with the Congress, participation in the open conferences is open to all and papers may be invited or submitted. Again, submitted papers are stringently refereed.

The working conferences are structured differently. They are usually run by a working group and attendance is small and by invitation only. Their purpose is to create an atmosphere conducive to innovation and development. Refereeing is less rigorous and papers are subjected to extensive group discussion.

Publications arising from IFIP events vary. The papers presented at the IFIP World Computer Congress and at open conferences are published as conference proceedings, while the results of the working conferences are often published as collections of selected and edited papers.

Any national society whose primary activity is in information may apply to become a full member of IFIP, although full membership is restricted to one society per country. Full members are entitled to vote at the annual General Assembly, National societies preferring a less committed involvement may apply for associate or corresponding membership. Associate members enjoy the same benefits as full members, but without voting rights. Corresponding members are not represented in IFIP bodies. Affiliated membership is open to non-national societies, and individual and honorary membership schemes are also offered.

Gurpreet Dhillon   Bernd Carsten Stahl
Richard Baskerville (Eds.)

Information Systems – Creativity and Innovation in Small and Medium-Sized Enterprises

IFIP WG 8.2 International Conference, CreativeSME 2009
Guimarães, Portugal, June 21-24, 2009
Proceedings

 Springer

Volume Editors

Gurpreet Dhillon
Virginia Commonwealth University, School of Business
301 W. Main Street, Richmond, VA 23284-4000, USA
E-mail: gdhillon@vcu.edu

Bernd Carsten Stahl
De Montfort University, Department of Informatics
The Gateway, Leicester LE1 9BH, UK
E-mail: bstahl@dmu.ac.uk

Richard Baskerville
Georgia State University, Department of Computer Information Systems
Atlanta, GA 30302-4015, USA
E-mail: baskerville@acm.org

CR Subject Classification (1998): D.2, D.1, J.1, K.8, K.7.2

ISSN   1868-4238

ISBN-13   978-3-642-10193-9   e-ISBN-13   978-3-642-02388-0

springer.com

© International Federation for Information Processing 2010
Printed in Germany

Printed on acid-free paper

Preface

This book contains the collection of papers presented at the conference of the International Federation for Information Processing Working Group 8.2 "Information and Organizations." The conference took place during June 21–24, 2009 at the Universidade do Minho in Guimarães, Portugal. The conference entitled "CreativeSME - The Role of IS in Leveraging the Intelligence and Creativity of SME's" attracted high-quality submissions from across the world.

Each paper was reviewed by at least two reviewers in a double-blind review process. In addition to the 19 papers presented at the conference, there were five panels and four workshops, which covered a range of issues relevant to SMEs, creativity and information systems.

We would like to show our appreciation of the efforts of our two invited keynote speakers, Michael Dowling of the University of Regensburg, Germany and Carlos Zorrinho, Portuguese coordinator of the Lisbon Strategy and the Technological Plan.

The following organizations supported the conference through financial or other contributions and we would like to thank them for their engagement:

- International Federation for Information Processing
- University of Minho, Portugal
- Portuguese Coordinator for the Lisbon Strategy and Technological Plan
- Multicert - Serviços de Cerificação Electrónica, S.A
- Virginia Commonwealth University, USA
- De Montfort University, UK
- Georgia State University, USA

Finally, we wish to thank a number of individuals who supported the conference in a variety of ways. Isabel Ramos and João Álvaro de Carvalho as local Organizing Chairs made huge efforts in facilitating and preparing the conference. Ravneet Gill helped with copyediting and formatting of the proceedings.

May 2009

Gurpreet Dhillon
Bernd Carsten Stahl
Richard Baskerville

Organization

Program Committee

Carl Adams	University of Portsmouth, UK
Rosio Alvarez	Lawrence Berkeley National Laboratory, USA
Liêda Amaral	Secretaria da Receita Federal Ministerio da Fazenda, Brazil
Olivier Braet	Vrije Universiteit Brussel, Belgium
Deborah Bunker	The University of New South Wales, Australia
Kevin Crowston	Syracuse University, USA
Dirk Deschoolmeester	Vlerick Leuven Gent Management School, Belgium
Kevin Desouza	University of Washington, USA
William Dixon	Ernst & Young, LLP, USA
António Dias Figueiredo	Universidade de Coimbra, Portugal
José Esteves	Instituto de Empresa, Spain
Andreas Gadatsch	Bonn-Rhein-Sieg University of Applied Sciences, Germany
Rui Gomes	Instituto Politécnico de Viana do Castelo, Portugal
Noriko Hara	SLIS Indiana University, USA
Juhani Iivari	University of Oulo, Finland
George M. Kasper	Virginia Commonwealth University, US
Julie Kendall	Rutgers University, USA
Kenneth Kendall	Rutgers University, USA
Frank Land	The London School of Economics and Political Science, UK
Karl Reiner Lang	City University of New York, USA
Tors J.Larsen	Norwegian School of Management, NO
Linda Levine	Software Engineering Institute of CMU, USA
Filomena Lopes	Universidade Portucalense, Portugal
Carolina Machado	University of Minho, Portugal
Paula Morais	Universidade Portucalense, Portugal
Michael Myers	University of Auckland, New Zealand
Jan Pries-Heje	Roskilde University, Denmark
Nancy Russo	Northern Illinois University, USA
António Lucas Soares	Faculdade de Engenharia da Universidàde do Porto e INESC Porto, Portugal
Dave Wastell	Nottingham University, UK

Table of Contents

Challenges in Managing Knowledge

Organizational Challenges, Power and Politics

Creativity and Intelligence in Small and Medium Sized Enterprises: The Role of Information Systems

Gurpreet Dhillon[1], Bernd Carsten Stahl[2], and Richard Baskerville[3]

[1] Virginia Commonwealth University, USA
[2] De Montfort University, UK
[3] Georgia State University, USA

1 Introduction

The work in this volume examines the real-world confluence of several concepts that are too often studied in isolation from each other. Research into creativity too rarely considers the presumed ability of smaller organisations to contribute a large proportion of the innovations introduced into the practical information systems field. There is also far too little research that addresses the notion that smaller organisations more intelligently manage their creativity and innovation, not only in the organisational signal products, but also in structures and processes found in smaller organisations.

Because organisational design itself benefits from creativity and innovation (Cooper, 2000), smaller organisations have an inbuilt advantage purely in terms of the smaller scope required to reorganise in innovative ways to match their projects and products. This smallness in scope also applies to the information systems of smaller organisations. Quite simply, innovations in smaller organisations do not have to diffuse their innovations as far as in larger organisations. The diffusion can happen faster, and without the need for complex knowledge management structures and agencies needed to make innovation happen in larger organisations (Datta, 2007). This difference in scope means that many of the innovation diffusion principles so important to larger organisations and markets, such as those of Rogers (Rogers, 2003), are less critical for the internal creativity of smaller organisations.

There are many good reasons for paying attention to small and medium sized enterprises (SMEs). They constitute the majority of organisations, they are a main source of employment, they are flexible, and they are often creative and innovative. Despite their economic and theoretical relevance, business-oriented research tends to concentrate on large and multinational organisations. This is true in business studies in general as well as in the field of information systems. That state of affairs is unfortunate because SMEs hold the potential to develop novel uses of technology and integrate them in interesting ways in their business processes. At the same time, information systems have the potential to make uniquely important contributions to SMEs, for example by extending markets or providing resources that individual SMEs typically do not have. These IFIP WG 8.2 proceedings aim to address the lacuna in the literature and provide a current discussion of the relationship between SMEs, creativity and innovation, and information systems.

The 8.2 working group is known for its innovative use of theory and its successful attempts to overcome the weaknesses of established approaches. The 2009 conference

G. Dhillon, B.C. Stahl, and R. Baskerville (Eds.): CreativeSME 2009, IFIP AICT 301, pp. 1–9, 2009.

in Portugal aimed at applying those non-conventional ideas to the area of SMEs. The organisers and chairs were curious to find out how the IFIP WG 8.2 community would take to a set of concrete business challenges that emerge from the context of IS use in SMEs. These proceedings show that the community has been successful in incorporating extant literature and developing it in new and interesting ways. In order to discuss the contributions of the authors in a coherent way, we have identified key challenges related to SME research. The papers pertaining to these have been grouped into the sections outlined below. In each section some novel ideas emerged, as we will show in this introduction.

- *Creativity and innovation challenges.* While many SMEs are creative and innovate partly because of their need to remain competitive, effective use of information and communication technologies helps in defining newer opportunities and sustainability in a marketplace.
- *Challenges in ensuring effective governance.* While it is easy for many SMEs to overlook the need for effective governance, the importance and need for good internal controls cannot be overstated. Often in the race to achieve high growth, internal control mechanisms get overlooked.
- *Challenges in managing knowledge.* Because of the very nature of SMEs, knowledge management is a challenge. The owner-manager structure of most SMEs introduces a lot of variance in managing knowledge and in satisfactory sharing of experiences.
- *Organizational challenges, power and politics.* Cultural differences amongst SMEs and power and politics of managing small firms pose numerous challenges. Foremost of these is the inter-organizational relationship and the role information systems play in facilitating or hindering progress.

2   Creativity and Innovation Challenges

It is a cliché that big organizations are bureaucratic and cumbersome, whereas smaller ones are more agile and flexible. There is nevertheless some truth in the observation that small companies can quickly react to changes in their environment and they can easily be redirected to take advantage of changing markets. This flexibility and maneuverability allows them to profit from creativity and be innovative. These views are probably not contentious. They nevertheless leave open a range of questions. What do we mean by these concepts? The definition of an SME is unproblematic because there are political views on this that are relatively straightforward, even if they may leave shades of grey. The situation is significantly different for the other terms involved. What happens if we undertake an analysis of terms such as creativity or innovation? Can one really allude to creativity with regard to an organization? And what does this have to do with technology?

Boden (2000) suggests that the core of creativity is always an idea. If creativity is linked to ideas then one can reasonably argue that the bearers and originators of ideas, namely human beings, can also be creative. It is much less simple to argue, however, that organizations can be the originators of ideas. Creativity of organizations is therefore presumably something different than creativity of individuals. It may be a property of an organization or an emerging characteristic of the way in which a social system develops. But where does this leave technology and specifically information systems? Lessig (2001) has argued that the development of the Internet was characterised by creativity and innovation. This leaves open the question whether it was the technology *per se* that had aspects of creativity or whether it was creativity of the individuals involved in building the technology that led to its phenomenal success.

Despite these and other conceptual uncertainties, innovation is often described as a consequence of creativity and is seen as an essential component of organizations in fast-moving markets. Creativity is seen as a key to organizational survival. While creativity and innovation are certainly important elements, especially for SMEs, to a large extent success at being creative and innovative depends on the market conditions. The chapters in the first section are those that deal directly with the conference theme of creativity and innovation in SMEs. They use a variety of approaches and theoretical lenses to increase our understanding of relevant phenomena.

A fitting starting chapter for this book is the one on "SMEs, IT, and the Third Space: Colonization and Creativity in the Theatre Industry" by Kendall and Kendall. This chapter draws on the rich tradition of social theory employed in the IFIP WG8.2 and uses this tradition to shine an interesting light on a very specific instance of small and medium sized enterprises, namely the management of theatres. Drawing on the concept of the third space, they develop a narrative of knowledge transfer, in particular the transfer of culture. This novel view of knowledge transfer is contextualised with the more established literature on knowledge management. As a result, the authors draw conclusions that allow a better understanding of the mechanisms that allow exchange between large commercial and small not-for-profit theatres.

Valcárcel offers a case study from Germany in her "SME 2.0: Roadmap towards Web 2.0-based Open Innovation in SME-Networks - A Case Study Based Research Framework" This case study is premised on the economic importance of SMEs and their well-known limitations with regards to innovations. The idea she develops and that reoccurs in a number of chapters in this book is that SMEs need to find ways of collaborating in order to ensure that they can make use of innovation. The specific interest of this chapter is the role that Web 2.0 technologies can play in facilitating such collaboration. The communicative features of Web 2.0 technologies are seen as a way of breaking down traditional barriers to knowledge creation and leading to open innovation. This communication can also create marketplaces, foster trust and lead to further collaboration. Valcárcel uses the findings of her case studies to develop a framework for better understanding the processes involved which also provide a basis for future research.

The following chapter on "Conducting Creativity Brainstorming Sessions in Small and Medium-Sized Enterprises Using Computer-Mediated Communication Tools" by Murthy offers a complementary view. Instead of Web 2.0 technologies, it uses computer-mediated communication tools that are in use by SMEs. These tools incorporate systems that are often related to Web 2.0 but in many instances go beyond what private individuals might use. In addition to chat and synchronous meeting facilities, these include electronic brainstorming technologies. Murthy investigates how such tools can be used for optimal results by SMEs. It derives recommendations from a set of experimental studies that require participants to use domain-specific knowledge. The resulting recommendations can be used as practical suggestions for SMEs to optimise their approach towards using brainstorming technologies.

The subsequent chapter by Nagle and Golden on "An Examination of the Disruptive Innovation Paradox: The Application of the Innovators Dilemma to SMEs" continues the theme of critical questioning of conventional wisdom concerning innovation in SMEs. The authors draw on the literature developed on paradoxes in modern organizations, in particular the innovator's dilemma. They apply a discussion developed in the context of large organisations to small and medium sized companies in order to investigate the consequences of the use of Web 2.0 technologies on multiple cases of e-learning companies. The study finds that the ability of companies to cope with the potential disruption caused by such technologies depends on the quality of their leadership which is related to the age of the organization and its risk profile.

In his chapter on "Two paths for innovation: Parvenu or Pariah", Bryant aims to cast doubt on much of the conventional wisdom concerning entrepreneurial creativity and innovation. Drawing on a rich background of economics and philosophy of science, he shows that the debate surrounding entrepreneurship is dangerously one-sided. Creativity and innovation are not and should not be limited to market interaction. Other aspects of society show aspects of creativity and innovation, and might indeed lead the way for commercial organisations to follow. Decades of unbridled market worship have, however, rendered these views relatively irrelevant, to the disadvantage of society in general, but also of businesses themselves. Bryant uses some of the current economical woes to support his argument that a broader understanding of innovation and creativity will be conducive in overcoming some of the societal issues we face.

Following from Bryant's critical evaluation of current discourses, Venable offers a similarly critical view of methodology in his "Identifying and Addressing Stakeholder Interests in Design Science Research: An Analysis Using Critical Systems Heuristics". He builds on the current debate surrounding design science research and explores the role that Critical Systems Heuristics can play in moving design science research forward. This chapter stands in the tradition of critical research that has often been the centre of attention in IFIP WG 8.2 work but it combines this critical tradition with an eminently practical intention. Using the ideas of Critical Systems Heuristics, Venable points out that design cannot and should not be exclusively geared towards the interests of those in power but that the whole range of stakeholders affected by a technology under development should be considered. The critical angle allows him to develop a philosophically and theoretically grounded framework that can inform stakeholder development in systems design. It addresses the difficult question of the representation of stakeholders who are unable to participate directly and introduces the idea of using witnesses in design processes.

Mamede and Santos address the question of creativity and innovation in IS from a very different angle. By commenting on "An Architecture for a Creative Innovation System", they move the focus away from human and organizational issues and open the discussion to include the question whether information systems themselves can be creative. The concept of creativity, they explore, is that of random word generation, also called brute thinking, which aims to develop new angles of problems that allow users to come up with new answers. The authors then go on to develop the architecture of a process that would allow the implementation of a system, fulfilling their definition of a creative information system.

The theme of creativity in systems design is then developed in a different direction in the last chapter of the section. Conboy, Wang and Fitzgerald look at current research on creativity in agile systems development. Their starting point is the proposition that agile methods foster creativity and there is lack of empirical research to support this assumption. The development of agile methods has been driven by the practitioner community, leaving questions of rigorous validation open, particularly in the area of SMEs. Using the theoretical lens of creativity theory, the authors discuss the extent to which creativity in agile projects actually occurs. The results of the study show gaps in current knowledge and points towards promising areas of further research.

3 Challenges in Ensuring Effective Governance

Governance relates to organizational processes dealing with internal control and ensuring effective utilization of information. Well-designed information systems are central to good governance. In many ways, correctness in system specification and the related organizational design helps ensure the establishment of good responsibility and accountability structures, which are central to good governance. In terms of SMEs, there are a number of governance challenges that need to be carefully understood and articulated. Some of these are addressed by the papers in this conference.

Devos, Landeghem and Deschoolmeester in their paper "IT Governance in SMEs: Trust or control?' start with the observation that it is futile to apply theories of IT governance which are relevant to large firms to SME's as the realities of both are diametrically opposite. In their paper, the authors try to address the very pertinent question of the reasons and manifestation of outsourced information system failure (OISF) in an SME. They try to bring this to light by qualitative and positivistic IS case study research, which delves into the on-ground scenario of as many as eight different cases of IS projects. They offer the premise that in SME's, theory of trust, fairness, intuition and empathy are more relevant and provide better guidelines for IT governance. This study sheds light on an aspect which has been widely accepted, but rarely documented - that trust and personal equations are the bedrock of systematic and procedural guidelines in SME's where people are more closely aligned with each other's aspirations, personality traits and operate with much more intimacy than is possible in a large organisation. The authors validate this understanding and also advise future researchers to hone on SME's specifically in their work, instead of drawing conclusions from observations made in large firms, which are largely redundant when applied to SME's.

Mamede and Amaral in their "Methodology for Electronic Business Initiatives" point out that the traditional systems development methodologies displays weaknesses that render them problematic, in particular for small and medium-sized organizations. In order for SMEs to make use of the potential offered by web-based technology, methodologies more specifically aimed at their needs are required. The authors use the chapter to argue for a methodology that is centred on the implementation lifecycle of electronic business in SMEs.

Taking this argument forward are Huang, Zmud and Price in their paper "IT Governance Practices in Small and Medium-Sized Enterprises: Recommendations from an Empirical Study", where they also contend that there is much documentation available about the concentration, flow and direction of decision-making in large organizations. While the need for better understanding of the same contexts in SME's is palpable, documentation and observation about these is lamentably lacking in the case of SME's. This leaves the field wide open for researchers, who must track, observe and record the shape and flow of decisions in small firms where the decision making authority is often confined to a group of individuals comprising the top management. The interesting facets of decision making, which this phenomenon results in, have been recorded through interviews with top managers from three SME's. Based on the insights gained from these interactions, the authors make thought provoking and pertinent recommendations, which invite further scrutiny and follow-ups.

It is indisputable that the high winds of current economic realities have greatly buffeted the mechanisms, which ensure effective governance across organisations. These have been more sharply felt in small firms where cost cutting has directly impacted IT processes by eroding into the investments on IT and decrease in the manpower running IT processes. There is little debate that this factor has caused a lot of disruption in the overall efficiency, market worthiness and competitiveness of the enterprise. In such a scenario, Albayrak and Gadatschhave tackled this pressing issue by presenting a reference model for IT controlling, "Life cycle Model for IT Performance Management: A reference model for small and medium enterprises". This model has the potential to bail out many a small firm embroiled in arbitrary cost cutting. It is founded on a performance oriented framework which is based on that most required but increasingly rare commodity-common sense. In the present economic situation, with resources drying up, this inexhaustible and germane commodity can prevent many firms from sacrificing efficiency and performance on the altar of forced economy. The authors present their model to be used in the organizations where it is most required and likely to succeed- small and medium firms.

4 Challenges in Managing Knowledge

The definition of knowledge as true justified beliefs is often ascribed to Plato. From the perspective of the scholar who is interested in knowledge management in SMEs this definition can offer the advantage of opening up new avenues of inquiry. Rather than getting caught in the difficult question of whether knowledge can be subject to management in the first place, one can look at more established epistemological issues of truth and justification and how these are affected by a particular organizational environment, such as an SME. Knowledge management is often taken for granted as a positive option that organizations should avail themselves of. This is somewhat surprising due to the conceptual uncertainty that surrounds it and much empirical research that sheds doubt on its effectiveness. If we are to understand knowledge management better, then research is needed into the conceptual basics as well as the organizational realities where the conceptual issues are filled with life. The chapters in this section all contribute to this and use an empirical study to investigate how knowledge can be shared and managed in SMEs.

In their "Knowledge Management in Small Firms", Panyasorn, Panteli and Powell describe experiences of the use of a particular technology, Lotus Notes, as a means to facilitate knowledge management in a developing country. This study aims to provide a counterpoint to the dominant focus on larger enterprises in IS and knowledge management research. They use an interpretive approach to develop three case studies. On the basis of the data they derive from this approach, they come up with taxonomy of the use of technology in different organizational processes that leads to or constitutes management of knowledge. The authors find evidence of knowledge creation on a lower hierarchical level whereas no such evidence is found at the organizational level. According to their structure, smaller companies can make better use of some technologies such as groupware than larger ones.

The subsequent chapter by Ramos, Cardoso and Carvalho offers further empirical evidence of the relevance of knowledge management to SMEs by exploring the idea of open innovation. A recurring theme of this book, namely that SMEs find it more difficult to institute regular R&D processes due to the smaller amount of resources they can dedicate to this, is addressed using the idea of open innovation. The chapter describes a piece of action research undertaken at the University of Minho with the aim of exploring how SMEs could be enabled to benefit from innovation developed elsewhere, i.e. in universities. Transfer of knowledge and technology, while politically desired by most government runs into a range of problems, from communication and technology to intellectual property regimes. Ramos et al. describe the development of a business model and a technology platform for an innovation broker that aims to connect ideas and technologies from a university to potential SME users. The chapter offers an evaluation of this strategy which may serve as a role model for future knowledge transfer.

The final chapter in the section on knowledge management and SMEs focuses on recent technological developments, notably on web 2.0 technologies. In his "Services Supporting Knowledge Maturing in Small and Medium-Sized Enterprises", Maier discusses reasons why much-hyped communication technologies have not yet been used successfully in knowledge management in SMEs. He argues that a general theoretical interest has not translated into practical guidance on how such technologies can be employed to address the knowledge needs of SMEs. Building on the theoretical basis of a knowledge-maturing model, the chapter offers the findings of an ethnographic study into the topic. The results are conducive to practical use in that they offer organizations ways in which to engage in knowledge sharing and cooperation with the main stakeholders of the organization.

5 Organizational Challenges, Power and Politics

SMEs are faced with a number of organizational challenges. While most SMEs may be in a rather steady state, aspiring to address the needs of their customers in an effective manner, there are an increasing number of SMEs that are innovative and responsive enough to be termed 'high growth' firms. Current research into SMEs suggests that there are a number of factors that come together to ensure their relative success or failure. Owner-manager characteristics and motivation is clearly an aspect that determines the nature and scope of leadership that a given SME might have. The nature of the business also plays an important role in defining SME challenges. For instance, in the traditional manufacturing enterprise, the power of large firms over smaller ones may be a significant influencer on their performance. In other cases however SMEs may be instrumental in defining the characteristic of a new market. Business characteristics, strategic influences and external environment may also define the direction of a given SME.

There is some similarity between the challenges that a SME, large enterprise or a government institution may face. Inadequacy of systems requirement assessment and an inability to integrate various user perspectives certainly causes problems. Wenger et al (2005) discuss how the implementation of an ERP system at a SME got off to a bad start when the owner-managers began using the system as a means of organizational restructuring. This led to different kinds of power getting manifested in the enterprise. Similarly, Yan and Panteli in their paper, "The Emergence of 'Power With': The Case of a Born Global Organization" discuss various organizational power issues with respect to Born Global organizations. Born Global enterprises are defined as businesses that are global, yet local, small but with a global outreach in terms of new product and services. Such enterprises have also been referred to as lean, mean and agile.

Along similar lines Wastell, White and Broadhurst in their paper "The Chiasmus of Design: paradoxical outcomes in the e-Government reform of UK Children's Services" presents an ethnography using McLuhan's concept of chiasmus. The study presents paradoxical outcomes of the use of an Integrated Children's System, where the intended outcome gets shelved and spawns contradictory effects. The flawed design and requirements assessments, as was also observed by Wenger et al (2005), resulted in compromises in record keeping, investigative approaches and generally a high level of risk. The paper ends by proposing an alternative approach to design, based on socio-technical precepts, emphasizing the principles of minimum critical specification, user-centeredness and local autonomy.

Other related challenges include aspects of technology acceptance, particularly evaluating factors that facilitate acceptance of systems in SMEs. At times it is perhaps a difference in perceptions that leads to or inhibits uptake of a given system. While SMEs, to some extent, present a collective mind, yet there are factors that enable successful adoption or non-adoption of systems. Many entrepreneurs recognize the challenges in SMEs and information systems and hence venture into establishing such an enterprise.

This intriguing aspect also forms the basis for Mourmant's study of "How and why do IT entrepreneurs leave their salaried employment to start a SME?- A mixed methods research design". The author sets himself a tall task and one, which has gained a lot of relevance and visibility in recent times. He explores the reasons and motivations that compel salaried IT professionals to leave the comparative security of their well paid jobs and venture into the untried and turbulent waters of entrepreneurship. The author has developed a conceptual framework that begins with the explanation and rebuttal of two streams of extant research. The first of these two streams refer to the literature pertaining to entrepreneurship, which is already developed and the second alludes to the characteristics and attributes of IT industry as a whole which significantly impacts employee turnover. From the vantage point of an observer seeking to note and record the exigencies that the present economic scenario necessitates, Mourmant forwards the argument that employee turnover is directly related and proportional to prevailing market conditions. He concludes his study with suggestions for IT managers and entrepreneurs to be able to cope better in trying times.

Continuing with the theme of power and politics present in organization, Costello and Moreton present their research in "Towards a Model of Technology Adoption: A Conceptual Model Proposition". They contend that Information Communication

Technology (ICT) practitioners in small and medium firms face the same issues and challenges which their larger counterparts face. The authors prepare a case for governmental intervention, which can facilitate the adoption of better and more efficient ICT. The present weaknesses in the ICT adoption are easily discernable and a new framework is presented which promises to provide an enhanced understanding of the ways in which ICT usage can be increased and improved.

6 Epilogue

Innovation and creativity are fundamental to the survival of SMEs. We are pleased that the range of papers being presented at the IFIP 8.2 creativeSME conference offer interesting insights into these two areas. There is no doubt that innovativeness nurtures creativity, which in turns allows SMEs to define distinctive competencies that are so necessary in a competitive marketplace. As has been recognized by many authors in these proceedings, majority of the research in innovativeness and creativity has remained focused on large corporations and relatively less in the context of SMEs. We are hopeful that the IFIP 8.2 creativeSME conference will set the tone for an interesting discourse in this rather important area. Some of the papers identified significant future research directions. For instance aspects of process integrity, organizational power, politics and information security have been identified. We are certain that many such issues will be discussed at this conference and beyond.

References

Boden, M.A.: Computing and Creativity. In: Baird, R.M., Ramsower, R., Rosenbaum, S.E. (eds.) Cyberethics - Social and Moral Issues in the Computer Age, pp. 308–319. Prometheus Books, New York (2000)

Cooper, R.B.: Information technology development creativity: A case study of attempted radical change. MIS Quarterly 24(2), 245–275 (2000)

Datta, P.: An Agent-Mediated Knowledge-in-Motion Model. Journal of the Association for Information Systems 8(5), 211–287 (2007)

Lessig, L.: The Future of Ideas - the Fate of the Commons in a Connected World. Vintage, New York (2001)

Rogers, E.M.: Diffusion of Innovations, 5th edn. The Free Press, New York (2003)

Wenger, M., Dhillon, G., Caldeira, M.: ERP Implementation in Portugal: interpreting dimensions of power. In: AMCIS, Omaha (2005)

SMEs, IT, and the Third Space: Colonization and Creativity in the Theatre Industry

Julie E. Kendall and Kenneth E. Kendall

Rutgers University, School of Business-Camden, USA

Abstract. We examine how small and medium-sized, professional, nonprofit performing arts theatres in the US can improve the strategic use of information technology (IT), as well as other aspects of theatre management for large, commercial theatre productions in the West End of London and on Broadway in New York City. In this article we use the epistemology of the third space developed by Bhabha (1994) and extended by Frenkel (2008). Although both authors were discussing knowledge transfer, we use their conceptualizations to characterize and explore more deeply the transfer process of culture (and thereby useful practices and worthwhile lessons) from small and medium-sized professional, nonprofit theaters to large-scale commercial theatres. We include a discussion of Nonaka's (1991) concept of ba, and how it relates to the third space. We specifically employ the metaphor of the third space developed by Bhabha (1994) to critique and understand the verbal and nonverbal cultural transmissions between small and large theatres. One of our contributions is to use the conceptualization and metaphor of the third space to understand the complex exchanges and relationships between small to medium-sized nonprofit professional theatres and large commercial theatres, and to identify what large commercial productions can learn from nonprofit theatres from these exchanges.

1 Introduction

Small nonprofit, professional theatres often struggle to live up to the creative, financial, marketing, IT, operational standards, and audience expectations of large, commercial productions[1]. Many times theatres denoted as "Off-Broadway," or "Off-Off-Broadway" are emblematic of the 1,800 or so small, professional, nonprofit performing arts organizations in the US, while the symbolic embodiment of the commercial heart of the theatre is widely acknowledged to reside in New York City's Broadway (Conte and Langley, 2007; Volz, 2004; & Webb, 2004). In London, the symbolic commercial center of productions is the famed West End. In London, while the small and medium-sized professional theatre is called "The Fringe."

It is striking to note that small nonprofit theatres typically have as part of their mission the purpose of "transmitting culture," rather than the *assimilation* of culture, which

[1] We would like to thank the nonprofit theatre companies in New York City and Philadelphia for providing access to the administrative and artistic staff, actors, and directors as well as the producers of Broadway productions who enabled us to gather the knowledge and data for this paper. We would also like to thank The Drama League for its ongoing help and support.

otherwise might be reasonably assumed due to their small production budgets and their geographic dispersion away from the cultural capitals of New York City and London. Since the inception of the nonprofit theatre movement in the US, there has been a noticeable flow and frequency of communication among the large-scale commercial productions and small local and regional nonprofit theatres. Local companies evidence this prominently in the movement of regional acting talent up from smaller venues to larger, mostly unionized commercial productions, for higher salaries, more notoriety and career exposure, and also via the licensing of copyright works for production.

Although communication, IT practices, and cultural content are often assumed to be trickling down *from* the large, commercial productions down to the small, nonprofit theatres, the actuality is far different. Small to medium sized nonprofit theatres can teach larger, commercial productions many lessons that can enhance and improve the strategic use of ICTs (information communication technologies), artistic expression, company creativity, financing, marketing, and operations of larger companies. Indeed, theatre researchers (Conte and Langley, 2007) note that in the last 30 years or so, commercial theatres have become increasingly dependent on original theatrical works (scripts and even productions) first developed regionally in nonprofit professional theatres. Often, these nonprofit organizations have as a primary goal the transmission of culture, via accomplishment of artistic and organizational goals, whereas the for-profit, commercial houses have the goal of becoming a financial success as their chief objective.

In this article we use the epistemology of the third space developed by Bhabha (1994) and extended by Frenkel (2008). Although both were discussing knowledge transfer, we use their conceptualizations to characterize and explore more deeply the transfer process of culture (and thereby useful practices and worthwhile lessons) from small and medium-sized professional, nonprofit theaters to large, for-profit commercial productions.

For the purposes of our study, it is possible to view the commercial theatre industry, symbolized by the Broadway houses, as the imperialist or colonialist power controlling the imagination of the audience and non-Broadway producers concerning what a good production is. Often the colonizing force has control of the labor, resources, and markets of those being colonized. As such, the imperialist power assumes it possesses superior culture, morals and values to those being colonized and is thus sanctioned to formally or informally enforce controls or set standards for the colonies. The language, culture, values, morals, laws and so on are all deemed to be flowing from the imperialist group to the colonists.

The colonialist's power may not even recognize or accept the principle of imposition. In fact the colonialist may see only the positive benefits of, for example, technology transfer. An example of this is the improved transportation systems, construction methods, disease prevention, and educational systems that the colonialist introduces to the colonies.

A colonial power receives (or even demands) certain benefits of being the colonial power. In world politics this could mean the exploitation of natural resources, or at its extreme, the enslavement of people. Although the consequences in the world of theatre may not be so severe, they are real. Some of the resources that large commercial productions take from the smaller nonprofit theatre companies are shown in Figure 1.

Large-Scale
Commercial
Productions

Small to Medium
Nonprofit Professional
Theatre Companies

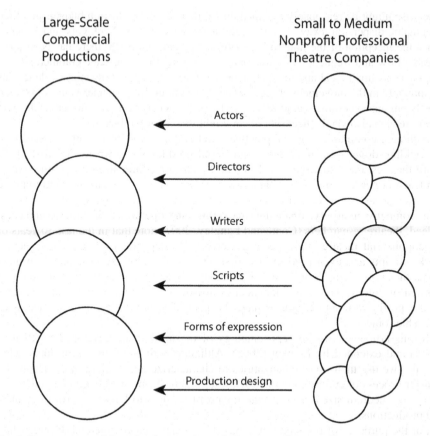

Actors

Directors

Writers

Scripts

Forms of expresssion

Production design

Fig. 1. Large commercial productions tend to take resources from small to medium nonprofit professional theatre companies

Small theatre companies provide a way for unknown actors and directors to enter the theatre world. When they become successful and are noticed, large productions hire them (even occasionally before the end of their current run) to perform or direct a large-scale production. Writers, in a similar fashion, will find that their scripts may soon be in demand on the commercial stage. Production design might be copied and forms of expression, for example ethnographic playscripts that were first performed on experimental stages have found their way to commercial productions. Two examples of this are the long-running and commercially successful musicals, *Hair* and *A Chorus Line,* which were originally developed Off-Broadway by The Public Theater.

We present this information in this way, because, a casual observer may see this transfer of resources occurring and think nothing of it. Perhaps they see movement from nonprofit to commercial venues as a career progression. However, there are more levels to reality than this somewhat superficial level. In many cases, there is some degree of a trading, mutually beneficial reality that needs to be explicitly identified.

If we adopt the use of the third space Bhabha, 1994) and Frenkel (2008), we are examining the relationship of the Broadway Theatres and the nonprofit professional theatres in the third space of mutually influential post-colonial exchanges. The use of the third space metaphor can help us understand more deeply the shaping that is going on between commercial Broadway productions and nonprofit professional theatres as they exchange ideas about the successful IT practices concerning scripts, actors, directors, forms of plays, and production design.

This paper uses the metaphor of colonialism to better understand the relationships between commercial theatre productions and small and medium nonprofit theatre companies. It is not a paper with a political mission to defend or subvert colonialism. Under no circumstances should this be considered a subaltern study or any other study about world politics. We only wish to say that colonialism is an appropriate metaphor for what happens in the business world and that, through a given lens, it is possible to see how IT can be used to be mutually beneficial to both large business and small and medium enterprises.

2   The Beginnings of the Nonprofit Professional Theatre In and Out of New York

Since the inception of the nonprofit professional theater, there has been a remarkable amount and variety of communication among large commercial productions and small and medium-sized nonprofit professional theatres. Small to medium-sized nonprofit, professional theatre can trace its origins to three or four key events and personalities, inside and outside of New York City, which proved to be the wellspring of inspiration for such theatres thereafter. Although we do not have space to recount all of the watershed artistic achievements during this period, the work of Conte and Langley (2007) is a recommended source. We are indebted to their insightful research in helping to inform and shape our view of this important era.

The beginning years span the decades from 1912 to the end of the 1940s, and they include the offering of an extremely influential playwriting class at Harvard University, the so-called defection of members of the New York Theatre Guild in New York to form the Group Theatre in 1929, the Federal Theatre Project which, along with its productions inspired the creation of the National Theatre Conference, and the establishment of important theatres and resident acting companies outside of New York such as the Cleveland Playhouse (1917); the Hedgerow Theatre of Philadelphia, established in 1923 by Jasper Deeter; the Playhouse Pittsburgh (1933); and the Barter Theatre, established by Robert Porterfield's in Abingdon, Virginia, also in 1933.

During this nascent period of 1912-1947, Conte and Langely (2007) describe the creation of the National Theatre Conference as "a collection of theatre people...who sought to reduce the dominance of commercial Broadway theatre and encourage artistically challenging work, not tied to the profit motive,"(p.115). Conte and Langely (2007) go on to summarize their observations by stating that " Much of the hope and passion engendered by the Federal Theatre Project activities (circa 1935-1939) seem to have taken root in the work of Margo Jones and her Theatre '47 in Texas, helping to inspire the subsequent proliferation of professional theatres outside of New York City. In 1947, Margo Jones' Theatre '47 was established in Texas and provided a prototype of a nonprofit organization, on which many new nonprofit theatres eventually would be based. (Conte and Langley, 2007, p. 115.) They further comment; "Jones combined the attributes of intelligence, professionalism, and dedication to artistic integrity that remain cornerstones of the majority of nonprofit theatres today," (p. 117).

The years from 1950 to 1960 in the US have been labeled as "the birth of the nonprofit theatre movement," (Conte and Langeley, p. 117). This was a time when productions Off-Broadway and Off-Off Broadway were created as a response to the rising production costs of putting on shows in commercial theatres. In 1954, Joseph Papp founded The Shakespeare Workshop, which later became known as The Public Theater (www.thepublictheater.org, 2009). The Public has since received countless awards and has transferred 52 shows from the non-profit arena to Broadway, including shows like *A Chorus Line* and *Hair*.

According to Conte and Langely, the almost 600 million dollar commitment of the Ford Foundation in 1957 was a crystallizing moment that turned the budding urges toward artistic expressionism, realism, and escape from commercialism into the "nonprofit theatre movement." For the first time the funding agency mandated that in order to receive a philanthropic gift, theatres, along with other types of "respectable" performing arts such as dance and classical music, must operate as "an ongoing, nonprofit organization." In addition it had to exist as a professional entity "both in terms of its objectives and employees," (p. 117).

Other important theatre alliances sprung up to help support and nurture the new nonprofit movement network including the Theatre Communications group (TCG) in New York City. During this same period, the actors' union, Actors' Equity, recognized that demands on actors in nonprofit professional companies would be essentially different than demands on Broadway actors, and a group of managers from the larger nonprofit theatres formed the League of Resident Theatres (LORT), which now negotiates contracts with unions on the part of theatres who are its members (Conte and Langely, 2007, p. 118). In 1965 the National Endowment for the Arts (NEA) was created via federal legislation. Federal, state and local funding for the arts became a reality, however, nonprofits (and explicitly *not* commercial productions), were the only entities eligible to receive this funding. (Subsequently strategic nonprofit and commercial alliances successfully skirted this prohibition, but more of that in an upcoming section.)

3 The Struggle for Artistic and Economic Freedom in Nonprofit Theatres

Thus, for the last forty years or so, the nonprofit small to medium-sized professional theatres either Off-Broadway, Off-Off Broadway, or dotted throughout small and medium-sized cities in the US, have forged a post-colonial identity in rebellion against and response to, the colonizing commercial force of Broadway theatre. Strong impulses surrounding longing for freedom of two kinds propel the nonprofit theatre movement freedom. These impulses embrace artistic expression and eschew staggering and oppressive production costs. Whereas colonization of artistic endeavors often means a homogenization of narrative into one mainstream voice that can fail to represent the multiple perspectives of the American story and lapses into a mainstream story that satisfies the masses but not the individual or minority, the nonprofit professional theatres provide the articulation of diverse voices, narratives, and experiences.

In this article we build on the metaphor of the third space created by Bhabha (1994) and successfully extended by Frenkel (2008). Although both were discussing knowledge transfer, we use their conceptualizations to specifically characterize and explore the transfer process of culture (and thereby best IT practices and good management lessons) to and from small and medium-sized nonprofit professional theaters to and from large, commercial theatre productions. We use the conceptual framework of Bhabha in understanding the dynamics of colonial and former colonies in a post-colonial relationship to critique and understand both the verbal (scripts, publications, marketing copy, and Web sites) and nonverbal discourse (i.e. tangible interchanges such as costumes, sets, actors, directors, and so on) as well as the combination of verbal and nonverbal acts that become known as a "production," including a script, direction, and so on used for cultural transmission between small performing arts organizations and large commercial productions.

4 Defining the Third Space for Cultural Exchanges between Nonprofit Professional Theatres and Commercial Productions

Bhabha (1994) and others are concerned with the "assumption that power relations between colonizer and colonized cannot be fully understood by focusing on the resources and structural forces that coerce the behavior of the dominated," (Peltonen, 2006, p. 530 as quoted in Frenkel, 2008). "Instead, power is seen as relational, emerging out of the mutual process of identity construction in both participants," (Frenkel, p. 926). Frenkel goes on to comment that Bhahha views knowledge as integral to the operation of power. So we see that the "formation of colonial knowledge" as emergent-being born of the "asymmetric and power-laden encounter between the colonizers and colonized, and as serving to naturalize and legitimize the colonizers' domination (Bhabha, 1994) as discussed in Frenkel (2008, p. 926).

Bhabha elaborates on the constructions of mimicry, hybridity, and the third space as they relate to the interactions of colonists and those being colonized. His comments illuminate a new way of seeing discourse between the colonized and the colonizer. Bhabha (1994) states:

> "The discourse of mimicry is constructed around an *ambivalence*; in order to be effective, mimicry must continually produce its slippage, its excess, its difference. The authority of that mode of colonial discourse that I have called mimicry is therefore stricken by indeterminacy; mimicry emerges as the representation of a difference that is itself a process of disavowal. Mimicry is, thus the sign of a double articulation: a complex strategy of reform, regulation and discipline, which 'appropriates' the Other as it visualizes power. Mimicry is also the sign of the inappropriate, however, a difference or recalcitrance which coheres the dominant strategic function of colonial power, intensifies surveillance, and possess an immanent threat to both 'normalized' knowledges and disciplinary powers." (pp. 122-123).

So colonial powers and the colonized might experience mimicry, and a state that Bhabha labels "hybridity" as well. In the case of hybridity, Bhabha departs from other colonial and post-colonial theorists. Frenkel (2008) reminds us, "In Bhabha's terms it is used to problematize the naturalized and ahistorical conceptualization of nation-hood in general and of national culture in particular," (p. 926). Bhabha instead claims that, according to Frenkel, "nations and cultures must be understood as "narrative" constructions that arise out of the hybrid interaction of competing national and cultural constituencies," (p. 927). Frenkel continues her analysis by noting that, "pro-ponents of Bhabhaian perspective would ask how the introduction of practices or technologies contributes to the reformulation of national identities and cultural be-liefs," (p. 927.) Frenkel notes that Bhabha emphasizes that individual characteristics … are subject to change and modification through experience, including the experi-ence of coping with an imposed body of foreign knowledge," (pp. 927 & 928).

5 The Third Space

In a liberating insight, that serves to free researchers and others from rigid interpreta-tions of "essentialism" and "naturalization" (Frenkel, 2008) of what happens in the exchanges between colonizers and colonies, Bhabha comes forth with a creative construction of what he calls the "third space." In the metaphor of the "third space of inbetween," (Bhabha, 1996) we find that there are no absolutes, and certainly no ab-solutes that pre-destine the direction of influence. Frenkel continues her excellent de-scription by stating," This space is not entirely governed by the laws of either ruler or ruled, and it is here that hybrid cultures are constructed that belong to neither of them but that are instead a fusion of the two," (p.928). She states, "From a Bhabhaiaian point of view, the third space is a liminal space in which the 'cutting edge of transla-tion and negotiation" between the colonizer and the colonized is to be found," (Bhabha, 1994, p. 38 as quoted in Frenkel, p. 928).

What is fascinating to us in this study is "the idea that the metaphor of the third space inspires us to think of the colonial encounter as a space of contradiction, repeti-tion, ambiguity, and the disavowal of colonial authority and as a space that does not allow for authentic and essentialist oppositional polarities," (Frenkel, p. 928). She continues by saying that, "within this metaphoric space we construct our identities in relation to these varied and often contradictory systems of meaning," (p. 928).

Nonaka and Konno (1998) are business scholars who have effectively identified and described the concept of *ba* drawn from Japanese philosophy, which might be usefully considered as somewhat akin to Bhabha's third space, "For those unfamiliar with the concept, *ba* can be thought of as a share space for emerging relationships. This space can be physical (e.g. office, dispersed business space), virtual (e.g. e-mail, teleconference), mental (e.g., shared experiences, ideas, ideals,), or any combination of them. What differentiates *ba* from ordinary human interaction is the concept of knowledge creation…. Thus, we consider *ba* to be a shared space that serves as foun-dation for knowledge creation," (Nonaka and Konno, 1998, p. 40).

Nonaka (1991; 2008) asserts that tacit knowledge resides in the individual and is evoked and evolved through individuals interactions. For Nonaka and Konno (1998) knowledge management is about humans and their relationships first, whereas IT for knowledge management is of secondary importance. Other researchers examining IT within small businesses have remarked on the importance of IT for maintaining the es-sence of small businesses, that is, their knowledge creation emanating from informal exchanges, "What surprised us in our research was how quickly internal transparency fell away and the need for an IS arose. This need translated into a requirement for the organizational IS to be used to maintain the informal cross-functional communication channels that used to be accomplished through face-to-face communication among top management, " (Street and Meister, 2004, p. 502). As noted in Pfughoeft, Rama-murthy, Soofi, Yasai-Ardekani, and Zahedi (2003), "…effective use of the Web (for small businesses) may lead to enhancement of interpersonal relationships," (p. 471.)

Perhaps the concept of *ba* coupled with the third space is a useful way to think about knowledge creation early in the process. Nonaka and Konno (1998) write of four characteristics of *ba*: *originating ba* which represents socialization, *interacting* ba which represents externalization, *exercising ba* which represents internalization, and *cyber ba* which represents combination.

Interacting ba is of special interest to us here, since it is the place for exchanges such as the ones we envision between nonprofit theatres and larger commercial pro-ductions. "Interacting *ba* is the place where tacit knowledge is made explicit, thus it represents the externalization proves. Dialogue is key for such conversions' and the extensive use of metaphors is one of the conversion skills required." (p. 47).

Also of keen interest to us, because it seems to harbor the spirit of the third space is "*cyber ba*" which is "a place of interaction in a virtual world instead of real space and time; and it represents the combination phased," (Nonaka and Konno , 1998, p. 47). They further describe *cyber ba*: "Here the combining of new explicit knowledge with existing knowledge generates and systematizes explicit knowledge throughout the or-ganization." and "The use of on-line networks, group-ware, documentations, and da-tabase has been growing rapidly …enhancing this conversion process," (p. 47).

While there are intriguing similarities between the third space and *ba*, two aspects are strikingly different. One is the collaboration which goes beyond sharing, adopting, and adapting of each other's best practices, moving to a relationship that is main-tained and advanced by actively *creating* together as embodied in the larger concept of *ba*. The other is the identification of explicit tension in collaborative relationships (Nonaka, 2008, p.1) that is necessary for "real exchange."

For nonprofit theatres interacting with large commercial theatrical enterprises, col-laborative knowledge creation certainly is an exciting prospect and holds out great promise. For some large and small theatres working together, knowledge creation is already taking place. Evidence of knowledge creation can be found in many joint pro-ductions in theatre and in opera, fostering of budding playwrights, and special "black box" theatrical creations that tap into what is being creating in *ba*. In addition, there is joint management of box offices, and there are joint promotional efforts that seek to boost the reputations of both for-profit productions and nonprofit theatres.

6   Analyzing the IT and Culture Transfer Process

In this section, we elaborate on our approach to analogize the work of Bhabha (1994), originally written to focus on "the distribution of knowledge and practices from the colonial metropole to the colonies — and the way that the distributed knowledge is as-similated and distorted as a reflection of the power relations between distributor and re-ceiver," (Frenkel, 2008, p. 925), in order to examine, interpret, and understand how the dominated forces (small, and medium-sized professional, nonprofit theatres) are able to transmit culture to the dominant forces (in our case, large-scale commercial productions). This analysis is undertaken to better understand how IT and people transmit the culture (lessons learned, best practices) of small, professional, nonprofit theatres to large-scale commercial productions, to suggest best practices that can be learned by large-scale commercial productions, and to suggest future research directions.

Conte and Langely (2007) comment "The nonprofit theatre and the commercial theatre have become dependent on each other for growth. Nonprofit theatres depend on the revenues from transferring their productions to commercial venues, and Broadway and West End producers depend on new and fully developed products to produce. Despite criticism from both industries suggesting that commercial and nonprofit theatre should function independently, the combination of business models is more economically realistic and viable for both parties," (p. 119).

Some examples of cooperation between large-scale commercial productions and small to medium-sized nonprofit professional theatres are shown in the third space in Figure 2. These areas of collaboration include learning, the creation and nurturing of

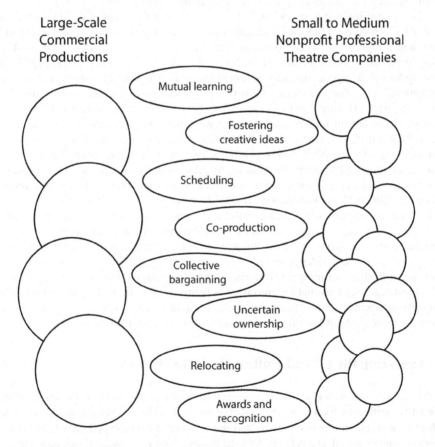

Large-Scale
Commercial
Productions

Small to Medium
Nonprofit Professional
Theatre Companies

Mutual learning

Fostering
creative ideas

Scheduling

Co-production

Collective
bargainning

Uncertain
ownership

Relocating

Awards and
recognition

Fig. 2. In the "third space" cooperation and collaboration can result in mutually beneficial activities that can help and improve the theatre industry

new ideas, and the art of scheduling productions. They also involve co-production, the relocation of a particular show, and a resolution to questions about ownership of the script or even production values.

Cooperation between commercial productions and nonprofit theatre companies may involve collective bargaining, where unions are able to recognize the risks and rewards of experimental, nonprofit theatre and their benefit to the theatre industry and to society as a whole. They can include shared values and agreement to participate in joint awards and recognition made possible by groups such as The Drama League and The Drama Desk, who evaluate and reward both commercial and nonprofit productions and the actors, directors, and crew that participate in either or both world.

In the following section we examine how information technology can be used in the third space to benefit both large-scale commercial productions and nonprofit theatre companies.

7 Cooperation and Collaboration in the Third Space

We can usefully examine the mutually beneficial exchanges that take place in the metaphorical third space between small and medium-sized professional nonprofit theatres and large-scale commercial productions. Recall that in the third space, there is much give and take between the colonizer and the colonized. There is a negotiated space that permits the emergent identities of those existing inside of it to take on sometimes surprisingly original shapes and dimensions, responding to each other, the old structure, and the newly emergent ways of doing things. The third space is dominated neither by the colonizer or the colonized. Emergent ways of thinking, speaking, and behaving are all in evidence here.

The use of IT in small to medium-sized theatres can improve the use of IT in large commercial productions in a number of ways. Commercial productions did not have the incentive to improve their IT, while the nonprofits did. Some nonprofits found it necessary to comply with reporting requirements mandated by government funding they had secured. Therefore, the IT systems had to be improved. In other cases, nonprofits needed to manage patron subscription databases. All needed to keep track of donors. Since commercial productions did not have government reporting requirements, a subscription audience, or charitable contributions, the incentives were not there to develop this part of the IT.

In some instances, nonprofit professional theatres have been able to surpass commercial productions saddled with legacy systems that required increasing amounts of maintenance just to keep them running. In addition, new technologies, including email applications and Web-based tools, afforded nonprofits the opportunity to adopt open source tools that leap-frogged over some commercial legacy systems and permitted them to take the upper hand in developing current content that met younger target audiences' expectations. Commercial productions rely on outsourcing and the IT provided by affiliations or parent groups. The 35 commercial physical Broadway theatres are owned by three organizations (The Shubert Organization, the Nederlander Producing Company of America, and the Jujamcyn Amusement Corporation). The Broadway productions rent the space from these established organizations.

Large-Scale
Commercial
Productions

Small to Medium
Nonprofit Professional
Theatre Companies

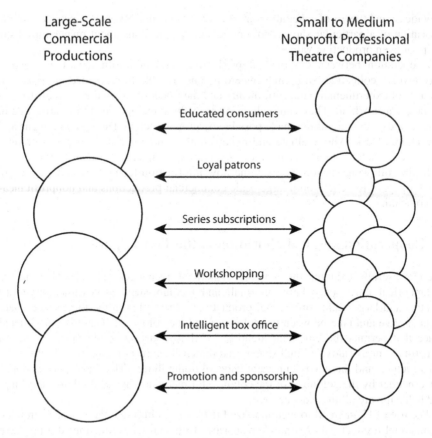

Educated consumers

Loyal patrons

Series subscriptions

Workshopping

Intelligent box office

Promotion and sponsorship

Fig. 3. Information technology can address the deliverables in the "third space" that are mutually beneficial to both large commercial productions and small to medium nonprofit professional theatre companies

Many nonprofit theatres might be classified as late adopters of information communication technologies (ICTs due to any number of reasons, which include the idea that priorities for funding went into productions not into IT, that there is a dearth of well-trained IT personnel available who will work at lower than industry-standard salaries; that there is a lack of budget for IT; that there exists a lack of a strategic plan for IT tied into a long term strategic plan for the organization's growth.

In the case of late IT adoptions of new tools, commercial productions existing in the third space learn the benefits of adopting newer, Web-based technologies; are influenced to catch up to the nonprofit theatres in the use of newer, IT-based media (rather than remain wedded to traditional print or television ads) to attract younger audiences accustomed to the Web, email, and social utility and networking Web sites including YouTube, Facebook, MySpace, Twitter, and many others.

In Figure 3 notice that there is mutual influence and exchange between large commercial productions and small to medium nonprofit professional theatre companies in the third space. It is our observation, based on our research with nonprofit professional theatres inside and outside of New York (Abuhamdieh, Kendall & Kendall, 2002 & 2007; Kendall, 2008; and Te'eni and Kendall, 2004) that there are at least six distinct deliverables that information technology can successfully address for large-scale commercial productions as well as small to medium nonprofit professional theatre companies. These include educated audience members; loyal patrons, theatre series subscriptions, workshopping of original theatrical musicals and plays (Martin, 2007); the implementation and use of intelligent box offices, and promotion and sponsorship. (For a revealing picture formed by the mosaic of use of technology and nonprofits see the research articles in the volume edited by Cortés and Rafter, 2007.)

In the third space, IT serves as a cultural facilitator for theatres sharing information with each other. Information technology in and of itself also shapes the culture into new forms, and provides new ways of organizing and thinking about the enterprise that can inspire or unlock creativity and bring new perspectives to the fore. While this assertion is innovative in the context of small to medium-sized theatres exchanging ideas with commercial theatres, many IT researchers, particularly over the last two decades or so, have examined how information systems can facilitate the internal work of a variety of small businesses; how they can extend small business strategies to become competitive with large firms by employing their ICTs or examined the importance of developing information systems specifically tailored for small businesses (Cragg and King, 1993; Cragg and Zinatelli, 1995; DeLone, 1988; Harrison, Mykytyn and Riemenschnieder, 1997; Hussin, King, and Cragg, 2002; Iacovou, Benbasat, and Dexter, 1995; Levy, Powell, and Yetton, 2001; Raymond, 1985; Winston and Dologite, 2002; and Zinatelli, Cragg, and Cavaye, 1996.)

There are many ways in which IT supports the development of knowledge sharing and the transfer of knowledge between and among nonprofit theatres and commercial houses in the third space of Bhabha (2004) and in the cyber *ba* described by Nonaka and Konno (1998). This includes educating audience members; capturing and retaining loyal theatre patrons; developing theatre series for large scale theatre productions; using the Web as a workspace to post casting calls for workshop actors; collaborating on creative works and technical designs for workshops; implementing and using intelligent box offices to fully integrate services for audience members; partnering with each other to secure government grants for future collaborations; and creating strategic alliances and partnerships of commercial ventures and nonprofits to gain corporate sponsorships promoted on the Web and through the use of other ICTs.

For example, theatres can work to develop their own audiences from the theatre-going public by using IT to educate and shape audience members. They can also use their Web site to inform other theatres of the activities that are surrounding their artistic decisions. The building of interactive Web sites, complete with biographies of actors and directors featured in current productions, notes from the director, synopsis and analysis from a dramaturge, and costume sketches from the designer, can comprise a Web site that will enhance the exchange between the nonprofit and commercial theatres and actually help grow an audience that that becomes participants in the creative processes.

Commercial theatres in the third space can also learn from small and medium-sized nonprofit theatres about maintaining loyal patrons. Small theatres often effectively cultivate loyal patrons through building and maintaining individual relationships over the course of many theatre seasons. Small theatres often focus on retention rather than selling a seat to an anonymous customer anew every time a new show is mounted. Large commercial productions can learn form them to see customers as partners in a relationship. IT enters in when customer relationship management systems (CRM) are developed or purchased. CRM can be developed around the patron, rather than emphasizing a numbered seat in the theatre. This value is one that can be exchanged in the third space, since small nonprofit theatres often maintain excellent patron communications, and large commercial productions are very organized in their approach to the box office.

Other low-cost and effective ways to cultivate loyal patrons are popular with nonprofit groups who use IT to send push emails of upcoming shows, sending a monthly or quarterly newsletter via push email, including insider news, casting updates, and industry gossip. Push emails can also be used to tie into seasonal calendars that relay changes in performance times and dates due to holidays. Theatres can also use IT to send early notification of special events via email. While traditional "save the date" post cards for upcoming benefits might still be posted in regular mail, early notification of patrons permits theatres to facilitate two-way communication with their patrons and also get the word out ahead of a mailed invitation campaign.

Web sites can also serve as a standard IT platform for offering an array of interactive features that are meant to retain audiences, and also meant to keep them returning to the Web site to see what's new. Smaller sites put up by the nonprofit theatres allow audience member feedback, online booking, online contributions, seat selection, and support many other functions. Sites can be customized so that subscribers log in with a secure password, are addressed by name, and encounter other personalization features such as including a recommendation system that features other shows that may appeal to the subscriber. In addition, subscribers could then access specially tailored content (videos of current and past productions, interviews with artistic talent including designers and so on).

In the third space, larger commercial productions can learn from nonprofit professional theatres by creating Web spaces that are easy to navigate, fun to visit, and personalized. Since IT budgets for larger productions are often a grater portion of their capital expenditures, Web sites can be updated more frequently, and the sophistication and range of ICTs available increases.

Commercial productions exchanging ideas in the third space can teach small, professional nonprofit theatres a great deal about creative marketing tie-ins hosted on the Web site. Nonprofits can learn to offer scripts for sale, T-shirts, and other clothing with production logos as exciting ways to engage with the production of a play and also donate to the organization. In addition, small theatres can offer lists of nearby recommended restaurants, often featuring a discount on a meal or beverage.

Stickiness of a Web site should be a concern of every Web site developer. Subscribers and potential subscribers could be encouraged to remain on the Web site and interact via blogs, chat rooms, watching video clips of current and past productions. Reviews of the show from a variety of sources, including subscriber reviews can be hosted on the site so that patrons are encouraged to return to the site often.

Other examples of commercial productions interacting with nonprofit theatres in the third space include extending the concept of subscriptions facilitated by IT to include large-scale, commercial productions. Many nonprofit theatres rely on the sale of subscriptions for 60 to 90 percent of their revenue. Subscriptions are advertised on theatre Web sites and through emails. In addition, sale of subscriptions permits budget forecasts and planning for future seasons that other types of one-time sales do not permit. This ties in well to the building of customer relationships discussed in the previous paragraph, and it is a good use of IT for commercial productions as well. While nonprofit theatres may rely on paper and pencil audience surveys to get feedback about what audiences prefer to see, commercial productions can learn the importance of customer feedback in planning too, but will be able to use more costly data mining techniques to identify audience preferences and custom-build a series based on their findings of past show-goers.

Often commercial productions go through a well-defined workshopping process to evaluate material (often musicals Workshopping requires the hiring of actors and musicians, as well as a space to rehearse and present the workshop, all in a highly compressed time period. Sometimes the workshopping space is a rental space the theatre owns or it can be an actual black box theatre that is used for development purposes. Information technology enters the picture because of the extensive and fast-paced collaborative effort required to workshop a show. Typically professional actors are cast for the parts (although often they will not be those who ultimately wind up with the roles) but their qualifications must be submitted and reviewed. Pushing those tasks to a workspace on the Web would be effective. Also, creating passworded workspace on the theatre's Web site for collaborating on music, scripts, and technical designs would satisfy the desire for intense, time driven-collaborations with people from all over the world. Nonprofit theatres can benefit from collaborating on the Web with commercial productions for workshopping new material.

In the third space, commercial productions and nonprofit theatres can learn from each other about the importance of the data that is collected and distributed by the box office. Small, nonprofit theatres, often seem to instinctually recognize that data from the box office is the lifeblood for not only generating revenues but for contact with audience members. If a theatre is outsourcing their box office (this can happened with either type of theatre), they still need to learn to capture and analyze the data being generated. IT can inform this process in powerful ways. These include tracking of patrons, and storing then honoring their seating preferences (including days of the week and performance times). Some patron programs use people in the role of directors of individual giving to perform these functions, but with a large subscriber base, the software is a necessity.

Theatres can also push emails to patrons notifying of them when it is permissible to book a show that is part of their theatre series. This serves as a welcome reminder, and also maintains a relationship with the patron. In more sophisticated application, intelligent agents can be used to search the Web for new commercial productions that fit an audience member's established and stored profile. Currently, these agents are somewhat clumsy, often organized around stored data that the audience member visits New York or some other city frequently, and so pushes shows opening in New York. Other times, the push email will be based on the patron's ticket purchase history, building a little bit of a profile from sales of previous show tickets; e.g. you just saw *Guys and Dolls*, you will enjoy another revival that is opening on Broadway, *Hair: The American tribal love-rock musical*. Although these shows have different producers, cooperation benefits the entire industry (Kendall, 2008).

Educated audience members
- Via Web sites, by providing playwright and actor bios, director notes, etc.
- Interactive Performance Calendars
- Open source content management systems
- Streaming video of former or current productions

Loyal patrons
- Customer relationship management (CRM) systems
- Push emails of upcoming productions, insider news, casting updates
- Push performance calendars around public holidays to show new performance times and changed performance dates
- Notification of special events via email

Theatre series subscriptions
- Extending the concept of subscriptions to include large-scale productions
- Building a long term relationship with audience members
- Using data mining to custom build subscription series

Workshopping of original theatrical musicals and plays
- Advertising for actors for workshops
- Notice of workshop electronically
- Use of Web space for collaborating on music, scripts, and technical designs

Implementation and use of intelligent box offices
- Tracking of patrons, their seating preferences including days of the week and performance times
- Push notification to patrons when productions open for booking
- Using intelligent agents to search for new commercial productions that fit an audience member's profile
- Using patron's history to build profile

Promotion and sponsorship
- Cooperatively promoting enthusiasm for all theatre
- Creating strategic alliances and partnerships of commercial ventures and nonprofits to gain corporate sponsorship

Fig. 4. Specific functions IT can perform in the third space involing both large-scale commercial productions and nonprofit theatre companies

Finally, nonprofit theatres and commercial productions in the third space can benefit from participating in promotion. Organizations such as The Drama League, which predates by 12 years the Broadway-only Tony Awards, and The Drama Desk, include both nonprofit theatres and commercial Broadway productions when they bestow their annual awards. Web sites that function as information aggregators such as play-bill.com, theatermania.com, and nytheatre.com do a satisfactory job of posting listings, reviews, interviews, and so on, but aggregators do not facilitate or encourage cooperation, they merely collect and display information. Commercial productions and nonprofits need to figure out ways to cooperate more using the Web.

Lastly, nonprofits and commercial ventures are working together in the third space to gain corporate sponsorship in order to fund innovative, socially conscious work in a larger venue, where all three work to form strategic alliances. The examples listed in Figure 4 summarize the foregoing specific instances of nonprofit theatres and commercial productions exchanging ideas and in turn being influenced in the third space.

8 Suggested Future Research Directions

There are many avenues of future research that can produce a lively dialectic and some very good ideas about transfer of IT and strategic management knowledge among and between theatres and productions of all sizes and financial status, whether commercial or not-for-profit. For example, it would be interesting to take a Bhabhaian perspective on Broadway theatre, examining it as postcolonial entity while examining the West End of London as the Colonial power, while assessing whether the metaphor of the third space is useful in understanding the dynamic interchange of ICTS, actors, directors, and productions that have become a hallmark of the US-British relationship over the last 40 years.

In the future, it would also be worthwhile to further elaborate and explore the interrelationship of the third space and *ba*, and to be able to identify where the two intersect and depart and what the meaning of those intersections and departures are for commercial productions and nonprofit theatres and their use of information technology.

9 Conclusion

In this article we examine the metaphor of the third space as proposed by Bhabha (1994), as a way to critique the discourse (both verbal and nonverbal) that encompasses IT, strategic management, and other exchanges between small and medium-sized nonprofit professional theatres symbolized by Off-Broadway and Off-Off Broadway theatres, and productions in London's Fringe, versus the large, commercial productions symbolized by Broadway and those in London's West End. Our motivation for this analysis is to deepen our understanding of the relationship of SMEs to large organizations, and to suggest that the mutual exchange of culture, including IT and other management practices from small theatres to large productions is usefully understood from a Bhabhaian perspective, with large, commercial productions learning from small and medium sized nonprofit theatres as well as the reverse, in what Bhabha envisions as the third space.

References

Abuhamdieh, A., Kendall, J.E., Kendall, K.E.: An Evaluation of the Web Presence of a Nonprofit Organization: Using the Balanced Scorecard Approach in Ecommerce. In: Traunmüller, R. (ed.) Information Systems: The E-Business Challenge, pp. 210–222. Kluwer Academic Publishers, Boston (2002)

Abuhamdieh, A., Kendall, J.E., Kendall, K.E.: E-commerce Opportunities in the Nonprofit Sector: The Case of New York Theatre Group. International Journal of Cases on Electronic Commerce 3(1), 29–48 (2007)

Bhabha, H.K.: The Location of Culture. Routledge Classics, New York (1994) (originally published 1994, reprinted 2008)

Bhabha, H.K.: Cultures in between. In: Hall, S., du Gay, P. (eds.) Questions of cultural identity, pp. 53–60. Sage, Thousand Oaks (1996)

Conte, D.M., Langley, S.: Theatre Management: Producing and Managing the Performing Arts. Entertainment Pro., and imprint of Quite Specific Media Group, Ltd., Hollywood, CA (2007)

Cortés, M., Rafter, K.M.: Nonprofits & Technology. Lyceum Books, Inc, Chicago (2007)

Cragg, P.B., King, M.: Small-Firm Computing: Motivators and Inhibitors. MIS Quarterly 17(1), 47–60 (1993)

Cragg, P.B., Zinatelli, N.: The Evolution of information Systems in Small Firms. Information & Management 29(1), 108 (1995)

DeLone, W.H.: Determinants of Success for Computer Usage in Small Business. MIS Quarterly 12(1), 51–61 (1988)

Frenkel, M.: The Multinational Corporation as a Third Space: Rethinking International Management Discourse on Knowledge Transfer Through Homi Bhaba. The Academy of Management Review 33(4), 924–942 (2008)

Harrison, D.A., Mykytyn Jr., P.P., Rimenschneider, C.K.: Executive Decisions About the Adoption of Information Technology in Small Business: Theory and Empirical Tests. Information Systems Research 9(2), 171–195 (1997)

Helgesen, S.: The Practical Wisdom of Ikujiro Nonaka, strategy+business (Winter), http://www.strategy-business.com/press/article/08407?gko=31376 (last accessed, March 5, 2009)

Hussin, H., King, M., Cragg, P.: IT Alignment in Small Firms. European Journal of Information Systems 11(2), 108–127 (2002)

Iacovou, C.L., Benbasat, I., Dexter, A.S.: Electronic Data Interchange and Small Organizations: Adoption and Impact of Technology. MIS Quarterly 19(4), 465–485 (1995)

Kendall, J.: Metaphors for E-Collaboration: A Study of Nonprofit Theatre Web Presence. In: Kock, N. (ed.) E-Collaboration in Modern Organizations: Initiating and Managing Distributed Projects, pp. 14–30. Information Science Reference, Hershey (2008)

Kendall, K.E., Kendall, J.E., Lee, K.C.: Understanding Disaster Recovery Planning through a Theatre Metaphor: Rehearsing for a Show that Might Never Open. Communications of AIS 16, 1001–1012 (2005)

Levy, M., Powell, P., Yetton, P.: SMEs: Aligning IS and the Strategic Context. Journal of Information Technology 16, 133–144 (2001)

Martin, J.S.J.: A Jesuit Off-Broadway. Loyola Press, Chicago (2007)

Nonaka, I.: The Knowledge-Creating Company. Harvard Business Review 69, 96–104 (1991)

Nonaka, I., Konno, N.: The Concept of "Ba": Building a Foundation for Knowledge Creation. California Management Review 40(3), 40–54 (1998)

Peltonen, T.: Critical theoretical perspectives on international human resource management. In: Stahl, G.K., Bjorkman, I. (eds.) Handbook of Research in International Human Resource Management, pp. 523–535. Edward Elgar, Cheltenham (2006)

Pflughoeft, K.A., Ramamurthy, K., Soofi, E.S., Yasai-Ardekani, M., Zahedi, F.: Multiple Conceptualizations of Small Business Web Use and Benefit. Decision Sciences 34(3), 467–512 (Summer 2003)

Raymond, L.: Organizational characteristics and MIS Success in the Context of Small Business. MIS Quarterly 9(1), 37–52 (1985)

Street, C.T., Meister, D.B.: Small Business Growth and Internal Transparency: The Role of Information Systems. MIS Quarterly 28(3), 473–506 (2004)

Te'eni, D., Kendall, J.E.: Internet Commerce and Fundraising. In: Young, D.R. (ed.) Effective Economic Decision-Making by Nonprofit Organizations, The Foundation Center, New York, NY, pp. 167–189 (2004)

Volz, J.: How to Run a Theater. Back Stage Books, New York (2004)

Webb, D.M.: Running Theaters: Best Practices for Leaders and Managers. Allworth Press, New York (2004)

Winston, E.R., Dologite, D.: How Does Attitude Impact IT Implementation: A Study of Small Business Owners. Journal of End User Computing 14(2), 16–29 (2002)

Zinatelli, N., Cragg, P.B., Cavaye, A.L.M.: End User Computing Sophistication and Success in Small Firms. European Journal of Information Systems 5(3), 172–181 (1996)

SME 2.0: Roadmap towards Web 2.0-Based Open Innovation in SME-Networks – A Case Study Based Research Framework

Nadine Lindermann, Sylvia Valcárcel, Mario Schaarschmidt,
and Harald von Kortzfleisch

University of Koblenz-Landau, Institute for Management,
Computer Science Faculty, Universitaetsstrasse 1, Germany

Abstract. Small- and medium sized enterprises (SMEs) are of high social and economic importance since they represent 99% of European enterprises. With regard to their restricted resources, SMEs are facing a limited capacity for innovation to compete with new challenges in a complex and dynamic competitive environment. Given this context, SMEs need to increasingly cooperate to generate innovations on an extended resource base. Our research project[1] focuses on the aspect of open innovation in SME-networks enabled by Web 2.0 applications and referring to innovative solutions of non-competitive daily life problems. Examples are industrial safety, work-life balance issues or pollution control. The project raises the question whether the use of Web 2.0 applications can foster the exchange of creativity and innovative ideas within a network of SMEs and hence catalyze new forms of innovation processes among its participants. Using Web 2.0 applications within SMEs implies consequently breaking down innovation processes to employees' level and thus systematically opening up a heterogeneous and broader knowledge base to idea generation. In this paper we address first steps on a roadmap towards Web 2.0-based open innovation processes within SME-networks. It presents a general framework for interaction activities leading to open innovation and recommends a regional marketplace as a viable, trust-building driver for further collaborative activities. These findings are based on field research within a specific SME-network in Rhineland-Palatinate Germany, the "WirtschaftsForum Neuwied e.V.", which consists of roughly 100 heterogeneous SMEs employing about 8,000 workers.

1 Introduction

Small- and medium sized enterprises (SMEs) are increasingly confronted with complex and dynamic problems of daily work life. Examples are worker's health protection, industrial safety, work-life balance issues, conservation of energy or pollution control. Since these non-competitive aspects are across all activities of a company's value chain, they also become important to primary activities and thus

---

[1] The research project is funded by the German Federal Ministry of Education and Research (BMBF).

G. Dhillon, B.C. Stahl, and R. Baskerville (Eds.): CreativeSME 2009, IFIP AICT 301, pp. 28–41, 2009.

require innovative solutions. SMEs need to cooperate in order to generate innovative solutions on an extended resource base.

Within our research project we explore new management strategies for collaboration in SME-networks related to innovative, cooperative solutions for daily work life problems. We systematically analyze concepts and models of self-organization and information technology (IT) in the context of Web 2.0 and assume that

- Many employees are confident in using Web 2.0-applications in their private lives and thus are motivated to participate on a Web 2.0-platform in a cross-organizational environment,
- Heterogeneous groups offer a high potential for creativity and innovation.

According to these assumptions we focus on the capability of Web 2.0 applications to integrate employees from different companies and to profit from their collaborative creativity. Thus the project raises the question- whether the use of Web 2.0 applications can foster the exchange of creativity and innovative ideas within a network of SMEs and hence catalyze new forms of innovation processes among its participants. We follow an incremental "action research design" (Romme 2003) collecting organizational and technical requirements for Web 2.0-based collaborative structures as well as developing and implementing a Web 2.0-application that supports inter-organizational creative processes within SME-networks. The project is based on field research within a specific SME-network in Rhineland-Palatinate Germany, the "WirtschaftsForum Neuwied e.V.".

This paper presents first results of our research project. It aims at depicting first steps on a roadmap towards Web 2.0-based open innovation processes within SME-networks. First of all we introduce the network "WirtschaftsForum Neuwied e.V." we are analyzing and give an overview of the characteristics and challenges it is facing with regard to Web 2.0 applications. We then focus on general aspects of Web 2.0-based open innovation. Afterwards we present first results of an interview series conducted with managers of the network's companies. Finally we introduce a general framework for interaction activities leading to open innovation and recommend a regional marketplace as a viable, trust-building driver for further collaborative activities.

2   SME 2.0: Challenges of a Cooperative Research Project

In the European economy, SMEs play a major role since they represent 99% of all Europe enterprises and thus are a main source of entrepreneurial skills, employment and innovation (European Commission 2003). In recent years, joining cross-organizational networks has become increasingly important for SMEs wishing to access an extended resource base and operate on the basis of it (Human and Provan 1996; Street and Cameron 2007). In general, a network is an association of at least three autonomous enterprises for the purpose of a corporate task fulfillment. By combining and coordinating resources and organizational functions, they aim at achieving competitive advantages to create win-win-situations for all participating partners (Corsten 2001; Picot et al. 2003). Thereby cooperation generates synergies for innovative business solutions where the combination of resources exceeds the sum of individual efforts

(European Commission 2003a). The "WirtschaftsForum Neuwied e.V." represents a SME-network in consideration which is described according to its characteristics and challenges below.

2.1 "WirtschaftsForum Neuwied e.V."

The "WirtschaftsForum Neuwied e.V." is a regional network in the north of Rhineland-Palatinate in Germany that consists of roughly 100 SMEs employing about 8,000 workers. It was founded in 2002 and comprises companies primarily from the industry and business sector in the surrounding area of Neuwied. The SME-network is heterogeneous in structure regarding respective size of the cooperating companies, represented branches, products and services and technological affinity. It focuses on non-competitive activities and aims at fostering knowledge transfer between its members and enhancing collaboration and business relations. In this regard it is facing challenges and problems generally related to SMEs (Bellmann and Gerster 2006; Street and Cameron 2007; Thielemann 1996):

- The management of SMEs is highly influenced by the personality of the owners and their attitude towards doing business. Joining a network is usually decided on the executives' level only, while employees are barely integrated into the collaborative work. This translates into scant use of expert knowledge on the operational level within the SME-network.
- IT is not yet widely implemented. Within the "WirtschaftsForum Neuwied e.V." many cooperating partners are hardly using IT, while others maintain a sophisticated internet-based IT infrastructure.
- The capability for innovation in SMEs is limited by restricted resources. Normally the business model is grouped around a core activity implying innovation efforts to be strictly targeted at the same field of activities.

The specific characteristics of SME-networks depicted above influence their use of Web 2.0-applications. In the following we outline the philosophy underlying Web 2.0.

2.2 SMEs and the Use of Web 2.0

Web 2.0 is a phenomenon that represents a changing trend in the World Wide Web (WWW). The term was coined by Tim O'Reilly in 2004 and is used for active user participation on the Internet (O'Reilly 2005). The idea of the concept is that internet content is not just to be read, listened to or observed, but also to be generated, commented on and shared with other users (O'Reilly 2005; Von Kortzfleisch et al. 2008). As it is heavily dependent on active participation on its users' side, Web 2.0 has an inherent potential for common problem solving and raising shared creativity. In this context "Enterprise 2.0" refers to the consequent application of Web 2.0 within an organizational context (McAfee 2006). Our research project broadens this perspective insofar as it addresses inter-organizational usage of Web 2.0 within a network of SMEs and introduces the term "SME 2.0".

In daily business practice, Web 2.0 use (e.g. wikis and blogs) has been observed as primarily being restricted to communication with the customer and internal information and knowledge management (CoreMedia and Berlecon Research 2007;

McKinsey and Company 2008; The Economist Intelligence Unit 2007). Within the context of SMEs, the potential of Web 2.0 is not yet fully perceived (De Saulles 2008a; De Saulles 2008b; Social Computing News Desk 2008). Given the creative potential of Web 2.0, we analyze whether and to what extent social software is used within a network of SMEs and thus can unfetter collective intelligence. Given the philosophy of SME 2.0 and the characteristics of SME-networks, the challenges shown in figure 1 have to be dealt with:

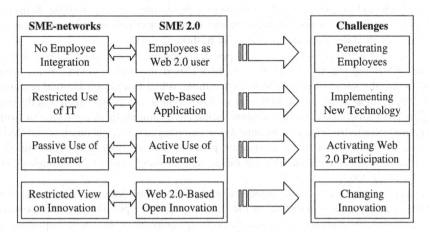

Fig. 1. Challenges of SME-networks using Web 2.0

- Within the network SMEs are primarily represented by their executives. Delegation to subordinates tends to be limited (Burns 2001), also implying they are not (sufficiently) integrated into the network's activities. According to our understanding of SME 2.0, employees should become Web 2.0-users who participate in collaborative work by transferring their knowledge across the internet platform. This requires penetrating the employees' level of the network.
- Currently, IT is hardly used within the SME-network, its use being confined to daily business matters and thus markedly short-termed (Levy and Powell 2005). Companies consequently need to be conducted to the new Web 2.0 approach.
- Internet content is passively consumed but not actively designed. User participation has to be activated (De Saulles 2008a; De Saulles 2008b).
- Our research project focuses on innovations regarding daily work life problems. Since innovations in SMEs are normally related to their primary activities, the companies have to be directed to this new aspect for innovation.

In our research project we focus on the question whether the use of Web 2.0-applications can foster the exchange of creativity and innovative ideas within a SME-network. A Web 2.0-application is planned to be developed to enable web-based collaborative idea generation. This approach is based on a roadmap defining the steps to be taken towards Web 2.0-based open innovation. According to the challenges we identified in figure 1, we first have to ensure acceptance and usage of the Web 2.0-based platform. Therefore we analyzed general requirements on Web 2.0-applications.

At the same time we considered aspects of Web 2.0-based open innovation that also have to be integrated into the model. These aspects are discussed in the section below.

3 Web 2.0-Based Collaborative Open Innovation

Open Innovation is a widely used term currently discussed in many contexts. At its core, it is the increasing usage of external sources for creating and developing new ideas which lead to innovation. In contrast to a closed innovation paradigm, firms try to include customers, users, universities and even competitors in different stages of their new product development processes (Chesbrough 2003).

The change from a closed to a more open development paradigm includes a change of the underlying mental model as well. In a closed innovation environment, firms tried to hire the smartest people to work for them, relied heavily on internal research and development activities (R&D), and tried to control and protect their Intellectual Property (IP). In contrast, in an open innovation environment, firms are trying to work with smart people from inside and outside the company, are recognising internal R&D activities as only a part of an innovation process, and are buying IP from outside, whenever it is needed and suitable for the current business model (Chesbrough 2003; Van der Meer 2007).

In recent years, many firms opened several parts of their innovation processes for external participation. According to the different types of possible external sources (users, customers, universities, research centres, competitors, etc) it is important to distinguish them with regard to the degree of their involvement. Most activities of integrating users or customers in innovation processes can be observed in early and late phases of the innovation process – like making use of lead users or mass customizing products (Von Hippel 2005; Piller and Walcher 2006) – whereas integrating external partners in core development activities is open to a lesser extend. In the latter case, firms mainly make use of industrial R&D consortiums and joint ventures which generally include contractual agreements – without integrating users or customers. Furthermore, research in the area of open innovation is concentrated mostly on single users rather than on groups or communities. However, the role of communities in creating, shaping and disseminating technological and social innovations outside the boundaries of the firm is a specially promising research area (West and Lakhani 2008). Since heterogeneity is known to be a driver for creativity and communities are heterogeneous in nature, they are offering a hidden creative potential (Oldman and Cummings 1996; Alves et al. 2007; Schaarschmidt and Von Kortzfleisch 2008). Furthermore, innovation networks, whether as networks of companies or persons have the potential to act as a proxy for innovation (Martins and Terblanche 2003; Kratzer et al. 2004; Birkinshaw et al. 2007).

To sum up, open innovation is a promising trend both in theory and practice. Communities are offering a high potential for generating innovative ideas and even products as is the case for development of open source software (Osterloh and Rota 2007) or idea generating platforms (Lakhani 2008). In addition to the use of Web 2.0 as basic-democratic and more or less non-hierarchical structures, this potential is even higher (Schaarschmidt and Von Kortzfleisch 2008). Willingness to take risk for example, as an important factor in generating innovative ideas, increases, when hierarchical structures are missing (Dewett 2007). The challenge firms are facing therefore is to canalize community activities to transform group creativity into useful ideas.

4 Open Innovation – Just a Theory in the Context of SME 2.0?

The first phase of the research project aims at analyzing the organizational and technical requirements to be met for the set-up of Web 2.0-applications within the "WirtschaftsForum Neuwied e.V.". This section outlines the results of explorative interviews with executives of the project's six value partners, both from a methodological as well as content-related perspective.

4.1 Setting Up of the Explorative Interview Phase

The chosen research design comprises two stages: the first stage is directed at generating recommendations for the enhancement of cooperation activities within a network of SMEs. Such an enhancement of cooperation activities is argued to be an indispensable prerequisite for open innovation activities within a network. Recommendations are generated on the basis of explorative, qualitative interviews, which provide for substantial insight into the given context and lay the ground for further generation of hypotheses (Miles and Huberman 1994). In a second stage of the research, a broad-based survey will be conducted, testing the hypotheses generated beforehand.

Concretely eight managing directors out of six partner firms ("value partners") were interviewed on the basis of a semi-standardized questionnaire. The value partners represent SMEs of different branches within the network and act as lead users who test the applications and diffuse them among the cooperating partners. The interviews were directed at determining the goals and needs of small and medium-sized companies cooperating within the network on a strategic level. They provide for general information about the company in question and its cooperation activities within "WirtschaftsForum Neuwied e.V.", as well as for requirements, benefits and objections concerning the use of Web 2.0. The following synthesis is elaborated along the thematic blocks of the questionnaire.

4.2 Requirements for SME 2.0: First Results of an Explorative Study

1. **Actual challenges of SMEs:** The main challenges of SMEs are customer loyalty and customer acquisition as well as market observation. Some SMEs are operating on nearly saturated markets and have to continuously generate new ideas and open up additional business segments. Since these companies might be founded on a single business idea, customer satisfaction is of primary importance ("We do not want to have just satisfied but enthused customers!"). Ideas are generated on the basis of internet research, journals, trade fairs or suppliers. However, a major source for idea generation lies in the customer needs gathered from personal counselling talks or surveys.
2. **Motives for joining a network of SMEs:** From the executives' perception, the "WirtschaftsForum Neuwied e.V." offers a regional platform, which enables

a) external presentation of the companies to communicate core business and services across the SME-network and b) exchange of services, especially requests received from other companies within the SME-network and orders placed with participating partners. The interview partners were primarily interested in gaining economical benefits from cooperation.

3. **Prerequisites for effective collaboration:** At present, the initial expectations of the interviewees when joining the "WirtschaftsForum Neuwied e.V." are not entirely met. In this regard the network has to address the requirements below:

   – General survey of the member structure. Interview partners expressed the wish to obtain relevant, useful information on other member firms on the network's website. So far, information on the member structure of "WirtschaftsForum Neuwied e.V.", i.e. represented industry sectors, business areas and services provided, is not available.
   – Cooperativeness- Collaboration requires continuous exchange of information and knowledge. The willingness to cooperate therefore depends on the company's economic benefit for all cooperating partners.
   – Integration of the employees' level- Employees have not been involved in network activities so far. At present, the companies of the network are exclusively collaborating on the executives' level. Integration of the operational employees' perspective is therefore required.

4. **Benefits of using Web 2.0:** Implementation of a Web 2.0-platform is expected to foster effective collaboration within the "WirtschaftsForum Neuwied e.V.". The managers propose a simple Web 2.0-application with network-members represented in a fact sheet. The application is supposed to provide a straightforward search function which allows easy access to the required enterprise information. In addition, regional customers might use this function to find solutions related to an individual problem. The Web 2.0-application is then to be gradually extended by additional functions such as a forum for exchanging experiences, idea generation or idea testing on the market.

5. **Success factors of SME 2.0:** SME 2.0 is vitally dependent on the participation of its users. The successful implementation of Web 2.0-applications within a network of SMEs requires active employees interacting on the overall platform. User participation itself is a question of trust, balance of effort and benefit as well as technical aspects: The Web 2.0-based platform needs to meet technical requirements such as easy access and use. The goals and benefits of the application have to be obvious for each enterprise and each single user. Security aspects such as preventing users from diffusing wrong or manipulated information that could negatively affect the company have to be addressed with priority. In order to cope with the problems of limited time resources and information overflow on the participants' side, all relevant information has to be rapidly and easily available.

4.3 SME 2.0 vs. Web 2.0-Based Open Innovation

As discussed in the previous section, open innovation needs a mental change from closed to open development of ideas based on external resources. Our research is focused on idea generation within employees' communities that are exchanging creativity and ideas in a Web 2.0-based environment of cooperating SMEs. This requires active participation of all employees acting independently of their companies' organizational structure. However, according to our results, the participation willingness rests upon conditions such as trust, security of sensitive data, and balance between effort and economical benefit. Given this context it can be assumed that the executives try to influence their employees' activities within SME 2.0 as well as the content that is generated with Web 2.0-applications. As a consequence we recommend an incremental approach towards Web 2.0-based open innovation as well as the direct implementation of first Web 2.0-applications. Since trust has to be built up by cooperation (Gambetta 2000), this approach enables the establishment of a Web 2.0-based platform meeting executives' needs but also objections. Thereby clearly described goals and rules of cooperation in SME 2.0 help to significantly reduce concerns towards the use of Web 2.0 (Volery and Mensik 1998).

5 A Roadmap towards Open Innovation within SME-Networks

Based on the analyzes of SMEs, their approach towards Web 2.0, and collaborative open innovation presented so far as well as the first interviews led with companies from "WirtschaftsForum Neuwied e.V.", the present section develops a general framework of interaction within networks of SMEs and outlines a roadmap for open innovation in this context. Interpretation of the research outcomes stemming from "WirtschaftsForum Neuwied e.V.", makes up for the first building block of the framework.

5.1 Interpreting the Case of "WirtschaftsForum Neuwied e.V."

The companies of the network "WirtschaftsForum Neuwied e.V." pursue the goal of "acting in common". As described beforehand and concretized on their common website, "acting in common" ranges from fostering company relations and cooperation activities among the networking partners to establishing a common (internet) appearance vis-à-vis the outside world.

The companies of the network are already taking an active part in cooperating within a range of areas which are non-critical from a competitive perspective. Basically they are engaging either in the bundling of needs and resources, such as is the case for procurement, or in sharing experience e.g. concerning issues of leadership and personnel. An important cooperation field at present is the set up of common standards for the training systems employed during apprenticeship of young workers. Because of its character, **shared resource use** is the term applied for this kind of cooperation activities within the network.

Looking at the case of "WirtschaftsForum Neuwied e.V." from this perspective shifts the initial research question into the question of how it is possible to move from a state of shared resource use to a state of open innovation within a network of SMEs. Within this context, the internet and especially Web 2.0 applications are seen as a means of stimulating interaction among the firms of the network.

On a very general level, the first set of interviews conducted so far suggests that companies of the heterogeneous network "WirtschaftsForum Neuwied e.V." prefer an incremental step-by-step-approach towards closer cooperation, thus slowly intensifying the interaction of the partners involved. Besides, the interviews show a strong need for a better market and thus customer access via the network. In more specific terms, the interviews reflect a demand for cooperating in different areas of activities. These areas of cooperation can be arrayed conforming to the degree of reciprocity they reflect in the following, increasing order:

- **Exchanging general information:** This activity is directed at promoting the network's partners main willingness to cooperate and at preparing the ground for further cooperation efforts. It is mutually trust-building on the one hand and meets a very practical need of exchanging basic information at an early stage of the cooperation on the other. Providing general information on the business activities of the company and details of contact persons engaged in cooperation activities are a typical example for this area of interaction. Exchanging general, useful information on business matters can be interpreted as a prerequisite for further cooperation within a network and also as a first step towards activating the partners' interaction willingness. As it can be helpful in the day-to-day work, it is furthermore a way of making employees of all hierarchical levels active partners of the cooperation.

- **Broadening market access:** This is the case where cooperation within the network by means of Web 2.0 is looked at as a way to becoming better known within the network and thus raising the number of demand-driven contacts – and probably business transactions – with potential customers. In more active terms, better knowledge of the networking partners can help firms approach potential customers within the network with attractive pricing models and customer-specific offers. An example could be a fitness and health centre giving special member discounts or holding in-house-courses at its partners' offices addressing the specific needs of their workforce. All cases of broadening market access planned so far have the common factor that firms look at partners of the network and their employees in their capacity as potential customers.

- **Establishing sales partnerships:** In this case the network is intended to be used in order to establish a partnership of suppliers. Cooperation within the network in this context is meant to create comprehensive business solutions for customers who would otherwise have to contract several suppliers and thereby incur higher transaction costs, saving them the cost of establishing additional business contacts. An example for this kind of cooperation could be the case of several manufacturers and traders of heating, isolating, and security systems providing an overall energy and safety solution to a future homeowner. In contrast to the case of broadening market access this type of cooperation activity is genuinely network-oriented, however frequently with view to a network-external, private customer.

- **Generating new ideas** by interacting with the customers: Central to this type of cooperation is the explicit interaction between a supplier and her customer for the sake of generating new ideas and business solutions. An example for this case could be a staff training institute developing new training methods and contents in close cooperation with its customers; or a software firm offering its customers the possibility of conjoint product development and testing, thus letting them exert influence on the design and functionality of its products and services. Of all the cases discussed so far, this one is the closest to open innovation and is characterized by the highest degree of reciprocity between the cooperating partners. This is true even if the interaction takes place at the boundaries of the network as is the case for network-external customers.

5.2   Interaction within Networks of SMEs: A General Framework

Analysis of the first interview results has helped systemize the cooperation activities the members of "WirtschaftsForum Neuwied e.V." are undertaking on the basis of potential **areas of interaction** the networking companies engages in. As for the areas of interaction, four types of network cooperation could be identified: information exchange, market access, sales, and idea generation. Since the present analysis is based on the outcomes of a few explorative interviews, the enumeration of interaction areas is most likely not to be exhaustive.

The empirical material gathered from the interviews as well as first theoretical considerations on this topic suggest that there might be yet another dimension of interaction important for achieving collaborative open innovation within company networks. This dimension is the general **focus of the interaction** in question. Looking at the focus of interaction two cases can be distinguished: the case of directly creating interaction value and the case of indirectly creating it.

- **Direct creation of interaction value** covers all interactions targeted at improving sales as well as resource and cost efficiency. Activities within this field of interaction are directly contributing to a firm's overall profit. The interviews show a strong preference for cooperation efforts along this line of reasoning. Companies of "WirtschaftsForum e.V." explicitly want to engage in "win-win-activities" with regard to short-term profits.
- **Indirect creation of interaction value** addresses all activities which are not creating direct value and at first sight maybe are not creating a value at all. The important thing about interaction activities which indirectly create value is that viewed from a broader perspective they are not only creating value for the business but can even become critical from a strategic point of view. This is the case for establishing favourable working conditions in order to attract excellent work force. With regard to the demographic developments that the societies of the Western World are facing, attracting highly motivated and skilled workforce is becoming increasingly difficult especially for small and medium-sized companies. Therefore, engaging in activities that improve working conditions and are thus render the working place more attractive might very well contribute to a firm's overall goal of profitable growth. Cooperation activities within this context can be especially promising, since they could make a business location as a whole – in this case the "WirtschaftsForum Neuwied e.V." – more attractive for highly skilled and motivated workforce. A long-term win-win-situation for networking partners can therefore be achieved.

Summing up, the analysis presented so far makes up for the following general framework of interactions within networks of SMEs:

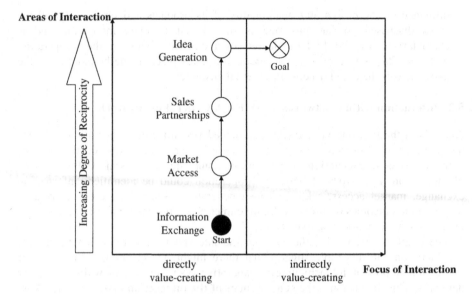

Fig. 2. Framework for Network Interaction

5.3 A Roadmap towards Web 2.0-Based Open Innovation

The general framework of interaction within SME-networks developed in the prior section builds the basis for the roadmap proposed towards Web 2.0-based open innovation. The previous sections covering the interview results and the theory of open innovation give essential clues for the concrete design of the approach recommended here. In accordance with the analyses made so far, the following recommendations hold:

- In order to generate short-term, direct value of interaction, firms should engage first in cooperation activities which are directly value-creating.
- As for the directly value-creating cooperation activities, companies should choose those areas of interaction that best fit their business needs. These can e.g. be in the fields of information exchange, market access, sales partnerships, or idea generation.
- A first step to build up trust among the networking partners and to activate their interaction willingness should be the mutual exchange of information.
- An efficient way to exchange information within a Web 2.0-based environment is the creation of a simple market platform.
- Moving towards collaborative open innovation means gradually shifting cooperation efforts towards (a) indirectly value-creating interaction activities and (b) interaction for the sake of common idea generation, be it within the network or at its boundaries.

6 Outlook

The properties of small and medium-sized companies on the one hand and the requirements for fruitful Web 2-0 based collaboration in company networks on the other hand make Web 2.0-based interaction activities within networks of SMEs a challenging field of research. Because of their inherently conflicting principles of (inter-)action, it is a demanding task to bring these two fields of research – networks of SMEs and Web 2.0 – together. Our paper points at the necessity of changing culture within SMEs in order to overcome the depicted gap: A corporate culture is required which not only accepts the employees of all hierarchical levels taking an active part in the cooperation, but also encourages them to do so.

Another area for future research lies at the heart of the following area of conflict which is distinctive for open innovation: The more partners involved in activities of common idea generation, the higher the probability of generating a truly new idea and business solution. The more partners who are interacting and generating vast amounts of ideas, the more important is the coordinating and channelling of interaction activities and outcomes, either from a security point of view or for content structuring reasons. These two research issues will have to be covered by subsequent research.

References

Alves, J., Marques, M.J., Saur, I., Marques, P.: Creativity and Innovation through Multidisciplinary and Multisectoral Cooperation. Creativity and Innovation Management 16(1), 27–34 (2007)

Bellmann, K., Gerster, B.: Netzwerkmanagement kleiner und mittlerer Unternehmen: Eine theoretische und empirische Untersuchung. In: Bellman, K., Becker, T. (eds.) Wertschöpfungsnetzwerke, pp. 53–68. Erich Schmidt Verlag, Berlin (2006)

Birkinshaw, J., Bessant, J., Delbridge, R.: Finding, Forming and Performing: Creating Networks for Discontinuous Innovation. California Management Review 43(3), 67–84 (2007)

Burns, P.: Entrepreneurship and Small Business. Palgrave, Hampshire (2001)

Chesbrough, H.: The Logic of Open Innovation: Managing Intellectual Property. California Management Review 45(3), 33–58 (2003)

CoreMedia, Berlecon Research: Enterprise 2.0 in Deutschland – Verbreitung, Chancen und Herausforderungen. A Study on behalf of CoreMedia conducted by Berlecon Research (2007)

Corsten, H.: Grundlagen der Koordination in Unternehmensnetzwerken. In: Corsten, H. (ed.) Unternehmensnetzwerke, Oldenburg, München, pp. 1–57 (2001)

De Saulles, M.: SMEs and the Web – Executive Summary. University of Brighton (2008a)

De Saulles, M.: Never too small to join the party. Information World Review (September 3, 2008b),
http://www.iwr.co.uk/information-world-review/features/2225252/never-small-join-party (last access: March 12, 2009)

Dewett, T.: Linking intrinsic motivation, risk taking, and employee creativity in an R&D environment. R&D Management 37(3), 197–208 (2007)

European Commission 2003: The new SME Definition – User guide and model declaration. Enterprise and Industry Publication (2003)

European Commission: Observatory of European SMEs – SMEs and cooperation. Enterpise Publication 2003/5 (2003a)

Gambetta, D.: Can We Trust? In: Gambetta, D. (ed.) Trust Making and Breaking Cooperative Relations, pp. 213–237. Basil Blackwell, London (2000)

Human, S.E., Provan, K.G.: External Resource Exchange and Perceptions of Competitiveness within Organizational Networks: An Organizational Learning Perspective. Frontiers of Entrepreneurship (1996)

Kratzer, J., Leenders, R.T., van Engelen, J.M.L.: Stimulating the potential: Creative performance and communication in innovation teams. Creativity and Innovation Management 13(1), 63–71 (2004)

Lakhani, K.R.: Innocentive.com. Harvard Business School case No. 9-608-170 (2008)

Levy, M., Powell, P.: Strategies for Growth in SMEs – The Role of Information and Information Systems. Information Systems Series (ISS). Elsevier, Oxford (2005)

Martins, E.C., Terblanche, F.: Building Organizational Culture that Stimulates Creativity and Innovation. European Journal of Innovation Management 6(1), 64–74 (2003)

McAfee, A.P.: Enterprise 2.0: The Drawn of Emergent Collaboration. Sloan Management Review 47(3), 21–28 (2006)

McKinsey and Company: Building the Web 2.0 Enterprise: Mc Kinsey Global Survey Results. The McKinsey Quarterly (July 2008)

Milles, M.B., Huberman, A.M.: Qualitative Data Analysis, 2nd edn. Sage Publications, Thousand Oaks (1994)

Oldham, G.R., Cummings, A.: Employee creativity: Personal and Contextual Factors at Work. The Academy of Management Journal 39(3), 607–634 (1996)

O'Reilly, T.: What Is Web 2.0 – Design Patterns and Business Models for the Next Generation of Software (2005),
http://www.oreillynet.com/pub/a/oreilly/tim/news/2005/09/30/
what-is-web-20.html (last access: March 12, 2009)

Osterloh, M., Rota, S.: Open Source development – Just another case of collective invention? Research Policy 36, 157–171 (2007)

Picot, A., Reichwald, R., Wigand, R.T.: Die grenzenlose Unternehmung – Information, Organisation und Management. Gabler, Wiesbaden (2003)

Piller, F.T., Walcher, D.: Toolkits for idea competitions: a novel method to integrate users in new product development. R&D Management 36(3), 307–318 (2006)

Romme, A.G.L.: Making a Difference: Organization as Design. Organization Science 14(5), 558–573 (2003)

Schaarschmidt, M., Von Kortzfleisch, H.: Social networking platforms as creativity fostering systems: Research model and exploratory study. University Koblenz-Landau, Computer Science Department Working Paper Series No. 9/2008 (2008)

Social Computing News Desk (2008): Web 2.0 is All About Using the Power of the Web Business Advantages, Says Expert. Social Computing Magazine (May 25, 2007) (2008) (last access: March 12, 2009),
http://www.socialcomputingmagazine.com/
viewcolumn.cfm?colid=249#bio

Street, C.T., Cameron, A.F.: External Relationships and the Small Business: A Review of Small Business Alliance and Network Research. Journal of Small Business Management 45(2), 239–266 (2007)

The Economist Intelligence Unit: Serious Business – Web 2.0 Goes Corporate. Report from the Economist Intelligence Unit Sponsored by FAST (2007)

Thielemann, F.: Die Gestaltung von Kooperationen kleiner und mittlerer Unternehmen. Innovation: Forschung und Management. No.7, IAI Institut für angewandte Innovationsforschung, Bochum (1996)

Tierney, P., Farmer, S.M., Graen, G.B.: An examination of leadership and employee creativity: the relevance of traits and relationships. Personnel Psychology 52, 591–620 (1999)

Van der Meer, H.: Open Innovation – The Dutch treat: Challenges in thinking in business models. Creativity and Innovation Management 16(2), 192–202 (2007)

Volery, T., Mensik, S.: The Role of Trust in Creating Effective Alliances: A Managerial Perspective. Journal of Business Ethics 17, 987–994 (1998)

Von Hippel, E.: Sticky Information and the Locus of Problem Solving. Management Science 40, 429–439 (1994)

Von Hippel, E.: Democratizing Innovation. MIT Press, Cambridge (2005)

Von Kortzfleisch, H., Mergel, I., Manouchehri, S., Schaarschmidt, M.: Corporate Web 2.0 Applications: Motives, Organizational Embeddedness, and Creativity. In: Hass, B., Walsh, G., Kilian, T. (eds.) Web 2.0: Neue Perspektiven für Marketing und Handel [trans. New Perspectives in Marketing and Business], pp. 73–89. Springer, Berlin (2008)

West, J., Lakhani, K.: Getting Clear About Communities in Open Innovation. Industry and Innovation 15(2), 223–231 (2008)

Conducting Creativity Brainstorming Sessions in Small and Medium-Sized Enterprises Using Computer-Mediated Communication Tools

Uday S. Murthy

School of Accountancy,
University of South Florida

Abstract. A variety of Web-based low cost computer-mediated communication (CMC) tools are now available for use by small and medium-sized enterprises (SME). These tools invariably incorporate chat systems that facilitate simultaneous input in synchronous electronic meeting environments, allowing what is referred to as "electronic brainstorming." Although prior research in information systems (IS) has established that electronic brainstorming can be superior to face-to-face brainstorming, there is a lack of detailed guidance regarding how CMC tools should be optimally configured to foster creativity in SMEs. This paper discusses factors to be considered in using CMC tools for creativity brainstorming and proposes recommendations for optimally configuring CMC tools to enhance creativity in SMEs. The recommendations are based on lessons learned from several recent experimental studies on the use of CMC tools for rich brainstorming tasks that require participants to invoke domain-specific knowledge. Based on a consideration of the advantages and disadvantages of the various configuration options, the recommendations provided can form the basis for selecting a CMC tool for creativity brainstorming or for creating an in-house CMC tool for the purpose.

Keywords: Computer-mediated communication (CMC), electronic brainstorming, creativity, small and medium-sized enterprises.

1 Introduction

Computer-mediated communication (CMC) technologies are increasingly being used to support communication between employees in small and medium-sized enterprises (SME), especially given their low cost and universal accessibility via the Internet. These technologies are unique in at least four ways. First, they allow participants to interact at varying levels of anonymity, thereby bypassing social cues that may negatively influence behaviour in face-to-face meetings. Second, they permit "any time, any place" meetings thus allowing employees of SMEs to work collaboratively regardless of time and geographical constraints. Third, they permit simultaneous input by multiple individuals—a key advantage over face-to-face meetings in a synchronous setting. Finally, an electronic log of the communication is automatically captured (a kind of "group memory"), which can be accessed subsequently by

G. Dhillon, B.C. Stahl, and R. Baskerville (Eds.): CreativeSME 2009, IFIP AICT 301, pp. 42–59, 2009.

employees and superiors for further processing. Not surprisingly, these technologies are increasingly being used in a wide array of business domains and are increasingly being viewed as indispensable for the conduct of collaborative work. Especially in light of the relatively low cost of Internet-based CMC tools for collaborative work, they can easily be deployed for both asynchronous work by "virtual teams" and also synchronous work by teams needing to work concurrently on business problems.

Organizations of all sizes, and especially SMEs, are constantly seeking ways to tap the creative potential of their employees. Mechanisms such as suggestion boxes and open-door policies encourage individual employees to offer their ideas for product and/or process improvement in the organization. Beyond such individual-based approaches, however, organizations realize that teams of employees can often come up with creative ideas that individuals acting alone cannot (Mohrman, Cohen, & Mohrman, 1995). As far back as the late 1930s, Osborn—who popularized the term "brainstorming"—proposed that groups could enhance their creative output by following a few rules. According to Osborn's rules, criticism of ideas proposed by others should be avoided, wild ideas are encouraged, groups should seek to maximize the quantity of ideas generated, and members are encouraged to combine and improve on ideas proposed by others. As opposed to working alone, a key reason why individuals interacting in a team can generate more ideas is that when working in a team members can build on the ideas proposed by others (Mednick, 1962; Milgram & Rabkin, 1980). Essentially, a good idea expressed by one team member can foster additional good ideas by other team members who are inspired by the original good idea. There are also socially desirable reasons for meeting in teams, for example greater sense of commitment to the outcomes from jointly performed work. It is for these reasons that creativity sessions often involve teams of employees brainstorming together.

There are, however, some drawbacks to face-to-face creativity sessions that can inhibit overall productivity, most notably social loafing, production blocking, and evaluation apprehension (Mullen, Johnson, & Salas, 1991). Social loafing, also known as free riding or shirking, manifests itself when individual team members do not contribute their fair share to the team effort. Especially when team sizes are large, it is easy for any one team member in a face-to-face environment to stay silent and simply allow others to speak. Unless the session has a facilitator or leader who specifically calls on individual team members, there is nothing to prevent an individual member from contributing little to nothing at all to the session. The second drawback of face-to-face meetings is the production blocking phenomenon. The consequence of this phenomenon is that in a face-to-face meeting a team member cannot contribute ideas as and when they arise in the mind, because some other team member may be speaking and social norms require that the speaker not be interrupted. Furthermore, social norms also dictate that one must pay attention to the person speaking, and the mental effort consumed by listening to the speaker detracts from effort that could otherwise be aimed at generating creative ideas. The third inhibitor of productivity in face-to-face creativity sessions is the evaluation apprehension phenomenon. In a team comprised of both senior and junior employees in an organization, the junior members are particular prone to this phenomenon. Essentially, the evaluation apprehension phenomenon means that junior members are unwilling to express their ideas freely, for fear that senior members may react negatively to the suggestions of junior members. A final drawback of face-to-face creativity sessions is that there is no real-time accessible "running log" of everything that is said during the session. Thus, it is difficult for individuals to recall ideas that have already been proposed, to avoid duplication and/or to build on previously mentioned ideas. Finally, it is important to note that face-to-face brainstorming requires all team members to be present at the same physical location at the same time.

The aforementioned three drawbacks, or process losses, of face-to-face creativity sessions can be overcome by employing CMC tools. In the information systems (IS) literature, there is considerable empirical evidence that brainstorming sessions held using CMC tools, referred to as "electronic brainstorming," is superior to face-to-face brainstorming (Gallupe et al. 1991; Nunamaker et al. 1991; Fjermestad & Hiltz 1998). The main reasons why teams using CMC tools generate more ideas than teams brainstorming face-to-face is because features of CMC tools allow computer-mediated teams to overcome the process losses inherent in face-to-face communication. Specifically, a CMC system used for creativity brainstorming offers four distinct advantages over face-to-face brainstorming: (1) parallel communication, also called simultaneous input, whereby each team member can simply type ideas into the system as they arise, (2) the possibility of anonymous or semi-anonymous input (to be explained later in the paper), whereby members can provide their input anonymously without fear of criticism, (3) a real-time accessible log of the creativity session, whereby ideas proposed by all members are accessible on a common screen that can be reviewed by all members at their convenience, and (4) members of the brainstorming team do not all have to be physically present at the same location; using Internet technologies members can log on from remote and still participate in the CMC-based brainstorming session. Parallel communication effectively overcomes the production blocking phenomenon and is one of the main reasons why CMC based brainstorming is more effective than face-to-face brainstorming (Nijstad, Stroebe, & Lodewijkx, 2003). The real-time log of the session in an electronic brainstorming session makes it easier to build on ideas proposed by others and also ensure that more ideas are read and processed by participants in the session. Using Internet protocols, members can participate from remote location, thus saving travel time and costs associated with assembling all participants at one physical location as must be done in face-to-face brainstorming.

Given these advantages of a CMC creativity brainstorming system, the question arises as to how the system can be configured to meet the needs of SMEs, considering the specific task types and individual characteristics that might affect the optimal use of such systems. Are there unique characteristics of certain brainstorming tasks that require the use of certain CMC features? What are the individual characteristics of employees, such as rank and position in the organization that might warrant the use of some CMC features but not others? Should the various CMC features be used in different ways at different phases in the brainstorming session? Answers to questions such as these would help SMEs harness the power of CMC tools for their creativity brainstorming sessions. This paper discusses the considerations involved and suggests configuration settings for CMC creativity brainstorming systems for SMEs so that they can obtain the maximum benefit from such systems.

2 Background on Brainstorming

The concept of brainstorming is not new. Osborn (1963), one of the original proponents of group brainstorming, proposed the following four rules for brainstorming:

1. Criticism is ruled out. Adverse judgment of ideas must be withheld;
2. "Free-wheeling" is welcomed. The wilder the idea, the better; it is easier to tame down than to think up;
3. Quantity is wanted. The greater the number of ideas, the more the likelihood of useful ideas; and
4. Combination and improvement are sought. In addition to contributing ideas of their own, participants should suggest how ideas of others can be turned into better ideas or how two or more ideas can be joined into still another idea.

The rationale for these rules is to reduce inhibitions and maximize the effectiveness of the brainstorming session, so that the largest number of good ideas can be generated. The first three rules seek to get participants to generate as many ideas as possible without regard to the ideas being proposed by others. The "free-wheeling" dictum seeks to get participants' creative juices flowing—to get them to "think outside the box." Sometimes, what may seem like a "wild" idea to the person proposing it may turn out to be the most original, innovative, and practical idea generated during the session. The last rule takes advantage of the fact that there are multiple participants in the team brainstorming session; it is logical to expect that ideas proposed by other team members might trigger ideas from another member that s/he would not have thought of alone.

Beyond the aforementioned four rules of brainstorming, however, there are other factors to consider in designing computer-mediated creativity brainstorming sessions. These include the use of alternative brainstorming techniques, facilitation techniques, and the role of the specific type of creativity task that the team addresses. These are now discussed.

2.1 Brainstorming Techniques

Following Osborn's approach, the most natural technique for conducting creativity brainstorming is the interactive technique, wherein participants brainstorm at the same time but possibly from different locations. In the interactive technique, participants see ideas proposed by others in real-time, since each participant can simultaneously type his or her ideas and all ideas' input appears in group memory. Interactive brainstorming thus facilitates Osborn's fourth rule of brainstorming, since it allows participants to build on ideas offered by others in the session. Indeed, the term "brainstorming" implies that individuals interact and jointly produce ideas. Interestingly, however, there is considerable research that shows that the *nominal group technique* is superior to interactive brainstorming, when the brainstorming session is conducted face-to-face. In the nominal group technique, individuals "brainstorm" by themselves—that is, they record their own ideas without interaction with anyone. Subsequently, members come together to share the ideas they had individually generated. All ideas individually produced are merged together. After eliminating duplicates, the merged set of ideas, constitutes the total number of unique ideas developed by the team, although they had "brainstormed" individually.

So which technique is "better" when using CMC to support creativity brainstorming—interactive or nominal brainstorming? There are both positive and negative aspects to each technique. Some researchers have argued that interactive brainstorming is necessary in order for group members to receive feedback and stimulation for generating ideas (Satzinger, Garfield, & Nagasundaram 1999). Satzinger et al. (1999) found that, through the group memory feature, interactive groups are exposed to the ideas of others while brainstorming and reading others' ideas can provide stimulus for generating new ideas of their own. This finding tends to validate the importance of Osborn's fourth rule of brainstorming, i.e., building off the ideas of others is a way to enhance creativity. However, one problem that can arise in interactive groups is cognitive inertia, which means that individuals tend to stay within the frame of previously submitted ideas. That is, individual members tend to "follow the lead" of others and offer only slight variations of previous ideas rather than entirely different, new, unique ideas. This phenomenon has been referred to as "groupthink"—a tendency for all group members to offer ideas that are essentially within the same realm, that is, ideas that do not differ substantially. The end result is a narrower range of ideas than if individuals were not subject to the cognitive inertia or groupthink phenomena. Another problem that can arise in interactive brainstorming is distraction conflict (Aiken & Sloan 1997; Pinsonneault & Barki 1999). In an interactive session, off-task comments made by others can be distracting, leading to a reduction in creative output. Although the group memory is a positive feature of electronic brainstorming, team members may become distracted by reading others' ideas, which takes time away from offering new ideas of their own.

The nominal brainstorming technique does have advantages. Pitfalls such as cognitive inertia and groupthink are not as likely in the nominal technique, since each participant generates ideas individually, at least initially. Additionally, since there is no real-time available group memory of ideas proposed by others, the nominal technique results in less distraction conflict—individuals cannot be distracted by off task comments or by reading the ideas put forth by others. The main drawback of the nominal group brainstorming technique, however, is that brainstorming by oneself makes it impossible to build off the ideas proposed by others. In effect, the nominal group technique violates Osborn's fourth rule of brainstorming. Therefore, the lack of interaction in nominal group brainstorming would seem to run counter to the concept of brainstorming as envisaged by Osborn (1963).

Whether interactive electronic or nominal electronic brainstorming is superior is an empirical question, which has been addressed to some extent in prior research. Interestingly, Gallupe et al. (1991) found no significant difference between interactive and nominal electronic brainstorming. Lynch, Murthy, & Engle (2009) also found no significant difference between the interactive and nominal group brainstorming techniques, in the context of a fraud brainstorming task. On the other hand, Valacich et al. (1994) found that larger groups brainstorming in interactive mode using technology produced a significantly higher number of ideas compared to electronic nominal groups. Given that there is no clear evidence that either technique dominates, the logical conclusion is that both techniques could be used with no substantial loss of effectiveness. Indeed, what might make the most sense is to use the techniques in conjunction—a phase of nominal group brainstorming, followed by a phase of interactive brainstorming, with perhaps a repetition of the sequence. Such an approach captures the benefits of both techniques, while mitigating the disadvantages of each.

One more brainstorming technique is worth discussing. Referred to as the "round-robin technique," it involves participants taking turns to propose ideas. In a face-to-face creativity brainstorming session, this technique makes sense, since it tends to equalize participation, i.e., the session cannot be dominated by one or a few members. Thus, in a face-to-face session, it makes sense to have participants take turns to speak. In an electronic creativity brainstorming session, however, given the parallel communication feature that allows simultaneous input by all participants, the question arises whether the round-robin technique applies, since there is less likelihood of the session being dominated by one or a few participants (i.e., every participant has an equal opportunity to input his or her ideas). I argue that the round-robin technique could still be productively employed even in an electronic creativity brainstorming session. Since the round-robin technique offers one participant's idea at a time for the group to consider, it directs attention towards that idea in a way that interactive brainstorming cannot. The round-robin technique could be programmed into the CMC tool, so that it automatically switches from participant to participant, obtains his/her idea, and posts it to group memory.

2.2 Interaction Mode

As indicated earlier, the use of CMC permits the creativity brainstorming sessions to be conducted with participants identified in one of three modes: anonymous, semi-anonymous, or non-anonymous. Anonymous interaction and non-anonymous interaction should be self-explanatory. In anonymous interaction, there is no identification at all of the author of an idea. Participant "A" could type an idea and the same participant could type a second comment indicating that the previously typed idea is an "excellent idea." The other participants would not know that it is in fact the very same participant who proposed the idea who is indicating that it is an excellent idea.

Non-anonymous brainstorming is the other extreme, where every idea is tagged with the full (real) name of the participant who input that idea. An intermediate identification mechanism is *semi-anonymous* brainstorming, in which each participant is assigned a unique code, which cannot be traced to the individual. Every idea input is tagged with this unique code. This approach would enhance transparency—an idea proposed by participant "X" cannot be touted as an excellent idea by participant "X" (or if that is the case, the other participants would see through it). If it is deemed essential for participants' identity to be hidden, semi-anonymous interaction is preferred to completely anonymous interaction, to prevent the sort of gaming alluded to here. That is, semi-anonymous interaction preserves anonymity while preventing "gaming" wherein a participant could anonymously comment on his/her own idea, as if the comment were coming from some other participant.

2.3 Facilitation

It is common for an expert facilitator to be used to run the brainstorming session. In an SME, the facilitator may be a senior member within the organization, rather than a hired consultant. The facilitator defines the problem, sets the agenda, and controls the flow of steps in the session. Prior to the session itself, the facilitator determines who will participate and might assign some background reading so that participants have a starting point and/or a common base of prior knowledge going into the session.

In preparation for the brainstorming session, the facilitator might also create a list of questions that could be used to stimulate discussion. For example, in a creativity session aimed at generating ideas for a new product, a few leading questions might be "What was the last successful new product introduced to the market? What were the unique attributes of that product? What made the product successful?" While not all of such advance questions may be actually posed during the session, the facilitator can judiciously propose a question if the session appears to be at an impasse. Another role the facilitator can play is to manage the session, so that it is not dominated by one or a few members. Some brainstorming techniques are aimed specifically at ensuring that all participants have their input attended to by other participants—these techniques will be discussed later in the paper.

So what exactly is "facilitation" in the context of a creativity brainstorming session? Bostrom et al. (1993, p. 147) defines facilitation as "...the set of functions or activities carried out before, during, and after a meeting to help the group achieve its own outcomes." There are two main types of facilitation—process facilitation and content facilitation. Process facilitation involves setting the agenda for the creativity session, determining and controlling who participates and when, and moving participants through the steps in a multi-step task. Content facilitation, on the other hand, involves efforts to influence the substance, or output, of the creativity session. One example of content facilitation is the facilitator suggesting specific alternatives for participants to consider. Another example of content facilitation is to provide props or prompts to lead participants in a certain direction.

There is evidence in the IS literature that facilitation improves group performance in many settings (Anson et al., 1995; Niederman et al., 1996; Wheeler and Valacich, 1996; Dennis and Wixom, 2001). For example, Wheeler and Valacich (1996) found that facilitated groups more faithfully followed the outlined heuristics and decision-making sequence, which in turn led to better decision quality, in comparison to groups that were not so facilitated. Santanen et al. (2004) found that groups who used a model of idea facilitation in which group goals were specified every two or eight minutes performed better than groups who brainstormed without the aid of such idea facilitation.

Although prior research generally supports the notion that facilitation results in positive group outcomes, it is noteworthy that the most prior studies on the use of facilitation techniques in conjunction with CMC tools has used a human facilitator. Naturally, some expert facilitators might be better than others. Thus, it is difficult to determine the extent to which the positive outcomes of a facilitated CMC session is a function of the specific human facilitator who led the session. One alternative to using an expert human facilitator is to *automate* facilitation, to the extent possible. When using CMC tools, it is possible to automate both process and content facilitation at least to some degree. For example, process facilitation steps that involve moving participants through a set agenda, making participants take turns to contribute ideas, and enforcing time limits for different phases of the session can be programmed into the CMC tool. Thus, rather than having a human facilitator perform these steps, they can be automated so that the CMC system "drives" participants through the creativity brainstorming session. Content facilitation can also similarly be automated. Specifically, the CMC tool can be configured to automatically offer alternatives for participants to consider. The author has developed an electronic brainstorming system that automates content facilitation for a fraud brainstorming scenario, whereby prompts appear on the screen at periodic intervals offering suggestions for participants to consider as they brainstorm (Lynch, Murthy, & Engle, 2009).

2.4 Consideration of Creativity Task Type

As indicated earlier, there is substantial evidence in the IS literature that teams brainstorming electronically outperform teams brainstorming face-to-face. One consideration in evaluating that body of research, however, is that the majority of studies used students as participants in experiments and had them brainstorm on relatively simple tasks that did not require significant domain-specific knowledge. As examples of tasks used, participants in these studies are asked to come up with solutions to the parking problem on campus, ideas for how tourism in their city could be improved, and what uses they could come up with for an extra thumb on a hand. These tasks do not require much domain-specific knowledge for generating ideas. If one has ever driven on campus and struggled to find parking, one can come up with ideas to improve the parking problem. If one has ever travelled, one has ideas about how tourism can be improved. Coming up with creative solutions to business problems, however, is another matter. Unless one has the requisite education and some experience working as an auditor in a public accounting firm, it would be difficult to come up with specific and relevant ideas on how auditing procedures could be improved.

For creativity brainstorming sessions aimed at generating ideas to solve specific business problems, it is important to consider the extent to which participants' background and experiences match the creativity task. For example, if the creativity task entails developing ideas for new products or services, it would be important for the brainstorming team to include one or more members from each of the following areas: sales, marketing, advertising, product design, manufacturing, and distribution. Within each of these areas, it is worth including both highly experienced and relatively inexperienced employees. While experienced employees can bring their wealth of experience to bear, inexperienced employees are often the ones who can engage in "outside the box" thinking to come up with fresh ideas. The idea of including members from all functional areas is to bring different perspectives to the brainstorming session, which is particularly important for leveraging Osborn's fourth rule of brainstorming—combining ideas proposed by others to form new innovative ideas.

Also depending on the specific business related reason for the creativity brainstorming session, it may be necessary to provide background reading to participants. This background reading should "set the stage" for the brainstorming session, ensuring that all participants come to the session with the same set of key assumptions. For example, for a creativity brainstorming session aimed at generating ideas for new products, participants could be given background material relating to the market, competitors' products, and prior failed and successful product ideas. In the United States, auditing standards require auditors to conduct a fraud brainstorming session at the beginning of the audit of publicly held companies. As background reading for such a fraud brainstorming session, participating auditors should be assigned to read material about the client, the industry in which the client operates, and other environmental factors that might impact the nature and type of fraud risks that might be present. The main purpose of such background reading is to get all participants "on the same page" and minimize the extent of irrelevant or impractical ideas that are proposed. It would also be important to make such background material available during the creativity brainstorming session itself, either in paper form or accessible on the computer. Participants can be encouraged to refer to these materials, especially in later stages of brainstorming when participants might be running out of ideas.

3   Using CMC Tools for Creativity Brainstorming

3.1   Sample Creativity Brainstorming Task

To provide a concrete example of a creativity brainstorming session for an SME, imagine that the management of the SME would like to solicit ideas from employees on how the firm's profits could be increased. They would first identify key employees from all departments who could contribute their expertise to such an endeavour. The task proposed to participating employees could be framed as follows:

> *Over the past several years, revenues and profitability have been declining for <<your SME>>. The firm's Chief Executive Officer has appointed you to a task force with ten other SME employees to generate ideas about how <<your SME>> can increase its revenues and profitability. He has specifically requested ideas for increasing the firm's share of the market by obtaining new clients, offering new products, and options for reducing expenses.*

The author has built a Web-based brainstorming system that could be used for conducting creativity sessions, shown in Figure 1 below.

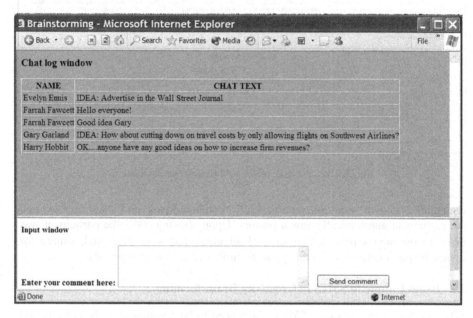

Fig. 1. Basic Web-based Brainstorming System

The system was built using Microsoft's Active Server Pages (ASP) technology. Tables holding configuration settings (e.g., duration of the session, number of participants, etc.), the real-time log of the session, and participant information (e.g., log on time, log off time, number of comments, etc.) are all housed in an open-source relational database system (MySQL). Participants log on to a web site, input their personal information such as their name (or logon ID, if so configured), and are taken to a page of instructions. After all participants are logged on, participants are allowed to move to the main brainstorming screen, shown in Figure 1. To use system, participants type their ideas in the input window at the bottom of their screen. Upon clicking 'Send comment' (or hitting Enter) the idea is transferred to the larger window above the input window. All participants' ideas appear sequentially in the large window, which in effect constitutes the "group memory" or real-time log of the creativity session. Ideas proposed by all participants appear in real-time in the group memory window. Prior comments made during the session are accessible by scrolling up through the group memory. In the rudimentary system that was developed, participants typed the word "IDEA" to distinguish between ideas being proposed about increasing revenues and profitability and comments that simply represented miscellaneous communication between team members."

Subsequently, an enhanced version of the system was created specifically for conducting a fraud brainstorming session. The resulting system is shown in Figure 2. As can be seen in Figure 2, there are some task-specific features that were built into the system. For example, the window at the top contains instructions specific to the fraud brainstorming scenario. At the top right of that window, the brainstorming time

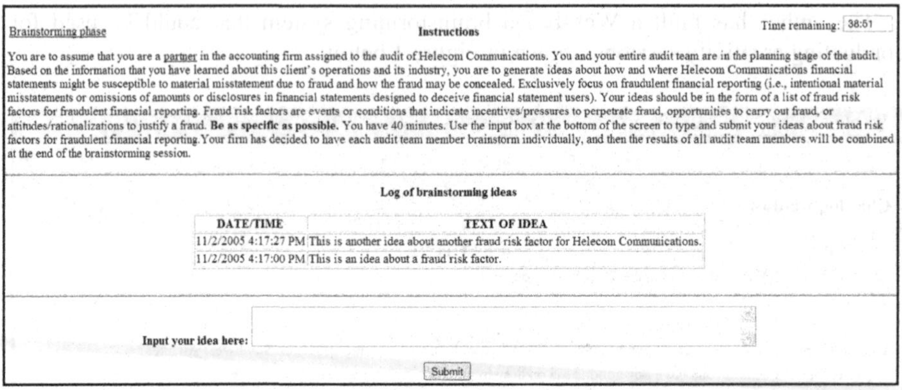

Fig. 2. Task-Specific Web-based Brainstorming System

remaining is shown—the time automatically "counted down" and when time expired the participant automatically saw a prompt. Upon clicking 'OK' the participant was taken to the next screen, which showed all ideas that were generated, simply for review by participants (i.e., at that point no further ideas could be added).

3.2 Issues Unique to SMEs in Creativity Brainstorming

What are the issues unique to SMEs which need to be considered in the conduct and optimization of computer-mediated creativity brainstorming sessions? First, by definition, SMEs have fewer employees than large organizations. One consequence of the smaller size is that the likelihood of employees having well-developed relational bonds is higher in an SME as compared to a very large organization. Another consequence of the smaller size of an SME is that there are likely to be fewer layers of hierarchy between top management and lower level employees. The implications of a "flatter" SME organization is that the employees who come together for the purpose of creativity brainstorming are likely to know one another very well. Second, SMEs very likely face significant resource constraints in comparison with large organizations. An SME, therefore, most likely will not have the resources at its disposal to purchase a high-end multi-featured group support system or to hire an expert facilitator to conduct creativity brainstorming sessions. Third, due to the relatively small size of an SME, the degree of specialization of jobs is likely to be lower as compared to a large organization. In other words, employees of SMEs very likely undertake multiple roles within the organization, even if only temporarily (e.g., to cover for an absent co-worker whose job might be fairly different). Since employees in an SME might be expected to be familiar with multiple job responsibilities, this means that they may not be able to develop a sufficiently high level of expertise in any one job. Accordingly, the expectations for specialized contributions in a creativity brainstorming session comprised of employees at an SME would be different in contrast to a similar session at a large organization with employees who have years of experience at one narrowly defined job role.

These three unique characteristics of SMEs have implications for the CMC tool configuration recommendations that would result in the most effective creativity brainstorming session for such organizations. To reiterate, the three significantly unique characteristics of SMEs in the context of creativity brainstorming are (1) relatively small size resulting in a "flatter" organization wherein employees who come together for brainstorming will know each other well, (2) resource constraints that limit the budget for a computer-mediated creativity brainstorming system, and (3) a lower degree of narrow specialization and potential expertise that SME employees can bring to the creativity brainstorming session, compared to large organizations. After first outlining recommendations for configuring CMC tools for creativity brainstorming in general, specific propositions are offered regarding the most effective configuration of CMC creativity brainstorming systems given the unique features of SMEs.

3.3 CMC Tool Configuration Recommendations

Having discussed the various factors that relate to the design of a CMC creativity brainstorming session, specific recommendations for configuring a CMC tool for use in a creativity brainstorming session are now offered. It is beyond the scope of this paper to review specific CMC tools for creativity brainstorming. The InnovationTools web site offers reviews of software tools for supporting creativity brainstorming.[1] While a number of Web-based CMC tools are available in the market, the extent to which each configuration recommendation can be implemented in any particular tool will require additional research. If resources and in-house expertise is available in the SME, it would be possible to build a custom CMC tool for creativity brainstorming that incorporates all configuration options, which can be customized as desired.

Before turning to the configuration recommendations, some general guidelines for conducting creativity brainstorming sessions are worth considering. It may be beneficial to remind participants of Osborn's rules of brainstorming at the beginning of the session. Specifically, participants should refrain from criticizing ideas proposed by others. The brainstorming session could then begin with a "warm up" task, where participants engage in brainstorming on an issue unrelated to the main purpose of the session. For example, if the brainstorming session is aimed at generating ideas for new products, the warm up session might involve asking participants to brainstorm about what they would do if they were unexpectedly given a day off at work. Such an exercise, which would very likely be viewed as a "fun" exercise, would probably put participants in a good, playful mood, ideal for fostering creativity for the "real" brainstorming task. Additionally, it may be worthwhile to refresh participants' memories regarding the Osborn rules in the middle of the session. For example, following rule 4 in Osborn's rules, after several ideas have been proposed and if participants appear to be stuck, the facilitator can encourage them to try to combine existing ideas to form a new idea.

In the previous section, four factors relevant for creativity brainstorming were outlined, namely brainstorming technique type, interaction mode, facilitation

---

[1] See http://www.innovationtools.com/Tools/SoftwareHeadlines.asp at the InnovationTools site.

technique, and task type. For the actual conduct of a computer-mediated creativity brainstorming session in an organization, several questions might be raised. Which particular brainstorming technique should be used? Should interaction be anonymous, non-anonymous, or semi-anonymous? Should process and/or content facilitation be used, and if so what specific types of process/content facilitation are to be deployed?

To complicate matters further, many of the options available are not "either or" options and can be used in conjunction with one another. Should the session begin with a phase of nominal group brainstorming followed by a phase of interactive brainstorming? Should the round-robin technique be introduced after a phase of interactive or nominal group brainstorming? Should the facilitator interject content facilitation if participants appear to be in a state of cognitive inertia? There is evidence in the literature that most innovative ideas come early in the session (Diehl and Stroebe 1991; Nijstad and Stroebe 2006). Thus, session management becomes more critical in the later stages of the brainstorming session, when participants are fatigued and should be spurred to produce additional ideas. Clearly, there are a host of options to consider, depending on the specific creativity task at hand for the SME.

Shown in Table 1 are the various factors discussed in the previous section, the options relating to the factor, and the recommendations relative to each factor option in designing the creativity brainstorming session.

Table 1. Recommendations for Creativity Brainstorming CMC Configuration

Factor	Option	Recommendation
Brainstorming technique	* Nominal	Use technique either at the beginning or the middle of the session, to allow participants to generate their own ideas without distraction conflict and to avoid "groupthink"
	* Interactive	Longest brainstorming time should be allocated to interactive brainstorming, to allow participants to see others' ideas and build off one another's ideas
	* Round-robin	Use to force each participant to offer an idea, in contexts where participants are likely to "loaf" (not offer their own ideas). Not appropriate when team size is large (e.g., greater than 10)
Interaction mode	* Anonymous	Configure session to be anonymous when creativity topic may be somewhat controversial and when it is not necessary to uniquely identify the author of each idea.
	* Semi-anonymous	Configure semi-anonymous identification when it is necessary to tag each idea's author, without revealing the author's full identity. Prevents "gaming" the session (author of an idea claiming in a subsequent posting that the idea is a good one).
	* Non-anonymous	Reveal full identity of each participant when there is little to no likelihood that participants will be inhibited from offering their ideas
Facilitation	* Content	Provide specific prompts, comprising subject-specific issues, to spur the generation of ideas relating to the prompt. Use later in the session, when participants may be running out of ideas.

Table 1. (*continued*)

	* Process	Have a set agenda and move participants through phases, with each phase being timed, when a large number of participants are involved, when multiple creativity tasks are to be undertaken, and when it is likely that participants may meander "off task."
	* Human	If an expert is available and has a successful track record, employ a human facilitator. If the content or process facilitation to be performed by the human facilitator is relatively generic, then consider whether the costs of the human facilitator are justified.
	* Automated	If human facilitators are not available or have resulted in variable outcomes, and if the content or process facilitation to be provided is generic, program the facilitation (content or process) into the CMC tool system.
Task type	* General (cross-department)	If the creativity brainstorming task is of the type that spans multiple department, involve employees from all departments involved, including departments that may only tangentially be related to the creativity brainstorming task. Consider the use of anonymous interactive brainstorming for a "free-wheeling" type of discussion.
	* Specialized (domain-specific)	If the creativity brainstorming task is highly specialized, requiring extensive domain-specific knowledge, select knowledgeable experts in the domain. It may be necessary to provide participants with background reading so that they are all "on the same page" during the brainstorming session.

3.4 Propositions for Computer-Mediated Creative Brainstorming in SMEs

It is important to note that the recommendations indicated in Table 1 are generic, in that they apply to large organizations as well as SMEs. In light of their unique features in comparison to large organizations, the question remains as to the implications of the broad recommendations for creativity brainstorming specifically for SMEs. Given that relatively little research has focused specifically on creativity brainstorming in the context of SMEs, the recommendations that follow are framed as propositions, which future research can subject to empirical testing. The list of propositions offered below is intended to be illustrative rather than exhaustive. Reviewing Table 1 and considering the unique features of SMEs, it would undoubtedly be possible to generate additional propositions and/or refine the ones suggested below.

Proposition 1: *For SMEs, creativity sessions will be more effective in interactive brainstorming mode than in nominal brainstorming mode.*

The rationale for Proposition 1 stems from SMEs being "flatter" with a higher likelihood of participants knowing one another and relating to one another well. Accordingly, participants are more likely to build off the ideas proposed by others, taking advantage of the benefits of interactivity. As additional support for this proposition, there is evidence in prior research that interacting groups feel better about electronic brainstorming than nominal groups (Gallupe et al. 1991). Given the higher degree of relational bonding among brainstorming participants in an SME, there should be a greater degree of cognitive stimulation resulting from viewing the ideas of other members (Connolly et al., 1993). As Paulus & Dzindolet (1993) suggest, interactive brainstorming should foster social influence processes that should promote a greater numbers of ideas. In contrast to interactive brainstorming, by definition nominal brainstorming does not provide cognitive stimulation from others' ideas nor are social influence processes possible (since each member "brainstorms" in isolation), both of which could inhibit creativity brainstorming productivity among employees in a closely knit SME.

Proposition 2: *When the brainstorming task is specialized (domain-specific) rather than general (cross-department), the round-robin brainstorming technique will be the most effective in an SME.*

Recall that the round-robin technique forces each participant to offer an idea. Due to the lower degree of narrow specialization among employees in an SME, it is likely that employees in other functional areas can offer constructive ideas because of the "cross pollination" of tasks across departments. Thus, in such situations, the round-robin technique elicits input from each employee who may have an interesting insight to offer, and there is a high likelihood that each idea thus proposed will be attended to by all other employees. In contrast to the round-robin technique, when either nominal or interactive brainstorming is employed individual ideas offered by an employee are not likely to be attended to by other employees to the same degree. When the brainstorming task is specialized it is important to obtain relatively equal levels of participation from all participants in the creativity brainstorming session, which the round-robin technique facilitates (Delbecq and Van de Ven 1971; Van de Ven and Delbecq 1974).

Proposition 3: *For SMEs, creativity sessions will be more effective in non-anonymous brainstorming mode than in the anonymous or semi-anonymous brainstorming modes.*

As Pinsonneault et al. (1999) indicate, non-anonymous brainstorming has two process gains in comparison to anonymous brainstorming: observational learning and social recognition. The idea of "observational learning" is that brainstorming participants can learn from and imitate the best performers in the session and "social recognition" means that individuals want their contributions to be recognized by others. Since it is quite likely that participants in a brainstorming session within an SME would have "bonded" well with one another, the interaction mode should be non-anonymous (i.e., identified) to foster both observational learning and social recognition anonymous. In contrast to non-anonymous brainstorming, both anonymous and semi-anonymous brainstorming modes will be viewed as "unnatural" and inhibiting. Not knowing the author of ideas being proposed is likely to be viewed negatively by participants, resulting in lower productivity, compared to when the session is non-anonymous. Given the likely high degree of relational bonding in an SME, it is also unlikely that the creativity brainstorming topic would be controversial, which is when anonymous or semi-anonymous brainstorming is advantageous. Finally, there is unlikely to be significant evaluation apprehension in an SME, which is also the condition when anonymous or semi-anonymous brainstorming is likely to be most effective.

Proposition 4: *Creativity brainstorming sessions in SMEs will be more effective when process facilitation (agenda setting) is employed than when the session is not facilitated.*

As indicated in Table 1, one reason to employ process facilitation is when it is likely that participants may meander "off task," i.e., engage in discussion that is unrelated to the issue at hand. Given that employees at SMEs would likely have bonded very well, it is natural to expect them to engage in some degree of "chit chat" in a computer-mediated session. Thus, the use of process facilitation techniques that involve setting an agenda and moving participants through the agenda should result in improved brainstorming effectiveness (Bostrom et al. 1993).

Proposition 5: *For specialized (domain-specific) creativity brainstorming tasks, effectiveness will be higher when content facilitation is provided for SME participants than when it is not provided.*

The logic underlying Proposition 5 stems from the lower likelihood of highly specialized domain knowledge in SME employees, given that they very likely perform a wider range of tasks than in large organizations wherein employees more likely perform narrow, highly specialized tasks. Content facilitation that seems to spur ideas by providing content related prompts should therefore be highly effective particularly for SMEs. Evidence consistent with this proposition is reported by Lynch, Murthy, & Engle (2009), who found that content facilitation by way of prompts about fraud risk categories resulted in greater brainstorming effectiveness.

Proposition 6: *For SME participants in a creativity brainstorming session, content facilitation will be more effective when interactive brainstorming is employed than when nominal brainstorming is employed.*

The rationale for Proposition 6 follows from the notion that employees in SMEs would likely have bonded together very well. Consequently, in response to content facilitation prompts, when the SME participants are engaged in interactive brainstorming, it is likely that the facilitation prompt would lead to discussion and the spurring of additional ideas as participants go back and forth in considering the prompt. Consistent with this idea, Miranda and Bostrom (1997) report that content facilitation can have a positive effect on group cohesiveness and participation, both of which are naturally facilitated if the brainstorming session is interactive. The lack of interactivity in the nominal technique would lead to decreased brainstorming effectiveness in such a scenario.

To reiterate, the propositions indicated above are not intended to be an exhaustive list. Additional propositions can almost certainly be generated by considering different combinations of brainstorming technique, interaction mode, facilitation technique, and task type, in light of the unique issues prevalent in SMEs. Using controlled laboratory experiments as well as field experiments, the propositions suggested above can be subjected to empirical testing to confirm (or disconfirm) their validity.

4 Summary and Conclusion

Given the availability of low-cost Web-based CMC tools, this paper discusses how these tools can be used for conducting creativity brainstorming sessions in an SME. In addition to discussing the various factors of relevance in using a CMC tool for creativity brainstorming, the paper provided recommendations regarding how the tool could be configured to maximize brainstorming effectiveness. The recommendations are based on lessons learned from several recent experimental studies on the use of CMC tools in brainstorming tasks that go beyond the relatively simplistic tasks used in the early IS research on electronic brainstorming. Alternative brainstorming techniques such as interactive, nominal, and round-robin brainstorming were discussed. Options for the interaction mode were presented, namely anonymous, non-anonymous and semi-anonymous brainstorming. The use of process and content facilitation was also discussed. It is clear that CMC tools can be effectively used to enhance brainstorming creativity in SMEs.

There are many potential avenues for future research to explore the effectiveness and limitations of CMC tools for creativity brainstorming sessions. For instance, future research should be conducted to examine whether there is an interactive effect between the extent of subjects' experience using CMC tools for brainstorming and the degree of creativity of their ideas. Future research could also explore whether the use of CMC tools for creativity brainstorming significantly alters the interpersonal dynamics of the brainstorming team, because of the absence of face-to-face contact and the loss of the rich visual and verbal cues that are present in face-to-face creativity brainstorming sessions. Finally, user surveys combined with expert evaluation of the quality of ideas generated from creativity brainstorming sessions configured in different ways would yield answers regarding the most optimal configuration from both an effectiveness and user satisfaction perspective. To conclude, this paper raises issues regarding the various possible configurations of computer-mediated creativity brainstorming sessions and provides recommendations for setting the configurations based on task, participant, and technology features.

References

Aiken, M., Sloan, H.: The use of two electronic idea generation techniques in strategy planning meetings. Journal of Business Communication 34(4), 370–382 (1997)

Anson, R., Bostrom, R., Wynne, B.: An experiment assessing group support system and facilitator effects on meeting outcomes. Management Science 41(2), 189–209 (1995)

Bostrom, R., Anson, R., Clawson, V.: Group facilitation and group support systems. In: Jessup, L., Valacich, J.S. (eds.) Group Support Systems: New Perspectives, pp. 146–168. Macmillan Publishing Co., New York (1993)

Dennis, A.R., Wixom, B.H.: Investigating the moderators of the group support systems use with meta-analysis. Journal of Management Information Systems 18(3), 235–257 (2001)

Diehl, M., Stroebe, W.: Productivity loss in idea-generation groups: Tracking down the blocking effect. Journal of Personality and Social Psychology 61(3), 392–403 (1991)

Fjermestad, J., Hiltz, S.R.: An assessment of group support systems experiment research: Methodology and results. Journal of Management Information Systems 15(3), 7–149 (1998)

Gallupe, R.B., Bastianutti, L.M., Cooper, W.H.: Unblocking brainstorms. Journal of Applied Psychology 76(1), 137–142 (1991)

Lynch, A.L., Murthy, U.S., Engle, T.: Fraud brainstorming using computer-mediated communication: The effects of brainstorming technique and facilitation. The Accounting Review (forthcoming, 2009)

Mednick, S.: The associative bias of the creative process. Psychological Review 69, 220–232 (1962)

Milgram, R.M., Rabkin, L.: Developmental test of Mednick's associative hierarchies of original thinking. Developmental Psychology 16, 157–158 (1980)

Mohrman, S.A., Cohen, S.G., Mohrman, A.M.: Designing team based organizations. Jossey-Bass, New York (1995)

Mullen, B., Johnson, C., Salas, E.: Productivity loss in brainstorming groups: A meta-analytic integration. Basic and Applied Social Psychology 12, 3–23 (1991)

Niederman, F., Beise, C.M., Beranek, P.M.: Issues and concerns about computer-supported meetings: The facilitator's perspective. MIS Quarterly 20(1), 1–22 (1996)

Nijstad, B.A., Stroebe, W.: How the group affects the mind: A cognitive model of idea generation in groups. Personality and Social Psychology Review 10(3), 186–213 (2006)

Nijstad, B.A., Stroebe, W., Lodewijkx, H.F.: Production blocking and idea generation: Does blocking interfere with cognitive processes? Journal of Experimental Social Psychology 39, 531–548 (2003)

Nunamaker, J.F., Dennis, A.R., Valacich, J.S., Vogel, D.R., George, J.F.: Electronic meeting systems to support group work. Communications of the ACM 34(7), 40–61 (1991)

Osborn, A.F.: Applied Imagination: Principles and Procedures of Creative Problem-Solving. Charles Scribner's Sons, New York (1963)

Pinsonneault, A., Barki, H.: Electronic brainstorming: The illusion of productivity. Information Systems Research 10(2), 110–133 (1999)

Santanen, E.L., Briggs, R.O., Vreede, G.: Causal relationships in creative problem solving: Comparing facilitation interventions for ideation. Journal of Management Information Systems 20(4), 167–197 (2004)

Satzinger, J.W., Garfield, M.J., Nagasundaram, M.: The creative process: The effects of group memory on individual idea generation. Journal of Management Information Systems 15(4), 143–160 (1999)

Valacich, J.S., Dennis, A.R., Connolly, T.: Idea generation in computer-based groups: A new ending to an old story. Organizational Behavior and Human Decision Processes 57(3), 448–467 (1994)

Wheeler, B.C., Valacich, J.S.: Facilitation, GSS, and training as sources of process restrictiveness and guidance for structured group decision making: An empirical assessment. Information Systems Research 7(4), 429–450 (1996)

An Examination of the Disruptive Innovation Paradox: The Application of the Innovators Dilemma to SME's

Tadhg Nagle[1] and William Golden[2]

[1] University College Cork
[2] National University of Ireland, Galway

Abstract. Managing strategic contradiction and paradoxical situations has been gaining importance in technological, innovation and management domains. As a result, more and more paradoxical instances and types have been documented in literature. The innovators dilemma is such an instance that gives a detailed description of how disruptive innovations affect firms. However, the innovators dilemma has only been applied to large organisations and more specifically industry incumbents. Through a multiple case study of six eLearning SME's, this paper investigates the applicability of the innovators dilemma as well as the disruptive effects of Web 2.0 on the organisations. Analysing the data collected over 18 months, it was found that the innovators dilemma did indeed apply to SME's. However, inline with the original thesis the dilemma only applied to the SME's established (pre-2002) before the development of Web 2.0 technologies began. Furthermore, the study highlights that the post-2002 firms were also partly vulnerable to the dilemma but were able to avoid any negative effects though technological visionary leadership. In contrast, the pre-2002 firms were lacking this visionary ability and were also constrained by low risk profiles.

1 Introduction

Increased technological change and global competition have required a need for managers to incorporate and integrate paradoxical thinking into their methodologies (Lewis, 2000). For instance, in the early 1990's IS researchers were drawn towards the productivity paradox, trying to understand the impact of information technology on organisations (Brynjolfsson, 1993). During the same period a number of wider organisational paradoxes were also identified. These included: the "basic unresolved problem" (Levinthal and March, 1993) the "competency trap" (Henderson and Clark, 1990) and "success syndrome" (Tushman and O' Reilly, 1996). The underlying theme in each of these studies highlights the need for IS and business managers alike to fully understand the possible paradoxical effects of their actions, especially if their actions are viewed as best practice by the wider community (Henderson and Clark, 1990; Tushman and O' Reilly, 1996). From this research, a number of frameworks have been developed to help organisations deal with the complexity of paradoxes (Lewis,

G. Dhillon, B.C. Stahl, and R. Baskerville (Eds.): CreativeSME 2009, IFIP AICT 301, pp. 60–72, 2009.
© IFIP International Federation for Information Processing 2009

2000). In particular, the "innovators dilemma" is one such framework that focuses on a very specific paradox within the innovation domain (Christensen and Bower, 1996; Christensen, 1997).

2 Innovation

The study of innovation has evolved as a multidisciplinary endeavour with numerous innovation types and definitions existing across many studies (Ettlie *et al.*, 1984; Garcia and Calantone, 2002). The idea that there are different forms of innovation with different competitive effects was first raised by Schumpeter (1942) through his notion of "creative destruction". Later termed as Schumptererian rents, Schumpeter described how value was appropriated from risky initiatives and entrepreneurial insights in uncertain and complex environments, which are subject to self-destruction as knowledge diffuses (Schumpeter, 1934). Following on from Schumpeter, the literature characterised different kinds of innovation based on their impact on the established capabilities of an organisation (Henderson and Clark, 1990). Disruptive innovation is one such form that has drawn the attention of both academics and practitioners alike, as being important in the long-term survival of an organisation (Linton, 2002; Danneels, 2004). Similar to what was termed as "Schumpterian shocks" (Barney, 1991), a disruptive change is one that changes the bases of competition by altering the performance metrics on which firms compete (Danneels, 2004). Initially, the disruptive nature of innovations was very loosely defined but it was later refined by Danneels (2004). He stated that a disruptive change was one that changes the bases of competition by altering the performance metrics on which firms compete. Moreover, research in the domain, such as: the phases of evolution of disruptive technologies   (Myers *et al.*, 2002), predictive models of disruptive innovation market diffusion (Linton, 2002), the definition of disruptive innovation and disruptive technologies (Danneels, 2004; Markides, 2006), have all added to the academic understanding and debate within the area.

3 ELearning and Disruptive Innovation

An example of the disruptive effects of innovation can be clearly seen in the eLearning industry. In 2006 a report highlighted that the industry was experiencing the disruptive impact of Web2.0 with the development of eLearning 2.0 (TerKeurst *et al.*, 2006). The term Web 2.0, which refers to the use of the internet to increase creativity, information sharing and collaboration between users, was officially coined in 2005 by O'Reilly. These concepts have led to the development and evolution of web-based communities and hosted services using platforms such as: social-networking sites, wikis, blogs, and folksonomies (O' Reilly, 2005). As an indication of how fast Web 2.0 was gaining traction in the IT industry, Facebook (a social network platform) was valued at $100 million after a mere 18 months of operation (Eisenmann and Feinstein, 2008).

The first of three findings from the 2006 eLearning report found Web2.0 to be at the core of many developments in eLearning. In addition, it estimated that 80% of learning is done informally compared to 20% of formal and structured learning (TerKeurst *et al.*, 2006). The later defining learning through defined courses or pedagogically defined methods, with the former defining learning through informal settings, conversations with peers or pedagogically undefined events (Cross, 2007). The potential for the web 2.0 technologies was thus seen supporting this new mode of eLearning as it moved from the distribution of formal content to a more learner centric environment (TerKeurst *et al.*, 2006). Examples of the effects of Web 2.0 on the wider eLearning industry are quite visible. In 2005, Wikipedia passed 750,000 articles (Wikipedia, 2008). Even though it has received mixed reviews, its popularity and ability to democratise information is quite unique (Korfiatis *et al.*, 2006). Furthermore, that year the "OpenCourseWare Consortium" was formed. The OpenCourseWare Consortium now consists of more than 200 higher education institutions and associated organisations from around the world. The primary aim of the consortium is to create a broad and deep body of open educational content using a free-sharing model. The possible effect of this is striking when Massachusetts Institute of Technology (MIT) openly admit that it costs them between $10,000 - $30,000 to publish a course through OpenCourseWare and in total costs $4 million a year to support the initiative.(OCW, 2008). In addition, Web 2.0 technologies have been supported by the rise of mobile and ubiquitous computing, which further disrupts the eLearning industry (Hall and Bannon, 2006; Clough *et al.*, 2008).

4 Innovators Dilemma

From a paradoxical perspective the innovators dilemma further adds to the domain of disruptive innovation. In essence, the innovators dilemma highlights the vulnerability of large industry incumbents when faced with a disruptive innovation in the form of a disruptive technology. An issue documented by many authors (McDermott and O'Connor, 2002), Christensen posits that the primary cause for the vulnerability lies in strong management paradigms that direct organisations to blindly focus on their current customers while ignoring innovations or technologies that appear inferior with potentially low financial returns (Christensen, 1997; Christensen and Raynor, 2003; Tellis, 2006). The dilemma then arises when the technology quickly outperforms current technologies leaving the large industry incumbents at a competitive disadvantage with a strong risk of loosing their current customers (Christensen, 1997).

Giving such examples of the mechanical excavator and hard disk drive industry, Christensen demonstrated how managers ignored new technologies which were economically unfeasible but later went on to become the underlying technologies of their markets. He found that organisations with technological leadership in an industry, tended to fall into the trap of aggressively pursuing high returns on innovations. This trap is indicative of the rule of thumb for only choosing product line extensions that promise to yield a higher net price (Calthrop, 2007). The fear is that if organisations do not follow this rule they may find themselves in the same situation as Hoover. Dyson entered the US market when Hoover was "innovating downward with simpler, cheaper products, reducing prices so that it could maintain its share of unit sales". Consequently Dyson gained the dollar share of the US market (Calthrop, 2007). However, avoiding a similar fate as befell Hoover by pursuing a long-term strategy of improving an existing product to further fulfil customer requirements, does not guarantee success. Such a course of action may lead to a situation wherein when the improved product is superseded by another technology, the organisation is unable to respond. The dilemma which lies in developing competing technologies at a time when the dominant market technology is currently and successfully employed by an organisation is a contradiction in managerial terms. This paradox is further defined through the five principles of the innovators dilemma, which have been further utilized in researching the phenomenon (Dhillion *et al.*, 2001). The principles explicitly specify key characteristics of a disruptive technological shift that cause large organisations to fail, which include:

Which explicitly specified key characteristics of a disruptive technological shift cause large organisations to fail? These principles include:

1. Companies depend on customers and investors for resources
2. Small markets don't solve the growth needs of large companies
3. Markets that don't exist can't be analysed
4. An organisation's capabilities define its disabilities
5. Technology supply may not equal market demand

Even though the theory has been supported by a number of authors such as Nault and Vandenbosch (2000), it has also had its critics (Danneels, 2004; Markides, 2006; Tellis, 2006). However, each of the critiques highlighted the complexity of the domain and the positive effect that research has made to the area. For instance, Danneels (2004) outlined a number of pitfalls in the theory (eg its ineffective predictive nature) but also highlighted its ability to "offer a really intricate picture of how firms react to technological shifts" and added to the theory by more tightly defining a disruptive innovation. Markides (2006) posited the need for a refined definition of disruptive innovations (to include (i) technologies, (ii) business models, and (iii) processes), but also stated that these three sub-categories may have the same effect on markets as outlined by Christensen. Finally, Tellis (2006) noted that the success and failure of an organisation is not determined by external impacts such as disruptive technologies, but by internal factors such as the culture of the firm. However, Christensen's theory does weigh heavily on the internal aspects of the firm as one of his key findings is that good management techniques are paradoxically the source of vulnerability and inertia in the face of disruptive innovations. As already outlined, the innovators dilemma specifically deals with large organisations with specific emphasis on incumbents. Nonetheless, the question arises; does the innovators dilemma also apply to other types of organisations? So far the debate has revolved around defining the different aspects of the theory with a distinct absence of research outside of these parameters. To this end the research question posited by this paper states:

RQ: Within the context of the eLearning industry, does the innovators dilemma apply to organisations other than large industry incumbents?

5 Research Method

The primary data of the study is collected through a multiple case study approach incorporating six eLearning organisations operating in Ireland. The study was categorised as exploratory due to the scarcity of empirical work in the area, the focus on discovery, and the aim of theory building. A number of authors have proposed that case studies constitute a suitable research methodology for exploratory research of this kind (Yin, 1984; Marshall and Rossman, 1989). The researchers also decided that a multiple case study would be the most appropriate method for this study as it would facilitate the collection of data from a larger number of organisations, and would form the basis for more focused research at a later stage. Moreover, case studies allow the study of phenomena in their proper contexts.

Highlighting the relevant context of the study, each of the organisations in the multiple case study were a part of an innovation network funded by Enterprise Ireland. Having identified eLearning as a high potential sector within the Irish economy (Forfás, 2002), Enterprise Ireland, a government body for supporting indigenous start-ups and SME's enabled an existing network of eLearning firms to gain access to substantial R&D resources. Each of the organisations in the study fell under the SME categorisation. Ranging in size from under 10 employees to between 100 and 150 employees, the SME's had also revenues of up to €15 million around that period. In addition, all of the organisations were primarily involved in the eLearning industry on a European and/or global basis and had been in existence between 2 and 20 years.

In 2006 and with the support of €2.5 million in funding, the organisations developed an innovation partnership with a third level institution, which specialised in Web 2.0 and semantic technologies. As a member of the third level institution the researcher was able to collect primary data over the first 18 months of innovation network, in which the eLearning SME's faced the technological disruption of Web 2.0. In all over 70 hours of primary data was collected from multiple sources and multiple informants using interviews and participant observation. Data was gathered from each of the eLearning organisations as well as the third level institution and Enterprise Ireland. In total, 7 interviews were undertaken, which lasted between 45 – 90 minutes and were all semi-structured. Participant observation was used throughout the 18 months and data was also gained from inter-organisational meetings and open days. Even though the meetings were not as formalised as interviews, the researcher was able to collect required data by asking questions or noting points of information that addressed the questions asked in previous interviews. Furthermore, on more than one occasion, meetings were conducted over a full business day. This gave the researcher time to talk freely with company employees and collect data in an unstructured manner that aligned with the research objectives of the study. Open days also consisted of one to two day events where all of the organisations in the innovation network were invited to one location to discuss current issues and topics associated with the network. Finally, analysis of company/industry reports and press releases that applied to period and organisations in question were also used to triangulate data used in the study. This data was then analysed through meta-matrices structured by the principles of the innovators dilemma. This enabled cross case comparisons as well as identification of common themes within the study.

6 Findings

Analysing the data gathered in the study, it became apparent that within the six organisations, two categories of firms existed. The first category, which was made up of the four firms (Companies A, B, C, D) established pre-2002 (before the beginning of Web 2.0) had done little to analyse, understand or deal with the technological shift in the industry. For instance the CTO of Company D saw very little change in the eLearning industry stating that *"courseware was much the same as it was 20 years ago"*.

Further evidence indicative of the inertia which the pre-2002 firms were experiencing was collected during an interview with a CTO of Company A. During this interview the CTO stated that *"we (Company A) don't have systems that are in any way sympathetic to where the web is. We are as much about Web1.0, big system in the sky with content. The content is multimedia and very engaging but there is no community, there is no collaboration, no sharing of content, in short, there is no Web2.0"*.

In contrast, the second category of organisations was made up of the two organisations that were established post-2002 and around the time that Web 2.0 technologies began to develop (Companies E and F). Taking the disruptive effects of ubiquitous computing as an underlying driver of the Web 2.0 technological shift in the eLearning industry, Company F had developed a product that would position them as an enabler of mobile eLearning by leveraging existing LMS resources. Company E, the organisation that made up the rest of the post-2002 category continued to use the advances in software and content delivery to their advantage. As an indication of how they were using Web2.0 to their advantage, the CTO stated that their biggest objective (early 2006) was to *"create a community around"* their product. This dichotomous classification of the pre and post-2002 firms is in line with Christensen and Bower's (1996) categorisation of existing and entrant organisations. In addition, the initial analysis is also in line with the thesis. However, to further explore the research question and determine whether the innovators dilemma applies to SME's, each of the firms are investigated in more detail using the five principles set out by Christensen.

Principle #1: Companies depend on customers and investors for resources

Evidence taken from each of the pre-2002 firms depicted in Table 1, explicitly demonstrates their over dependence on current customers for resources and innovation direction. All innovation efforts were primarily focused on getting extra value from current customers. For instance, the COO of Company A stated that they would rather gain more revenue off existing customers then look for new customers. In addition, in-line with the Theory of resource dependence from which this principle is based, the CEO of Company C highlighted that it is customers that control what type of technology an organization explores. Moreover, evidence from Company D illustrated that the process of exploration only went as far as the current customers of the organisation. Furthermore, evidence from a senior member in Enterprise Ireland suggested that innovation initiatives that did not intend to generate revenue from their current customers within the short-to-medium term meant too much high risk for the

Table 1. Data demonstrating the dependence on customers for resources

Quote	Interviewee	Company
"Rather than worry about solving a new problem for a new client. I much rather double the amount of money each client pays me every year then going out to find the same number customers paying me the same amount every year"	COO	Company A Pre-2002
Talking about the next generation of customer and user of eLearning it was highlighted "that they are geared to think". The CTO added "yes but this generation pays the cheque".	CTO	Company B Pre-2002
"clients push the technology in a very tight market"	CEO	Company C Pre-2002
"We typically start off by researching the market or from demand from clients. As for the financial sector there maybe a new derivative product on the market and a client might need"	COO	Company D Pre-2002
"In terms in overall product direction, probably not an awful lot at the moment as it is ahead of the curve, they haven't seen it before"	COO	Company E Post-2002

eLearning SME's to manage. This limitation in-turn put a big restriction on their ability to look beyond their existing market or existing customers. In contrast, the post-2002 firms were in process of building a customer base and were not strongly dependent on existing customers. In addition, input from customers in the development of their products was minimal. Moreover, during an interview the COO of one of the post-2002 firms stated the input that was received was not of great use as *"they (customers) haven't seen it before"*.

Principle #2: Small markets don't solve the growth needs of large companies
With particular emphasis on eLearning 2.0 and mobile Learning, Table 2 highlights that the pre-2002 firms felt the markets were too small for them. For instance, Company C felt that the potential market constituted of *"geeks"* alone. These could be viewed as early adopters and as potential lead users. However, the pre-2002 firms viewed this type of market as low demand and low value, which highlights a lack of vision. Demonstrating this point, the CTO of Company D felt that this new type of eLearning 2.0 could be compared to *"dumpster diving"*. The markets were also small for the post-2002 firms but as they were in the early growth stages of organisational development. There was a sufficiently large enough market for them to survive. In the case of Company E, they used venture capital to cover any shortfalls due to the lack of demand from the emerging markets.

Table 2. Data demonstrating the applicability of principle two to the SME's

Quote	Interviewee	Company
"all you have is the geeks that love blogging and write all the time"	CTO	Company C Pre-2002
"we have to develop ourselves to make it normal to read an email off a blackberry. People are only coming to that and there is not that much demand for it."	CTO	Company C Pre-2002
"dumpster diving"	CTO	Company D Pre-2002
"we have come from start-up stage to initial growth stage"	COO	Company E Post-2002

Principle #3: Markets that don't exist can't be analysed
Indicative of the organisations in its category, Company A primarily did market analysis on their current customers (as highlighted in Table 4). In addition, the majority of the data analysed points to the fact that very little market analysis was carried out beyond the scope of their market segments. In fact there is evidence to suggest that the organisations felt that trying to analyse future markets was of no benefit. The clearest indication of this futility experienced by organisations was given by a partner of Company B during a meeting. The partner felt that an organisation should not look too much far ahead as the potential for generating revenue is primarily in the short-term future. The partner states that analysis only works when you go "*one and a half steps ahead*" compared to "*ten and a half steps ahead*". Moreover, the quote from Company C indicates that the organisation did not have the ability to envision a future for technologies (such as mobile computing) within eLearning. This is in contrast to Company F of the post-2002 firms who saw big potential in the technology and developed a project around it. In addition, both of the post-2002 firms had quite clear visions of the future of the eLearning industry. As already mentioned, Company F viewed mobile computing to be a big driver within the industry, whereas Company E saw the industry being disruptive by Web 2.0. Furthermore, it was not just Web 2.0 social networking but "*social networking in an Enterprise sense*" (COO, Company E). What this shows is that the post-2002 organisations faced the same hurdles in analysing the future eLearning markets, but were better able to create a clear vision around where their organisation could utilise the potential of new technologies.

Table 3. Data demonstrating difficulties experienced by the organisations in analysing new markets

Quote	Interviewee	Company
"*My management team spends a lot of time in the field and detects a pattern in the market place and says something like our customer base could do with something that does this.*"	COO	Company A Pre-2002
"*I have lived my life ten and a half steps ahead of the market, what I have learned is to make money you can only be one and a half steps ahead*"	Partner	Company B Pre-2002
"*A lot of people are talking about m-learning or learning on PDA's. I don't see it happening yet, I still think there is too much to do for a person to do a course on their PDA*".	CTO	Company C Pre-2002
"*social networking in an Enterprise sense*"	COO	Company E Post-2002

Principle #4: An organisation's capabilities defines its disabilities
Throughout the 18 month study it was found that the core competence of the pre-2002 organisations lay in fulfilling the regulatory/compliance needs of their customers by producing eLearning courses. In addition, as the data (see Table 4) demonstrates, the

main capabilities of these firms leaned more towards customer relationship management than technological expertise. For instance the COO from Company A explicitly stated that their core competence was their Sales department. The CEO of Company D also noted that in the competitive market of eLearning, their organisation strength lay in knowing their market. However, the strongest evidence of the shift away from a technological emphasis can be found in Company C, where the CEO admitted that he consistently chose short-term revenue opportunities over technological R&D investment. In contrast, both of the post-2002 firms were not tied to the compliance/regulation market. Furthermore, they both believed that the compliance/regulation market was at the low end of the value scale. In addition, their capabilities were strongest on the technological aspect and as a result they found it easier to take advantage of the new technological trends emerging. As a result their existing capabilities did not tie them to specific markets or specific technologies.

Table 4. Data demonstrating the different impacts of the pre and post-2002 firm's capabilities

Quote	Interviewee	Company
"Its not the customisability of our products but the fact that we can produce a custom built product for whatever the need is."	CTO	Company C Pre-2002
Asked what is the core competence of the firm the COO "I'm always going to say sales"	COO	Company A Pre-2002
"We are very good at keeping a close eye on our niche and knowing our customers"	CEO	Company D Pre-2002
"The CTO has always shown the need for an R&D department but I always say that we need to make money" (CEO)	CEO/CTO	Company C Pre-2002
"value in certification. Certification as it is now is nothing but a set of multiple choice questions".	COO	Company E Post-2002
"Compliance has driven eLearning but that is not where the future of the industry lies"	CTO	Company F Post-2002

Principle #5: Technology supply may not equal market demand
There is strong evidence that suggests that both the current and new technologies within the industry were overshooting the need of the organisations customers of both the pre and post-2002 firms. Furthermore, table 5 illustrates that the pre-2002 firms were struggling to balance the technological oversupply within their current products with the weak demand for newer technologies. The CTO of Company C pointed out that there are excellent technologies available to support social networking and collaboration. However, this was of no value if there was no demand for the technology and number of people collaborating was none. Indicative of all the firms, the COO of Company A explicitly stated that the technology was *"way ahead of the market"*. However, instead of just staying away from new technologies, the post-2002 firms took it upon themselves to *"educate the market"* (CTO, Company F). In addition, Company E used new business models to drive the adoption of their new eLearning product.

Table 5. Data demonstrating that technology supply in the eLearning industry did not meet the demand of both types of firms

Quote	Interviewee	Company
Semantic web and stuff..... yea, we don't see the value in it yet as customers haven't asked for it.	COO	Company D Pre-2002
"Wisdom of crowds is useless if you're the only one there"	CTO	Company B Pre-2002
"There is all the great stuff that we can do for customers, multiple ways of delivering content, if wake up in the morning and decide to take the train to work they can get it on their phone and when they get into the office they can carry on with their PC. But from my point of view is who is going to pay for the extra layers"	CTO	Company C Pre-2002
"The technology is way ahead of what the market can bare and what the market will pay for and we have to run a business and the business is a slave to the market."	COO	Company A Pre-2002
"I find myself educating the market"	CTO	Company F Post-2002
"we are evangelising, going out getting in front of users, telling them what you do."	COO	Company E Post-2002

7 Summary of Findings

Summarising the applicability of the innovators dilemma to the SME's in the study, Table 6 demonstrates that the pre-2002 firms were caught in the dilemma. Moreover, in the case of the pre-2002 firms, their inability to handle medium to long-term risks placed strong restrictions on their ability to reduce their dependence on current customers and invest in Web 2.0 innovations. Highlighted in Table 6, only two of the principles could be adequately applied to the post-2002 firms. However, their ability to create a clear vision and the realisation of their role in educating the market helped

Table 6. Summary of the applicability of the Innovators Dilemma to the pre and post-2002 firms

	Principles of the Innovators Dilemma				
	#1	#2	#3	#4	#5
Pre-2002	Applied	Applied	Applied	Applied	Applied
Post-2002	Did not apply as (i) the organisations were building a customer base, and (ii) due to the novelty of their products had minimal input from customers.	Did not apply as (i) the firms were in an early growth stage and the small markets were sufficient, (ii) venture capital enabled the firms to build up small markets	Applied	Did not apply as the capabilities of firms worked to their advantage rather than disadvantage when exploiting the disruptive innovations	Applied

the firms overcome the negative consequences of the principles. This ability to create a vision was clearly lacking in the pre-2002 firms. In addition, Table 6 also highlights the reasons why principles 1, 2 and 4 did not apply to the organisations.

8 Conclusions

Christensen specifically focuses on large and successful organisations in his research to highlight the discontinuous nature of disruptive innovations. In doing so, he highlights that one of the causes of innovation inertia is the size of the organisation, but fails to analyse any organisation falling within the SME categorisation. For instance, principle two of the innovators dilemma states that "small markets don't solve the growth needs of large organisations". However, evidence from our findings demonstrates that all five principles of the innovators dilemma apply to SME's just as they apply to large organisations in the face of disruptive innovations. In particular, it was found that the dilemma only applied to the pre-2002 firms. This is inline with the dilemma and further emphasises the relevance of the paradox to incumbent or established firms in comparison to start-ups or new market entrants. However, the issue of risk and the risk profile of firms played a much bigger role than was documented by Christensen. This would support research that shows a positive link between resource availability and risk-taking, which in-turn impacts the innovativeness of an organisation (Entrialgo et al., 2001).

The findings also highlighted that the post-2002 firms were able to avoid the negative effects of principle 3 (markets that don't exist cannot be analysed) by creating a clear vision of potential opportunities in the industry and by working towards making those visions a reality. This was done by both post-2002 firms as they went about evangelising and educating the market. These findings bring further light to bear on how "visionary leadership that embraces change" (Tellis, 2006), can be used to manage the disruptive paradox.

Overall, the study shows that SME's are not different from large business units (Lubatkin et al., 2006) in their need to overcome organisational and innovation challenges. This further suggests that SME's are just as susceptible to innovation inertia and disruptive technologies as large organisations and also forges a link between the general corpus on innovation and literature on SME innovation, which is currently lacking in research (Edwards et al., 2005).

References

Barney, J.: Firm Resources and Sustained Competitive Advantage. Journal of Management 17, 99–120 (1991)

Brynjolfsson, E.: The Productivity Paradox of Information Technology. Communications of the ACM 36, 67–77 (1993)

Calthrop, P.: Higher Net Price–Or Bust. Harvard Business Review 85, 30 (2007)

Christensen, C.: The innovator's dilemma: when new technologies cause great firms to fail. Business School Press, Boston (1997)

Christensen, C.M., Bower, J.L.: Customer power, strategic investment, and the failure of leading firms. Strategic Management Journal 17, 197–218 (1996)

Christensen, C.M., Raynor, M.E.: The Innovator's Solution. Creating and Sustaining Successful Growth. Harvard Business School Press, Boston (2003)

Clough, G., Jones, A.C., McAndrew, P., Scanlon, E.: Informal learning with PDAs and smartphones. Journal of Computer Assisted Learning 24, 359–371 (2008)

Cross, J.: Informal Learning: Rediscovering the Natural Pathways That Inspire Innovation and Performance. Pfeiffer, San Francisco (2007)

Danneels, E.: Disruptive technology reconsidered: A critique and research agenda. Journal of Product Innovation Management 21, 246–258 (2004)

Dhillion, G., Coss, D., Hackney, R.: Interpreting the role of disruptive technologies in e-business. Logistics Information Management 14, 163–171 (2001)

Edwards, T., Delbridge, R., Munday, M.: Understanding innovation in small and medium-sized enterprises: a process manifest. Technovation 25, 1119–1127 (2005)

Eisenmann, T.R., Feinstein, B.: Harvard Business School, pp. 1–30 (2008)

Entrialgo, M., Fernandez, E., Vazquez, C.J.: The effect of the organizational context on SME's entrepreneurship: Some Spanish evidence. Small Business Economics 16, 223–236 (2001)

Ettlie, J.E., Bridges, W.P., Okeefe, R.D.: Organization Strategy and Structural Differences for Radical Versus Incremental Innovation. Management Science 30, 682–695 (1984)

Forfás: A Strategy for the Digital Content Industry in Ireland (2002)

Garcia, R., Calantone, R.: A critical look at technological innovation typology and innovativeness terminology: a literature review. Journal of Product Innovation Management 19, 110–132 (2002)

Hall, T., Bannon, L.: Designing ubiquitous computing to enhance children's learning in museums. Journal of Computer Assisted Learning 22, 231–243 (2006)

Henderson, R.M., Clark, K.B.: Architectural Innovation - the Reconfiguration of Existing Product Technologies and the Failure of Established Firms. Administrative Science Quarterly 35, 9–30 (1990)

Korfiatis, N.T., Poulos, M., Bokos, G.: Evaluating authoritative sources using social networks: an insight from Wikipedia. Online Information Review 30, 252–262 (2006)

Levinthal, D.A., March, J.G.: The Myopia of Learning. Strategic Management Journal 14, 95–112 (1993)

Lewis, M.W.: Exploring paradox: Toward a more comprehensive guide. Academy of Management Review 25, 760–776 (2000)

Linton, J.D.: Forecasting the market diffusion of disruptive and discontinuous innovation. IEEE Transactions on Engineering Management 49, 365–374 (2002)

Lubatkin, M.H., Simsek, Z., Ling, Y., Veiga, J.F.: Ambidexterity and performance in small- to medium-sized firms: The pivotal role of top management team behavioral integration. Journal of Management 32, 646–672 (2006)

Markides, C.: Disruptive innovation: In need of better theory. Journal of Product Innovation Management 23, 19–25 (2006)

Marshall, C., Rossman, B.G.: Designing Qualitative Research. Sage Publications, Newbury Park (1989)

McDermott, C.M., O'Connor, G.C.: Managing radical innovation: an overview of emergent strategy issues. Journal of Product Innovation Management (2002)

Myers, D.R., Sumpter, C.W., Walsh, S.T., Kirchhoff, B.A.: A practitioner's view: Evolutionary stages of disruptive technologies. IEEE Transactions on Engineering Management 49, 322–329 (2002)

Nault, B.R., Vandenbosch, M.B.: Research report: Disruptive technologies - Explaining entry in next generation information technology markets. Information Systems Research 11, 304–319 (2000)

O' Reilly, T.: vol. 2008. O' Reilly, CA (2005),
http://www.oreillynet.com/pub/a/oreilly/tim/news/2005/09/30/
what-is-web-20.html
OCW, vol. 2008 (2008),
http://www.ocwconsortium.org/about-us/about-us.html
Schumpeter, J.A.: The Theory of Economic Development: An Inquiry into Profits, Capital,
    Credit, Interest, and the Business Cycle. Harvard University Press, Cambridge (1934)
Schumpeter, J.A.: Capitalism, Socialism and Democracy. Havard University Press, Cambridge
    (1942)
Tellis, G.J.: Disruptive technology or visionary leadership? Journal of Product Innovation
    Management 23, 34–38 (2006)
TerKeurst, J., Keith, A., Hyland, L., Bull, G., Mackenzie, E., Woolard, A., Turner, S.: DTI and
    University of Abertay Dundee (2006)
Tushman, M.L., O' Reilly, C.A.: Ambidextrous organizations: Managing evolutionary and
    revolutionary change. California Management Review 38, 8 (1996)
Wikipedia (2008), http://en.wikipedia.org/wiki/History_of_Wikipedia
Yin, R.K.: Case Study Research: Design and Methods. Sage Publications, Beverly Hills (1984)

Two Paths for Innovation: Parvenu or Pariah

Antony Bryant

Leeds Metropolitan University

"The intuitive mind is a sacred gift and the rational mind is a faithful servant. We have created a society that honors the servant and has forgotten the gift."

Albert Einstein

Abstract. In recent years the innovator has invariably been seen as an entrepreneur, wedded to a market philosophy that extends beyond any narrow confines of business or commerce, becoming all pervasive. With regard to the public and third sectors, there was some justification for this as a useful corrective to an over-centralized concept of government which almost by definition precluded genuine innovation and enterprise. On the other hand, there was always the concomitant danger that the balance sheet would gradually efface any concerns with issues such as social justice and inequality. Recent state interventions resulting from the credit crunch and general concerns with financial liquidity, have dramatically altered the focus on the relationship and balance between the private, public, and third sectors. This in turn, requires a revised understanding of innovation and entrepreneurship across all sectors of society, as well as highlighting the role played by ICT.

Keywords: Innovation, Entrepreneurship, Social Entrepreneurship, Civil Society, Liquid Modernity, Hannah Arendt, Zygmunt Bauman, Albert Camus, Peter Drucker, Karl Polanyi, Jean-Baptiste Say, Joseph Schumpeter.

1 Introduction

Many years ago, when Calvin Coolidge returned from a church service he told his wife that the sermon had been on the topic of sin. His wife asked him what the minister had said; opting for brevity, Coolidge replied; 'On the whole he was against it'. Conversely, someone giving a presentation on creativity and innovation would, on the whole, be in favour of them. In recent years this auspiciousness has been virtually unchallenged, particularly with the concepts becoming increasingly allied with a business-like orientation to the world in general. This is exemplified in the call for papers for this workshop which included the phrase *'leveraging* the intelligence and creativity of SMEs': Also the ways in which terms such as 'social innovation', 'social enterprise', and 'social entrepreneur' have gained currency and kudos. Innovation is seen as 'a good thing' – understood primarily in business terms; moreover this approach is understood to have applicability to virtually all aspects of everyday life.

G. Dhillon, B.C. Stahl, and R. Baskerville (Eds.): CreativeSME 2009, IFIP AICT 301, pp. 73–92, 2009.

During the period from the end of the bursting of the DotCom bubble (2001), which itself coincided with the dissipation of endeavours connected with Y2K (remember that?), until at least the latter half of 2007, discussion of innovation and creativity took place against a backdrop of seemingly endless economic growth, in part founded on increasingly sophisticated use of ICT/IS.[1] Indeed the DotCom bust began to recede, both in time and significance, against an apparently inexorable tale of innovation and growth that extended from the early 1990s into a future promising near-global prosperity. This was accompanied by a belief that the best way in which to foster innovation and creativity was to reduce regulation and centralized control, giving free rein – or reign – to the market; encouraging the private sector to participate in or even take control of what had traditionally been thought of as specifically public sector responsibilities.

By the middle of this decade there was a strong clamour for these trends to be expanded on a global scale; although there was an equally vociferous counter force which claimed that such unfettered markets lead to increased disparities in wealth, ever-increasing injustice and inequality, and significant propensities for unrest and discord. The former proved to be very much more powerful and influential – Davos won out over Porto Alegre.[2] The result was an ever-shrinking public domain, while whatever remained of the public sector was increasingly market-oriented. This led to diminishing opportunities for collective and social action. Yet at the same time there was a general expansion in the number and role of NGOs and Civil Society Organizations [CSOs]. Governments were keen to reduce the size and scope of their public sector and associated expenditure, but the issues of social justice, equality, security and basic living standards did not disappear; on the contrary, in many cases they were exacerbated, often leaving the voluntary sector, NGOs and other CSOs as the last safety net or recourse for those cast aside, as the welfare state, in any meaningful and universal sense, was replaced by something more akin to a Dickensian one.

Against this context the concepts of innovation and creativity took on important new features; specifically becoming wedded to the development and promotion of enterprise and entrepreneurialism in the public sector and civil society in general. Moreover such civil society projects and third sector initiatives came to be judged in terms of their ambition, innovation and initiative – criteria emanating from the domain of the commercial entrepreneur: Hence the concept of the *Social* Entrepreneur.

2 The Social Entrepreneur

Social entrepreneurs can be seen as those who work on social issues and public sector projects, linking ideas of innovation, creativity, and change to a business-oriented

[1] For the purposes of what follows and given the CFP which alludes to 'IS', I shall treat the technological aspect (ICT) as coterminous with the systems aspect (IS). Thus phenomena such as ERP, CRM, E-Commerce, E-Government exemplify different forms of this combination.

[2] Davos being the location of the annual gathering of the rich and powerful – The World Economic Forum; Porto Alegre on the other hand hosts The World Social Forum, and is itself famous as a city that has fostered participatory budgeting and aims at redistributive democracy. See respectively
http://www.weforum.org/en/index.htm
http://www.portoalegre2002.org/homepage.html.

approach. But in itself this is not sufficient; it simply stresses the second term at the expense of the first. If there is a really *social* weight to the appellation then there must also be some clearly delineated ethical stance, giving a distinctively social and collective orientation to such endeavours. If this aspect was not obvious before the current economic meltdown – credit crunch, sub-prime crisis, or whatever term is preferred – then there can be little justification for ignoring it under the present circumstances.[3]

In what follows, an effort will be made to outline the context against which this association of entrepreneurialism and civil society has been invoked, and the implications of this linkage; also the ways in which recent economic developments now necessitate its re-examination. In turn, this will demand clarification and revision of the concepts of entrepreneurialism and of innovation in the context of civil society and society in general. The result will be to question whether or not innovation and creativity can be seen as best engendered by the desire for maximizing private gain: A position founded on the belief that "from this emerges the good-of-all" in the manner of Adam Smith's *invisible hand* – i.e. leading to the promotion of an end which was no particular person's intention. Perhaps it is now time to reconsider the entrepreneurial orientation, so that it involves a primary focus on the *collective good* with moral concerns from the outset. This will have implications for discussions about leveraging creativity and innovation, the nature of SMEs, and the role of ICTs.

3 Innovation and Entrepreneurship

These two terms are so *obviously* related that it is not surprising that they are often confused, and any distinction between them is lost. An authoritative source in recent decades that links the two is Peter Drucker's book *Innovation and Entrepreneurship* (1994), originally dating from the 1980s: Although as we shall see, Drucker demonstrates and perpetuates many shortcomings and misconceptions in his writing.

Drucker draws on the earlier work of Jean-Baptiste Say (1767-1832) and Joseph Schumpeter (1883-1950) in his discussion. He refers to Say's dictum that '[T]he entrepreneur shifts economic resources out of an area of lower and into an area of higher productivity and greater yield' (1994: 20). Say is credited with coining the term entrepreneur, although he also uses a term that can be translated as 'master-agent'.[4] This aligns well with Drucker's argument that entrepreneurship is as much about effective management – of a particular sort – as it is about innovation. For Say, the primary determining factor of value was the usefulness placed on a commodity by the buyer. The entrepreneur was the agent who managed to identify new sources of untapped demand that could be met by new ways of combining the key three resources of land, labour and capital.[5]

---

[3] An equivalent point holds true for AI – which to date has proved far more *artificial* than *intelligent*.

[4] It is also often given as 'master-agent or adventurer'.

[5] Say is credited with introducing this three-fold distinction of resources. He is best known for Say's Law – 'supply creates its own demand'; he also translated Adam Smith's work into French, although he criticized the labour-theory of value as found, for example, in the work of Adam Smith; seeing it as misguided or incomplete, needing to be replaced by or complemented with a utility-oriented theory.

For Say, this 'master-agent' offers a very specific form of expertise in an economy; an ability to act in ways in which existing resources can be re-combined in novel ways to produce higher returns and more effective use of resources, resulting in the final product having a higher utility value for potential buyers. Drucker develops this insight as a central part of his argument that entrepreneurship is something that should and can be systematized and taught, relying on a specific 'technology' which offers the perfect 'vehicle of this profound change in attitudes, values, and above all in behaviour' (1994: 13) – the technology 'is called management'.

Thus for Drucker, the entrepreneur is someone who changes or transmutes value; and writing for his readership in the late 20th century Drucker wished to advance the idea that rather than simply waiting for such people to appear, it is necessary, feasible, and desirable to develop these activities in a systematic manner. Just as the haphazard and near-magical process of invention was transformed in the 20th century into an institutionalized practice of research, and in particular of R&D; so too must innovation and entrepreneurship be systematized and institutionalized. 'Entrepreneurs will have to learn to *practise systematic innovation.* ... *Systematic innovation therefore consists in the purposeful and organized search for changes, and in the systematic analysis of the opportunities such changes might offer for economic or social innovation.*' (1994: 30-31 – stress in the original – NB Drucker here clearly uses the term *innovation* to define a *process* not an artefact or outcome.)

4   Schumpeter: The Entrepreneur as *Super*-Rational or *Non*-Rational?

Joseph Schumpeter drew on Say's work in his arguments about the nature of entrepreneurship, and the 'creative destruction' that was the key feature of capitalism. Schumpeter's concept of the entrepreneur changed in the course of his writing, but the essential point of the role of entrepreneur*ship* did not. The onward drive of capitalism emanated from the disturbances caused by entrepreneurial activities. Without entrepreneurship there would be stasis. In systems predating capitalism, entrepreneurship relied on specific individuals upsetting the *status quo* and releasing new potentialities; even in early capitalism this was still very much the case. Entrepreneurs were those people who created new possibilities, often going against conventional and accepted ideas. Although once the new ideas became the conventional ones, the entrepreneur might cease to act in this manner and become more of an executive or administrator; or might continue to act the entrepreneur, but now in contrast to the new form of what constituted the normal and the routine – 'the distinctive element is readily recognized so soon as we make clear to ourselves what it means to act outside the pale of routine. The distinction between adaptive and creative response to given conditions may or may not be felicitous, but it conveys an essential point; it conveys an essential difference.' (Schumpeter, quoted in Langlois 2002)

Some commentators such as Langlois (2002) have drawn the distinction between two conflicting strands in Schumpeter's work – either arguing that they coexist throughout his work, or differ between early and later writings: One strand centres on the argument that the spirit of the entrepreneur will gradually become obsolete as rational calculation encroaches further into everyday activities.[6] If our knowledge increases, we can become more readily aware of the possibilities for innovation, and so rely less on the insights of the entrepreneurs. This implies that entrepreneurial insights make up for gaps or failings in current knowledge, so to an extent the entrepreneur is not only more insightful, but also more knowledgeable – i.e. *supra*-rational. Thus according to this view, potential innovations become more apparent with more knowledge. This implies a divergence between innovation and entrepreneurship, since as innovation, or the potential for innovation, increases, the need for or the call for entrepreneurship decreases.

The second strand is the exact opposite of this. Here the *spirit of the entrepreneur* will always be needed, because the ability to see things differently is precisely at odds with things as they are. This will apply however well-informed people might be. The key implication is that entrepreneurial insight is something *non*-rational; knowledge and rational calculation might be available, but there will always be a demand to go beyond the planned and the calculated, or at least to take an unorthodox and unconventional perspective.

This tension can be found in many writings on entrepreneurship and innovation; as well as embedded in many national and governmental policies designed to encourage such activities. Is the source of innovation and the entrepreneurial spirit to be found *within* the corporations and multi-nationals, with their plans and strategies centred on research departments and R&D budgets, or is this large-scale organization inimical to precisely these tendencies? Are the innovations of the future primarily to be found *outside* these large-scale organizations? Are large-scale organizations able to foster the process of innovation? Are SMEs the best sources of innovation, or should the sources and processes of innovations be sought beyond the confines of the private sector? Moreover how can the resources of the public and private sectors best be marshalled to ensure that such activities are encouraged and fostered? Are strategic plans designed to encourage innovation a contradiction in terms?

5 Entrepreneurialism – Systematized or Situated?

Drucker, writing in the 1980s and 1990s, argued in favour of systematizing entrepreneurship and innovation. He identified the five elements of the process of innovation, and linked these with a framework of opportunities for innovation set against an account of entrepreneurship practices and strategies. Peter Denning (2004), amongst others, has argued that, had Drucker's maxims been adhered to, the *dotcom* boom and bust might have been avoided. Yet this is not borne out either by a careful reading of Drucker's categories or by some reflection on the bases of the *dotcom* boom.[7] Drucker's categories, although useful as guides, are far too ambiguous to serve as clear indicators in a fast-developing, fast-changing context. Furthermore, falling back on Say's position, those who acted in an entrepreneurial fashion at the start of the

---

[6] Schumpeter coined the term *Unternehmergeist* – usually translated as 'spirit of the entrepreneur' – although *entrepreneurship* seems a less clumsy form.

[7] A glance at Drucker's maxims in the light of the sub-prime fiasco indicates severe weaknesses in Drucker's position – but there is no space to develop this further at this juncture. See also Drucker's Top 10 Tips from 2005.

dotcom boom were able to do so precisely because the resources were so readily available since companies and investors were falling over each other in the rush to ensure that resources were on tap for start-up *dotcoms.*[8]

Drucker offers a number of examples of innovations and entrepreneurs, often reusing them in different ways to underline his main arguments. This fails to resolve the issue of the distinctions between *invention, innovation,* and *entrepreneurship.* Furthermore there is a paradox in pointing to past innovations as guides to future ones. Schumpeter is adamant that *the entrepreneur sees things differently* – creatively rather than adaptively; but the new situation that arises as a result of entrepreneurship is then the one that becomes commonplace; hence the response of many people to some innovation – 'Well I could have thought of that!'

It is noteworthy that Drucker omits any mention of invention, preferring to focus on the term innovation. Yet from the outset any reader might be confused by his various uses of the term. He defines innovation as

> *[a] specific tool of entrepreneurs, the means by which they exploit change as opportunity for a different business or a different service. It is capable of being presented as a discipline, capable of being learned, capable of being practised. Entrepreneurs need to search purposefully for the sources of innovation, the changes and their symptoms that indicate opportunities for successful innovation. And they need to know and to apply the principles of successful innovation. (1994: 17)*

This clearly defines innovation as a process and a tool; one that entrepreneurs have to understand and employ. But what does Drucker mean by the term 'successful innovation'? In the context of a discussion of innovation, creativity, and entrepreneurship surely a successful innovation is one that has achieved success – however that might be defined – precisely after being subject to some entrepreneurial activity. This might be accomplished through a re-combination of resources to provide higher utility and greater effectiveness (Say), or as part of the process of creative destruction (Schumpeter). So entrepreneurship is the activity that ensures that an innovation becomes successful – in which case Drucker's invocation seems to be that entrepreneurs have to act as entrepreneurs; his definition is circular. On the other hand the first part of the extract implies that innovation itself is something distinct from entrepreneurship; the entrepreneur has to 'search purposefully' for the sources of innovation, and perhaps for the innovations themselves. The net result is that Drucker seems unable to distinguish between his two terms; hence his inability to separate them in one of his concluding remarks about the three factors which together 'make up *innovation and entrepreneurship*' (p233 – stress in the original) - these are purposeful innovation, entrepreneurial management, and entrepreneurial strategies.[9]

A careful reading of his book indicates that this is an understandable source of confusion, with Drucker acting as a master-agent re-combining two conceptual resources

---

[8] And the lead in to the sub-prime fiasco was even more marked an example of a context which impelled entrepreneurialism of a sort.

[9] Denning argues that Drucker does have a clear distinction – innovation is the search for opportunities, which then are transformed into practices and taken to the market place; entrepreneurship is the institutionalization of the practice of innovation in an organization.

into a single term 'innovation-and-entrepreneurship'. The examples he uses throughout the book are illustrative of this; Gillette's pricing of safety razors and blades; Sony's application of transistor technology; public sector policies in Lincoln, Nebraska: All are used in various places throughout the book as examples of either innovation or entrepreneurialism, or both, depending on the point that Drucker wishes to make. The result is that the two become indistinguishable.

Moreover Drucker implies that his hybrid innovation-and-entrepreneurship is predominantly located within organizations – primarily in the private sector. He does seek to distance these activities from 'centralized planning', and so allow for individual idiosyncrasies. But largely the assumption is that the entrepreneurial spirit is one to be systematized within an organizational context; by default, the private corporate kind. Drucker evades some of the issues around this assumption with recourse to what he terms 'the entrepreneurial society' – but how this has come about, or exactly what it means is never clarified. The argument for this purposeful, systematized entrepreneurialism is ultimately incoherent; although it has been influential since it has come from the pen of Peter Drucker.

6   Innovation and Invention

A more helpful approach can be found in the work of John Howells (2005). His work focuses on innovation, with only passing reference to entrepreneurship; but in so doing he offers a far more profound analysis of the reality of the process itself. He distinguishes invention from innovation. Invention is defined as 'the generation of the idea of an innovation' (2005: 1) – which implies that an invention only becomes an innovation when it achieves some form of embodiment or actualization. This is similar to the work of Brian Winston (1998) whose model of invention is premised on the distinction between science or competence, and technology or performance. For Winston the move from competence to performance and beyond involves a series of socially mediated transformations. Just as Howells defines an invention as an idea, so Winston talks of ideation as the basis of the process of invention; although he sees this as including some initial move from competence to performance, at the very least demonstrating that the idea has some feasibility in the form of a prototype. Winston argues that the route from the laboratory into a wider context is often lengthy and always uncertain and precarious. Moreover the determining factor is rarely the nature of the invention itself, but rather what he terms 'supervening social necessity'. Howells develops this insight, albeit without reference to Winston, describing the process as a 'socio-cognitive' one – i.e. one with perceptual features as well as social ones. Winston, Howells and others stress that innovation must be seen as a situated process. Howells, in characterizing his approach offers a succinct description – 'A striking feature of the stories of invention was the role of social context and prior expertise for the cognitive act of insight. ... it seems important to capture the sense that social context and expertise influence the act of insight that is more commonly understood as the inventive process.' (2005: 33-34)

Howells gives detailed accounts of many innovations, showing how their route from conception to commonplace was far more complicated than is usually understood. In so doing he discusses the ways in which management within private firms acts both to promote and constrain innovation. His focus is specifically technological development, but his insights apply generally to the issues of the management of innovation. As he states in his preface

> *The overall object of the book is to convey an understanding of technology as immediately shaped by the firm, but situated in 'society' – and situated in the particular form of society that is the market economy, understood as the working set of institutions and governance procedures that have evolved to sometimes limit and sometimes enable technology-shaping decisions by management and entrepreneurs.*

This is echoed by Manuel Castells in the introduction to *The Information Age*, where he offers a cogent dismissal of technological determinism.

> *Of course technology does not determine society. Nor does society script the course of technological change, since many factors, including individual intuitiveness and entrepreneurialism, intervene in the process of scientific discovery, technological innovation, and social applications, so that the final outcome depends on a complex pattern of interaction. Indeed the dilemma of technological determinism is probably a false problem, since technology is society, and society cannot be understood or represented without its technological tools.*

The issue, addressed below, is: 'What kind of society?'

The work of those such as Howells and Winston offers a basis for grasping that innovation is a process that has to be understood in relationship to its social context; a situated practice with cognitive features and ramifications. This leads to three issues, amongst many others, that will be addressed in the remaining sections of this paper: What is the specific social context of the early 21st century? Why is the concept of social entrepreneurship critical to our current context? How have recent economic upheavals altered the context and our understanding of terms such as innovation, creativity, and social entrepreneurship?

7 The Current Context – Liquid Modernity

Drucker used the term 'the entrepreneurial society', but offered nothing further other than that he hoped it would be a social context which encouraged and enhanced innovation-and-entrepreneurship. Howells locates innovation within the market economy, and Winston talks of the social forces that can either prevent innovations moving from the laboratory to the market place, or propel them there. But, particularly with regard to innovation, there are specific and critical characteristics of the current social context that are not brought out in the work of Howells, Winston and others. Say saw the entrepreneur as 'necessary for the setting in motion of every class of industry whatever; that is to say, the application of acquired knowledge to the creation of a product for human consumption' (stress added). Schumpeter made similar claims, seeing entrepreneurship as the motor that propelled capitalism. The common implication is that without this impetus there would be stasis, or at best only restricted movement. This may have been the case in the past, but the current context is markedly different.

Zygmunt Bauman has labelled our current era as 'Liquid Modernity', which 'sets itself no objective, draws no finishing line, and assigns the quality of permanence solely to the state of transience. Time flows; but it no longer marches on to any destination'. Bauman's imagery of liquidity draws its resonance from The Communist Manifesto with its declaration – 'All that is solid melts into air, all that is holy is profaned, the need of a constantly expanding market for its products chases the bourgeoisie over the entire surface of the globe, it must nestle everywhere, settle everywhere, establish connections everywhere.' (see Bauman 2000: Foreword). The next sentence, not quoted by Bauman, continues thus: 'All fixed, fast frozen relations, with their train of ancient and venerable prejudices and opinions, are swept away, all new-formed ones become antiquated before they can ossify.'

The declaration itself is paradoxical, and Bauman specifically draws our attention to this in his work. The idea of sweeping things away is an iterative and never-ending process. It is not simply a case of a once-and-for-all eradication of the old, and emergence of the new. The new rapidly becomes the old, and is itself swept away; and so on, indefinitely. The word 'liquidity' evokes the idea of flow, incessant movement, and change; it raises the question 'flow towards what'? But in the context of Liquid Modernity as Bauman characterizes it there is only flow *away from* the present, it has no ultimate destination or objective.

At this juncture, without seeking to offer any extended account of Bauman's recent work, the key points for present purposes are that; society may no longer need the powers of impulsion and momentum of the entrepreneur – at least not in the ways Say, Schumpeter, and Drucker envisaged them; the process of innovation needs to be re-examined, re-conceptualized and re-evaluated; our understanding of entrepreneurialism and the role of the entrepreneur will have to be revised and enhanced. This was already evident once one grasps Bauman's arguments, but is more so in the light of the sub-prime crisis and its aftermath.

8 Innovation as an End in Itself

In the context of Liquid Modernity, innovation is not the exception but the rule. There is an incessant demand for something new, purely because there is a craving for novelty, which, once delivered, rapidly becomes outdated; fit only for the scrap heap. Drucker's dream of an 'entrepreneurial society' has become a nightmarish reality, akin to Italo Calvino's city of *Leonia* which 'refashions itself every day'; with all the remains of yesterday 'encased in spotless plastic bags' placed carefully on the sidewalk waiting for the refuse collectors.

Drucker viewed such a society as comprising 'purposeful innovation, entrepreneurial management, and entrepreneurial strategies'. In the current context, innovation is indeed purposeful; paradoxically it has the prime purpose of being 'innovative', rather than meeting any actual need: The means has become an end in itself. In Say's terms, we might argue that the measure of utility is now innovation itself; with the supply of innovations now creating its own demand. Hence any innovative quality must have appeal first-and-foremost to the consumer, but this will be transitory. No-one wants yesterday's innovation; they want tomorrow's or at the very least today's. Schumpeter's concept of creative destruction becomes a cycle of creation-production-consumption-disposal. This applies not only to the products and services themselves, as in Leonia, but also to the people and organizations involved in bringing them to market.[10]

The recent economic upheavals demonstrate that this cycle can extend not only to corporate giants such as Ford, General Motors, and Chrysler, but even to entire countries such as Iceland. Even prior to the third quarter of 2008, corporate strategies and management policies were creative-destructive, but usually with the destructive part falling on the shoulders of those working in or for the companies producing the innovations, rather than, as now seems to be the case, on entire companies themselves: Although companies that failed to heed this message were themselves destroyed or dismantled, often including those which until recently appeared to be well-established and long-lived.[11]

This might be taken to mean that there is now a free-for-all, with many innovations vying for market space to the ultimate benefit of all. This is often cited as one of the *raisons d'être* for policies that encourage SMEs, since they have the agility to respond swiftly to rapidly changing contexts, producing innovative ideas and strategies. But as Howells and others demonstrate, there is a tendency for innovations to become institutionalized inside large and powerful companies. This is something akin to Schumpeter's belief that eventually there will be a declining role for the entrepreneur, as knowledge and rational calculation are perfected; although in the context of research and innovation in corporations in the late 20th and early 21st centuries this is not based primarily on the nature of knowledge but on control of resources, expertise and R&D budgets.[12] Thus, even the ability to develop competence, in Winston's sense, may be outside the scope of all but a few with access to the requisite resources: Performance is virtually unattainable by those outside the relevant institutional settings.

9   The Great Transformation and the Double Movement

On the other hand, against this background of increased concentration of a small number of 'master-agents or adventurers', and sources of and possibilities for innovation, there was, until recently, the parallel one of fragmentation as the centralizing and co-ordinating roles of the state and the public sector were dismantled. In many regards this

---

[10] And unlike the people of Leonia, the waste and detritus is not placed neatly into plastic bags as Sennett (1999) and Bauman (2004) make all too clear – the 'waste' from liquid modern society includes people as well as out-dated consumer goods.

[11] See Sennett 1999.

[12] This is not to rule out the role of serendipity and individual insight, but in many areas – e.g. medical research, bio-informatics, aeronautics, etc. – it is almost impossible to undertake anything beyond pure speculation and ideation outside the confines of the major corporations involved in those areas. Is this the way ahead for other aspects of research and innovation? It has even be noted that the outputs of R&D endeavours in some organizations produced inventions with no obvious market, until one is later created: And even inventions which are solutions to 'problems 'that did not exist prior to the invention itself.

was a continuation of Karl Polanyi's *Great Transformation*[13] (1944) whereby the self-regulating market gradually comes to take over all other aspects of social interaction and strategy, such that 'the market' is seen as something natural, inevitable, and universal. This lifts a great number of issues out of the realm of public debate and discourse, and the extent to which the great transformation developed above and beyond anything that Polanyi envisaged can be seen by the way in which the concept of the self-regulating market became the *fons et origo* or be-all and end-all for all manner of discourses and domains; including education, welfare, justice, and governance. Polanyi saw the creation of the modern economy and modern nation state as two parts of the same innovation, which he termed *Market Society*. Writing in 1940s as WWII was coming to a close, Polanyi was convinced that the post-war era would mark a qualitative move away from the cataclysm that had resulted from 'the utopian endeavour of economic liberalism to set up a self-regulating market system'. Unfortunately, precisely the opposite proved to be the case, in some countries after a brief interlude of centralized planning.

Polanyi's argument was that this transformation did not occur by force of nature, but rather as a result of institutional changes emanating from governments and powerful interests in the economy. Even the general acceptance of land, labour and capital as commodities was the result of a cognitive transformation; an example of Howells' concept of innovation with its stress on socio-cognitive changes. What Polanyi also argued, however, was that this continued colonization of everyday life by the self-regulating market was part of a *double movement*; whereby the force in favour of unfettered 'market forces' was tempered by moves towards increased intervention aimed at offsetting the excesses and evils that were unleashed by the market itself. Polanyi argued that prior to the Great Transformation 'production for gain' was held in check by 'production for use'; a distinction that Aristotle had made between 'householding proper' and 'production for gain'. This dichotomy is effaced once 'Market Society' emerges and develops in the 19th century.

Social solidarity was then dismantled, and the main unifying force put in its place was 'the market'. Moreover, what at first was a set of public policy recommendations, becomes seen as a force of nature, and the basis of natural order. When this does not seem to be working in a satisfactory manner, governments may try to take steps to intervene, either by dismantling constraints or imposing new ones. Sometimes both strategies are taken simultaneously to the consternation of all involved; and ultimately with diminished effect or unintended consequences. Polanyi pointed both at government policies projected to protect workers from poverty, and those to protect businesses from monopolies or other market developments. He defined the double movement as 'the principle of economic liberalism, aiming at the establishment of a self-regulating market ... [and] the principle of social protection aiming at the conservation of man and nature as well as productive organization'.

For the past few decades the double movement has clearly been slanted in favour of the self-regulating market; with some efforts enacted by governments to offset the

---

[13] Karl was the brother of Michael (Personal Knowledge), and uncle of John (Nobel Laureate for Chemistry). It would be useful if the IS world paid at least as much attention to Karl's work as they have to Michael's; and even better if the ideas of both were understood in a more nuanced manner. Michael's concept of tacit knowledge has been dreadfully misconstrued in much of the work on knowledge management.

most palpable and blatant inequities. As the lure of the market has come to dominate all discourses, however, the extent to which governments and the public sector as a whole should take responsibility for its citizens has diminished, or been itself couched in market terms. One result has been an ironic twist to the double movement and great transformation; sometimes termed philanthro-capitalism or social entrepreneurship.

10 Social Entrepreneurship

Schumpeter's argument that the role of the entrepreneur will disappear as rational calculation extends into evermore aspects of social and economic life was never convincing; the limitations of 'rational planning' and 'perfectible knowledge' have always been evident, and his alternative concept of the entrepreneur as '*non*-rational' was more persuasive. Yet the growing dominance of the market in ever-increasing aspects of society, particularly the public sector, seemed to portend the ultimate and universal applicability of business models – rational or otherwise. Moreover people could point to this encroachment or re-orientation as a source of new opportunities for innovation and entrepreneurial activities. Services and support activities that were once the monopoly of government or the state in one form or another were now being offered by private sector organizations and Civil Society Organizations [CSOs], or combinations of all three – public, private, and third sectors. In all cases the era seemed to be one where there was an unquestioned primacy for a business-oriented approach.

This was all part of a trend in many societies for private providers to take on many of the roles previously seen as inherently part of the public sector.[14] Thus health, education, law enforcement and the like have increasingly been privatized. This has opened up opportunities for entrepreneurship in the public sector in Say's sense of re-focusing resources in a new and more productive manner – although many of the claims that private provision of such services is more efficient, effective and profitable than public ones are widely challenged. (For present purposes, however, this is not the point at issue.) More important is the way in which the evolving relationship between different sectors of society brings to the fore the idea that entrepreneurship is not simply confined to the private sector. This has led to the use of the term 'social entrepreneurship' – also of 'philanthro-capitalism'. In some cases these are seen as ways of addressing social issues by linking ideas for public sector innovation and change to a business-oriented approach. Hence such comments as the following; 'The past two decades have seen an explosion of entrepreneurship and a healthy competition in the social sector, which has discovered what the business sector learned from the railroad, the stock market and the digital revolution: Nothing is as powerful as a big new idea if it is in the hands of a first class entrepreneur.'

This is entirely laudable, but it can quickly become simply another form of profit-driven entrepreneurship, shaking off any distinctively social and collective orientation. An example of this can be found on the website of *The Institute for Social*

---

[14] This has been seen as opening up a range of new opportunities for SMEs, although to a large extent provision has been dominated by large multinational and consortia. In any case it is equally important to understand that there needs to be a role for other organizational forms, including those developed bottom-up often in the manner of open source models of collaboration. I intend to develop this in further contributions at a later date.

Entrepreneurs where a *social entrepreneur* is defined as 'any person, in any sector, who runs a social enterprise'; a *social enterprise* is "any organization, in any sector, that uses earned income strategies to pursue a double or triple bottom line, either alone (as a social sector business) or as part of a mixed revenue stream that includes charitable contributions and public sector subsidies'.

Even before the credit-crunch and ensuing bail-outs from the public purse undermined such statements, the overall ideas behind social entrepreneurship and philanthro-capitalism were far too restrictive. In many cases even the most 'successful' and visible exemplars were no more than small efforts to re-balance the excesses of the double movement that had swung so far in favour of the self-regulating market. Indeed as Michael Edwards (2008) points out in his extended critique of philanthro-capitalism, the figures used to proclaim its importance and impact are dwarfed by those of more conventional methods such as charities and the public sector *per se*. The key issue, which has become more evident and more important in the light of recent developments, is that the application of entrepreneurialism to civil society and the public sector has been far too inhibited and unimaginative: It needs to be far more wide-reaching and ambitious. This involves the realization that the concept of re-combining resources in an ambitious and innovative manner needs to be applied well beyond the confines of a business model and the private sector – although it may still retain some aspects of this approach.

11 SMEs, IS/ICT, Creativity, and Innovation

The Call for Papers for this working group specifically links SMEs with IS/ICT, creativity and innovation: Also making mention of KM, knowledge transfer and various other terms lifted from the optimistic lexicon of business-as-usual – e.g. *leveraging*; although now ineluctably overtaken by intervening events. The general intent would appear to be that prevailing conditions are conducive to agility and change as long as the correct strategies and models can be articulated; in many cases such opportunities being rendered feasible through use of IS/ICT. There is, of course, no reason why the convenors of the workshop should have had any inkling of the dramatic events of the past few months, since almost no-one else did – even those allegedly with the relevant expertise. But even so, it is critical that we begin to dismantle this conceptual amalgam, questioning the implied linkages and opening up issues which otherwise might fall outside our purview (leaving aside, for the moment, who exactly is included in 'our').

The relationships between creativity, invention, innovation, and entrepreneurship need to be set against the current social context of liquid modernity – currently going through a crisis of illiquidity; building on and accounting for Winston's and Howells' respective ideas, and also offering a new understanding of Drucker, Say, and Schumpeter, amongst others. First it must be stressed that creativity is at work at all times and emanates from all manner of sources. Occasionally it finds form in invention, and some inventions become innovations, in line with Winston's concept of the transition from competence to performance. The arguments of Winston and Howells also have a further implication that needs to be grasped: Much creativity remains firmly wedded to the creator, never leading to innovation or a move into the market. This is well understood by Castells and Daniel Bell, both of whom use Harvey Brooks' definition of technology – 'the use of scientific knowledge to specify ways of doing things in a *re-producible* manner'. If an invention or ideation cannot be reproduced, in both the technical and economic senses of the term, it will not become an innovation; yet that is a necessary, but not sufficient condition.

In a society centred on the self-regulating market the transition from invention to innovation will necessarily involve entrepreneurship – in both Say's sense of the 'master-agent or adventurer' and Schumpeter's of 'creativity' rather than 'adaptivity'. But as Winston and Howells argue, such forces operate against a context of socio-economic characteristics that can impel or impede the move from competence to performance. In the current and extreme form of market society – Liquid Modernity – this entrepreneurship or adventurism runs amok. Everyone is encouraged, even prompted, to become an entrepreneur or a master-agent. The most successful being those able to find new ways of combining or *leveraging* the 'natural' resources of market society; what Polanyi terms the fictitious commodities of land, labour and capital. The result is that creativity, in its affirmative and imaginative, actually becomes divorced from innovation and entrepreneurship. The paradigmatic innovators-cum-entrepreneurs of early 21st century liquid modernity are those financiers, hedge-fund managers, whiz-kids and maestros of arbitrage and other forms of transactional prestidigitation who have brought us to the current crisis. They have indeed transmuted value in Say's terms, shifting economic resources from lower into higher productivity and greater yield, but not in the substantive fashion that Say had in mind. Unfortunately the transmutation has proved as chimerical as that of the alchemists. There is no ultimate consumer whose needs are satisfied; only the chump finally left holding the 'assets' that are now revealed to be liabilities. The transmutation, if any, has been from lead to gold, rather than vice versa.

To an extent much of this innovation and entrepreneurialism, if not driven by the opportunities afforded by IS/ICT, has certainly benefited from the technology that facilitates and promotes the marshalling and consolidation of huge amounts of information, round-the-clock and near-instantaneous trading, infinitesimal transaction costs, all set against a global financial system that knows no boundaries and seemingly allows or even encourages evasion of all impediments and controls.[15] Those advocating and encouraging the use of IS/ICT for all manner of improvements in efficiency and effectiveness have been far too ready to adopt and accept the breathless language of relentless encroachment of the market. In the IS/ICT academy we have been complicit with the chimerical innovators-cum-entrepreneurs who have proved to be the exact opposite of Schumpeter's concept. Rather than being creative and *supra*-rational, they have in fact been *supra*-adaptive and conventional; following the logic of the market in fictitious commodities, and ultimately producing fictitious and spectral innovations.

12 The Entreprenuer: *Pariah* or *Parvenu*?

The true role of the entrepreneur is to see things differently. Yet the entrepreneurs and innovators of liquid modernity appear to be the ultimate conformists; taking the concept of innovation as an end in itself to new extremes. In an age where we are all pressed to recreate ourselves on an almost daily basis, the entrepreneur has become the rule rather than the exception; and innovation has become the commonplace, the

---

[15] And if that fails, there is always straight forward mendacity, larceny, and dishonesty.

routine and the humdrum: Oxymoronic as that may appear. This can be understood in terms of Hannah Arendt's concepts of the pariah and the parvenu (1951), and Albert Camus' distinction between two forms of rebellion (1951).

For Arendt, the parvenu is an upstart and a social climber: Someone who seeks to conform and so adapts to the established norms – stated and tacit – of the surrounding milieu; often excelling in performing whatever it is that is most highly regarded or rewarded. The parvenu is devoid of political ideas or wider social agendas, being entirely focused on personal interests and aggrandisement. The pariah on the other hand stands outside and apart from 'the conventional wisdom'; either by choice, or out of necessity: Arendt's initial discussion of the terms is couched in the context and her own experience of being Jewish in Germany in the 1920s and 1930s. The pariah sees things differently, which is both a precondition for and a result of being a pariah. The overall effect is that pariahs see the bigger picture, the social whole; often leading to utopianism, advocacy of social change, and political ideas that go beyond personal interests. The pariah often becomes the rebel.

Camus' discussion of rebellion brings out a further critical distinction, derived from his experience and observation of those who engaged with communism in the middle of the 20th century. Those who saw the need for social change in terms aiming at perfection of society, based on some set of 'absolute values', were likely to follow even the most dictatorial and totalitarian tendencies and actual regimes. Camus termed this 'revolution' or 'historical rebellion'. While those who recognized the absurd, while still striving for change and improvement, engage in 'metaphysical rebellion', based on a lucidity that accepts the absurdity of the drama of social existence and the 'unreasonable silence of the world'.

Today we might understand Camus' concept of 'the absurd' in terms such as 'uncertainty', 'complexity' or 'chaos'; and this resonates with Bauman's Liquid Modernity particularly if, as I have argued elsewhere (Bryant,2007; Bryant et al 2007), the fluid metaphor is extended to incorporate a consideration of 'turbulence'. In terms of the current discussion, acceptance of absurdity or complexity effectively subverts any idea that perfection of knowledge and rationality will result in the demise of innovation and creativity – a reading of Schumpeter that sees the entrepreneur as *supra*-rational – and instead heavily favours the alternative reading – the entrepreneur as *non*-rational. This leads to a focus on serendipity, rather than any misguided expectation of perfection or certainty.

So in the light of the credit-crunch, and the continuing exposure of the ways in which 'rational calculation' lay at the base of the fiasco in which we are all mired, it can be seen that many of the self-proclaimed entrepreneurs are parvenus rather pariahs; while the chorus of supporters, until recently urging general emulation of their efforts, are historical rebels quick to proclaim perfection and nirvana. To an extent this was understandable given the realities of Soviet-style Communism and its final demise, which exacerbated the enthusiasm for and growth of market society; on several occasions such has been its supremacy that many have heralded a new utopia of frictionless growth, universal prosperity, the end of boom and bust. Of course there were warnings from some sources, and even strong indications of precedents. J K Galbraith, one of the most astute writers on economics, often warned that when people herald a new age of universal prosperity it is time to take cover. Bauman has referred to Emerson's dictum that when skating on thin ice, the only strategy is speed.

What we now realize is that we are like those cartoon characters who continue on their way beyond the edge of the cliff, only falling once they look down to see that they have no visible means of support.

The current solutions to this crisis appear to be very much more-of-the-same; hence people's consternation that while the problem is proclaimed to be caused by over-borrowing and over-spending, the solution appears to involve further borrowing and spending on an even larger scale. In some regions a different solution is already in place – either by accident or design: state capitalism as found in China, Russia and some of the countries that operate with what are termed 'sovereign wealth funds'. This can be seen as a triumph of aiming for perfection, either dispensing with democratic participation altogether, or effectively limiting or precluding it. In more established democracies the welfare state has suddenly re-emerged, but only for the rich, a somewhat different form of the double movement from that envisaged by Polanyi; but effectively still with the same aim of saving the self-regulating market from its own excesses.

In fact Polanyi himself warned about the fracturing effects of market society, saying that it 'should need no elaboration that a process of undirected change, the pace of which is deemed too fast, should be slowed down, if possible, so as to safeguard the welfare of the community': and commentators as different as Bauman and Theodore Dalrymple (2005) now argue that perhaps the social fabric has been destroyed beyond repair. The socio-cognitive context has become so reliant on an individuated, market-oriented view of the world that people cannot see any solutions other than those couched in terms of a re-invigoration of the market, and a plethora of SME-led, IS/ICT-supported innovations.

13 The *Agora* – The Social Entrepreneur, Social Innovation and Civil Society

What is needed now is not more-of-the-same, the entrepreneur as parvenu; but new ways of seeing, the entrepreneur as pariah. This will involve a re-orientation of what is actually involved in creativity and innovation, stressing the importance of fostering genuinely new ways of seeing in a re-invigorated social context drawing on the possibilities and propensities of IS/ICT. In recent times the concept of a third sector, incorporating charities, voluntary organizations and NGOs, has come to the fore; as distinct from the private and public sectors. This sector is seen as part of the more amorphous and ambiguous 'civil society', which might best be characterized by the following definition from the Centre for Civil Society at the LSE.

> *Civil society refers to the arena of uncoerced collective action around shared interests, purposes and values. In theory, its institutional forms are distinct from those of the state, family and market, though in practice, the boundaries between state, civil society, family and market are often complex, blurred and negotiated. Civil society commonly embraces a diversity of spaces, actors and institutional forms, varying in their degree of formality, autonomy and power. Civil societies are often populated by organisations such as registered charities, development non-governmental organisations, community groups, women's organisations, faith-based*

> *organisations, professional associations, trades unions, self-help*
> *groups, social movements, business associations, coalitions and ad-*
> *vocacy group.*

In many regards this is akin to the *Agora*; initially a specific location in Athens, but later a conceptual space which as Bauman explains was

> *neither private nor public, but more exactly private and public at*
> *the same time. The space where private problems meet in a*
> *meaningful way – that is, not just to draw narcissistic pleasures*
> *or in search of some therapy through public display, but to seek*
> *collectively managed levers powerful enough to lift individuals*
> *from their privately suffered misery; the space where such ideas*
> *may be born and take shape as the 'public good', the 'just soci-*
> *ety' or 'shared values'. (1999, pp.3-4)*

For Bauman, the history of modern societies has been a long war of attrition 'launched against the agora from the side of the ecclesia'. In other words there has been a sustained effort to curtail or eradicate any space in which issues pertaining to the collective, the shared, the communal, might be raised and discussed. Concomitant with Polanyi's Great Transformation, the encroachment of market society has resulted in the subversion of any claims for legitimacy for the social and communal, fostering the expansion of the operation and calculus of the market flooding into all aspects of human existence – social and personal, the public and the private. Yet the novelty of this as part of modernity and liquid modernity has been in its intensity rather than its actual occurrence, since, as Arendt (1958) pointed out, the pressure from the *ecclesia* often took the form of efforts to transform the *agora* 'into an assemblage of shops *like the bazaars of oriental despotism'*.

If IS/ICT has anything to offer in the present crisis, it is the ways in which new technologies present opportunities for civil society to flourish; the internet, social networking, the *blogosphere*, *wikis* and so forth might well be the bases for a renewed if virtual *agora*: *Agora 2.0*. But the actual motivation behind some of this technology, particularly the Open Source movement, in fact exemplifies the ways in which the Great Transformation has continued to exert its power. Eric Raymond's *The Cathedral and The Bazaar* is rightly regarded as the *de facto* manifesto of the Open Source movement. Yet as Raymond (1997) noted some years later, 'I very nearly called this paper *The Cathedral and the Agora*, the latter term being the Greek for an open market or public meeting place.' In a brief email exchange with Raymond it became clear that his concept of the *agora* was profoundly market-oriented and bazaar-like. Thus he distinguished between the 'monetary market' and the market *per se* which, quoting Drexler and Miller (1988), he explained is 'the sum total of all voluntary interactions': Also stating that the *agora* is a subset of the market.

Raymond is, of course, entitled to this view; but it should not preclude consideration of the alternative on offer from Arendt and Bauman amongst others. More importantly, if we take up the challenge implicit in Arendt's and Bauman's critique we can see that discussions around IS/ICT-based innovation should indeed engage with the concerns of civil society. In this sense the real social entrepreneurs include those who have sought to counteract the forces of market society; often by giving impetus to the countervailing forces of the double movement. So Beveridge, Bevan, Brandt should be regarded as exemplary figures – and it is left to the reader to suggest others of this ilk. Polanyi singled out Robert Owen in this regard, someone who understood that *society* was the prime phenomenon; wanting to harness the state and the machine to positive effect. He attacked Christianity because it displaced society by individualization. 'He grasped the fact that what appeared primarily as an economic problem was essentially a social one.' He advocated the self-protection of society, something that, Polanyi observes, was in fact incompatible with the economic system itself.

It is well beyond the skills and capabilities of this author to offer anything by way of a definitive explanation for the current crisis, but Polanyi offers a glimpse of what needs to be done to enact some form of transformation that goes beyond policies that amount to little more than cosmetic forms of more-of-the-same. Howells correctly alludes to the socio-cognitive aspects of innovation, but he fails to say whether the socio-cognitive change comes before or after the innovation: I suspect he would argue that either sequence is possible. In terms of the current crisis, however, the socio-cognitive change has to start off the process of innovation, with people beginning to grasp that the foisting of the market on society as a whole did not occur naturally, but was the result of a series of deliberate policies and transformations along the lines suggested by Polanyi.

What we are now witnessing is state intervention with a vengeance; but largely on behalf of the rich. This might be simply a case of business-as-usual – albeit in unusual circumstances – but it might also be that there is no way for genuinely new ways of seeing things to find an audience and serious consideration. The babble of the internet remains just that, unless ways can be found to 'leverage' the technology and the participants to a more authoritative level: That will be truly innovative IS/ICT; truly creative use of technology to foster social entrepreneur*ship* that can be encouraged to flourish and have genuine influence, understood in terms of a collective process with firm ethical underpinnings. This will also move innovation-cum-entrepreneurship from rational-economic compulsive obsession, to its original and more affirmative meaning. As Camus asserted, it is the artist who discerns a privation of certain things in the world and attempts to recreate the world in acts of creation:

> In every rebellion is to be found the metaphysical demand for
> unity, the impossibility of capturing it, and the construction of a
> substitute universe. Rebellion, from this point of view, is a fabri-
> cator of universes. This also defines art.34

14   Conclusion – The Post Credit-Crunch Context of Innovation, ICT and SMEs

What then are the lessons for SMEs in their role as sources of innovation and creativity in the current context of an ICT-oriented network society in which the economic certainties have been replaced by stimulus packages and bail-outs that not even Nobel laureates such as Paul Krugman understand?[16] At the very least there must be a reconsideration of concepts such as creativity, innovation, and entrepreneurialism. These will not disappear as the world moves towards ever greater rationality and

---

[16] Paul Krugman column, New York Times, February 10, 2009.

planning, on the contrary, rational models themselves have been found wanting in the extreme. Bauman's concept of liquid modernity centres on this; the current context of *ill*iquidity makes it even more evident.

This has severe implications for IS/ICT and computability since models that seem to indicate the possible perfection of calculability and computability of complex decisions have proved wanting. Indeed there are good reasons to point to computer-based models and ICT-based transaction systems as very much part of the problem. Moreover the flow of information, given the reality of ICT, the internet and so on, has played a significant role in persuading people of the power and promise of innovation; with innovation having become an end in itself. Thus *leveraging* IS/ICT is perhaps a misleading image since it can be taken to imply that use of ICTs by SMEs is inevitably going to be 'a good thing', resulting in significant benefits derived from small, agile sources and resources. The IS world's enthusiasm for knowledge management has often exhibited this partiality in both regards; with knowledge seen as something that is inherently perfectible and manageable, and with more meaning better. The current crisis, and its precursors in scandals such as Enron and WorldCom, demonstrates the darker aspects of knowledge management as well as the risks and dangers of *leveraging*.

In the light of all these developments the spirit of the entrepreneur has to be recognized as something that will always be required, but Drucker's dream of a society of entrepreneurs and SMEs may in fact be far more of a nightmare, made even worse with the advent of ICTs.

What is needed is a re-interpretation or revision of our concepts of innovation. We have lived through a period where inventions were themselves commodified, with even cases of people inventing things and then looking for the problem for which the invention might be a saleable solution. Using Winston's terms this is a case of the brake disappearing, and the accelerator being full on for innovation; moving even minor competences to fully fledged, marketable performances. Socio-cognitively, as Howell suggests, innovation and creativity came to encompass financial sleights of hand whereby liabilities were treated as assets, and other such absurdities. We now see the necessity to move away from this, while retaining an impetus in favour of creativity amidst a modernity that is not characterized by order, planning and calculation; but rather by complexity, chaos and turbulence. This may also offer an opportunity to rebalance the forces behind the double movement, and ICT has a key part to play in this, particularly drawing on the inspiration offered by the Open Source movement and its derivatives. (What can be termed *Mutuality 2.0*, but that is a subject for whole new paper.)

The context within which SMEs now operate requires a rethinking of their role as sources of innovation and creativity; not least because many of them will be unable to attract the investments needed to progress their ideas. Here again ICT has a part to play since it has resulted in fractional transaction costs and allowed new forms of networking to develop that might provide alternative routes to obtain funding or other resources – again Open Source is an archetype. Crises represent opportunities for entrepreneurs to flourish, but the present one also offers the prospect to change the way in which innovation, creativity, and entrepreneurship are envisaged and nurtured. The literal translation of *Der Unternehmer* is *The Undertaker*; and it may now be time to inter one form of innovation in favour of another: Or as Einstein noted in the quote above; it may be time for us to attend more to the gift and less to the servant.

References

Arendt, H.: The Origins of Totalitarianism. Harcourt, San Diego (1994, orig 1951)
Arendt, H.: The Human Condition. University of Chicago Press, Chicago (1998, orig 1958)
Bauman, Z.: In Search of Politics. Polity, Cambridge (1999)
Bauman, Z.: Liquid Modernity. Polity, Cambridge (2000)
Bauman, Z.: Wasted Lives. Polity, Cambridge (2004)
Bryant, A.: Liquid Modernity, Complexity and Turbulence. Theory, Culture & Society 24, 127–136 (2007)
Bryant, A., Pollock, G., Bauman, Z., Metzger, G.: Liquid Arts. Theory, Culture & Society 24(1) (2007)
Calvino, I.: Invisible Cities. Harcourt, Orlando (1974)
Camus, A.: The Rebel. Penguin, Harmondsworth (2000, orig 1951)
Castells, M.: The Rise of the Network Society: Economy, Society and Culture. Blackwell, Oxford (2000, orig 1996)
Dalrymple, T.: Our Culture What's Left of it. Ivan Dee, London (2005)
Denning, P.: The Social Life of Innovation. Communications of the ACM 47(4), 15–19 (2004)
Drucker, P.: Innovation & Entrepreneurship, 2nd revised edn. Butterworth-Heinemann, Oxford (1994)
Edwards, M.: Just Another Emperor? The Myths and Realities of Philanthrocapitalism. The Young Foundation/DEMOS, London (2008)
Howells, J.: The Management of Innovation & Technology. SAGE, London (2005)
Langlois, R.: Schumpeter and the Obsolescence of the Entrepreneur. Announced as due to appear in Advances in Austrian Economics (2002),
   http://ideas.repec.org/p/uct/uconnp/2002-19.html
Miller, M.S., Drexler, K.E.: The Agoric Papers. In: Huberman, B. (ed.) First published in The Ecology of Computation. Elsevier Science Publishers/North-Holland (1988),
   http://www.agorics.com/Library/agoricpapers.html
Peters, T., Waterman, R.: In Search of Excellence. Harper & Row, New York (1982)
Polanyi, K.: The Great Transformation. Beacon, Boston (2001, orig 1944)
Raymond, E.: The Cathedral and the Bazaar. First given at the Linux Kongress, 1997; subsequently republished and revised on several occasions and in several places; the version referenced here is the title essay in Raymond's book, The Cathedral and The Bazaar: Musings on Linux and Open Source by an Accidental Revolutionary. O'Reilly (page references are for the latter edition) (1997)
Sennett, R.: The Corrosion of Character. Norton, London (1999)
Winston, B.: Media, Technology & Society. Routledge, London (1998)

Identifying and Addressing Stakeholder Interests in Design Science Research: An Analysis Using Critical Systems Heuristics

John R. Venable

School of Information Systems,
Curtin University of Technology,
Perth, Western Australia

Abstract. This paper utilises the Critical Systems Heuristics (CSH) framework developed by Werner Ulrich to critically consider the stakeholders and design goals that should be considered as relevant by researchers conducing Design Science Research (DSR). CSH provides a philosophically and theoretically grounded framework and means for critical consideration of the choices of stakeholders considered to be relevant to any system under design consideration. The paper recommends that legitimately undertaken DSR should include witnesses to represent the interests of the future consumers of the outcomes of DSR, i.e., the future clients, decision makers, professionals, and other non-included stakeholders in the future use of the solution technologies to be invented in DSR. The paper further discusses options for how witnesses might be included, who should be witnessed for and obstacles to implementing the recommendations.

Keywords: Critical Systems Heuristics, Design Science Research, Stakeholder Analysis, Design Goals, Critical Research, Ethics, Participation.

1 Introduction

Design Science Research (DSR) has recently received much attention in the Information Systems literature. MIS Quarterly, the IS field's flagship publication, has published a seminal article (Hevner et al, 2004) and a special issue on DSR. Three international conferences on the topic have now been held focusing on the topic (Hevner and Chatterjee, 2006, Chatterjee and Rossi, 2007, Baskerville and Vaishnavi, 2008) with a fourth to be held soon. Web pages on the topic have been created and incorporated into IS World Net (Vaishnavi and Kuechler, 2005).

DSR is a paradigm or stream of IS research that aims to help solve important human, organisational, and business problems through the invention, design, and development of new "solution technologies" (Venable, 2006a). DSR has been touted by many (e.g. March and Smith, 1995, Hevner et al 2004, Venable 2006a, 2006b) as an important stream of research for improving the relevance of IS research (or addressing what Robey and Markus (1998) called the "relevance crisis" in the IS field).

G. Dhillon, B.C. Stahl, and R. Baskerville (Eds.): CreativeSME 2009, IFIP AICT 301, pp. 93–112, 2009.

One motivation for the recent emphasis on DSR as a research approach is that design as an activity has been viewed by many in the IS field (particularly in North America) as practice, rather than research, and therefore illegitimate as a research activity. Proponents of DSR attempt to legitimate its practice (and publishability) both by noting its relevance (as above) and also by distinguishing Design Science Research from (ordinary) design practice. The key distinguishing characteristic is that DSR attempts to solve problems that are general in nature, with generic solutions that can be applied in multiple situations. Design practice, on the other hand, solves particular, situated problems with particular stakeholders. Another distinguishing characteristic is that in DSR, outcomes are published, while in ordinary design practice they are not.

While the term "Design Science Research" (often just "Design Science") is relatively new, the roots of its practice go far back in IS research practice and tradition, arising out of computer science and software engineering. What *is* new in DSR is the newfound care with which the field considers and reflects upon how DSR should be conducted to improve its rigour and relevance. A growing number of papers have made recommendations about how DSR should be conducted, how its results should be communicated, and standards for acceptable quality of DSR (Nunamaker et al, 1991, Walls et al, 1992, March and Smith, 1995, Hevner et al, 2004, Vaishnavi and Kuechler, 2005, Venable, 2006a, 2006b, Baskerville et al, 2007, Gregor and Jones, 2007). These lessons, recommendations and standards are also potentially applicable to research approaches used in computer science and software engineering.

However, there remain important questions to be asked about the goals and ethical practice of DSR. Baskerville et al (2007) note that the goals to be addressed by DSR depend on the view of the problem to be solved, and that there are multiple such views. Cranefield and Yoong (2007) in particular have asked the question "To whom should Information Systems Research be relevant?" (also asked by Keen, 1991). They develop an "Ecology of IS Practice" (i.e. potential stakeholders in IS Research) including levels ranging from the individual up to society as a whole. Furthermore, at a recent panel at ECIS on the promise of DSR to improve the relevance of IS Research (Pries-Heje et al, 2007), Prof Michael Myers (then AIS president) noted the absence of ethics as a concern in the standards for the conduct of DSR. Unfortunately, the existing literature on DSR does not address these concerns.

Critical Research takes an ethical stance on both research and practice (Stahl, 2008). Stahl (2008) defines critical research as "research characterized by an intention to change the status quo, overcome injustice and alienation, and promote emancipation" (p. 139). Most DSR authors do not take a stance with respect to this intention, by default leaving the intention up to the researcher. Where guidance is provided on what kinds of goals should be addressed, these are explicitly supposed to align with "business strategy" (e.g. Hevner et al, 2004, figure 1) or "business needs" (e.g. Hevner et al, 2004, figure 2). Indeed, much of the published DSR literature could be characterised (and criticised) as serving the interests of "efficiency, rationalization and progress", which are viewed as increasing "social control and domination" (Cecez-Kecmanovic et al, 2008, p. 123). Cecez-Kecmanovic et al, (2008) further note that Critical Research in IS should also investigate "the practice, purpose, implications, and institutional constraints under which" IS research operates (p. 123), presumably including DSR in IS.

This paper partially addresses the above concerns by critically examining the issue of stakeholders and design goals in DSR. The identification, selection and inclusion of stakeholders and their participation in determining goals are (or should be) key issues in both design practice and in DSR. Failure to consider and include possible stakeholders in DSR (or in design practice) can be viewed as a form of systematic communication distortion, resulting in the loss of communicative action in favour of instrumental action (Habermas, 1983). Such communication distortion is perpetrated by IS Design Science researchers in the interest of business (managers and owners). It is potentially at the expense of others, by preventing them from representing their own interests (e.g., their own emancipation).

But, how can and should we judge which stakeholders to include and how to avoid such distortion? What about DSR (as opposed to design practice) affects our answer to this question? What guidance should we give to the Design Science Researcher? To analyse and answer these questions, this paper employs Critical Systems Heuristics (CSH) (Ulrich, 1983, 1987, 2002). Werner Ulrich, who was a student of Churchman, developed CSH to provide a philosophically and theoretically grounded framework and means for critical consideration of the choices of stakeholders considered to be relevant to any system under design consideration. DSR is at a higher level than design practice, but still is confronted with issues of goals, boundaries, and stakeholders, for which CSH is a useful framework for analysis.

The next section reviews relevant IS research literature to establish a clear context for the work in this paper. The subsequent section introduces the CSH framework as published by Ulrich. Next, the paper applies the CSH framework to DSR. The paper concludes with an analysis of some implications arising from the CSH analysis of DSR.

2 Literature Review

Literature relevant to the topic of this paper comes from the DSR, IS relevance, and stakeholder analysis literatures. We consider each of these briefly in turn.

2.1 Research Goals and Stakeholders in the DSR Literature

As noted above, key papers in the DSR literature make recommendations about how DSR should be conducted, how its results should be communicated, and standards for acceptable quality (Nunamaker et al, 1991, Walls et al, 1992, March and Smith, 1995, Hevner et al, 2004, Vaishnavi and Kuechler, 2005, Venable, 2006a, 2006b, Baskerville et al, 2007).

Nunamaker et al (1991) justified system development as a research methodology (an early form of DSR in IS). They develop a multi-methodological framework for IS Research, including four major types of activity: (1) theory building, (2) experimentation, (3) observation, and (4) systems development. Of these types of activities, only (3) observation, which is concerned with observing a problem domain to get an appreciation of its circumstances, provides guidance for what problems are to be addressed. However, in describing this activity, Nunamaker et al (1991) provide no guidance about stakeholders or how one focuses on particular aspects of the problem domain.

Nunamaker et al further describe a five-step System Development Research Methodology: (1) Construct a Conceptual Framework, (2) Develop a System

Architecture, (3) Analyse and Design the System, (4) Build the (Prototype) System, and (5) Observe & Evaluate the System. The first step includes "state a meaningful research question." Presumably this draws on information garnered from observation (above). The only guidance provided is that the question should draw on a research problem that is "new, creative, and important in the field" (p. 98). This still leaves the question, "Important according to whom?"

Walls et al (1992) develop the concept of an IS Design Theory (ISDT), which has seven components. The main component of interest here is that of Meta-Requirements, which represent the goals or contingencies to be addressed by a particular kind of solution to be designed. However, the paper provides neither a process-oriented view of DSR nor any advice about where those meta-requirements should come from or how they should be established.

March and Smith (1995) emphasise that DSR is oriented toward problem solving and that "Problems must be properly conceptualised …" (p. 251). They identify the main research activities of build (a technology/systema), evaluate (the built technology/system), theorise (about how/why the technology/system works or not), and justify (the resulting theory). They further identify four products of DSR: representational constructs, models, methods, and instantiations. The products of DSR ate to be evaluated against criteria of value and utility. However, March and Smith do not address questions about problems, value or utility for whom or the choices of which problems should be addressed. They do not provide guidance about how problems can be "properly conceptualised".

Hevner et al (2004), like March and Smith (1995), emphasise the problem solving orientation of DSR and the main DSR activities, which they group into a cycle of Develop/Build (artifact instance and theory, respectively) and Evaluate/Justify (the same). The goals to be addressed by DSR are derived by "business needs", which are obtained from the environment, or the part of it that constitutes the "problem space". According to Hevner et al (2004),

The DSR environment or problem space "is composed of people, (business) organizations, and their existing or planned technologies. In it are the goals, tasks, problems and opportunities that define business needs as they are perceived by people within the organization. … Together these define the business need or 'problem' as perceived by the researcher. Framing research activities to address business needs assures research relevance." (Hevner et al, 2004, p. 79)

Clearly, Hevner et al (2004) acknowledge that problems are perceived (by various stakeholders). However, it can also be seen that according to Hevner et al (2004), DSR should serve the needs of business organisations (as a whole). For example, in describing their second guideline (problem relevance) for evaluating DSR projects or publications, they note that the main goal or business need to be addressed in DSR is profit maximisation. They are also quite clear about the stakeholders that they see as relevant when they state the following.

"The relevance of any design science research effort is with respect to a constituent community. For IS researchers, that constituent community is the practitioners who plan, manage, design, implement, operate, and evaluate information systems and those who plan, manage, design, implement, operate and evaluate the technologies that enable their development and implementation." (Hevner et al, 2004, p. 85)

The needs of various other stakeholders are therefore not addressed by Hevner et al (2004). Further, despite their recognition of the perceived nature of problems, they provide no guidance about how one should identify who should determine, represent or provide those needs to the researcher.

Vaishnavi and Kuechler (2004), in their Design Research website on AIS World, describe various aspects of DSR, including its philosophical foundations, its outputs, and a general methodology for DSR. The methodology contains five steps (awareness of problem, suggestion, development, evaluation, and conclusion), with feedback loops from later steps to earlier steps. Of these, awareness of problem is relevant to design research goals and stakeholders.

"Awareness of Problem: An awareness of an interesting problem may come from multiple sources: new developments in industry or in a reference discipline. Reading in an allied discipline may also provide the opportunity for application of new findings to the researcher's field. The output of this phase is a Proposal, formal or informal, for a new research effort." (Vaishnavi and Kuechler, 2004, n.p.)

From this it can be seen that Vaishnavi and Kuechler (2004) are open to input from different stakeholders (not just business organisations or IS practitioners), but provide no guidance for what sorts of goals DSR should pursue or how to select appropriate stakeholders.

Venable (2006a) explicitly recognises and emphasises the perceived nature of problems and that different stakeholders (and IS Design Science Researchers) may have different perceptions of a problem space and disagreements about it. However, he does not offer any advice on how to select from among different competing views of different stakeholders; he only advises that Design Science Researchers therefore need to be precise in their statements about what problem or problems they are trying to solve in any particular piece of DSR so as to avoid misunderstandings.

Baskerville et al (2007) also recognise the perceived nature of problems. However, their concern is with the evaluation of designed artifacts and IS Design Theories. The import of the perceived nature of problems is that evaluation results are different depending on the goals and interests of those involved in the evaluation (and in the determination of the original problem formulation). They also do not provide any guidance about selection of stakeholders and their interests or in goals or problems to be solved, except to suggest the use of soft methods, such as Soft Systems Methodology (SSM) (Checkland, 1981, Checkland and Scholes, 1990, Checkland and Holwell, 1998).

To summarise the DSR literature overall, some of it does not recognise (or deal at all) with the issue of different perceptions of problems; some of it recognises the perceived nature of problems, but emphasises the needs and problems of business organisations; some of it recognises the perceived nature of problems and the possibility of disagreement about what problem(s) should be solved, but is silent about how to choose. Most importantly, none of the DSR literature either considers what stakeholders (beyond "IS practitioners" or "business organisations") should be consulted about problems and how to choose among them or makes any sort of critical examination of what problem(s) should be solved or how one should arrive at that decision.

2.2   Research Goals and Stakeholders in the IS Relevance Literature

A number of papers over the past few years have addressed relevance in IS Research more generally (as opposed to in IS DSR).

Benbasat and Zmud (1999) identified four aspects of relevance for IS Research: interest, applicability, currency, and accessibility. They further identified recommend-dations for actions that IS researchers could take to improve relevance, including, among other things, identifying topics from IS practice, reaching agreement within the IS community on likely future issues, focusing on the future interests of key stakeholders, and providing contingency approaches for managerial action. Implicit in their discussion are stakeholders such as "IS practice", "the IS community", and management. Both "IS practice" and "key stakeholders" seem to refer to IS practitioners, especially managers. They do not acknowledge any stakeholders outside of IS practice or offer any research goals beyond those that serve IS practice.

Moody and Buist (1999, Moody, 2000) lamented the disconnect between IS research and IS practice, particularly the lack of input from IS practice to IS research about practical problems to be addressed. However, they do not provide guidance on which stakeholders within IS practice or acknowledge any research goals or stakeholders outside of IS practice.

Recently, Cranefield and Yoong (2007) directly considered the question "To whom should Information Systems Research be relevant?" Consistent with the vision for the purpose of the IS field as stated in Weber (1997) to serve "individuals, groups, organisations, societies, and nations" (p. 1), they develop an "Ecology of IS Practice" (i.e. potential stakeholders in IS Research) including various levels of increasing scope: individual (e.g., a practitioner or user), interpersonal (group), individual organisation, group of organisations (e.g. an industry), community, and society (e.g. a nation). Interestingly, they do not mention a trans-national, international or world level, although this would seem a logical extension. Very appropriately, the authors argue that "if IT practitioners, CIOs, and even CEOs are viewed as the only people to whom IS research is relevant, then IS research is unlikely to lead to improvements above the organisational level. … The ecological perspective would reposition the IS practitioner as only one member of a richer web of consumers."

To summarise the IS relevance literature, broadly characterised, most of it considers the stakeholders and interests of IS practitioners and managers as the source of relevance and hence as the source of goals for IS Research (and hence DSR more specifically). On the other hand, Cranefield and Yoong (2007) specifically go beyond that view to propose higher levels of increasingly broad scope of stakeholders.

2.3   Socio-technical Design and Participative/Participatory Design Literature

Stakeholders have long been recognised in the IS Development literature. Nearly any textbook would refer to users, indirect users, system professionals, and managers as stakeholders in IS development. As noted earlier, the identification, selection and inclusion of stakeholders and their participation in determining goals are (or should be) key issues in both design practice and DSR.

Several areas of research in IS (and other system) development have particularly emphasised participation. Socio-technical design methods, such as ETHICS (Mumford, 1983, 1996) give equal weight to performance improvement and quality of working life goals by giving workers the means to participate in setting their own design goals and designing and selecting systems that meet those goals. Participative design (e.g. Emery, 1989), coming out of the socio-technical systems/design movement, also emphasises giving users the means to participate in design. Heavily overlapping, if not interchangeable, but with a slightly different name, participatory design (e.g. Schuler & Namioka, 1993; Kyng et al, 1997) has a long history in Scandinavia, including a series of decennial conferences at Aarhus University. Research in this stream has looked at many options for participation, including who, when, and how. See Mumford (2006) for a history of socio-technical design, which covers some of the overlap with the Scandinavian and participatory design traditions.

While there is much in this literature about how and why to achieve participation, it has a key weakness with respect to our purposes here; research in participatory design concerns how to perform (participatory) design *in practice* rather than how to perform DSR. I.e., participatory design defines the topic of the research rather than the method or means of doing the research. Now, it is true that many pieces of research on participative design actually *are* pieces of DSR, i.e. that they invent or develop new, generically applicable methods for doing participative design. They also conduct such DSR from a critical perspective, but by and large they are not systematically reflective about the stakeholders in research on participative design. Such pieces may consider who to include in the research and how, but for practical, epistemological reasons; it usually takes the research goals for granted and does not enlist stakeholders in determining them. Thus, while participatory design research may provide suggestions for methods of participation during design, it does not provide suggestions for how to critically select stakeholders in DSR.

2.4 Stakeholder Analysis Literature

In addition to the ISD literature, there is also a literature that looks at stakeholders in situations generally. In particular, frameworks have been identified for determining appropriate stakeholders to consider, including Qualitative Classes of Stakeholders (QCoS, Mitchell et al, 1997) and Critical System Heuristics (CSH, Ulrich, 1983, 1987, 2002).

Before considering these questions, it is worth introducing the concept of a stakeholder. Just what is a stakeholder? Checkland (1981) defines a stakeholder as a "beneficiary or victim" of an organisation, system, action or change. Freedman (1984) defines a stakeholder as "any group or individual who can affect or is affected by the achievement of the organisation's objectives." The definition that we will use here is "a person or organisation with an interest in a problematic situation or in actions taken to 'improve' the problematic situation."

As described by Cranefield and Yoong (2007), there are many things that can be stakeholders and at many levels, including: individual people, groups, neighbourhoods, organisations, institutions, societies, and even future generations. Generally we are concerned with humans, but some people consider non-human nature (animals, plants, etc.) as stakeholders (even though they cannot represent their own interests). Infants, other children, and future generations are similar in that regard.

Another question we might consider re. stakeholders is "What is a stake (or at stake)?" A stake can be any relevant interest, benefit, or loss, including (but not limited to) money, possessions, power, legal rights or options, customs, norms, expectations, relationships to other people (social relations), activities (work or leisure), or quality of life (working or otherwise). A stake can literally be anything that someone thinks is relevant because they have an interest in it and it will or might be changed.

Mitchell et al (1997) approach the issue of stakeholders from the perspective of concern for identifying those stakeholders in companies/firms (and their decisions) who warrant managerial attention before they can interfere with organisational actions. They developed a framework entitled Qualitative Classes of Stakeholders (QCoS). This framework distinguishes three "relationship attributes", which describe the form and strength of the relationship between (putative) stakeholders and an organisation.

- Power – The stakeholder's power to influence the firm
- Legitimacy – The legitimacy of the stakeholder's relationship with the firm
- Urgency – The urgency of the stakeholder's claim on the firm

Any particular stakeholder will have at least one of these attributes, to a varying degree, and possibly (commonly) in combination. Figure 1 illustrates how these attributes can be in combination and characterizes the eight different combinations that are possible. The strongest claim for relevance as a stakeholder is to have all three (a "definitive" stakeholder in figure 1) and strongly; the weakest is to have only one attribute and weakly.

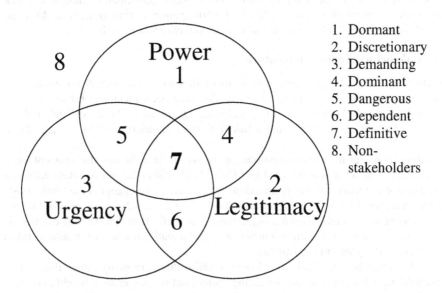

1. Dormant
2. Discretionary
3. Demanding
4. Dominant
5. Dangerous
6. Dependent
7. Definitive
8. Non-stakeholders

Fig. 1. Qualtitative Classes of Stakeholders (QCoS) Framework (Mitchell et al, 1997)

The framework highlights why management ignores some stakeholders (weak, unconsidered claims). However, ignoring stakeholders can lead to lack of cooperation, resistance, and system/solution failures – as well as inappropriate systems.

While interesting and informative, QCoS can be strongly criticised from a Critical Research perspective. The means of picking stakeholders to include as ones whose needs should be addressed is rooted in an analysis of their power and status. In a nutshell, the method serves managerial interests in identifying stakeholders whose needs must be addressed in order to achieve managerial goals. Implied is the ability to ignore certain classes of stakeholders a long as the organisation has the power to overcome them. It does not seek to increase discursive communication (Habermas, 1983) for its own sake and those of the stakeholders, but to manipulate it through instrumental action (Habermas, 1983). Thus, the method fails the critical test of advancing emancipation interests.

Critical Systems Heuristics (CSH, Ulrich, 1983), unlike QCoS, is strongly concerned with ethical interests and adopts a critical perspective. CSH is based on systems theory and has a firm philosophical grounding. Because of its critical perspective and grounding, it is the approach used in this paper. CSH is described in more detail in the following section.

3 Critical Systems Heuristics (CSH)

Ulrich (1983, 1987, 2002) proposed and developed Critical System Heuristics in order to address a concern arising from general systems theory. That issue is that systems theory provides guidance that the scope of a system under consideration must be decided that is wide enough to prevent local decisions from causing significant problems in the larger system(s) within which the system under consideration can be considered as a component. Thus, for example, the scope of a marketing system under consideration must (should) be considered broadly enough that sales or production do not incur problems.

However, one cannot practically continue to expand and expand the scope of a system under consideration indefinitely, because one does not have the resources to do so (i.e., one cannot design the universe or consider all its potential problems). Therefore, one needs an appropriate means to guide the boundary decision – What will we consider to be within the scope of the situation and what will we exclude?

Critical Systems Heuristics (CSH - Ulrich 1983, 1987, 2002) provides a reasoned guideline (heuristic) to guide such boundary definitions. The CSH framework incorporates 12 questions for system developers (no matter what kind of system) to answer in order to define a system's boundary or scope. Figure 2 provides an overview of the framework and its concerns. The questions are grouped according to four different boundary issues, each of which has its own kind of stakeholders, the nature of their interests, and their relevance as stakeholders.

Each of the four groups in figure 2, together with the 12 questions relating to each of the 12 areas above, is described below (Ulrich 1983, 1987, 2002).

Boundary categories   Boundary issues

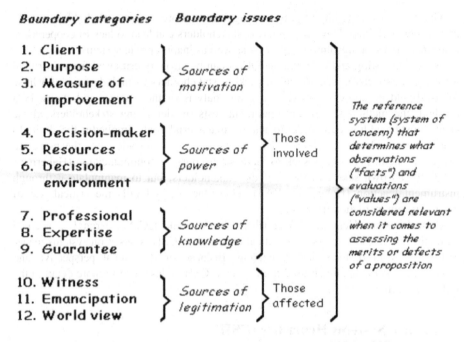

1. **Client**
2. **Purpose**
3. **Measure of improvement**

} *Sources of motivation*

4. **Decision-maker**
5. **Resources**
6. **Decision environment**

} *Sources of power*   } Those involved

7. **Professional**
8. **Expertise**
9. **Guarantee**

} *Sources of knowledge*

10. **Witness**
11. **Emancipation**
12. **World view**

} *Sources of legitimation*   } Those affected

The reference system (system of concern) that determines what observations ("facts") and evaluations ("values") are considered relevant when it comes to assessing the merits or defects of a proposition

Fig. 2. Critical Systems Heuristics (CSH) Framework (Ulrich, 1983)

Sources of Motivation

1. Who is (ought to be) the client? That is, whose interests are (should be) served?
2. What is (ought to be) the purpose? That is, what are (should be) the consequences?
3. What is (ought to be) the measure of improvement? That is, how can (should) we determine that the consequences, taken together, constitute an improvement?

Sources of Power

4. Who is (ought to be) the decision-maker? That is, who is (should be) in a position to change the measure of improvement?
5. What resources are (ought to be) controlled by the decision-maker? That is, what conditions of success can (should) those involved control?
6. What conditions are (ought to be) part of the decision environment? That is, what conditions lie outside the decision-maker's control (or should lie outside, e.g., from the viewpoint of those not involved)?

Sources of Knowledge

7. Who is (ought to be) considered a professional? That is, who is (should be) involved as an expert, e.g., as a systems designer, researcher, or consultant?
8. What expertise is (ought to be) consulted? That is, what counts (should count) as relevant knowledge?

9. What or who is (ought to be) assumed to be a guarantor of success? That is, what serves (should serve) as a guarantee that improvement will be achieved – for example, consensus among experts, the involvement of stakeholders, the experience and intuition of those involved, or political support?

Sources of Legitimation

10. Who is (ought to be) witness to the interests of those affected but not involved? That is, who voices (should voice) the concerns of stakeholders who are not involved or cannot speak for themselves, including future generations and non-human nature?

11. What secures (ought to secure) the emancipation of those affected from the premises and promises of those involved? That is, where does (should) legitimacy lie?

12. What worldview is (ought to be) determining? That is, what different visions of "improvement" are (should be) considered, and how are they (should they be) reconciled?

All of the above questions have critical emphasis and implications. They all exist to guide people endeavouring to make "improvements" via systemic interventions to think explicitly and critically about what perspectives and goals should guide their choices and actions. Making the choice of client and purpose explicit (rather than leaving it implicit) forces a critical perspective. Explicitly considering who will make a decision on an intervention and how to decide forces a critical perspective. Explicitly considering what will guarantee success forces critical consideration of the ability and feasibility of making change responsibly, rather than putting stakeholders at risk of going through all the effort and pain of implementing change that in the end does not work. The last three questions have a particularly strong critical appeal in considering how to accommodate the interests of those who aren't even part of the process and otherwise have no voice.

Having sketched out the basics of the CSH approach and framework, the next section applies the framework to analyse the area of Design Science Research.

4   A Critical Systems Heuristics Analysis of Design Science Research

In this section we apply the CSH framework to Design Science Research (DSR) in order to analyse potential difficulties and to provide guidance for the conduct of DSR. But first, we should consider why it is relevant to apply CSH to DSR.

Design Science Research is all about solving problems and making improvements. The means for doing so is to invent new or improved solution technologies (Venable, 2006a, b) as the means for solving (or partially solving) a class or classes of problems, possibly problems that have never been addressed or solved before. By such invention, DSR produces and disseminates knowledge about how to solve the the class of problems so that others can apply that knowledge to solving their own problems or making improvements in their own situations. Applying knowledge to solve a problem requires intervention in a system, a system that almost always has multiple stakeholders and interests; therefore CSH is applicable. Design Science researchers then have an opportunity (and arguably an obligation) to consider how solutions that they invent will or can be used or applied and the scope of the problem or system that they should be considering when inventing new means or technologies to solve problems. Design Science researchers also need to design the technologies, practices, and knowledge they invent so that their inventions are likely to be employed appropriately.

Before applying the CSH framework, we should also consider why DSR is different from ordinary design and what implications that may have for a CSH analysis. Why is DSR a special case of design? Why might CSH apply differently to DSR than to 'ordinary' design – i.e. to design practice?

Ordinary design, or design practice, is related to a particular, situated problem (or group of problems). It has particular stakeholders with particular interests in the problem(s) and its/their potential solution(s). On the other hand, Design Science Research should be related to a type, kind, or class of problems (an abstract problem), which has characteristics that are generalised from typical, similar problems. It is relevant to typical classes of stakeholders rather than to particular people or organisations. The scope of both the problem to be addressed by the new solution technology and of the system in which intervention is to occur is generalised from the scopes of typical problems in typical systems. The applicability of the proposed new solutions is intended for situations of that type. Therefore, the stakeholders in these future problems are hypothetical and the scope of the problem to be addressed is intentional and hypothetical as well. Furthermore, rather than actually solving the situated problems (via design practice), it only indirectly contributes to their solution by developing new forms of solution and communicating them to would-be problem solvers. Therefore, the Design Science researcher must anticipate how others will put the solutions technologies that they invent into practice; the researchers themselves (for the most part) will not apply the solutions to ordinary design practice. [Note: An exception is Action Research, which may comprise both Design Practice (and intervention) and Design Science Research.] Design Science researchers must take into account that they are one step removed from actual problem solution when designing and inventing generalised solutions. They have a responsibility to consider how the things they invent will be used and whether they will achieve appropriate ends and outcomes through their use (and not achieve inappropriate ones!).

Having identified that CSH is appropriate for Design Science Research, the next four sections analyse DSR using the CSH lens, considering in turn the roles of client, decision maker, professional, and witness and that Design Science researchers may have to answer some of the above questions for themselves based on the particular types of problems, stakeholders, and situations intended (and unintended!) to be addressed.

4.1 The Client Role in Design Science Research

As discussed above, the Client is the role of the person/people/organisation(s) with an interest in solving the problem, or in the case of DSR, the type of hypothetical people with potential future interest in solving problems of the particular type(s) to be addressed by the new solution technology. The key issues for the client role are the purpose and the measure of improvement.

One could take a very narrow view and say that it is only the Design Science Researcher who determines the purpose(s) in solving a generalised problem. Design Science researchers might be considered to be their own clients in satisfying their own curiosity and in creating publishing opportunities. One could say that the readers of the published knowledge either find the information relevant and useful or not, but the researcher has no real obligation to anticipate their needs. However, I do not find this position tenable, particularly for employees who conduct research for the public good and have an obligation to publish (without which it is not really research).

Another perspective is that the nature of the client depends on who funds the research and on whose behalf the Design Science researcher is acting. Where this is a private organisation, it may be fairly narrowly defined as the client and have key interests. However, even if the funding organisation has an important and non-public interest, if research outcomes are published for consumption by the general public as would-be problem solvers, isn't the public a client?

For DSR, then, we could broadly define the Client role as "The set of all members of the generalised class of all people or organisations who could potentially be motivated to solve instances of the generalised class of problem(s)".

But who would this actually be? Can the Design Science researcher anticipate this correctly and select client stakeholder groups accordingly? Or, should we assume that the public (or even, if taken to extreme, all of humanity) are the clients of DSR? The real issue is who determines (or is involved in determining) the purpose(s) of the Design Science Research and the associated measure(s) of improvement. These issues are considered further later in this paper.

4.2 The Decision Maker Role in Design Science Research

The Decision Maker role is that of the person who decides which actions will be taken to intervene in the system and make an "improvement". Typically, they are the people who fund the intervention. In the case of DSR, the direct nature of the improvement is to publish and disseminate the ideas. The key issues for the decision maker role are resources and the decision environment.

A narrow view would hold that, with academic freedom, it is the Design Science researcher who decides what research will be undertaken and what they will do. The researcher can decide what research work to do and what to publish. However, the researcher is generally paid by someone else – a public or private institution, such as a university or a research funding agency. Funding agencies in particular are only rarely concerned just with the publication. They are interested in the possibility for actual improvement and problem solving following publication through the use of the new solution technology and make funding decisions accordingly. They expect the Design Science research to consider the needs of those who will be deciding whether and how to employ the new solution technology (or not).

For DSR then, we could broadly define the Decision Maker role as "The set of all members of the generalised class of all who might need to decide whether to employ the result of the research to the solution of the generalised class of problem(s)". Again, we can consider whether we can know in advance who the actual future decision makers will be. It would seem that any members of the public or humanity are potential future decision makers about deploying the new solution technology.

4.3 The Professional Role in Design Science Research

The Professional role is that of the person with appropriate expertise, who actually takes action to intervene in a system and generate the improvement. The key issues for the professional role are expertise and what guarantees success in the intervention.

Narrowly defined, the Design Science Researcher has expertise in DSR and takes the action to generate and publish the knowledge, which is the Design Science researcher's intervention in the system called "the world".

However, DSR and especially publication is not done in isolation, so there are other involved expert roles. Reviewers (of grant applications and of publications) and editors of publications also have important professional roles in the evaluation of the DSR and outcomes before publication. Reviewers and editors must therefore have appropriate expertise in DSR.

Furthermore, one could say that the entire research community has a professional role to play in its reaction to published research, e.g. in discussion at conferences or in pointing out flaws in research (e.g. through letters to the editor) or in replicating, extending, and/or refuting published results.

But viewed in the large as including deployment of the new solution technology, professional role includes those who learn about, develop expertise in, and employ (or deploy) the solution technology. Viewed from this perspective, we could broadly define the Professional role in DSR as "The set of all members of the generalised class of all who could apply the solution technology developed in the Design Science research to the solution of an instance of the generalised class of problem(s)". Again this is potentially any member of the public or humanity.

The key issue here is what guarantees that the DSR will be successful, not just in being published (the immediate goal), but in the long-term goal of making improvement in the world, through the action of those who learn about and employ the newly invented and published solution technologies (or even old ones long after publication). In the case of DSR, there are issues of the correct appraisal of generalised organisational or other problems, the efficacy of the solutions, and of technology transfer. All of these are dependent on the expertise of the design researchers and others involved in DSR, and particularly the consideration and involvement of potential future stakeholders.

4.4 The Witness Role in Design Science Research

As described above, the Witness role is that of anyone who represents the interests of those who could be affected by the intervention and who are not able to represent their own interests in the intervention problem formulation, solution design and deployment process. The key issues in the Witness role are emancipation of affected parties, legitimacy of the intervention, and the appropriateness of the worldview(s) governing the intervention.

From the critical point of view, those who cannot represent their own interests need to have them represented in some legitimate way (informed and effective). In DSR, people are affected both directly by the DSR (by reading and employing the knowledge outcomes in the DSR publications) and indirectly by the DSR (by being affected by the employment of the new solution technologies).

Following from this, we could broadly define the Witness role in DSR as "The set of all who could represent the interests of all members of the generalised class(es) of all who would be affected by the publication and/or application of the new solution technology". Again, the whole of the public or humanity are potentially affected indirectly (most likely), or even directly (less likely).

From a critical perspective, DSR should be conducted in a way and with a worldview that the emancipation and other interests of those who are not directly involved will be legitimately represented. But how should that be done? Is it enough for the Design Science researcher to (say paternalistically or maternalistically) look after the interests of those potentially affected? These questions are considered further below.

5   Discussion and Implications for Design Science Research

In the broader definitions of the roles suggested above, members of the public have a direct interest and role to play in the conduct of DSR as a way of improving the state of the world by solving or making improvements on various types of problems. However, the practicality of their involvement seems unreasonable and impracticable. One cannot consult all of humanity! Furthermore, most if not all of us members of humanity would not want to be consulted by every Design Science researcher on how we might be affected by their particular DSR project!

In the narrower definitions of the roles above, the key direct participants are (1) the Design Science Researcher, (2) the employers of Design Science Researchers, (3) Research Funding Agencies who fund DSR projects, (4) Reviewers and Editors (and Publishers) of DSR results, and (5) (possibly) Governments and Regulatory Agencies. The Design Science Researcher may act in the roles of client (following his/her own interest), decision-maker (allocating their own time), professional (expert in DSR and the problem domain), and even witness (perhaps by reading literature, drawing on experience, or even imagining what effects the new solution technology might have on others). Employers may have a role in decision making about what DSR is done and how (client and decision maker roles or even witnesses for the public). For example, ethics review and approval bodies at universities may have an important role to play. Research Funding Agencies (whether public or private) can also play a decision maker role, but also a client role in setting out problems to be solved and priorities. Reviewers (both for publication and for competitive funding) and Editors play an important quality control role and are thus Professionals, collaborating (in some sense) with the Design Science researcher as a professional. They also decide whether research is relevant for their audience, which is a client role. Governments have a role to play as client (setting the agenda), decision maker (about funding), and possibly as witnesses for the public. Regulatory Agencies primarily could play a witness role.

By taking these narrower role definitions, all of the other roles broadly defined above as potentially being played by the rest of the public and humanity are only indirectly affected by or involved with DSR. Future clients benefiting from new solution technology usage, future decision makers about new solution technology usage, future professionals employing/deploying new solution technologies, future witnesses for those affected by the usage of new solution technologies, and those potentially affected in the future by the application of new solution technologies, but not involved in their deployment/use need witnesses to protect their interests. Having witnesses for the public, as in the narrow definition and approach, rather than open participation by the public, seems more realistic and practicable.

This, however, leaves a few key questions. First, how should the interests of society/humanity be represented in the design science research process, i.e., who should legitimately witness for the public and how? Second, what should guide these decisions? Third, what are the obstacles to making such decisions and ensuring that the many interests of the public are legitimately represented during DSR?

5.1 How Should the Public/Humanity Be Consulted, Involved, or Witnessed for?

As suggested above, one possibility is that it could be the researcher who fills the witness role by understanding and/or imagining what effects the solution means might have on others. However, is the researcher capable of doing this? The question is one of expertise and ability, but also of legitimacy. This might be considered more appropriate where the researcher actually is personally confronted with the same problem(s) that he or she is trying to solve. However, the researcher's personal interest will likely be narrow and not representative of the breadth of different interests held by the diverse members of the public.

Another possibility is that the public's interests can be represented by the community of experts, including not only the researcher, but ethics review and approval bodies, funding agencies, reviewers, editors, and the like. For example, university ethics committees, reviewers, or editors might consider the potential long-term consequences of DSR outcomes in use by the public. The expert community brings more expertise and broader knowledge about the needs of others and possible consequences to them to bear. However, is that knowledge broad enough? Is it legitimate to represent the interests of the public?

Another possibility is that the interests of the public are represented through rigourous evaluation of the solution technology before publication. Evaluation is a key activity in DSR. Really rigorous evaluation requires naturalistic evaluation (Venable, 2006b), which requires involving real people with real problems using the real solution technology (Sun and Kantor, 2006). However, evaluation is already down the track and the purpose(s) have already by then been long determined, so this seems inappropriate. Furthermore, questions of appropriate forms of evaluation in DSR are currently under considerable debate in the DSR community (e.g. see Baskerville et al 2007).

A fourth possibility is that representation of the interests of future users naturally follows from their involvement in forms of research such as Action Research. Action research includes real stakeholder involvement in the development of solution(s) of their real problems. As such, it is both Design Practice and Design Research at the same time. However, there is still a possible issue with generalisability of the solution technology because the worldview of the action research client and their problem(s) may be too narrow, idiosyncratic, and not representative of the interests of the public. Furthermore, the choice and inclusion of clients may be opportunistic and ad hoc, leading to a lack of representativeness.

A fifth possibility is that the interests of future users of the solution technology should be represented by government, who funds much of research and is commonly involved in driving the goals influencing competitive grant funding and selection. However, not all of DSR is funded in such a way and much DSR may be little influenced by government.

The final possibility considered here (there may be others) is some form of direct participation by and involvement of the public. Focus groups might be conducted to gather information about needs. Surveys might be conducted. Advisory boards might be created to advise DSR projects. Other forms of broader participation might be created, such as public forums, online discussion groups, and open calls for participation.

While this last possibility would seem to be the most legitimate, there would still be important questions and issues. Importantly, which public do we mean by "the public"? Do we mean the local community or municipality, the state, the country, the region, or the whole world? What about other cultures, countries, etc.? In today's global economy, with global education and global dissemination of ideas, what is published in one context may be used in other contexts for which it was not intended or designed. Should those alternative cultures and societies have their interests and peculiarities of worldview and need be represented in some way? Or can we design for one community and culture and let other communities and cultures decide for themselves whether new solution technologies are appropriate for their context or not (Caveat emptor!)?

Another important question is what should guide decisions about how to represent the needs of the public from among the different possibilities described above. An important issue in answering this question is the amount of resources required to represent the interests of the public and whether they are well spent. One could say that the cost and resources used must be balanced against the need and risk. What is the importance and significance of the problem? Who is affected by it and what are the costs? What are the potential impacts – how widespread or serious? What are the risks to the public? Are there any issues of ethics of the research method and conduct? How important and serious are they? Are there other factors that should be considered? One can also ask whether such questions can even be answered a priori. To some extent, the answers can't be predicted reliably and aren't known until after the research is conducted.

A final question for this paper concerns the practicality and applicability of this whole discussion. Is it possible to influence and change the way that DSR is conducted in order to accommodate the above concerns? There are a number of factors that argue against Design Science researchers accepting any of these ideas and putting them into practice. First, there is the issue of the effort required to learn about these issues, to reflect on them, and to change one's practice. Second, researchers will naturally worry that choosing to involve other stakeholders will take additional (very precious) time and thereby reduce their research productivity. For example, processes to obtain ethical approval may become bureaucratic and time consuming. Third, the values, goals, and objectives of those in other roles, not to mention the approach taken, may lead to solutions and work that are different from the vision and designs already held by, created by, and of interest to the researcher. Fourth, any outcome that is different may be less publishable than what the researcher intended to do, so there is less control over outcomes. Finally, if others are involved, the researcher may receive less credit due to the shared effort in the design of a new approach. For these reasons, Design Science researchers may naturally resist accommodating the witnessing activity in their DSR efforts.

6   Summary and Conclusions

This paper has applied the Critical System Heuristics perspective to critically analyse Design Science Research. Doing so has raised some issues concerning the way in which DSR should and could be legitimately conducted. The analysis has shown that future clients, decision makers, professionals, and other non-included stakeholders in the future employment of new solution technologies to be invented via DSR, who may potentially be any member of the public or humanity, may well need to have their interests represented by witnesses during DSR. However, there are open questions about the form by which the witness activity should be undertaken and how the resource costs for that activity can be balanced against the interests of and risks to the public. Further, there are questions about who constitute the public that needs to be witnessed for, with the answers ranging from only locally affected groups through all of humanity, including people in other countries and cultures. Finally, there are open questions about how the recommended inclusion of a witness role and activity can be raised, accepted, and included in DSR as practiced.

References

Baskerville, R., Pries-Heje, J., Venable, J.: Soft Design Science Research: Extending the Boundaries of Evaluation in Design Science Research. In: Chatterjee, S., Rossi, M. (eds.) Proceedings of the 2nd International Conference on Design Science Research in Information Systems and Technology (DESRIST 2007), Pasadena, California, USA, May 13-15 (2007)

Baskerville, R., Vaishnavi, V. (eds.): Proceedings of the 3rd International Conference on Design Science Research in Information Systems and Technology (DESRIST 2008), Atlanta, Georgia, USA, May 7-9, 2008 (2007)

Cecez-Kecmanovic, D., Klein, H.K., Brooke, C.: Exploring the Critical Agenda in Information Systems Research. Information Systems Journal 18(2), 123–135 (2008)

Chatterjee, S., Rossi, M. (eds.): Proceedings of the 2nd International Conference on Design Science Research in Information Systems and Technology (DESRIST 2007), Pasadena, California, USA, May 13-15 (2007)

Checkland, P.: Systems Thinking, Systems Practice. John Wiley & Sons, Chichester (1981)

Checkland, P., Holwell, S.: Information, Systems and Information Systems. John Wiley & Sons, Chichester (1998)

Checkland, P., Scholes, J.: Soft Systems Methodology in Action. John Wiley & Sons, Chichester (1990)

Cranefield, J., Yoong, P.: To Whom Should Information Systems Research Be Relevant: The Case for an Ecological Perspective. In: Österle, H., Schelp, J., Winter, R. (eds.) Proceedings of the 15th European Conference on Information Systems (ECIS 2007, on CD), St Gallen, Switzerland, 7-9 June 2007, pp. 1313–1324 (2007)

Emery, M. (ed.): Participative Design for Participative Democracy. Centre for Continuing Education. Australian National University, Canberra (1989)

Gregor, S., Jones, D.: The Anatomy of a Design Theory. Journal of the Association for Information Systems 8(5), article 2, 312–335 (2007)

Habermas, J.: Moral Consciousness and Communicative Action. MIT Press, Cambridge (1983) (English translation 1991)

Hevner, A., Chatterjee, S. (eds.): Proceedings of the 1st International Conference on Design Science in Information Systems and Technology (DESRIST 2006),, Claremont, California, USA, February 24-26, 2005 (2006), http://ncl.cgu.edu/firstdesignconf/Cochairmsg.htm (viewed 18 June 2007)

Hevner, A.R., March, S.T., Park, J., Ram, S.: Design Science in Information Systems Research. MIS Quarterly 28(1), 75–105 (2004)

Keen, P.: Relevance and rigour in information systems research: Improving quality, confidence, cohesion and impact. In: Nissen, H.-E., Klein, H.K., Hirschheim, R. (eds.) Information Systems Research: Contemporary Approaches and Emergent Traditions (Proceedings of the IFIP WG 8.2 Working Conference in Copenhagen), pp. 27–49. North-Holland, Amsterdam (1991)

Kyng, M., Beardon, C., Mathiassen, L. (eds.): Computers and Design in Context. MIT Press, Cambridge (1997)

March, S.T., Smith, G.F.: Design and Natural Science Research on Information Technology. Decision Support Systems 15(4), 251–266 (1995)

Mitchell, R.K., Agle, B.R., Wood, D.J.: Toward a Theory of Stakeholder Identification and Salience: Defining the Principle of Who and What Really Counts. Academy of Management Journal 22(4), 853–886 (1997)

Moody, D.: Building links between IS research and professional practice: improving the relevance and impact of IS research. In: Proceedings of the Twenty First International Conference on Information Systems, Brisbane, Queensland, Australia, pp. 351–360 (2000)

Moody, D., Buist, A.: Improving Links Between Information Systems Research and Practice – Lessons from the Medical Profession. In: Proceedings of the 10th Australasian Conference on Information Systems, Wellington, New Zealand, pp. 645–659 (1999)

Mumford, E.: Designing Human Systems: The ETHICS Method. Manchester Business School (1983)

Mumford, E.: Systems Design: Ethical Tools for Ethical Change. Macmillan, London (1996)

Mumford, E.: The Story of Socio-Technical Design: Reflections on its successes, failures and potential. Information Systems Journal 16, 317–342 (2006)

Nunamaker Jr., J.F., Chen, M., Purdin, T.D.M.: Systems Development in Information Systems Research. Journal of Management Information Systems 7(3), 89–106 (1991)

Schuler, D., Namioka, A.: Participatory Design: Principles and Practices. Lawrence Erlbaum Associates, Mahwah (1993)

Stahl, B.C.: The Ethical Nature of Critical Research in Information Systems. Information Systems Journal 18(2), 137–163 (2008)

Sun, Y., Kantor, P.B.: Cross-Evaluation: A new model for information system evaluation. Journal of the American Society for Information Science and Technology 57(5), 614–628 (2006)

Ulrich, W.: Critical Heuristics of Social Planning: A New Approach to Practical Philosophy. Paul Hapt, Bern/Stuttgart (1983)

Ulrich, W.: Critical Heuristics of Social Systems Design. European Journal of Operational Research 31, 276–283 (1987)

Ulrich, W.: Critical Systems Heuristics. In: Daellenbach, H.G., Flood, R.L. (eds.) The Informed Student Guide to Management Science. Thomson Learning, London (2002)

Vaishnavi, V., Kuechler, B.: Design Research in Information Systems. in ISWorldNet website (2004),
http://www.isworld.org/Researchdesign/drisISworld.htm (viewed 9 January 2006)

Venable, J.R.: The Role of Theory and Theorising in Design Science Research. In: Hevner, A., Chatterjee, S. (eds.) Proceedings of the 1st International Conference on Design Science in Information Systems and Technology (DESRIST 2006), Claremont, California, USA, February 24-26 (2006a),
http://ncl.cgu.edu/firstdesignconf/
DESRIST%202006%20Proceedings/2A_1.pdf (viewed June 18, 2007)

Venable, J.: A Framework for Design Science Research Activities. In: Proceedings of the 2006 Information Resource Management Association Conference, Washington, DC, USA (2006b)

Walls, J.G., Widmeyer, G.R., El Sawy, O.A.: Building an information system design theory for vigilant EIS. Information Systems Research 3(1), 36–59 (1992)

Architecture for a Creative Information System

Henrique São Mamede[1] and Vitor Santos[2]

[1] Universidade Aberta, Rua da Escola Politécnica, nº 141-147, 1269-001 Lisboa, Portugal
[2] Microsoft, Edifício Qualidade, C1-C2, Av. Prof. Doutor Aníbal Cavaco Silva, Tagus Park

Abstract. Considering that the capacity to innovate is increasingly becoming a decisive factor in the competition between organisations, the study and conception of systems that help the birth of new ideas, products and solutions is rising in importance. In this article, the authors consider the concept of Creative Information Systems and present a proposal for the development of architecture for such a system based on the creative technique of brute thinking.

Keywords: Information Systems, Creative Thinking, Innovation.

1 Introduction

There are many definitions of creativity presented by various schools of thought. As an example, and coming from distinct environments, we can consider two different approaches presented by John Kao and Stan Gryskiewicz (Kao 1996, Gryskiewicz 1993). The first defines creativity as the process through which ideas are generated, developed and transformed into value. The second defines creativity as a useful novelty.

For the context of the present article, we will define creativity as the ability to imagine, invent and create new solutions, unexpected, original, useful, and capable of solving problems of unknown forms or to present things that where never thought of before. Creativity is the result of an intentional thought, with the aim of finding new solutions to problems or to guarantee already known solutions (Adams 1986). All human beings have the potential to be creative, some more than others, and everyone can develop and improve their creative capacity.

There is a great diversity of techniques that support creative thinking and a large array of tools which perform some of those techniques[1]. All the creativity techniques have strong and weak points and can be more or less useful depending on the kind of problem (Jay 2000).

Considering that the capacity to innovate is becoming more and more a decisive factor in enterprise competition and in everyday life, the study and conception of systems that help to innovate have an increasing importance (Bennetti 1999).

---

[1] Creative techniques list, http://www.mycoted.com/creativity/techniques/
Creative thinking techniques and lateral thinking,
http://www.brainstorming.co.uk/tutorials/creativethinkingcontents.html
Creative thinking techniques, http://members.optusnet.com.au/~charles57/Creative/Techniques

G. Dhillon, B.C. Stahl, and R. Baskerville (Eds.): CreativeSME 2009, IFIP AICT 301, pp. 113–121, 2009.
© IFIP International Federation for Information Processing 2009

In this context, the hypothesis which would appeal to the capacity of computer systems, based on knowledge or on adaptations of creativity techniques in order to help to produce new combinations and to give unexpected, original, useful and satisfactory answers, focused in one specific context, is something extremely challenging. In this article, we consider the concept of "Creative Information System" which introduces us to a proposal of a concrete architecture based on the technique of creativity named brute thinking (Michalko 1991). This technique is a powerful lateral-thinking technique that is very easy to use. It is by far the simplest of all creative techniques and is now widely used by people who need to create new ideas[2].

2 About Creative Thinking

While enquiring into creativity, we come across a variety of theories and models that explain the creative thought and its mental procedures (Koestler 1964). The most well known theory is the concept of the divergent thought by the American J. P. Guilford (Gardner 1998, Arieti 1993), a decisive theory in the inquiry of creativity in the United States between the 1960s and 1970s, and the theory of the lateral thought, developed by Edward De Bono (Binnig 1997, Baxter 2000) between the 1970s and 1980s.

Later on, in a conference about 'Design Thinking', Nigel Cross criticized those creators, stating that frequently, they have difficulties in departing from an initial idea and to choose a new path for the search of a new solution (Binnig 1997), bringing into attention the necessity for a wider use of lateral thought in creativity.

Other aspects of scant consideration by Guilford and De Bono are the personal characteristics and the cognitive styles of an individual, the bio-social conditions (work structures, communication styles, conflict management, hierarchies) and environments (colors and shapes in-house, temperature, light, noise, etc.) where individuals work. All these aspects had already been identified by one of the most recent theories that explain creativity – the Theory of the Systems (Cardoso de Sousa 1998).

The systemic vision of creativity is based on the General Theory of the Systems, from the biologist Ludwig von Bertalaffy, who applied this term in the 1970s to frequently describe points of the biological, physical and social systems. Previously, systemic theories had been developed within the cybernetics (Wiener 1950), where the objectives were to dominate the complexity of technical and economic systems (Bono 1994). On the base of the von Bertalaffy and Wiener's work, a theory of systems was largely developed and it leads us to the explanation, simulation and manipulation of the Nature process evolution. Currently, the main goal is to find a universal theory on the common systemic principles to different sciences (Jonas 1994).

The majority of the investigators in the creativity field agree with the three main features that characterize a creative person: the fluidity, the flexibility and the originality of the thought. These three pointers are the criteria of evaluation in many tests of creativity (Cross et al. 1992). The fluidity of thought points out the ease of producing ideas in quantity within a limited time frame. This is about a non critical

---

[2] Edward de Bono, http://www.edwarddebono.com/PassageDetail.php?passage_id=692&

thought which can be stimulated by techniques such as brainstorming or brainwriting (Guilford 1986).

The flexibility of the thought is characterized by ease not only of producing ideas in quantity, but also in quality and to find answers that allow different classifications. As opposed to flexibility there is rigidity, immobility and incapability to change attitudes, behaviors or points of view, the impossibility to offer other alternatives or to change an already applied method. When a proposal is created, if it is different from the existing ones, within a certain context, because it is uncommon or unusual, then it is considered originality of thought.

The analytical thought is the process to recognize, classify and describe the elements of a problem. Humans describe themselves to others and to the world as analytical beings, able to study and decompose everything in parts. The conclusions of the analysis can give us tracks to the accomplishment of a hypothesis, an analogy or a new synthesis. As the traditions of the western thought are based on analysis and logical reasoning, analysis is being increasingly used as one of the abilities of creative thought; however, it is known that many students have difficulties to accomplish functional and morphological analyses problems (Ferreras 1999).

The accomplishment of hypotheses is another procedure of the creative thought. It is the ability to assume and to establish. In the experimental sciences, a reasonable explanation of the facts is provisionally adopted with the aim to submit it to a methodical verification for the experience. It is the search of causes and consequences. An important procedure of the hypothetical thought is the divergent interrogation. Divergent questions allow some valid answers. These are inducing because they are open, thus stimulating a diversity of ideas, images, feelings and immediate reactions.

In order to understand relations and interconnections, it is necessary to compare and relate. Another elementary operation to solve a problem in a creative way is the analogical-comparative thought. It is about a mental process of bi-association of ideas (Smith 1990) which allows establishing a new and uncommon relation between objects and situations. The ideas are bi-associations; to create is to recombine the available knowledge. The development of the analogical thought demands imagination training and the use of metaphors.

The synthetic thought is a combinational thought that carries through a new synthesis in an individual or group base. It is the dispersed integration of fragmentary elements and information in a new combination (Gogatz and Mondejar 2005). To create an innovative product through an original synthesis, it is necessary to have an open attitude to different stimulations in order to have the maximum possible choice. Finally, but just as important, the mental procedure to process creation is intuition. It is linked with the direct and immediate contemplation of the reality or a problem for which a different solution from the one that could be obtained by a logical reasoning is being sought. It is an unconscious thought, where the procedure is not explainable. According to the physicist Gerd Binnig, intuition is a kind of analysis or synthesis that is not processed logically when the problem is too complex (Smith 1990). Thus, the intuitive thought helps the designer to take a decision if the situation is not well defined and unclear and data is contradictory, incomplete or too subjective, which occurs with the majority of situations concerning design projects.

3 The Creative Information System

3.1 Creativity Techniques

To the creativity process, one or more available techniques are referred for the desired effect. Overall there are hundreds of techniques published in the works of Michael Michalko (Michalko 2000), Van Gundy (Van Gundy, 2007), James Higgins (Higgins, 1996), Dilip Mukerjea (Mukerjea, 2003) among other authors. These techniques are tools able to suit different approaches for different creative parties. For example, techniques for the definition of existing problems, to explore attributes of a problem, to generate alternatives, for visual explorations, metaphors, analogies and evaluation and implementation of ideas. A few groups of techniques will be presented in the following text as a small example. In this sense, we have the technique of random word or image, false rules, random website, the SCAMPER, research and the reusing, role-play, escaped and analogies.

The random word technique, also called brute thinking, refers to the random generation of a word that will work as an initial stimulation, extracting its underlying principles and applying them to the problem. The technique of the random image is by all means similar to the previous one, except its resource, which is an image instead of a word. The technique of false rules applies rules that previously were not considered possible to the problems, hence the name "false". Making the false rule and forcing its use in the new situation, forces it in differentiated directions, which normally would not be followed.

The random website technique consists of finding and consulting sites randomly, collecting ideas and using those ideas to generate new ideas. The SCAMPER technique is a good example of a elaborate technique that uses a set of directed questions that you answer about your problem in order to come up with new ideas. The stimulus comes from forcing yourself to answer those questions which you would not normally pose. The questions direct you to thinking about a problem in ways which typically throw up new ideas.

The role play technique involves changing the perspective of the problem, acting like another person and trying to determine the way he would face the question.

The escaped technique consists in generating the wildest proposals without possible limits, without any moral, rules, labels, laws or standards.

The technique of analogies refers to the use of an analogy or a metaphor in a particular situation in order to locate similar opportunities or solutions in other areas.

More information and hyperlinks for related web pages with techniques of creative thought can be found in the website of Andy Beckett[3] who is promoting a body of work of compilation of various techniques[4]. We also appreciate the recent work of Hudson (Hudson 2007).

3.2 Definition of "Creative Information System"

We define "Creative Information System" (CIS) as an information system that, facing a concrete problem in a certain context and using an adjusted creativity technique, is

---

[3] http://members.optusnet.com.au/~charles57/Creative/Techniques/
[4] http://www.mycoted.com/creativity/techniques/

able to generate automatically a potentially innovative set of answers for the solution of a problem (Santos and Mamede 2007).

The information system that we consider, does not cover all the development cycle of the creative process, but allows relying on the computer system in terms of all the direct creativity techniques application, with a larger or smaller sophistication degree, as shown in fig. 1 (Santos and Mamede 2006).

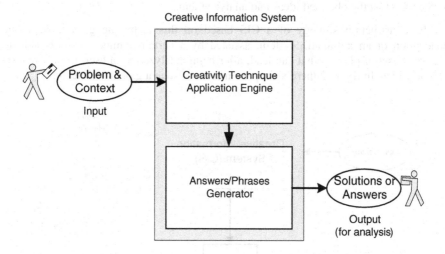

Fig. 1. General scheme of a Creative Information System

To be able to work, the information system has to receive the necessary minimum inputs as a starting point, namely the specification of the problem, the context and the restrictions to the generated solutions. The answers are generated through the application of one or more techniques of creativity or by the combination of those adapted in order to be implemented through computer applications, with a larger or smaller degree of sophistication.

As far as we can tell, all the known techniques of creativity can be implemented with larger or smaller adaptations, without restrictions (Mamede and Santos 2005).

The generated answers or solutions can be direct or indirect proposal solutions. A solution is considered to be direct when the answer possesses an immediate applicability for the resolution of the problem. On the other hand a solution is considered as indirect when the answer cannot be applied immediately but has potential to lead to the appearance of a direct solution. The degree of sophistication of the system can be measured by the number of supplied answers that can be considered more or less direct.

4   The Architecture of a CIS

The architecture for a creative information system that we consider in this section is based on a technique from Michael Michalko named brute thinking. This simple technique is based on a very simplified process, which is developed in four steps, as follows:

- Step 1 – Choose randomly a word
- Step 2 – Choose things/elements associated with the random word obtained
- Step 3 – Force links between the word and the problem and also between the associations and the problem
- Step 4 – List the obtained ideas and analyze them.

The construction strategy of a CIS based on this technique goes through the conception of an automatic system, assisted by a certain number of tools able to generate a set of phrases that can lead, after being analyzed by a user, to the creation of a new idea. In figure 2 there's a representation of such a global architecture.

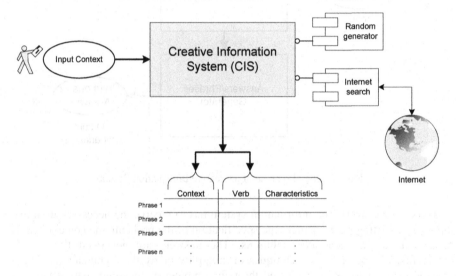

Fig. 2. Global architecture of a creativity information system based in brute thinking

In order for this to become possible, a context is supplied to the system by the user. This context will be used later, in the final phase of the sentences composition, attempting to generate a new idea based on the user's context. Simultaneously, a set of words representing tangible or intangible objects are generated, in a perfectly random form. For each one of these objects a set of key characteristics associated with it is determined. For this task of determination, a dictionary of characteristics from the Internet can be used.

After obtaining all those elements, the system should be able to generate phrases with a predetermined structure. Then, they are constituted by context – the verb, that will be also be randomly generated, and one of the predetermined key characteristics. The sentences will be generated and presented to the user for analysis; we estimate that only a very small percentage may have some meaning for the user. However, this will be the result of the exclusively random combinations, without any base in other previously existing ideas which could restrict the generator.

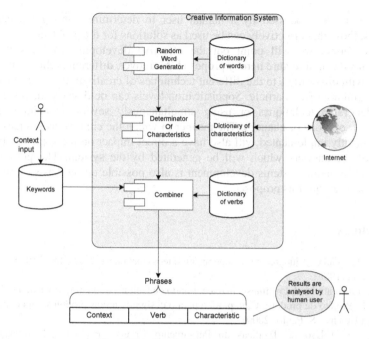

Fig. 3. Detailed architecture of a CSI

It is now possible to determine which of the elements shall constitute the central core of our creative information system needed to implement this architecture. We will need a random generator of words, an element capable of determining the characteristics of a given object and a module with the capacity to combine all of these elements with the keywords that describe the context generating phrases.

In this document, the element that comprises the architecture proposal is represented in figure 3. The central element of the system architecture is a module capable of combining the objects and its characteristics with words, which describe the context where the generation of new ideas is demanded and the verb, giving origin to a phrase that might or might not constitute a new idea. To determine the use of the characteristics, the system carries out the creation of objects, based on a dictionary. For each one of these objects there are some characteristics which are common to all, supported or based on a dictionary, which searches it in the Internet and stores it for later reference. These are transferred into the combiner that conjugates them with the keywords, which describe the context of the user, and with a verb which is taken in turn from a proper dictionary. With the capacity to combine these elements, a set of phrases is generated and then analyzed by the user who will collect those that are effectively representing a new idea or proposal and will discard the rest.

5 Conclusion and Future Work

It becomes possible to use an information system that supports most automatic functions of the creative process by implementing different techniques. The final part requires it to be processed by a human user to determine, among the generated solutions, those that effectively can be used as solutions for the problem.

In the future, we will point out the effective development of a system that implements the architecture hereby proposed. Moreover, different architectures can be defined, with direct links to the different techniques of creativity that were mentioned in the beginning of this article. Sophistication levels can be developed, consisting of more elaborated techniques or using simultaneously several techniques for the creation of solutions or chances. The manner in which the creative techniques will be algorithmically implemented will also have a direct impact on the sophistication and quality of the answers which will be generated by the system. The possibility of creative information systems development is also possible on the basis of new ideas that can appear with this proposal.

References

Adams, J.L.: Guía y juegos para superar bloqueos mentales, 2nd edn. Editorial Gedisa, Barcelona (1986)

Arieti, S.: La creatividad, La síntesis mágica. Fondo de Cultura Económica, México (1993)

Baxter, M.: Projeto de produto: Guia prático para o design de novos produtos, 2nd edn. Editora Edgard Blücher, S. Paulo (2000)

Bennetti, P.: O Uso de Técnicas do Pensamento Criativo Facilita a Participação e o Comprometimento do Corpo Gerencial de uma Empresa com o Planeamento Estratégico. Tese de Mestrado em Criatividade Aplicada Total, Universidade de Santiago de Compostela (1999)

Binnig, G.: Aus dem Nichts: Über die Kreativität von Natur und Mensch. Piper Verlag, München (1997)

Bono, E.: De Bono's Thinking Course. BBC Books, London (1994)

Cardoso de Sousa, F.: A criatividade como disciplina científica. Colecção de Monografias Master de Creatividad, Servicio de Publicacións da Universidade de Santiago de Compostela, Santiago (1998)

Cross, N., Dorst, K., Roozenburg, N. (eds.): Research in Design Thinking. Delft University Press, Delft (1992)

Ferreras, A.P.: El cerebro creador. Psicologia, Alianza Editorial, Madrid (1999)

Gardner, H.: Mentes Creativas, una anatomía de la creatividad. Paidós, Barcelona (1998)

Gogatz, A., Mondejar, R.: Business Creativity – Breaking the Invisible Barrier. Palgrave Macmillan, New York (2005)

Gryskiewicz, S.: Discovering Creativity. Center Creative Leadership Press, USA (1993)

Guilford, J.P.: Creative talents: their nature, uses and development. Bearly Limited, Buffalo (1986)

Higgins, J.M.: Innovate or evaporate: Creative techniques for strategists. Long Range Planning Journal 29(3), 370–380 (1996)

Hudson, K.: The Idea Generator – Tools For Business Growth. Allen & Unwin, Crows Nest (2007)

Jay, R.: The Ultimate Book of Business Creativity. Capstone Publishing Limited, Oxford (2000)

Jonas, W.: Design –System – Theorie, Überlegungen zu einem systemtheoretischen Modell von Design-Theorie. Ed. Die Blaue Eule, Essen (1994)

Kao, J.: Jamming. HarperBusiness, New York (1996)

Koestler, A.: The act of creation. Arkana Penguin Books, London (1964)

Mamede, H.S., Santos, V.: Uma Arquitectura para um Sistema de Informação Criativo. 6ª Conferência da Associação Portuguesa de Sistemas de Informação, Bragança, Portugal (2005)

Michalko, M.: Thinkertoys: A Handbook of Business Creativity For the 90s. Ten Speed Press, USA (1991)

Michalko, M.: Los secretos de los genios de la creatividad. Ed. Gestión, Barcelona (2000)

Mukerjea, D.: Brain Symphony. The Brainware Press, Singapore (2003)

Santos, V., Mamede, H.S.: Um Sistema de Informação Criativo baseado na técnica de criatividade whiteboard. In: Actas da 1ª CISTI (Conferência Ibérica de Sistemas e Tecnologias de Informação), Esposende, Portugal (2006)

Santos, V., Mamede, H.S.: Creative Information Systems. In: Freire, M., Pereira, M. (eds.) Encyclopedia of Internet Technologies and Applications, IGI Global, USA (2007)

Smith, F.: Pensar, Epigénese e Desenvolvimento. Instituto Piaget, Lisboa (1990)

Van Gundy, A.B.: Getting to Innovation: How Asking the Right Questions Generates the Great Ideas Your Company Needs. AMACOM, Boston (2007)

Wiener, N.: The Human Use of Human Beings: Cybernetics and Society. Houghton Mifflin Company, Boston (1950)

Creativity in Agile Systems Development:
A Literature Review

Kieran Conboy[1], Xiaofeng Wang[2], and Brian Fitzgerald[2]

[1] National University of Ireland,
Galway, Ireland
[2] Lero Software Engineering Research Centre,
University of Limerick, Castletroy, Limerick, Ireland

Abstract. Proponents of agile methods claim that enabling, fostering and driving creativity is the key motivation that differentiates agile methods from their more traditional, beauraucratic counterparts. However, there is very little rigorous research to support this claim. Like most of their predecessors, the development and promotion of these methods has been almost entirely driven by practitioners and consultants, with little objective validation from the research community. This lack of validation is particularly relevant for SMEs, given that many of their project teams typify the environment to which agile methods are most suited i.e. small, co-located teams with diverse, blended skills in unstructured, sometimes even chaotic surroundings. This paper uses creativity theory as a lens to review the current agile method literature to understand exactly how much we know about the extent to which creativity actually occurs in these agile environments. The study reveals many gaps and conflict of opinion in the body of knowledge in its current state and identifies many avenues for further research.

1 Introduction

The last decade or so has seen the emergence of a number of software development methods as a response to the inefficiency of existing software development methods in rapidly changing environments (Highsmith, 2004). Some of the most popular include eXtreme Programming (XP) (Beck, 2000) and Scrum (Schwaber and Beedle, 2002). This family of methods are now commonly known as 'agile', primarily through the formation of the Agile Alliance and the publication of the Agile Manifesto (Agile Manifesto 2001). Agile methods have been well received by those in the system development community and there is strong anecdotal evidence to suggest that awareness and indeed use of these methods is highly prevalent across the community. Agile methods, given their flexible and light-weight processes, place emphasis on close communication and collaboration in project teams (Beck, 2000; Schwaber and Beedle, 2002). These approaches are typical of the development environments of small to medium software organizations.

Creativity has been advocated as a core part of Information Systems Development (ISD) for many years (Brooks 1987; Elam and Mead 1987; Cougar 1990; Sampler

G. Dhillon, B.C. Stahl, and R. Baskerville (Eds.): CreativeSME 2009, IFIP AICT 301, pp. 122–134, 2009.

and Galleta 1991; Lobert and Dologite 1994; Gallivan 2003; Carayannis and Coleman 2005). Cougar (1990) believed that creative activities should play a pivotal role "in all aspects of IT development, from requirements definition through program design". Lobert and Dologite (1994) propose three reasons for this. Firstly, "technology is evolving on a daily basis and we can continually look for new ways to utilise resources". Secondly, "most simple systems have already been developed and the challenging ones are still ahead". Finally, "many information systems are old, not meeting existing demand, and will soon become obsolete". Researchers such as Gallivan (2003) highlight the importance of creative developers, and Brooks (1987) even contends that the critical problems in ISD may not be addressed by ISD methods per se, but rather how those methods facilitate creativity and improvisation.

The importance of creativity has also been highlighted and the support to creativity claimed within the agile method movement (Highsmith and Cockburn, 2001; Highsmith, 2004; Cockburn and Highsmith, 2001; Highsmith, 2002; Highsmith, 2002a). Agile advocates believe that "creativity, not voluminous written rules, is the only way to manage complex software development problems" (Highsmith and Cockburn, 2001). Cockburn and Highsmith (2001) claim that "Agile methodologies deal with unpredictability by relying on people and their creativity rather than on processes". Highsmith (2002a) contends that "agile approaches are best employed to explore new ground and to power teams for which innovation and creativity are paramount". The literature also illustrates the fact that the requirement for creativity has been highlighted in discussions of specific agile methods, such as eXtreme Programming (XP), one of the most popular agile methods (Highsmith, 2002a; Crispin and House, 2003; Benediktsson et al, 2004). Highsmith (2002a) observers that "although XP contains certain disciplined practices, its intent is to foster creativity and communication". Benediktsson et al (2004) claim that "given the benefits of XP in terms of creativity, value delivery and higher satisfaction levels, it is not surprising that many managers and developers have adopted such practices".

Despite these claims, however, there is a lack of understanding of what constitute creativity in software development in general and to which extent agile methods actually facilitate creativity. The aim of this paper is thus to get a better understanding of the extent to which agile methods facilitate creativity. For our theoretical base we propose a conceptual framework drawn from existing creativity literature, and then use this as a lens to analyse the relevant agile method literature. The paper concludes with a set of recommendations for possible future research.

2 Creativity Constructs

Creativity, typically referring to the act of producing new ideas, approaches or actions, is crucial to the success of organizations (Nonaka, 1991; Amabile, 1998). It is seen as a starting point and a necessary but not sufficient condition for organizational innovation, which often refers to the entire process by which an organization generates creative new ideas and converts them into novel, useful and viable commercial products, services, and business practices (Amabile et al., 1996).

A careful literature review reveals a set of creativity constructs-elements that constitute or facilitate creativity of an organization.

3 Generation of New Ideas

One of the simplest work practices facilitating creativity is setting aside time for *idea generation* (Woodman, Sawyer et al. 1993; Ekvall 1996). However, organisations often tend to over-simplify the creative process, and often misconstrue the setting aside of some "idea time" (Ekvall 1996) as being the only thing needed to be a creative organisation. A number of researchers highlight the distinct lack of resources explicitly dedicated by most organisations to the creative process (Payne 1990). Amabile (1996) details this proposition further, stating that creativity tasks are often bereft of "funds, facilities, materials and information". The critical enablers of creativity which are often ignored include time and resources for *testing and experimentation* to validate ideas once they have been generated (Anderson and West 1996; Ekvall 1996). Prototyping is often cited as the most important, but most under-funded activity across organisations (Leonard-Barton 1995).

Stakeholder involvement is considered imperative to the creative process, yet many with vested interest are never involved (Nonaka and Takeuchi 1995; Amabile 1996; Ekvall 1996; Mathisen and Einarsen 2004). Flores (1993) exemplifies this by discussing the merits of involving the customer in the innovation process. In a truly creative environment, an organisation's internal and external communication boundaries should be as porous as possible (Leonard-Barton 1995).

Creativity supports also include mechanisms to *store* knowledge, both tacit and explicit, and *distribute* that knowledge in order to facilitate creativity (Nonaka and Takeuchi 1995). It is also highly beneficial to *measure the creative output* produced at the end of a process, both to motivate the team, and to refine the creative process in the next development cycle (Eccles 1991; Grupp 1998; Canibano, Garcia-Ayuso et al. 2000).

4 Freedom to Act

The most commonly cited factor of creativity is personnel *autonomy*, defined by Amabile (1996) as "the ability to decide what work to do and how to do it", where group members are free to define most of their work, and have the freedom to deviate and tailor work practices (Nonaka 1991; Amabile 1996; Ekvall 1996; Mathisen and Einarsen 2004). For many years, empirical research has been showing that creativity is fostered in autonomous work environments (Pelz and Andrews 1966; Paolillo and Brown 1978; Bailyn 1985). According to Siegel and Kaemmerer (1978), *ownership of work* is an extension of autonomy and a critical driver of creativity. This refers to situations where "group members....originate and develop the ideas, processes and solutions with which they work, as opposed to simply using previously determined solutions" (Mathisen and Einarsen 2004). Anderson and West (1996) found that work practices must do more than just facilitate ownership, but must also encourage *participative safety*. They found that group members are often adverse to the development of new ideas and processes. In order for ownership of work to actually enhance creativity, the group members must inhabit a "non-threatening environment"

(Mathisen and Einarsen 2004), built on "trust and openness" (Ekvall 1996) where they know it is safe to present new ideas and ways of doing things.

5 Vision

Although autonomy is a key enabler of creativity, the role of the leader is not removed but simply altered. Anderson and West (1996) stress that reckless creativity is often detrimental to an organisation, and that in order for "structured creativity" to flourish, objectives and visions must be "clearly defined, shared, valued and attainable" and all members of the team must have a clear *understanding of business goals*. In other words, when a new idea is born, there must be a clear value addition to the organisation underpinning that idea (Siegel and Kaemmerer 1978; Amabile 1996; Anderson and West 1996; Amabile 1998). Nonaka and Takeuchi (1995) refers to this concept as "strategic intent", while Siegel and Kaemmerer (1978) referred to this as "consistency" across creative processes "so that members do not choose lines of action which might conflict with the objective of the activity". Along the same vein of thought, Amabile (1996) deem "supervisory encouragement" to be a dimension of creativity, where the role of the manager or the process is to provide "goal clarity". This need to ensure that all creative initiatives follow an aligned path requires *creative reality checks* to be put in place (Nakamura and Csikszentmihalyi 2001).

6 Creative Abrasion

Creative abrasion is a term coined by Hirschberg, the director of Nissan Design International. It is "the recognition of the potential inherent in a portfolio of often conflicting signature skills". It encourages the interaction of individuals who are different in their ideas, biases, personalities, values and skills, as opposed to keeping them apart (Siegel and Kaemmerer 1978; Nonaka 1991; Leonard-Barton 1995). This mode of thinking can be linked back to Plato:

"Only if the various principles – names, definitions, intimations and perceptions – are laboriously tested and rubbed against one another in a reconciliatory tone, without ill will during the discussion, only then will insight and reason radiate forth in each case, and achieve for man the highest possible force".

Outcomes of abrasion include "healthy encounters, exchanges, debates, and viewpoints supported by differing experiences and knowledge" (Leonard-Barton 1995). In operational terms this may be facilitated through co-locating the team and allowing them to observe or swap roles and responsibilities. Leonard-Barton (1995) advocates *observation and swapping of roles and responsibilities* to encourage creative abrasion. It is important, however, to draw a distinction between creative abrasion and what Ekvall (1996) calls "conflict". In climates where conflict is rife, groups and individuals dislike each other and there is considerable gossip and slander (Mathisen and Einarsen 2004). With regard to creative abrasion however, Leonard-Barton (1995) states that although sparks fly, "the sparks are creative not personal".

Creative abrasion can also be facilitated by *diversity,* which has been viewed as a central requirement of the creative enterprise for many years, with Andrews (1979) stating that it accounts for 10% of the variance in creativity across R&D teams. Siegel and Kaemmerer (1978) suggest a "norms for diversity" stance to be adopted across the organisation, pertaining toward a "positive attitude toward diversity where few behaviours are judged as being deviant". Similarly, Nonaka (1991) calls for "requisite variety", where the group aiming to be creative needs to possess elements of diversity. Leonard-Barton (1995) identifies three types of "signature skill" on which the diversity of a team can be assessed:

- *Diverse Task Preferences:* People tend to gravitate toward specialisations in certain activities and tasks. As Leonard-Barton (1995) states "specialisation leads to expertise" and the "availability of deep knowledge to apply to problems". However, Leonard-Barton (1995) cites Dougherty's (1992) notion that increasing specialisation also results in "distinct thought worlds" that rarely intersect.
- *Diverse Tool and Method Preferences:* Leonard-Barton (1995) acknowledges that, as well as having distinct task preferences, people are also diverse in the methods they use to accomplish those tasks.
- *Diverse Cognitive Style:* Diversity across group members can extend beyond their range of skills and experience. Leonard-Barton (1995) stresses the importance of acknowledging differences in cognitive style, and ensuring that varying styles are used to best effect within the organisation. She cites examples of "personalysis" tests carried out within Nissan Design, where the cognitive preferences of employees were assessed, allowing management to identify those who veered toward rational reasoning as opposed to intuition, or decisive action as opposed to needing larger volumes of information.

7 Continuous Creativity

Creativity is often carried out in one-off or very sporadic initiatives. Research following the history of industries over generations has shown that there is always sharp discontinuities with sporadic innovations from time to time (Leonard-Barton 1995). Siegel and Kaemmerer (1978) propose a number of reasons why the creative process must be *continuous* rather than periodic. For example, creativity revolving around organisational goals must acknowledge that those goals are in a constant state of flux. Therefore outputs of a creative brainstorming session may be obsolete soon after the event. As well as being continuous, creativity thrives on *challenging* work and work environments (Leonard-Barton 1995; Ekvall 1996). At an operational level, individuals should be emotionally attached to their tasks (Ekvall 1996), regard their tasks as being important and worthwhile (Amabile 1996), and should be intellectually challenged by that work (Amabile 1996). In order to ensure these are achieved, some creativity constructs proposed revolve around the incorporation of "dynamism", "liveliness" , "playfulness" and "humorous" (Ekvall 1996) elements of work.

Table 1 is a summary of the creativity constructs suggested in the literature.

Table 1. Creativity Constructs

Construct	Sub-construct	Creativity Literature
Generation of New Ideas	Idea Generation, Tests & Experiments	(Woodman, Sawyer et al. 1993; Anderson and West 1996; Ekvall 1996)
	Stakeholder Involvement	(Nonaka 1991; Flores 1993; Leonard-Barton 1995; Nonaka and Takeuchi 1995; Amabile 1996; Ekvall 1996; Mathisen and Einarsen 2004)
	Information Storage & Distribution	(Nonaka 1991; Nonaka and Takeuchi 1995)
	Measurement of Output	(Eccles 1991; Grupp 1998; Canibano, Garcia-Ayuso et al. 2000)
Freedom to Act	Autonomy, Ownership & Safety	(Pelz and Andrews 1966; Paolillo and Brown 1978; Siegel and Kaemmerer 1978; Bailyn 1985; Nonaka 1991; Amabile 1996; Ekvall 1996; Mathisen and Einarsen 2004)
Vision	Understanding of Business Goals	(Siegel and Kaemmerer 1978; Shiba, Graham et al. 1992; Amabile 1996; Anderson and West 1996; Amabile 1998)
	Creative Reality Checks	(Nakamura and Csikszentmihalyi 2001)
Creative Abrasion	Observation/ Swapping of Roles/ Responsibilities	(Siegel and Kaemmerer 1978; Nonaka 1991; Leonard-Barton 1995)
	Task, Method, & Cognitive Diversity	(Siegel and Kaemmerer 1978; Andrews 1979; Nonaka 1991; Leonard-Barton 1995)
Continuous Creativity	Continuous Development	(Allen 1977; Siegel and Kaemmerer 1978; Leonard-Barton 1995)
	Challenging Work	(Leonard-Barton 1995; Amabile 1996; Ekvall 1996)

8   A Critical Consideration of Creativity Constructs in Agile Methods

This section examines the agile methods literature in general, and XP literature in particular, for evidence of the various constructs of creativity listed in the framework.

9 Generation of New Ideas

There are various principles and practices across the agile method spectrum that could be classified as *idea generation, tests* or *experiments.* Requirements development is referred to as "exploration" in XP (Stephens and Rosenberg 2003), as "exploratory 360°" in Crystal (Cockburn 2001), and "speculation" in ASD (Highsmith 1999). Highsmith (2004) calls for the setting of "Big Hairy Audacious Goals (BHAGS)" in ASD, and for developers to follow in the footsteps of "great explorers such as Cook, Magellan, Shackleton and Columbus". He is also one of the only authors to show how current agile practices such as self-organising teams, encouraging interaction and participatory decision-making all have the potential to facilitate creativity and exploration.

However, there is little evidence throughout the literature that suggests these phases go beyond the traditional elicitation of standard requirements to activities which result in new ground-breaking and innovative requirements and functionality. In fact, the exploration phase of XP is the only instance where the execution of *tests and experiments* are explicitly stated (Jeffries, Anderson et al. 2000; Auer and Miller 2002). As Jeffries et al (2000) describe, during the exploration phase, "the programmers will be experimenting with ways of building the system", and "trying experiments that inform them how costly the various stories and features will be".

Regarding *stakeholder involvement,* the on-site customer has made the single most significant contribution (Beck 1999; Beck 1999; Jeffries, Anderson et al. 2000; Beck and Fowler 2001; Auer and Miller 2002). The purveyors of agile methods have indeed recognised that "a good customer collaborating with a good development team can significantly increase the success of a project" (Schuh 2005). This has grown from a single on-site customer, which has been dismissed by Beck himself as "an error of early XP thinking", and many agile method texts now recommend customer teams be "equal to or larger in size than the programming team" (McBreen 2003). However, there are two shortcomings of the agile methods research in this area:

- Firstly, to date, all of the discussion on agile methods has focused on the on-site customer where the customer travels to the development site or area. The concept of an on-site developer who travels to the customer's area of work to get a true feeling of what the customer wants and does on a day-to-day basis has received no attention.
- Secondly, Augustine (2005) is one of the few researchers in the agile method arena who explicitly extends the notion of the stakeholder beyond the customer. He recommends the development of a stakeholder map (see Figure 1). None of the proprietary agile method texts focus on this broader notion of stakeholder as far as this study is aware.

The extent to which agile methods facilitate *information storage and distribution* is certainly a matter for debate. On one hand, circulation of information is increased due to co-located teams, pair programming, daily meetings and other practices (Beck 1999; Beck 1999; Jeffries, Anderson et al. 2000; Beck and Fowler 2001; Auer and Miller 2002; Cockburn 2002; Schwaber and Beedle 2002). Indeed one of the core values of the Manifesto is to value "individuals and *interactions* over processes and tools". On the other hand however, reduced documentation and increased reliance on "oral documentation" (McBreen 2003) has significant negative consequences on the quantity and quality of information stored and distributed to various team members and groups (see McBreen (2003) and Stephens and Rosenberg (2003) for a more extensive discussion of these problems). Regardless of the debate as to whether agile methods improve the circulation of information, no literature focuses on the relationship between creativity and information storage or distribution in an agile method context.

There is also a distinct lack of discussion regarding the *measurement of creativity* in the agile method literature to date. This includes both assessment of creative behaviours and processes, as well as any attempts to assess how innovative the final system is.

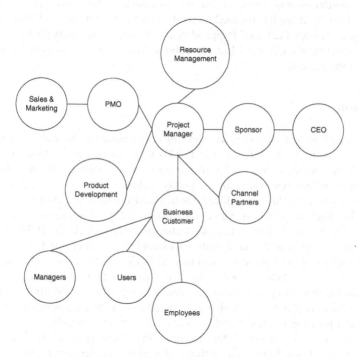

Fig. 1. Stakeholder Map (Augustine, 2005)

10 Freedom to Act

Unlike many of the exemplars listed in Table 1, *autonomy* and *ownership* are constructs of creativity often cited in agile method research. The Agile Manifesto devotes a section to conveying the belief that "the best architectures, requirements, and designs emerge from self-organising teams" (Fowler and Highsmith 2001). Koch (2005) senses that the agile community has done a lot more than just introduce self-organisation, and that "the agile methods embrace the recent movement toward self-managed, self-directed and self-organising teams". Referring to Amabile's (1996) definition of autonomy where the team possesses "the ability to decide what work and how to do it", it is clear that the agile method purveyors have adopted an interpretation that is not too dissimilar. Agile methods require a shift from command-and-control management to "leadership-and-collaboration" (Nerur, Mahapatra et al. 2005), or what Highsmith (2004) refers to as an "egalitarian workplace". According to the agile belief structure, the team are counted "as an entity that has its own knowledge, perspective, motivation and expertise", "are treated as a partner with management and the customer", and are "capable of providing insight, affecting decisions, and negotiating commitments" (Koch 2005). Method-specific examples include Scrum which holds self-organising teams as one of its principles (Schwaber and Beedle 2002).

The notion of *participative safety* was proposed as a key exemplar of creativity, where a non-threatening environment was deemed to be a critical facilitator of creativity. Past literature has focused on trust in ISD (e.g. Hohnmann 1997), and in an agile context, Poppendieck and Poppendieck (2003) refer to safety in the context of LSD, and Cockburn's Crystal Clear (Cockburn 2001) also lists personal safety as a property of the method.

11 Vision

The *understanding of business goals and objectives* seems to be well catered for by today's agile methods. As Jeffries et al (2000) state, "your chief weapon is business value". "Agile methods are popular in the business community because they force concentration on business value above purely technical pursuits" (Augustine 2005). Agile methods achieve this through various mechanisms such as constant prioritisation of work in order of business value (Augustine 2005). Prioritisation is done by customers through user stories and not technical personnel (Beck 1999; Augustine 2005), as is the case with Scrum sprints for example (Schwaber and Beedle 2002). A further example is ASD's project vision that "defines the commissioned system by its business objectives" (Schuh 2005). Also, the on-site customer provides frequent "checks and balances" to ensure business value is being achieved (McBreen 2003).

With regard to *reality checks*, it should be noted that McBreen's point above cites the customer as a provider of checks and balances to ensure new ideas have some business value. Conversely, Highsmith (2004) indicates that there is a similar role required within the team of developers. He outlines two groups of developers; the "creators", who "always want to go for the big prize", and are constantly seeking "innovation, new product development, new processes and practices", while on the other hand, "we also require stewards who can't get excited about an innovation until .... they understand how the economic value will be created".

12 Creative Abrasion

Observation and swapping of roles and responsibilities is commonplace on agile ISD projects, although again this is not explicitly stated as a goal. Rather it is achieved implicitly through other agile practices, where multitasking and self-organisation are encouraged (Augustine 2005), roles and responsibilities are stated at a much higher level of granularity (Beck and Fowler 2001), short iterations mean that a developer need not be tied to a specific role for a long period of time (Beck 1999; Cockburn 2001; Schwaber and Beedle 2002), and pair programming and co-located teams allow easy observation between developers (Williams, Kessler et al. 2000; Canfora, Cimitile et al. 2005). Few researchers have examined the impact of creative abrasion and conflict in the ISD process (see Domino, Collins et al. 2003 for a comprehensive literature review), despite the fact that Cohen et al (2003) found such conflict to be a frequent and significant occurrence on ISD projects. Newman and Robey (1992) state that the generation and resolution of conflict is of central theoretical interest to ISD researchers, yet there is "little empirical work relating to conflict handling styles and ISD" (Domino, Collins et al. 2003). There is no agile method research which focuses on the potential for conflict to contribute to creativity, which is strange given agile method practices such as co-located teams and pair programming increase personal interaction and the potential for such conflict to occur (Domino, Collins et al. 2003).

Diversity of any form is rarely discussed throughout the agile method literature, and Coplien and Harrison (2005), in their discussion of organisational patterns in agile development, are the only authors to explicitly demand group diversity as a tenet of an agile approach. The mainstream methods such as XP and Scrum make no reference to any form of group diversity.

13 Continuous Creativity

Continuous development is encouraged throughout the agile method literature via continuous evaluation (Schuh 2005), continuous testing (Beck 1999; Crispin and House 2003), continuous integration (Beck 1999; Jeffries, Anderson et al. 2000; Highsmith 2002; Augustine 2005), and frequent and continuous code releases (Beck 1999; Jeffries, Anderson et al. 2000; Cockburn 2001; Augustine 2005). In Scrum, the product and sprint backlogs ensure that there is always more functionality to be developed even if all of the initial requirements set out for a sprint are completed ahead of time (Schwaber and Beedle 2002). Also, the fact that agile methods such as Scrum, XP and Crystal Clear all recommend daily meetings also encourages continuous work (Cockburn 2001; Schwaber and Beedle 2002). The 40-hour week is a rule of XP that is said to contribute to continuous development, but as McBreen (2003) notes, this has been renamed "sustainable pace", which gives further credence to the fact that XP emphasises "long term, continuous performance".

In terms of *challenging work*, Beck (1999) claims that the developer should be "fresh and eager every morning, and tired and satisfied every night". McBreen (2003) describes XP as "a high-intensity approach to software development". His rationale for this is that (i) the planning practices "are geared toward delivering maximal value in minimum calendar time", and (ii) "delivering incrementally in short time-boxed iterations to exacting test standards is rewarding but difficult". Many of the agile method practices such as on-site customer, daily meetings, and pair programming can all be argued to contribute to a more challenging environment for the ISD team. However, again these are suppositions that have not been covered in any depth by existing research.

14 Conclusions and Further Research

To summarise, the general ISD literature validates creativity as being relevant to the field, and has frequently called for recognition of the critical role creativity plays in the successful development of a system. In relation to agile methods research, the literature points to a number of quotes and references that not only validate the relevance of creativity to agile methods, but highlight it as a key driving force behind their emergence. However, the extent to which agile methods handle the various exemplars of creativity is very inconclusive. The literature identified some exemplars which are handled by agile methods, some which are not, and in some cases it could be argued that agile methods may even act as inhibitors to some exemplars.

Some of the most prominent issues identified in this study which may warrant further research include:

- regarding generation of new ideas, study of routinising exploratory activities and allocating organizational resources to them in software development projects; understanding the involvement of stakeholders other than customers in software development; investigating the relationship between creativity and information storage or distribution in an agile method context where there is an un-emphasis of formal methods to storing and distributing information; and assessing creative behaviours and processes of agile method projects, including the measurement of how creative the final software system is.
- in terms of creative abrasion, examining the impact of creative abrasion and conflict in agile processes to understand the impact of agile practices on project teams and their contribution to creativity; and study of how agile methods influence team diversity.
- with respect to continuous creativity construct, establishing empirical evidence of the contribution of agile practices to create a challenging but rewarding working environment for agile method teams.

References

Allen, T.: Managing the flow of technology: Technology transfer and the dissemination of technological information within the R&D organization. MIT Press, Cambridge (1977)

Amabile, T.: Creativity in Context. Westview Press, Boulder (1996)

Amabile, T.: How to Kill Creativity. Harvard Business Review 76(5), 77–87 (1998)

Anderson, N., West, M.: The team Climate Inventory Development Exercises. Windsor, England (1996)

Andrews, F.: Scientific Productivity. Cambridge University Press, Cambridge (1979)

Auer, K., Miller, R.: Extreme Programming Applied - Playing to Win. Addison-Wesley, Reading (2002)

Augustine, S.: Managing Agile Projects. Prentice-Hall, Upper Saddle River (2005)

Bailyn, L.: Autonomy in the Industrial R&D Laboratory. Human Resource Management 24(1), 129–146 (1985)

Beck, K.: Embracing change with extreme programming. IEEE Computer 32(10), 70–77 (1999)

Beck, K.: Extreme Programming Explained. Addison Wesley, Reading (1999)

Beck, K., Fowler, M.: Planning eXtreme Programming. Addison-Wesley, Boston (2001)

Brooks, F.: No Silver Bullet: Essence and Accidents of Software Engineering. IEEE Computer 20(4), 10–19 (1987)

Canfora, G., Cimitile, A., et al.: Empirical study on the productivity of the pair programming. In: Baumeister, H., Marchesi, M., Holcombe, M. (eds.) XP 2005. LNCS, vol. 3556, pp. 92–99. Springer, Heidelberg (2005)

Canibano, L., Garcia-Ayuso, M., et al.: Shortcomings in the Measurement of Innovation: Implications for Accounting Standard Setting. Journal of Management and Governance 4(4), 319–342 (2000)

Carayannis, E., Coleman, J.: Creative system design methodologies. Technovation 25(3), 831–840 (2005)

Cockburn, A.: Crystal Clear: A human-powered software development methodology for small teams. Addison-Wesley, Reading (2001)

Cockburn, A.: Agile Software Development. Addison-Wesley, Reading (2002)

Cohen, C., Birkin, S., et al.: Managing Conflict in Software Testing: Lessons from the Field. Communications of the ACM 47(1), 76–81 (2003)

Coplien, J., Harrison, R.: Organisational Patterns of Agile Software Development. Pearson, Upper Saddle River (2005)

Cougar, J.: Ensuring creative approaches in information system design. Managerial and Decision Economics 11(2), 281–295 (1990)

Crispin, L., House, T.: Testing Extreme Programming. Pearson, Boston (2003)

Domino, M., Collins, R., et al.: Conflict in Collaborative Software Development. In: SIGMIS Conference 2003, Philadelphia, PA, pp. 44–51 (2003)

Dougherty, D.: The Illegitimacy of Successful Product Innovation in Established Firms. Organisation Science 5(2), 200–218 (1992)

Eccles, R.: The Performance Measurement Manifesto. Harvard Business Review 69(1), 131–137 (1991)

Ekvall, G.: Organisational Climate for Creativity and Innovation. European Journal of Work and Organisational Psychology 5(1), 105–123 (1996)

Elam, J., Mead, M.: Designing for creativity: considerations for DSS development. Information & Management 13(2), 215–222 (1987)

Flores, F.: Innovation by Listening Carefully to Customers. Long Range Planning 26(3), 95–102 (1993)

Fowler, M., Highsmith, J.: The Agile Manifesto. Software Development 9(8), 28–32 (2001)

Gallivan, M.: The Influence of Software Developer's Creative Style on Their Attitudes To and Assimilation of a Software Process Innovation. Information & Management 40(1), 443–465 (2003)

Grupp, H.: Foundations of the Economics of Innovation Theory, Measurement and Practice. Elgar Publishing, Cheltenham (1998)

Highsmith, J.: Adaptive Software Development. Dorset House, NY (1999)

Highsmith, J.: Agile Software Development Ecosystems. Pearson, Boston (2002)

Highsmith, J.: Agile Project Management. Addison-Wesley, Boston (2004)

Hohnmann, L.: Journey of the Software Professional. Prentice-Hall, Upper Saddle River (1997)

Jeffries, R., Anderson, A., et al.: Extreme Programming Installed. Addison-Wesley, Reading (2000)

Koch, A.: Agile Software Development: Evaluating the Methods for Your Organisation. Artech House, Norwood (2005)

Leonard-Barton, D.: Wellsprings of Knowledge: Building and Sustaining the Sources of Innovation. Harvard Business School Press, Boston (1995)

Lobert, B., Dologite, D.: Measuring creativity of information system ideas: an exploratory investigation. In: IEEE Proceedings of the Annual Hawaii International Conference on Systems Science, Hawaii. IEEE Computer Society Press, Los Alamitos (1994)

Mathisen, G., Einarsen, S.: A Review of Instruments Assessing Creative and Innovative Environments Within Organisations. Creativity Research Journal 16(1), 119–140 (2004)

McBreen, P.: Questioning Extreme Programming. Addison-Wesley, Boston (2003)

Nakamura, J., Csikszentmihalyi: Catalytic Creativity: The Case of Linus Pauling. American Psychologist 56(4), 360–362 (2001)

Nerur, S., Mahapatra, R., et al.: Challenges of Migrating to Agile Methodologies. Communication of the ACM 48(5), 72–78 (2005)

Newman, M., Robey, D.: A Social Process Model of User-Analyst Relationships. MIS Quarterly 16(2), 249–266 (1992)

Nonaka, I.: The Knowledge-Creating Company. Harvard Business Review 69(6), 96–104 (1991)

Nonaka, I., Takeuchi, H.: The Knowledge-Creating Company. Oxford University Press, Oxford (1995)

Paolillo, J., Brown, W.: How Organisational Factors Affect R&D Innovation. Research Management 21(1), 12–15 (1978)

Payne, R.: The effectiveness of research teams: A review. In: West, M., Farr, J. (eds.) Innovation & Creativity at Work, pp. 101–122. Wiley, Chichester (1990)

Pelz, D., Andrews, F.: Scientists in Organisations. Wiley, NY (1966)

Poppendieck, M., Poppendieck, T.: Lean Software Development: An Agile Toolkit. Addison-Wesley, Reading (2003)

Sampler, J., Galleta, D.: Individual and organisational changes necessary for the application of creativity techniques in the development of information systems. In: Proceedings of the 24th Annual Hawaii International Conference on System Sciences, Hawaii. IEEE Society Press, Los Alamitos (1991)

Schuh, P.: Integrating Agile Development in the Real World. Charles River Media, Hingham (2005)

Schwaber, K., Beedle, M.: Agile Software Development with Scrum. Prentice-Hall, Upper Saddle River (2002)

Shiba, S., Graham, A., et al.: A New American TQM: Four Practical Revolutions in Management. The Center for Quality Management and Productivity Press, Boston (1992)

Siegel, S., Kaemmerer, W.: Measuring the Pereived Support for Innovation in Organisations. Journal of Applied Pschology 63(3), 553–562 (1978)

Stephens, M., Rosenberg, D.: Extreme Programming Refactored. Apress (2003) ISBN 1-59059-096-1

Williams, L., Kessler, R., et al.: Strengthening the Case for Pair-Programming. IEEE Software 17(4), 19–25 (2000)

Woodman, R., Sawyer, J., et al.: Toward a Theory of Organisational Creativity. Academy of Management Review 18(2), 293–321 (1993)

IT Governance in SMEs: Trust or Control?

Jan Devos[1], Hendrik Van Landeghem[2], and Dirk Deschoolmeester[2]

[1] Ghent University Association
[2] Ghent University

Abstract. It is believed by many scholars that a small and medium-sized enterprise (SME) cannot be seen through the lens of a large firm. Theories which explain IT governance in large organizations and methodologies used by practitioners can therefore not be extrapolated to SMEs, which have a completely different economic, cultural and managerial environment. SMEs suffer from resource poverty, have less IS experience and need more external support. SMEs largely contribute to the failure of many IS projects. We define an outsourced information system failure (OISF) as a failure of IT governance in an SME environment and propose a structure for stating propositions derived from both agency theory and theory of trust. The theoretical question addressed in this paper is: how and why do OISFs occur in SMEs? We have chosen a qualitative and positivistic IS case study research strategy based on multiple cases. Eight cases of IS projects were selected. We found that trust is more important than control issues like output-based contracts and structured controls for eliminating opportunistic behaviour in SMEs. We conclude that the world of SMEs is significantly different from that of large companies. This necessitates extra care to be taken on the part of researchers and practitioners when designing artefacts for SMEs.

Keywords: SMEs, Agency Theory, Trust, Case Study.

1 Introduction

It is believed by many scholars that a small and medium-sized enterprise (SME) cannot be seen through the lens of a large firm. Therefore theories which explain IT governance in large organisations and methodologies used by practitioners cannot be extrapolated to SMEs, since they have a completely different economical, cultural and managerial environment (Welsh and White 1981). Despite the efforts to develop methods for IT governance in SMEs, like the Cobit QuickStart method, the adoption rate is rather disappointing (IT Governance Institute 2003). IT governance in SMEs is still immature. Both scholars and practitioners, too grounded in their way of thinking, hold simplistic vision of an SME as a small scale model of a large firm (Raymond 1985). We still lack genuine SME-centred theories that can lead to general inferences about how SMEs should conduct IT governance. Riemenschneider et al. stated that: '[...]May be organizational theories and practices, such as bureaucratic structure and organizational behaviour, applicable to large organizations may not be valid in small ones' (Riemenschneider 2003).

G. Dhillon, B.C. Stahl, and R. Baskerville (Eds.): CreativeSME 2009, IFIP AICT 301, pp. 135–149, 2009.
© IFIP International Federation for Information Processing 2009

In this work, we focus on the constructs of trust and control in relation to IS projects in SME environments. This paper is based on an ongoing research on IT governance in SMEs and reports on recent research based on a qualitative, positivistic and multiple case study research strategy where we investigate IS failures in an outsourced SME environment. Due to their small scale and hence a lack of in house IT-skills, SMEs depend more on IT vendors than large companies (Thong 2001, Thong et al. 1997). However this does not mean that outsourcing is without risks or problems. From a managerial point of view we associate risk in IT outsourcing with negative outcomes. A risk scenario that is of special interest for this research is the occurrence of IS failures. We elaborate on IS failures further in this paper. IS failures can lead to disputes which can be divided into litigation and non-litigation issues since not all IS failures lead to litigation.

Following this introduction, this paper is structured into five parts. The specific relationships between SMEs and IT, with particular focus on the phenomenon of outsourced IS failures, is reviewed in the next part. We elaborate on the theoretical foundations of trust and control in part three. Part four details the research methodology and the research design. Part five presents the results of testing the propositions by the multiple case study method and our empirical observations along with a discussion of our findings and conclusions.

2 Outsourced IS Failures in SMEs

Research and literature have highlighted the definitional problems of SMEs. Companies differ in size, location, ownership structure, financial performance, maturity and management style. It is advisable to clearly define an SME before venturing into any research. However this is not obvious. There are many characteristics which identify an SME. The European Commission took an initiative to define a SME in terms of microeconomic characteristics like turnover (not exceeding 50 million euro), annual balance sheet total (not exceeding 43 million euro) and headcount (fewer than 250 persons) (European Commission 2003). This definition is derived from a legal and economic point of view and is not always found accurate when it comes to the study of the relationship between the company and IT. However, this definition is used for our research.

In the years of the dotcom hype, many believed that IT would enable SMEs to compete with large companies. However a lack of readiness towards networking with other enterprises and reluctance to use advanced IT proved otherwise (European Commission 2004). SMEs perceive little incentive to change business models when returns are unclear (OECD 2004). Research also showed that SMEs do not excel in knowledge retention and obtaining a sustainable competitive advantage. There is a slower adoption of IT in SMEs than in large enterprises (Lia et al. 2004, Premkumar 2003). Existing mechanisms of IT governance build on a strong belief that IT creates values for the business; but these do not hold true for SMEs where decision making is mostly centred round one person (Levy et al. 2003, Southern et al. 2000, Lefebvre et al. 1997). SMEs also cannot learn and benefit from past experiences because there are not enough IS projects conducted.

Existing research on IT and SMEs is fragmented in terms of findings and conceptual approaches (Harrison et al. 1997). In this research, we focus on two major findings: the role of the CEO as the principal decision maker in SMEs (Southern et al. 2000; Lefebvre et al. 1997) and the dependency of SMEs on external IT expertise (Thong 2001, Thong et al. 1997). Thong has shown that both findings are related: "The results show that the most effective IS implementation environment is one in which both top management support and external IS experts work as a team".

Despite the numerous success stories illustrating the advantages of bringing Information Technology into organisations, it is broadly accepted that the processes of designing, developing and implementing are cumbersome and not straightforward. Both recent and older reports show that IS projects frequently fail. A broad and elaborate research on IS failures has been conducted for more than four decennia (Ackoff 1967, Lucas 1975, Lyytinen et al. 1987, Sauer 1993, Keil 1995, Beynon-Davies 1999, Ewushi-Mensah 2003, Iacovou et al. 2005, Avison et al. 2006). Practitioners and expert witnesses report frequent IS failures in SMEs as well as in large companies (Standish Group 2004, Webster 2000).

IS failures can be divided into expectation (Lyytinen et al. 1987) and termination (Sauer 1993) failures. Expectation failures can be categorised into correspondence, process and interaction failures. Correspondence failures occur when IS are oriented towards previous defined design objectives. A lack of correspondence between design objectives and evaluation is seen as a failure. Process failures occur when there is unsatisfactory development performance, i.e., one fails to produce a workable system or to deliver within the budget constraints of time and costs. Process failures are sometimes called 'runaways' or escalating projects (Iacovou 2004, Keil 1995). Interaction failures are situated within the mismatch between requirements and user acceptance. An interaction failure appears when an IS remains unused. In summary, an IS expectation failure is the inability of an IS to meet the expectations of the stakeholders.

Sauer brought up the more pragmatic concept of the termination failure (Sauer 1993). According to Sauer an IS failure can only occur when the development process or operation of an IS causes dissatisfied stakeholders to abandon the project.

We argue that there is an extra dimension to IS failures that is not covered by those descriptive models, which we call the Outsourced IS Failure (OISF). An OISF is a failure that occurs during an IS project in an outsourced environment. We use the taxonomy of Lacity and Hirschheim (Dibbern et al. 2004) of outsourcing options and focus on Project Management. Some academics have already pointed out that outsourcing increases risks leading to IS failures (Natovich 2003, Aubert et al. 2003).

We see an OSIF in a SME as a failure of governing IT in a SME environment and propose a structure for stating propositions derived from both agency theory and the theory of trust in the following section. The theoretical question addressed in this paper is: How and why do OISFs occur in SMEs? An overview of the literature provides strong support for the belief that a lot of OISFs do occur in SMEs and that the construct of trust is of significant importance. Mohtashami et al. stated that: '[...]the absence of a proper level of trust is the primary reason for a larger percentage (40 to 70%) of collaboration failure' (Mohtashami et al. 2006).

3 Theory: Trust and Control

The concept of trust is subtle, diffuse and elusive. Although there is agreement on the importance of trust, there also appears disagreement on a suitable definition of the construct (Bigley and Pearce 1998). Trust can be seen as a co-ordinating mechanism based on shared moral values and norms supporting collective co-operation and collaboration within uncertain environments (Reed 2001). Blois gives a number of definitions of trust appearing in frequently quoted papers (Blois 1999). Trust/control relations between organisations can be seen as highly complex structures of social relations and processes which are needed for the generation and maintenance of collective action. The concept of trust is crucial in business interactions that are characterised by mutual dependency combined with a lack of mutual control. Some researchers argue that trust is also reciprocal. According to Reed: ...the essential character of all trust relations is their reciprocal nature. Trust tends to evoke trust, distrust to evoke distrust... . As trust shrinks, distrust takes over... (Reed 2001).

The concept of trust was already used in IS research (Mohtashami et al. 2006, Gefen 2004, Lander et al. 2004, Sahberwal 1999) and in related environments as R&D (Blomqvist 2005) and business to business relationships (Blois 1999).

A working definition of trust already used in IS research and most suitable for our empirical setting is given by Gefen: 'Trust is the belief that others upon whom one depends, yet has little control over, will not take advantage of the situation by behaving in an opportunistic manner but, rather, will fulfil their expected commitments by behaving ethically, dependably and fairly especially under conditions involving risk and potential loss' (Gefen 2004).

Trust can occur on the personal level or on the organisational level. The latter is also known as institutionalized trust. The concept of personal trust seems to be relevant in family-owned SMEs since in those organizations the central role of the CEO has been identified as a key factor for effective IS implementation (Thong et al. 1997). However, Zaheer et al found interpersonal and organizational trust to be highly correlated (Zaheer et al. 1998).

Sabherwal states that inter-organisational relationships involve a psychological contract and a formal written contract. The written contract is negotiated and well understood, while the psychological contract consists of unwritten and largely unspoken sets of expectations held by the transacting parties about each other's prerogatives and obligations (Sabherwal 1999). Governing IT in an outsourced environment requires dealing with both types of contracts. Trust supports the psychological contract. An outsourced IT project in an SME environment can be seen as an interpersonal cooperation and exchange. Trust limits the need for structured controls by reducing the perceived need to guard against opportunistic behaviour when unexpected changes occur in an IT project. Structural controls are appropriate mechanisms including deliverables, reporting arrangements, meeting schedules, penalty clauses for governing the project and to address compliance with the contract (Sabherwal 1999). Trust can also be seen as a mechanism for reducing complexity. Trust does not go into the complexity itself but tries to avoid or reduce it. Theoretically, the role of trust in an outsourced IS environment, amongst others things, appears to be important.

A predominant theory central to Western management thinking and one of the cornerstones for governance is the Agency Theory (Jensen et al. 1976, Eisenhardt 1986). Agency theory has his roots in the research of decision making and was used as an explanation for the theory of firm. Its original setting was the principal as the firm's owner(s) and the agent as the manager(s). Agency theory and derivative theories like formal control theory and IT governance are also very popular theories used in IS research (Aubert et al. 2005, Weil et al. 2004, Choudhury and Sabherwal 2003, Kirsch 2002, Kirsch 1997). Together with transaction cost economy theory, agency theory is seen as a foundation for IS outsourcing (Dibbern et al. 2004). However its contribution is not always very clear since the excessive truth-claims and assumptions of the agency theory are entirely based on analysis in environments other then IT/IS.

Agency theory views problems that occur in outsourced environments as the results of three factors: goal differences, risk behaviour differences and information asymmetry. It is assumed that the agent vendor has private information about the quality of the IS that is not available to the principal (SME). According to agent theory agents can therefore act in their own best interest and exposing opportunistic behaviour which can lead to moral hazard (Tuttle 1997). However when principal and agent are contracting the negotiated transaction can never be described perfectly. Anderlini and Felli state that: '[...]the contracting parties may lack the necessary degree of rationality necessary to describe exactly the various states of nature in the ex-ante contract they draw up.' (Anderline and Felli 2004).

Unlike most theories, agency theory incorporates strongly the concept of the Homo Economicus: a model of people as rational self-interest maximizers. Agency theory inhales a deep mistrust of the principal in the agent and his actions (Ghoshal 2005, Lubatkin 2005). It is precisely in that mistrust where the theory fails to act as a grand IS theory for inducing normative IT governance principles for SMEs.

The complex balancing relationship between trust and control is elaborated by Reed (Reed 2001). Although this relationship can be seen as a nexus there is also rivalry in the theoretical underpinnings. However this rivalry must be seen as commingled rivalry (Yin 2003). The relation of both theories is brought together by Sahberwal (see Figure 1).

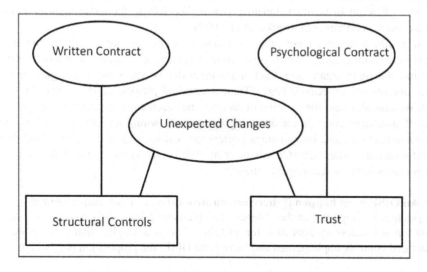

Fig. 1. The complementary nature of structure and trust (R. Sabherwal)

4   Research Methodology and Design

We have chosen a qualitative and positivistic IS case study research strategy based on multiple cases. The choice for qualitative research is based on the accessibility of well documented secondary data in litigation files of failed IS projects in SMEs. Eight cases of IS projects were selected. Most of the projects were subject to litigation. To avoid the difficult problem of defining a failed project, we used the concept of a termination error (Sauer 1993).

OISFs are embedded in an organizational context which is not divisible from the unit of analysis. There are definitely more variables to be studied than there is available data. This is a situation where the case study is an ideal research strategy (Yin 2003, Lee 1989). According to Yin a case study research strategy is useful when a phenomenon cannot be studied outside the context in which it occurs or where the boundaries between phenomenon and context are not clearly evident. Sauer shares the opinion that research in relation to IS failures is best done by case study method (Sauer 1993). The development of the research design and methodology is inspired by the work of researchers experienced in case study research (Eisenhardt 1989, Lee 1989, Dubé et al. 2003).

To explain OISF and the failure of IT governance in SMEs, we draw on agency theory and on the theory of institutional trust to induce test-worthy propositions for our cases. We consider both theories as process theories (Soh et al. 1995, Markus 1988) and as rival or competing theories. Both theories have discrete outcomes that may not occur even when conditions are present and have a logical form in which conditions are expressed in qualifications as necessary or sufficient rather than dependent and independent variables. Time is a crucial factor in both theories since conditions are built up during the course of an IT project. Both theories were studied and can be considered as falsifiable with the potential of deducing logical and consistent propositions (Lee 1989). We also craft rival propositions from the theories. The theories all seem to have explanatory power. We follow the same logic to induce propositions as Sarker et al. (Sarker et al. 1998).

According to agency theory the opportunistic behaviour that eventually can occur is corrected with control. Kirsch views control as encompassing all attempts to ensure that individuals in organisations act in a manner that is consistent with organizational goals and objectives (Kirsch 1997). There are several possibilities to deploy this control. We consider here the creation of an outcome based contract and the implementation of structured controls for obtaining compliance within the contract. It has been shown that an outcome based contract offers the best solution in a setting where there is information asymmetry (Grossman et al. 1983). We come to the following two propositions induced from agency theory:

P1. An OISF must happen if there are no structured controls implemented
Proposition P1 implies that the absence of implemented structured controls is a sufficient but not necessary condition for an OISF. This also implies that if there are no structured controls implemented and there is no OISF, the proposition is falsified.

P2. An OISF must happen if the contract is not outcome-based
Proposition P2 implies that the absence of an outcome-based contract is a sufficient but not necessary condition for an OISF. This also implies that if there is not an outcome-based contract and there is no OISF, the proposition is falsified.

P3. An OISF must happen if (there are no structured controls implemented and the contract is not outcome-based)
Proposition P3 implies that an outcome-based contract together with (logically "and") the absence of implemented structured controls is a sufficient but not necessary condition for an OISF. This also implies that if the combined condition is true and there is no OISF, the proposition is falsified. Proposition P3 is much stronger than P1 and P1, since both condition (outcome-based contract and structured controls) must appear simultaneously.

We induced also a proposition from institutional trust theory. The operationalisation of the construct trust is based on the work of Lander and Sabherwal who build a classification of trust into three types: calculus-based, knowledge-based and identification-based trust (Sabherwal, 1999, Lander et al. 2004)

Calculus-based or deterrence-based trust is the lowest form of trust and exists when both parties can be trusted to keep their word. The deterrence is rooted in the rewards and punishment of the project and can be found in the project contract. Knowledge-based trust is based on the predictability of the other party developed though knowing the other sufficiently well so that their behaviour is predictable. The highest order of trust is identification-based trust and is developed when one party has "fully internalized the other's wants, and this mutual understanding is developed to the point that each can effectively act for the other" (Lander et al., 2004). The former authors also developed a list with trust-building mechanisms for each level of trust. Based on the characteristic of trust having a reciprocal nature, we looked for distrust evoking events and for trust-building mechanisms in the observations.

We come to the following proposition:

P4. An OISF must happen if there is no trust between the principal (SME CEO) and the agent
Proposition P4 implies that the absence of trust (or distrust) between both parties in the exchange is a sufficient but not necessary condition for an OISF. This also implies that if there is trust between the principal and the agent and there is an OISF, the proposition is falsified.

The unit of analysis in every case is the IS project in an SME environment that was subject to an OISF. This narrowed down our focus to a bounded system (Paré 2004). Since this is a multiple-case study design we will follow replication logic to offer external validity. Generalisability is of major concern in every research but cannot be of a statistical kind in this work. The kind of generalisation that will be established here is an analytical generalisation (Yin 2003) or generalising from case study findings to theory (Lee and Baskerville 2003). The theoretical generalisation from the empirical description in our case study has no value beyond the given cases. However the generalisation from ideographic details to theory is important for offering clarification of theoretical concepts. The cases are therefore carefully chosen to accomplish literal replication logic (7 cases) as well as theoretical replication logic (1 case). In each case there is at least some evidence of incomplete and asymmetric information, hidden actions and hidden intentions on behalf of the agent.

We used a longitudinal approach in all cases. Three sources of evidence were used to ensure construct validity: 1) documents, 2) focus and open-ended interviews and 3) direct and participant observations. Project documentation, minutes from steering committee meetings, memorandums and letters were analyzed. Documents were delivered by three sources: plaintiff, defendant and expert witness. The plaintiff and defendant documents were often the same but were brought into litigation for opposed opinions. All expert witness reports were exposed through cross examination of all parties and were corrected if material errors did occur. This resulted in an extra triangulation of the available data. The interviews were recorded on audiotapes and written down in reports and sent to all parties for cross examination. All interviews took place in the present of all parties and the expert witness. The case study sites were visited at least four times for the purpose of doing interviews and direct observations. Additional data was collected during those site visits. In three cases (Rockit, Stones and Boxcars) evidence was obtained as participant observer. The data coming from all sources was coded by means of a coding scheme, which is part of the case study protocol. The coding scheme separates the basic data from the metadata (the documents, reports and sheets). The coding scheme was designed to avoid data contamination. All data is stored in a computerised case study database and links are made between basic data and metadata. The data is retrievable by computer but is also available in original and raw format for reviewers.

Data was analyzed in two steps. First step was a within-case analysis to review the unique patterns of each case. Second a cross-case analysis was conducted in search for common patterns. The cases were selected to allow comparison and to maximise variation while respecting the ceteris paribus criteria so our multiple case study is analogous to multiple experiments as shown in Table 1.

Table 1. The selected cases

Case Name	Sector	Ownership Structure	Turnover (million)	Staff	Type of Project	Cost of Project	Result	Dispute Resolution
Rockit	Textile	Family	€11.64	67	ERP	€644000	No failure	-
Woody	Trading	Family	n.a.	< 200	SDI	€372000	Process Failure	Litigation
Mach	Manufacturing	Family	€12.75	146	ERP	€90000	Expectation Failure	Litigation
Bupo	Software	Family	€0.475	8	SD	€50000	Process Failure	Litigation
Dybo	Trading	Family	€15.65	16	SDI	€50000	Process Failure	Litigation
Stones	Manufacturing	Family	€31.25	200	ERP	€750000	Expectation Failure	ADR
Boxcars	Service	Family	€5.00 - €20.00	10-30	DIS	60x €75000	Expectation Failure	ADR
Hero	Service	Family	€4.00	5	SDI	€75000	Escalation Failure	Litigation

Table 2. Overview and summary of case observations

Observation	Case Rockit	Case Woody	Case Mach	Case Bupo
IT Maturity	CMM level 1	CMM level 1	CMM level 1	CMM level 1
Type of contract	Behaviour-based	Outcome-based	Mixed	Outcome-based
Structural controls in contract / in project	Yes/No	Yes/Yes	Yes/No	Yes/No
Private information (agent)	Yes	Yes	Yes	Yes
Private information (principal)	Yes	No	Yes	No
Hidden actions agent	No	Yes	Yes	Yes
Hidden actions principal	No	No	Yes	No
Lack of commitment (agent)	No	Yes	Yes	Yes
Lack of commitment (principal)	No	No	No	No
Level of trust	Identification	Deterrence	Deterrence	Deterrence
Distrust evocation	No	Yes	Yes	Yes
Trust deterioration	No	Yes	Yes	Yes
Trust-building mechanisms	Yes	No	No	No
Observation	Case Dybo	Case Stones	Case Boxcars	Case Hero
IT Maturity	CMM level 0	CMM Level 2	CMM level 1	CMM level 0
Type of contract	Mixed	Behaviour-based	Mixed	Outcome-based
Structural controls in contract / in project	No/No	Yes/Yes	Yes/Yes	Yes/No
Private information (agent)	Yes	Yes	Yes	Yes
Private information (principal)	No	No	No	Yes
Hidden actions agent	No	Yes	Yes	No
Hidden actions principal	No	No	No	No
Lack of commitment (agent)	No	No	No	No
Lack of commitment (principal)	Yes	No	Yes	Yes
Level of trust	Deterrence	Knowledge	Deterrence	Deterrence
Distrust evocation	Yes	Yes	Yes	Yes
Trust deterioration	Yes	No	No	Yes
Trust-building mechanisms	No	No	No	No

Similarities pertain to the size of the enterprises: all principal sites are family owned SMEs, and there is a strategic importance of the IS project. In terms of variation three projects are ERP implementations, three projects are software development and implementation projects (SDI) and one project is a software development project without implementation (SD). Case Boxcars is a consortium of 60 car dealers who contracted together for a Dealer Information System (DIS). Customizing took place for all ERP projects and the DIS project in the observed cases. The turnover of those firm lays between €5 million and €20 million and the headcount between 10 and 30 people. Two cases (Stones and Boxcars) were subject to alternative dispute resolution (ADR).

Table 2 gives an overview of the observations in our research. For each case we looked at:

- Type of contract: two types of contracts are possible: outcome-based and behaviour-based. In some cases a mixed type was discovered in which some parts of the contact were outcome-based (in particular software licences) and others (in particular consultancy fees) were behaviour-based.

- Structural controls: structural controls appropriate mechanisms including deliverables, reporting arrangements, meeting schedules, penalty clauses for governing the project. We searched for two aspects of structural controls: those stipulated in the contract and those applied during the course of the project.
- Information asymmetry (private information of agent and of principal): traces of private information at both parties.
- Hidden actions (of principal and of agent): traces of hidden actions.
- Lack of commitment: includes the lack of oversight and engagement by executives
- Level of trust: three levels of trust are considered: deterrence-based or calculus-based, knowledge-based and identification-based trust.
- Distrust evocation: f.e. broken promises, lies and personnel changes in the project team.
- Trust deterioration or decline of trust: f.e. parties reacting with formal writings.
- Trust building mechanisms: integrity (fulfilling promises, telling the truth), predictability (consistency, clear roles with responsibilities and accountabilities), communications (openness, receptivity, creating common language), commitment and sharing control.

We summarized the major observations of structural controls (applied during the course of the project), trust and type of contract in table 3.

Table 3. Summary of the findings

Trust	Outcome based contract	Structural controls	OISF	Case
Yes	Yes	Yes	No	-
Yes	Yes	No	No	-
Yes	No	Yes	No	Stones, Boxcars
Yes	No	No	No	Rockit
No	Yes	Yes	Yes	Foam, Woody
No	Yes	No	Yes	Bupo, Hero
No	No	Yes	Yes	-
No	No	No	Yes	Dybo

5 Discussion and Conclusions

Observations indicate that agency theory has certainly predicting power in showing opportunistic behaviour in situations where there is information asymmetry. In all cases we could observe information asymmetry and in five cases this was followed by hidden actions by the agent or the principal. However in one case (Mach) we could also observe hidden actions on behalf of the principal. This is a finding which was already suggested by Moynihan and Aubert:

'Agency theory views the exchange primarily from the perspective of the principal. But what of the agent's perspective? What strategies can agents use to protect themselves from potentially opportunistic or other unfavourable forms of behaviour on the part of the principal?' (Moynihan 2002)

'Both clients and vendors tend to behave opportunistically when entering into a contract and this can lead to mutual disadvantage.' (Aubert 2003)

Hidden actions on behalf of the agent, once revealed were always leading to an evocation of distrust with the principal.

A match of the findings with proposition P1 are cases Bupo, Hero and Dybo. However in case Rockit we could observe absence of structural controls and no OISF occurred. This leads to the conclusion that proposition P1 is falsified. OISFs do not always happen if there are no structured controls.

Only case Dybo follows a pattern that matches with proposition P2. The cases Stones and Boxcars had no outcome based contracts but an OISF did not occur. Both parties went to alternative dispute resolution. In both cases the CEOs went sitting around the table to work on a solution to save the project and save their future collaboration. An initially OISF which was already ripe to bring into litigation was removed. This leads to the conclusion that proposition P2 is falsified.

The most compelling proposition was P3 in which only case Dybo and Rockit shows a match which the conditions. However in case Rockit there was no OISF, leading to the conclusion that also proposition P3 is falsified.

Finally, all empirical patterns in the cases matches with proposition P4. An OSIF must happen if there is no trust between the principal and the agent.

We can conclude that trust is more important than output-based contracts for eliminating opportunistic behaviour in family-owned SMEs. Even with structural controls in place, trust is necessary to prevent from IS failure. Trust is also more important than structural controls for eliminating opportunistic behaviour in SMEs. The propositions deduced from agency theory are theoretical but not empirical logical. The world of family-owned SMEs is significant different than this of large companies. Although we did not show any evidence that the same findings perhaps also hold for non-SMEs. However we believe that the specific management structure in family-owned SMEs, centred round the CEO as the main decision maker is a discriminating factor.

There is another intriguing finding. In all cases, except case Rockit, we could observe evocation of distrust on behalf of the agent. In those cases we could observe that representatives of the agent made promises in the tender of the outsourced project that could not stand once the project was started. This is due to the lack of observation power of the principal ex ante. These promises often touched the essentials of the projects like commitments on price, budget and quality (functionality). Ex post, when the contract is signed and the endeavour with the agent takes a real start, the agent denies his promises which evokes very early in the project trajectory a mistrust with the principal that could not always be mended during the course of the project since there were no trust-building mechanisms. Those observations are predicted by agency theory and lead to the adverse selection by the principal. This is a most interesting topic which need further investigation.

Our findings are rather surprising for structural controls seeming less important than trust. However we do not conclude that structural controls are pointless in SME environments. This could also mean that trust and control are not necessarily full rivalry theories. As Reed stated: ...In short, the conventional dichotomy between normatively-based trust and politically-based control has become unsustainable, as the theoretical and empirical work in organizational analysis has consistently blurred the putative analytical and substantive boundaries between them (Reed, 2001).

We cannot neglect the descriptive power of agency theory in an SME – OISF setting, but the theory evade the issue of trust. Nooteboom comes to similar results in his work on trust, opportunism and governance with the transaction cost economy as underlying theory (Nooteboom 1996). Since transaction cost economy theory is also seen as a founding theory for IS outsourcing this may lead to suggestions for further research on TCE and trust in the same SME-OISF settings.

We argue that in an SME environment social-psychological processes with constructs like trust (and probably also fairness, intuition and empathy) are of more importance to explain the complex IT governance phenomena and therefore are more appropriate for deriving guidelines for practitioners than agency theory and (formal) control theory. Rather the ramifications of our findings is that managerial focus in SMEs is completely different compared to large companies. Since the SME-CEO is the crucial stakeholder of an IS project and taking into account that CEO often lacks commitment, time and knowledge this needs further empirical research. For researchers and practitioners this could means that it would be meaningful to start from the beginning with an focussed orientation to SMEs in their work instead of a derived vision on how things are going in large companies.

We conclude with Claudio Ciborra (2002) who stated that: "We can envisage an alternative approach to overcome the crisis generated by an overdose of methodologies. Let us go back to the basics and encounter the world as it presents itself in our everyday experience. We rely on evidence, intuition, and empathy".

References

Ackoff, R.L.: Management misinformation systems. Management Science 14(4), 147–156 (1967)

Anderlini, L., Felli, L.: Bounded rationality and incomplete contracts. Research in Economics 58(2004), 3–30 (2004)

Aubert, B.A., Patry, M., Rivard, S.: A tale of two outsourcing contracts - An agency-theoretical perpective. Wirtschaftsinformatik 45(2), 181–190 (2003)

Aubert, B.A., Patry, M., Rivard, S.: A Framework for Information Technology Outsourcing Risk Management. Database for Advances In Information Systems 36(4), 9–28 (2005)

Avison, D., Gregor, S., Wilson, M.: Managerial IT Unconsciousness. Communications of the ACM 49(7), 89–93 (2006)

Bahli, B., Rivard, S.: The information technology outsourcing risk: a transaction cost and agency theory-based perspective. Journal of Information Technology 18(9), 211–221 (2003)

Beynon-Davies, P.: Information systems 'failure': The case of the London ambulance service's computer aided despatch project. European Journal of Information Systems 4(3), 171–184 (1995)

Bigley, G.A., Pearce, J.L.: Straining for Shared Meaning in Organization Science: Problems of Trust and Distrust. Academy of Management Review 23(3), 405–421 (1998)

Blois, K.J.: Trust in Business to Business Relationships: An Evaluation of Its Status. Journal of Management Studies 36(2), 197–215 (1999)

Blomqvist, K., Hurmelinna, P., Seppänen, R.: Playing the collaboration game right - balancing trust and contracting. Technovation 25(2005), 497–504 (2005)

Choudhury, V., Sabherwal, R.: Portfolios of Control in Outsourced Software development Projects. Information Systems Research 14(3), 291–314 (2003)

Ciborra, C.: The Labyrinths of Information - Challenging the Wisdom of Systems. Oxford University Press, Oxford (2002)

Dibbern, J., Goles, T., Hirschheim, R.: Information Systems Outsourcing: A Survey and Analysis of the Literature. Database for Advances In Information Systems 35(4), 6–102 (2004)

Dubé, L., Paré, G.: Rigor in Information Systems Positivist Case Research: Current Practices, Trends and Recommendations. MIS Quarterly 27(4), 597–635 (2003)

Eisenhardt, K.M.: Agency theory: an assessment and review. Academy of Management Review 14(1), 57–74 (1989)

Eisenhardt, K.M.: Control: Organizational and Economic Approaches. Management Science 31(2), 134–149 (1985)

European Commission, The new SME definition: User guide and model declaration (2003)

European Commission, The Go Digital Awareness Campaign 2001-2003: The main lessons to be learnt (2004)

Ewusi-Mensah, K.: Software Development Failures. MIT Press, Cambridge (2003)

Fink, D.: Guidelines for the successful adoption of information technology in small and medium enterprises. International Journal of Information Management 18(4), 243–253 (1999)

Gefen, D.: What makes an ERP implementation relationship worthwhile: Linking trust mechanisms and ERP usefulness. Journal of Management Information Systems 21(1), 263–288 (2004)

Ghoshal, S.: Bad Management Theories Are Destroying Good Management Practices. Academy of Management Learning & Education 4(1), 75–91 (2005)

Grossman, S.J., Hart, O.D.: An Analysis of the Principal-Agent Problem. Econometrica 51(1), 7–45 (1983)

Harrison, D.A., Mykytyn Jr., P.P., Riemenschneider, C.K.: Executive Decisions About Adoption of Information Technology in Small Business: Theory and Empirical Tests. Information Systems Research 8(2), 171–195 (1997)

Iacovou, C.L.: Managing MIS Project Failures: A Crisis Management Perspective. PhD dissertation (1999)

IT Governance Institute, Cobit Quickstart, IT Governance Institute (2003)

Jensen, M.C., Meckling, W.H.: Theory of the Firm: Managerial Behavior, Agency Costs and Ownership Structure. Journal of Financial Economics 3(4), 305–360 (1976)

Keil, M.: Pulling the Plug: Software Project Management and the Problem of Project Escalation. MIS Quarterly 19(4), 421–431 (1995)

Kirsch, L.J., Sambamurthy, V., Ko, D.G.: Controlling Information Systems Development Projects: The View from the Client. Management Science 48(4), 484–498 (2002)

Kirsch, L.J.: Portfolios of Control Modes and IS Project Management. Information Systems Research 8(3), 215–239 (1997)

Lander, M.C., Purvis, R.L., McCray, G.E., Leigh, W.: Trust-building mechanisms uitlized in outsourced IS development projects: a case study. Information & Management 41(2004), 509–528 (2004)

Lee, G., Xia, W.: Organizational size and IT innovation adoption: A meta-analysis. Information & Management 43(2006), 975–985 (2006)

Lee, A.S., Baskerville, R.L.: Generalizing generalizability in information system research. Information Systems Research 14(3), 221–243 (2003)

Lee, A.S.: A Scientific Methodology for MIS Case Studies. MIS Quarterly 13(1), 33–50 (1989)

Lefebvre, L.A., Mason, R., Lefebvre, E.: The influence prism in SMEs: The power of CEO's perceptions on technology policy and its organizational impacts. Management Science 43(6), 856–878 (1997)

Levy, M., Loebbecke, C., Powell, P.: SMEs, Co-opetition and Knowledge sharing: The IS role. European Journal of information Systems 12(1), 3–17 (2003)

Lubatkin, M.H.: A Theory of the Firm Only a Microeconomist Could Love. Journal of Management Inquiry 14(2005), 213–216 (2005)

Lucas, H.C.: Why Information Systems Fail. Columbia University Press (1975)

Lyytinen, K., Hirschheim, R.: Information systems failures - a survey and classification of the empirical literature. In: Zorkoczy, P.I. (ed.) Oxford Surveys in Information Technology, vol. 4(1987), pp. 257–309. Oxford University Press, Oxford (1987)

Markus, M.L., Robey, D.: Information Technology and Organizational Change: Causal Structure in Theory and Research. Management Science 34(5), 583–598 (1988)

Mohtashami, M., Marlowe, T., Kirova, V.: Risk Management For Collaborative Software Development. Information Systems Management, 20–30 (2006)

Montazemi, A.R.: How They Manage IT: SMEs in Canada and the US. Communications of the ACM 49(12), 109–112 (2006)

Moynihan, T.: Coping with client-based 'people-problems': the theories-of-action of experienced IS/software project managers. Information & Management 39, 377–390 (2001)

Natovich, J.: Vendor Related Risks in IT Development: A Chronology of an Outsourced Project Failure. Technology Analysis & Strategic Management 15(4), 409–419 (2003)

Nooteboom, B.: Trust, Opportunism and Governance: A Process and Control Model. Organization Studies 17(6), 985–1010 (1996)

OECD, ICT, E-Business and SMEs, Paris (2004)

Paré, G.: Investigating Information Systems with Positivist Case Study Research. Communications of the AIS 13(2004), 233–264 (2004)

Raymond, L.: Organizational characteristics and MIS success in the context of small business. MIS Quarterly 9(1), 37–52 (1985)

Reed, I.M.: Organization, Trust and Control: A Realist Analist. Organization Studies 22(2), 201–228 (2001)

Riemenschneider, C.K., Mykytyn Jr., P.P.: What small business executives have learned about managing information technology. Information & Management 37(2000), 257–269 (2000)

Riemenschneider, C.K., Harrison, P., Mykytyn Jr., P.P.: Understanding IT adoption decisions in small business: integrating current theories. Information & Management 40(2003), 269–285 (2003)

Ring, P.S., Van De Ven, A.H.: Developmental Processes of Cooperative Interorganizational Relationships. Academy of Management Review 19(1), 90–118 (1994)

Sabherwal, R.: The Role of Trust in Outsourced IS Development Projects. Communications of the ACM 42(2), 80–86 (1999)

Sarker, S., Lee, A.S.: Using A Positivistic Case Research Methodology to Test a Theory about IT-Enabled BPR. In: Proceedings of the 19th ICIS 1998, Helsinki, vol. (7), pp. 237–252 (2002)

Sauer, C.: Why Information Systems Fail: A Case Study Approach, Alfred Wailer, Henley-on-Thames (1993)

Soh, C., Markus, M.L.: How IT creates business value: a proces theory synthesis. In: Proceedings of the 16th ICIS 1995, Amsterdam, pp. 29–42 (1995)

Standish Group International, Inc., 2004 Third Quarter Research Report, The Standish Group International, Inc. (2004)

Thong, J., Yap, C.S., Raman, K.S.: Environments for Information Systems Implementation in Small Businesses. Journal of Organizational Computing and Electronic Commerce 7(4), 253–278 (1997)

Thong, J.: Resource constraints and information systems implementation in Singaporean small business. Omega - The International Journal of Management Science 29(2001), 143–156 (2001)

Tuttle, B., Harrell, A., Harrison, P.: Moral Hazard, Ethical Considerations, and the Decision to Implement an Information System. Journal of Management Information Systems 13(4), 7–77 (1997)

Webster, B.F.: Patterns in IT Litigation: Systems Failure (1976-2000), A Study By PricewaterhousCoopers LLP (2000)

Weill, P., Ross, J.W.: IT Governance - How top Performers Manage IT Decisions Rights for Superior Results. Harvard Business School Press (2004)

Welsh, J.A., White, J.F.: A Small Business Is Not a Little Big Business. Harvard Business Review 59(4), 18–32 (1981)

Yin, R.K.: Case Study Research: Design and Methods. Sage Publications, Thousand Oaks (2003)

Zaheer, A., McEvily, B., Perrone, V.: Does trust matter? Exploring the effects of interorganizational and interpersonal trust on performance. Organization Science 9(2), 141–159 (1998)

A Methodology for Electronic Business Initiatives Implementation in SME

Henrique S. Mamede[1] and Luís Amaral[2]

[1] Universidade Aberta
[2] Universidade do Minho

Abstract. The World Wide Web technology, supported on Internet, is transforming all business activities into information-based activities. As a result, one can see a radical change in the traditional theoretical models and organisation. The small and medium enterprises (SME) are the type of enterprises that can reap more advantages with the usage of Internet for electronic business. We found that current methodologies present gaps which make them inadequate and unable to help the small and medium enterprises define an effective strategy and follow an plausible implementation path. This being so, we propose a methodology to support the complete implementation lifecycle of electronic business in small and medium enterprises.

1 Introduction

The Internet had made and continues to make a great impact on society. The way it shapes and handles the business is no exception. The systematic usage of the Internet, World Wide Web (Web) and Systems and Information Technology (SIT) has revolutionized traditional markets and business. It is now in the midst of intense global competition, even in areas where Small and Medium Enterprises (SME) need to participate. Never before have companies, especially SME's, have had to face such global and open competition. It is these small firms who are required to meet the new demands of customers and business partners, which are putting enormous pressure on these organisations.

The environment for e-business has also offered many opportunities to improve and expand the internal processes and interactions and transactions between business-to-business (B2B), business-to-consumer (B2C) and business-to-administration (B2A), among others.

The business processes which have been e-enabled, supported by digital media, accelerate and facilitate the flow of information, allow the sharing of information and knowledge and thus create new opportunities for expansion and development of new connections between the various business partners around the globe (Ballou et al. 2000; Cross 2000). Those are the processes that allow the contribution of participants in a distributed business process: end users, suppliers, producers, responsible for marketing and others, from different geographical locations.

At the heart of the transformation process is the level of integration of electronic business (EB) and trade between external and internal processes and systems. These

G. Dhillon, B.C. Stahl, and R. Baskerville (Eds.): CreativeSME 2009, IFIP AICT 301, pp. 150–157, 2009.

enable enterprises develop successful and sustainable digital business models. Such companies are in a privileged position to digitize their processes, products and distribution agents (Choi et al. 1997). Apart from the perspective of the product or area of activity, the depth of the impact of electronic commerce and business, or conversion, the size of the impact of the transformation etc depends on several internal organisational factors, such as products, management, structure and employees, and the external environment, political, economic, social and technological. In addition to these there exist micro forces such as competition, suppliers, customers and technology suppliers (Al-Qirim and Corbitt 2002a; Al-Qirim and Corbitt 2002b).

SME are very susceptible to environmental forces (Blili and Raymond 1993). Consequently, the identification of contexts and significant factors for the success of digital initiatives and an explanation of their impact is crucial. However the representation of the two extremes in Figure 2-9, in an organisation purely physical versus purely virtual organisation does not imply that SMEs should elevate to the level of exclusive digital market, thus making it virtual. Rather, depending on certain contextual impacts, organisations can be represented along the continuous line that separates the two extremes. For example, Adam and Deans (Adam and Deans 2000) suggest that there is a tendency in organisations to migrate from both ends to a mixture of physical and virtual organisation, or bricks and clicks (Gulati and Garino 2000). Moreover, some organisations have started tgeir existence only in digital markets, never having existed in the physical markets, whereas other companies may have decided to start simultaneously with presence in both types of market.

2   The Need for Methodological Support

Digital business has its own characteristics and it is accepted that their operations allow a greater level of efficiency than a traditional business. The introduction of electronic commerce and electronic business requires the company to rethink and redefine both the business strategy and the processes that exist, with the e-transformation in mind.

We made a literature review of the models and standards and other efforts made till date in a bid to help the organisations in this process. Following the decision of e-adoption, we concluded that there is an absence of a methodology that covers the entire cycle of development which would lend necessary support to the company that decides to follow the path of e-business (Mamede et al. 2007).

It is thus important to propose a methodology to support the adoption of such characteristics by an existing business, particularly in the case of an SME. Different companies have implemented various business processes and these are in some cases closer to the electronic business than others. Further, different companies have different levels of sophistication in terms of systems and technologies of information and internal knowledge in this field. The important question which rises is-what steps must be taken in addition to examining the current organisation and the subsequent development of a guiding plan so that the company might move in the direction of becoming an electronic business.

3 The MICEP Methodology

Due to the lack of methodologies to support the electronic business implementation in SME, we developed the "Metodologia para a Implementação de Comércio e Negócio Electrónico nas Pequenas e Médias Empresas" (MICEP).

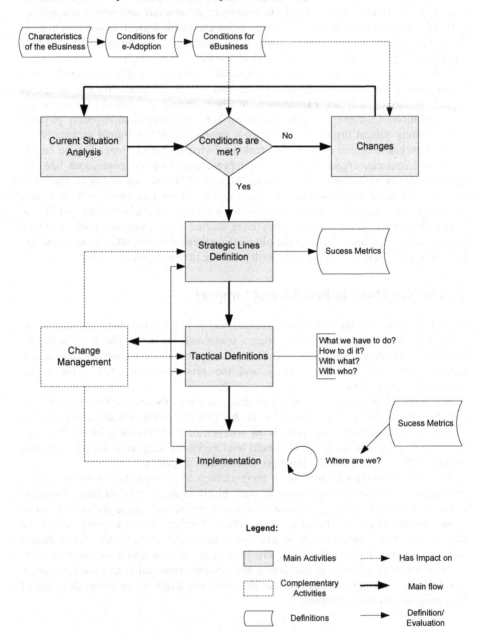

Fig. 1. The MICEP methodology

The methodology we are going to propose can be seen as a set of guidelines for organisational transformation. It provides a visual representation of the major steps needed to progress towards the transformation to electronic business. Each step represents a level of sophistication in particular. This allows a company to see its current position and plan its future path.

The methodology, shown in Fig. 1, consists of several stages and sets up its implementation in continuous cycles, following a spiral. The proposed methodology is made of activities which can be divided into two parts: first, a group of main activities (MA), which constitute the core of the methodology, prominently represented in figure 1; on the other hand, a set of complementary activities (CA), which support the realization of main activities.

One can look to MICEP as being made of two different parts, as shown in Fig. 2. Once the implementation stage, the last activity of the first part is finished, the second part of the methodology starts, with a full analysis of the work done and the results achieved in order to define future paths for improvement.

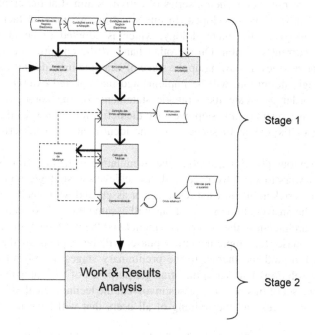

Fig. 2. The macro view of MICEP methodology

As main activities, we have the following:

MA 1. Current Situation Analysis
MA 2. Verification of the existence of conditions for the EB
MA 3. Amendments to the creation of conditions for the EB
MA 4. Strategic Definition
MA 5. Tactical Definitions
MA 6. Implementation
MA 7. Analysis of Results and Impacts

As complementary activities, we define the following ones:

CA1. Initial Settings (Characteristics of Electronic Business, Conditions for e-Adoption, Conditions for Electronic Business)
CA2. Change Management
CA3. Definition of Success Metrics

The main activities begin with the assessment of the initial situation, with the intent to determine whether the basic premises for the implementation of mechanisms for e-business and application of the methodology actually exist in the organisation.

The next step is to validate whether the conditions exist or if such changes are required and possible to realize. This initial step is crucial to the success of the whole project, because if the organisation has not met the basic premises, then never, or only with great difficulty, it will be possible to realize the implementation of e-business. If the conditions are not found, then a series of activities aimed at the creation of such conditions will have to be developed. In this situation, we may be facing a critical factor for the usage of the methodology, which is adopted to begin drafting the portrait of the current situation. On the other hand, if the conditions exist, then you can move to the next level, starting up the stage of strategic lines definition.

In the strategic definition, will be implemented internal and external reviews and reflections in order to create the strategic statement for the company's electronic business. Also as a result of this step, we have the definition of metrics that will allow the measuring of the extent of success and the identification of the critical success factors.

After the previous phase, takes place the formulation of tactics. In this phase will be obtained answers to what we need to do to achieve the strategic objectives, what actions to be undertaken, using what resources or assets and who, inside or outside the organisation. The answers to those questions will assume the form of deliverables like the integration architecture, the governance model and the implementation plan.

In the next phase, the implementation phase, will be applied all the knowledge already created around the theme, in the preliminary stages, in order to effectively implement the solutions that serve the strategic purposes of the company. As results we will have the set of business processes involved, the technological infrastructure to support those processes and the training of all users that will have to deal with the new tools.

When the implementation phase is finished, we consider the first stage of the methodology to have been achieved. The next stage means analysis of outcomes and impacts of all projects in order to influence improvements and help define future paths.

The complementary activities complement the nuclear activities, and the first of them begins by establishing the initial settings, CA1, where the characteristics for EB in the specific market are analyzed, and the conditions for e-adoption and implementation of EB in the company are evaluated. The CA2 is also very important, and it has a development plan itself that is connected to the implementation plan that is set in MA5. Nevertheless, this sideline has an impact on virtually all the main activities.

The CA3 is developed in the same period of time as MA4 and establishes the conditions that will determine the success of the implementation of the remaining MA.

For each MA there are one or more tools that support the activities to be undertaken, like shown in table 1.

Table 1. Support tools used in MICEP

Activity	Tool
Current Situation Analysis (MA1)	Levels of Organisational Transformation
	Matrix for transformation opportunity analysis
	EB Opportunity/Threat indicator
	Nolan model (adapted)
	Matrix for modeling opportunities/capacities
Strategic Lines Definition (MA4)	EB initiatives modeling
	Critical Sucess Factors listing
Tactical Definition (MA5)	Integration architecture for infrastructure
	Implementation plan
	Governance model
Implementation (MA6)	Business Process description (BPMN)
	Process reengineering (Muthu, Whitman e Cheraghi (Muthu et al. 1999) methodology)
Change Management (CA2)	Frame model

4 Methodology Validation

For the validation of the methodology we decided to follow the application of a real-world case. This application was directed at reviewing the applicability and usefulness of the MICEP methodology as a tool to support the implementation of mechanisms for electronic business. Thus, a Portuguese SME which has evinced interest in this project has been selected and we were able to full apply MICEP.

In reviewing the work done, two main observations can be forwarded: first, we saw the usefulness and support that the use of methodology provides to a company that has determined its strategic objective as the desire to be electronically linked with the entities to which it relates; second, we noted that the methodology covers the whole cycle concerning the implementation of mechanisms for electronic business, from the strategic assessment till the evaluation of what is implemented and the impact that such projects may have on the strategic review of the organisation. The use of MICEP was important to successfully implement the initiatives of EB in an SME. As the methodology goes from strategic planning to implementation itself, including change management, this makes the decision of e-adoption and its consequences directly linked to the business strategy, which involves the management of the organisation. Moreover, completing all the steps foreseen in MICEP, all ideas and all aspects related to the EB initiatives are compiled and sorted, helping to determine what may indeed be implemented. Thus, it is fair to say that MICEP is a contributor to change, which ensures that all EB related aspects are well covered, leading to success in such projects.

Therefore, we can conclude from this case study that the proposed methodology allows organisations to successfully complete all activities related to the e-adoption decision. Any future refinement in the methodology, which could be achieved through the study of more application cases, will result in improvement of efficiency.

5 Conclusion

How should the organisation change and the methodologies and standards that partially support the move towards the implementation of e-business be adopted was presented and discussed in previous work by Mamede, Amaral and Coelho (Mamede et al. 2007). It was the absence of a methodology that could support the development of EB initiatives, leading to the definition and automation of business processes, and their implementation that motivated the development of a proposal translated in the form of the MICEP methodology.

The MICEP methodology is comprehensive and complex. It is complete because it covers the entire cycle from the analysis of the situation of the company, to the definition of initiatives, which must be selected and implemented in the initial stage itself. Peripheral issues such as change management and reassessment of all the work done to serve as inputs for a new cycle, also lies in the scope. But the methodology is complex because it incorporates a relatively wide range of tools, fitting them in some other form of meshing. This is also a strong point of MICEP, as a tool can always be replaced by another identical one, provided that they both accept the same inputs and produce the same kind of results, so as to continue to function in coordination with the others. Thus, as the methodology matures, we can come to the conclusion that there is a need to use other tools to the detriment of some of the existing ones, and perform this simple amendment.

References

Adam, S., Deans, K.: Online business in Australia and New Zealand: Crossing a chasm. In: Proceedings of AusWeb2k – The Sixth Australian World Wide Web Conference, Rihga Colonial Club Resort, Cairns (2000)

Al-Qirim, N., Corbitt, B.: Critical factors for electronic commerce success in small business: A meta study. In: 2002 Information Resources Management Association (IRMA) International Conference, Seattle, pp. 798–202 (2002a)

Al-Qirim, N., Corbitt, B.: An empirical investigation of an e-commerce adoption model in small to medium-sized enterprises in New Zealand. In: 6th Pacific Asia Conference on Information Systems (PACIS 2002): The Next e-What? For Business and Communities, Tokyo, pp. 343–362 (2002b)

Ballou, R.H., Gilbert, S.M., et al.: New Managerial Challenges From Supply Chain Opportunities. Industrial Marketing Management 29, 7–18 (2000)

Blili, S., Raymond, L.: Information technology: Threats and opportunities for small and medium-sized enterprises. International Journal of Information Management 13(6), 439–448 (1993)

Choi, S.Y., Whinston, A.B., et al.: The Economics of Electronic Commerce. Macmillan Technical Publications, Indianapolis (1997)

Cross, G.J.: How E-Business is Transforming Supply Chain Management. The Journal of Business Strategy 21(2), 36–39 (2000)

Gulati, R., Garino, J.: Get the right mix of bricks & clicks. Harvard Business Review 78(3), 107–114 (2000)

Mamede, H.S., Amaral, L., et al.: A Necessidade de uma Metodologia para a Definição Estratégica da Digitalização do Negócio das PME. Revista de Ciências da Computação da Universidade Aberta II 2, 65–84 (2007)

Muthu, S., Whitman, L., et al.: Business Process Reengineering: A Consolidated Methodology. In: 4th Annual International Conference on Industrial Engineering Theory, Applications and Practice, San Antonio, Texas, USA (1999)

IT Governance Practices in Small and Medium-Sized Enterprises: Recommendations from an Empirical Study

Rui Huang[1], Robert W. Zmud[2], and R. Leon Price[2]

[1] School of Management
State University of New York at Binghamton
[2] Michael F. Price College of Business
University of Oklahoma

Abstract. Much has been learned through IT governance research about the nature of IT-related decisions, the location of decision rights for these decisions, and governance mechanisms applied to facilitate associated decision processes in large organisations. Our knowledge about IT governance structures in small and medium-sized enterprises (SME), on the other hand, is quite limited. Adopting a qualitative and inductive approach, this study examines the nature and influence of IT governance in SMEs through interviews with executives from three SMEs. Our results demonstrate that IT decision authority was centralized in all three SMEs but that senior management involvement in governance procedures and communication practices about governance policies were observed to explain differences in these organisations' IT use. We propose recommendations based on the findings of this study.

1 Introduction

Organisations introduce IT governance mechanisms in order to rationalize and coordinate their IT-related decision making so that IT assets, efforts and investments are aligned with the organisation's strategic and tactical intents. Well-architected IT governance mechanisms involve careful consideration of a variety of issues: what are an organisation's critical IT decisions, what policies need to be put in place to guide these decisions, who should be accountable for and who should contribute to these decisions, what procedures should be followed in carrying out these decisions, and which type of coordination mechanisms are most appropriate given the natures of these decisions (Sambamurthy and Zmud 1999; Weill and Ross 2004).

Research on the nature and influence of IT governance mechanisms can be traced back to the 1960's (Brown 2005) with researchers examining a variety of fundamental issues including the definition of IT governance (Weill 2004), structural options for IT governance (Jenkins and Santos 1982; Zmud et al. 1986), and the drivers of IT governance structural forms (Brown and Magill 1998; Sambamurthy and Zmud 1999). Further, it is generally accepted that IT governance does matter. For example, consistent results have been observed regarding relationships between the centralization of IT

G. Dhillon, B.C. Stahl, and R. Baskerville (Eds.): CreativeSME 2009, IFIP AICT 301, pp. 158–179, 2009.

governance and the patterns of IT use (e.g., Brown 1997): centralized IT governance tends to improve enterprise-wide efficiencies but suboptimizes in delivering value to local work units; and, decentralized IT governance tends to optimize in delivering value to local work units but yields enterprise-wide inefficiencies. Such enterprise-versus-local tensions is a recurrent theme of the IT governance literature (Weill and Ross 2004).

While most research on IT governance has been conducted within large enterprises, the organisational (i.e., institutional and managerial) structures of large enterprises tend to be quite distinct from those of small- and medium-sized enterprises (SMEs) (Meyer 1972). Along with other factors (e.g., technology and environment), organisational size (Starbuck 1965) and structural differentiation (Blau and Schoenherr 1971) induce considerable variation in organisational structures which in turn influence the nature of instituted decision structures (Ein-Dor and Segev 1982), including IT governance structures (Cross et al. 1997). In particular, SMEs tend to be characterized by centralized decision structures (Wilensky 1967), which engender centralized IT governance structures (Brown 1997; Sambamurthy and Zmud 1999).

Given the prior literature on IT governance and the likelihood of centralized IT governance, should it be expected that well-managed SMEs applying centralized IT governance structures would experience efficiencies in their use of IT but suboptimize in exploiting local work unit IT-related opportunities? Or, would the relatively smaller size of SMEs diminish enterprise-local tensions and enable both efficiencies and local effectiveness to be observed? In the absence of empirical evidence in the SME context, it is difficult to say.

The research question of this study therefore is: *how can SMEs optimize IT performance through governance practices?* In the following sections, we provide overviews of what is currently known about the SME context (i.e., SME organisational structures, IT endowments, and IT management posture) and about IT steering committees, a key IT governance mechanism. We next describe three case studies, and then use observations drawn from within and across case analyses to propose recommendations for optimizing IT performance in SMEs.

2 The Small- and Medium-Sized Enterprise (SME) Context

SMEs constitute the great majority of all organisations and represent a vibrant economic engine with significant potential to drive economic and employment growth as well as poverty alleviation[1]. Generally, the term SME applies to firms employing fewer than 500 workers (Levy and Powell 2005). Given their size and market reach, SMEs generally hold small market shares and tend to manoeuvre in operating regimes much more characteristic of classic perfect competition, relative to their larger counterparts, as they are less able to influence market prices through strategic actions (Storey and Sykes 1996). On the other hand, their smaller size enables SMEs to be nimbler (flexible, innovative, etc.) in responding to customer and market demands (Hay and Kamshad 1994). The remainder of this section synthesizes extant research in characterizing SMEs with regard to their organisational structures, their IT endowments and their IT management postures.

---

[1] "World Bank Review of Small Business". IFC, World Bank, MIGA. 2001.

2.1 SME Organisational Structures

Complexity, formalization and centralization are three commonly examined attributes of organisational structure (Hall 1972; Pugh et al. 1968). Complexity refers to the number of hierarchical levels, the number of departments or functions, and the extent of specialization (Blau and Schoenherr 1971). Formalization defines the degree to which rules and procedures are specified, promoted and adhered to (Hall 1972). Centralization reflects the extent to which the locus of formal control is held by a central decision-making authority (Child 1972).

Regarding their organisational structures, SMEs tend to exhibit low levels of formalization and complexity when compared to large firms (Ghobadian and Gallear 1996; Storey 1994). Along with flatter organisational structures and simpler organisational processes, SMEs tend to exhibit rich information networks (employees at all levels are likely to interact with one another on a regular basis) and a high degree of internal transparency (employees at all levels are likely to be cognizant of others' work assignments and roles, perspectives and taken decisions) thus allowing coordination in the absence for formalized rules and procedures (Street and Meister 2004). The SME owner/CEO has considerably more personal influence over a firm's strategies, tactics and operations than her peers in larger enterprises as well as considerable personal opportunity to engage in decision processes across the firm (Levy and Powell 2005). As a result, although a flat, informal organisational structure is likely to exist, decision making tends to be quite centralized around the owner/CEO (Bianchi 2002).

2.2 IT Endowments

Relative to larger enterprises, SMEs tend to be constrained regarding their endowments of financial resources and IT capabilities, prompting many SMEs to make extensive use of packaged solutions, third party service providers and external consultants (Keasey and Watson 1993). Not surprisingly, Thong (2001) has observed that SMEs spend proportionally less on IT than larger businesses. Three primary explanations validate this reality. First, SMEs' very influential owner/founders tend to have limited prior IT expertise and experience, unless the business itself is IT-enabled or IT-based (Hadjimanoulis 2000). Not unexpected, the expertise of SME owners/founders typically lays in one or more non-IT aspects of the business, e.g., the product or service offered, external constituencies (customers, suppliers, regulators, etc.), operational processes, etc. In the absence of strong understanding of IT issues, owners/founders decision styles regarding IT tend to be reactive (Bianchi 2002) and, when exercised, tend to be operational rather than strategic and tactical (Lybaert 1998). Second, SMEs' employees tend to be generalists, rather than specialists, hired for their business skills, not necessarily their technology skills. The IT knowledge held by these employees is often quite limited, as their attention is most often directed toward ensuring core business survival rather than driving IT innovation regarding products, services or processes (Levy and Powell 2005). As a result, employees of SMEs generally hold low awareness of the potential benefits and costs of IT (Thong 1999). Third, given available resources as well as the nature of the IT work carried out, it is often difficult, and generally unnecessary, for SMEs to attract and retain highly capable IT professionals.

2.3 IT Management Posture

Because of the limited IT perspectives of owners/founders and a lack of IT proficiency across these firms' employees, most SMEs maintain quite small internal IT groups that tend to look outside the firm for identifying, acquiring, developing, installing and supporting IT-enabled business solutions (Thong 2001). Invariably, the decision orientation of this internal IT group tends to be focused on the short-term (e.g., little time spent on IT planning, repairing rather than upgrading existing systems) and on operational efficiency (Hagmann and McCahon 1993; Levy and Powell 2005). Further, the work processes and decision processes associated with this internal IT group tend to be less mature, lacking both rigor and consistency (Thong 1999), compared to those of IT groups in larger organisations. As a result, the introduction of new IT-enabled business solutions often occurs in a fragmented manner without systematic strategic foresight (Foong 1999).

2.4 Summary

SMEs are associated with a number of characteristics that distinguish them from larger organisations, particularly with regard to their organisational structures, IT endowments, and IT management postures. The decision structures of SMEs tend to be centralized, flat and informal. Financial constraints limit their abilities to invest in IT and to attract highly capable IT professionals. Finally, the internal IT groups of SMEs often lack process maturity and a long-term focus.

3   IT Steering Committees

IT steering committees represent a governance mechanism frequently applied to ensure the alignment of IT investments with business priorities and to otherwise provide oversight of organisations' IT-related activities. As typically established, the IT steering committee is a formally recognized group of senior executives representing differing perspectives that meets on a regular basis (McKeen and Guimaraes 1985, p. 1344). IT steering committees function as a "board of directors" and act as a liaison device among various functional groups by facilitating inter-unit coordination, setting IT policies, allocating resources, and monitoring progress of IT projects (Torkzadeh and Xia 1992). Without steering committees, "individual managers are left to resolve isolated issues as they arise, and those individual actions can often be at odds with each other" (Weill and Ross 2005, p. 26).

Firms using IT steering committees have been found to exhibit greater executive attention to IT-related activities (Vadapalli and Mone 2000), a greater commitment to planning practices (Doll and Torkzadeh 1987), and a forward-looking IT project portfolio (McKeen and Guimaraes 1985). In addition, steering committees set the tone of business-IT relationships at an enterprise level (Ross et al. 1996) as business executives interact with the CIO in deliberating on IT-related issues and initiatives.

The design (i.e., who participates) and focus of IT steering committees varies considerably. The CIO typically plays a proactive role (Earl and Feeny 1994). Besides the CIO, participants might involve senior executives, other IT executives and representatives from functional areas, business units and/or process leaders. Steering committees largely comprised of executive-level participants tend to emphasize standardization and efficiency as well as better leveraging of IT to improve profitability; steering committees largely comprised of participants representing operating areas tend to focus on improving operating performance; and steering committees largely comprised of senior managers representing business operating area and IT operating areas tend to focus on achieving optimal asset utilization (Weill and Ross 2005).

To summarize, IT steering committees provide overview of IT-related activities. They serve as a channel for business and IT executives to collaboratively initiate, plan, and manage IT projects. The design of IT steering committees differentiates an organisation's focus on IT issues at either enterprise-level or operational-level.

4   Research Design

To examine IT governance practices in SMEs and the impacts of these governance practices on the success achieved by SMEs in their IT use, a qualitative analysis of three case sites was undertaken (Yin 1984). By using the interview as the primary collection device, the cues used are framed within the interviewee's specific context (Kaplan and Maxwell 1994), and data could be collected from interviewees (i.e., senior managers in SMEs) whose organisational roles were most appropriate given the questions being asked.

The three SMEs selected – two for-profit SMEs (a manufacturing firm and a health services firm) and a non-profit SME – achieved a sampling strategy aimed at realizing variation in organisational objectives, strategies, structures and processes so as to reduce contextual biases (Dubé and Paré 2003; Rumelt 1991). Pharma is a manufacture subsidiary of an international pharmaceutical company, with businesses in Asia Pacific, North America, and Europe. HealthCare is a health care management organisation with multiple offices in three U.S. States that provides patient care services to their physician partners. Agriculture is a non-profit research foundation that engages in applied research as well as provides consultation services in agriculture techniques and advanced plant science. Demographic data along with interviewees from the field sites are provided in Table 1.

Table 1. Demographic Information on Research Sites

	HealthCare	Agriculture	Pharma
Firm Size	182	300	360
IT Group Size	12	14	10
Interviewees	CIO	CIO	CIO
	4 Divisional VPs	2 Divisional Directors	Controller, Divisional VP

Entry to a organisation occurred through the CIO. After this initial interview, other interviewees were identified based on snowball sampling, in which the CIO was asked for suggestions of the appropriate senior managers of operational or staff units with the greatest potential to obtain value from IT use. All interviewees were asked questions about their understanding of the organisation's business tactics and strategies, IT governance structure, and IT use[2]. Each interview lasted between 30 and 50 minutes.

4.1 A Priori Specification of Constructs

Following Bourgeois and Eisenhardt (1988), we identified four potentially important constructs from the literature: decision loci, senior management involvement in IT governance processes, IT governance communication practices, and IT success. A priori specification of constructs helps shape the initial research design and analysis, and permits researchers to measure constructs more accurately (Eisenhardt 1989). We now provide a brief description of each of these constructs.

Decision Loci.
Previous studies in IT governance indicate that three governance structures are most prevalent: centralized, decentralized, and hybrid structures. Specifically, with centralized governance structures, IT decisions are made from a top-down, enterprise-wide perspective. With decentralized governance structures, IT decisions are made from a bottom-up, localized (e.g., business unit, functional department, etc.) perspective. Hybrid structures (a.k.a. the federal governance mode) finds IT decisions being made collaboratively by representatives holding enterprise-wide and local perspectives. The primary advantage of centralized structures are the operational efficiencies and enterprise-wide synergies that result, whereas the major advantage of

Table 2. Centralized and Decentralized Governance Structures

Decision Structure	Advantages	Disadvantages
Centralization	- Enterprise-wide infrastructure - Economies of scale and scope - Cost control - Enterprise-wide project prioritization - Elimination of redundant functions	- Loss of local autonomy - Overlooking local needs - Bureaucracy - Slow response times
Decentralization	- Locally-customized business solutions - Fast, flexible responses to customers - Fast, flexible responses to competition	- Duplication of business solutions and IT services - Higher operational costs - Loss of a single-enterprise view

---

[2] Interview protocol is available upon requests.

decentralized structures is the local control enabling flexibility in responding to customer needs and competitive requirements (Brown 1997). A federal governance mode potentially provides for the advantages of both centralized and decentralized structures by centralizing certain IT decisions and decentralizing others (Zmud et al. 1986). Studies have sought to understand why organisations adopt specific IT governance structures (e.g., Sambamurthy and Zmud 1999) and under what conditions do firms choose to implement a hybrid IT governance solution (Brown 1997). Researchers have concluded that organisational choices of IT governance structures depend on numerous factors, including organisational structure, business strategy, industry, and firm size (Brown 2005; Sambamurthy and Zmud 1999; Weill and Ross 2004). Table 2 summarizes the advantages/disadvantages of centralized and decentralized governance structures.

Senior Management Involvement in IT Governance Processes
To ensure the alignment between business and IT and provide a high-level overview of IT practices, senior management is often involved in IT governance processes (Weill and Ross 2005). Senior management involvement refers to personal interventions and participation of executive managers in the decision-making processes of IT-related issues. The involvement of executives in IT decisions occurs through formal and informal pathways. Formally, senior management gets involved in IT decisions through governance bodies – such as steering committees – that shape strategies and policies (Doll 1985). Informally, senior IT decision makers interact with executive-level and senior operating managers to derive strategic IT directions and to deliberate on alternative solutions for critical business and IT issues.

IT Governance Communication Practices
In order for an organisation's members to behave appropriately as they engage with others when contributing to IT-related actions, it is beneficial that a mutually-understood view of what represents enterprise-appropriate IT actions is held by these interacting members (Lind and Zmud 1995). For such a common understanding to emerge, it is desirable that enterprise policies, guidelines, and practices regarding appropriate and deviant IT-related behaviors be disseminated (Uzzi 1996; Walker et al. 1997). IT governance policies, guidelines and practices can be communicated through a variety of communication channels, each of which is characterized by distinctive capabilities (Carlson and Zmud 1999; Daft and Lengel 1986). The identification of these communication channels will help us categorize the impacts of communication practices on IT performance.

IT Success
Applying the lens of Porter's value chain (Porter 1985), IT has the potential to enable or support most organisational core work and managerial processes. Strategically, organisations can apply IT to enhance business flexibility, reduce operation costs, innovate new products or processes, create and penetrate new markets, and provide value-added services to stakeholders (Sambamurthy et al. 2003). Tactically and operationally, organisations can apply IT across the value chain activities to improve work process efficiency and effectiveness internally and, increasingly, also externally (Krishnan et al. 2007).

Table 3. Variable Operationalization

Construct	Sub-Category	Description
Decision Loci	Centralization	Decisions made by corporate-level IT/business senior managers
	Hybrid	Decisions jointly made by corporate and divisional senior managers
	Decentralization	Decisions made by divisional senior managers
Senior Management Involvement in IT Governance Processes	Formal Involvement	Active participation of executive managers in formal IT steering committees
	Informal Involvement	Senior managers, categorized as corporate senior managers, divisional senior managers or both, having regular interactions with the CIO
IT Governance Communication Practices	Number of Channels	Number (and types) of communication channels used to communicate IT governance policies, guidelines and practices throughout the SME.
	Primary Communication Channel	The primary communication channel used to communicate IT policies, guidelines and procedures throughout the SME.
IT Success	Efficiency of IT Use	How efficient the firm has been in its use of IT (a 5-point scale with 5 representing the highest efficiency; averaged by number of respondents).
	Breadth of current IT use	The number of distinct areas identified, aggregated across interviewees, where IT is being appropriately used
	Breadth of potential IT use	The number of distinct work processes identified, by any interviewees, as being actively considered or planned for future IT use.

There are several ways of assessing organisational success in IT use. Following Edmondson, Winslow, Bohmer, and Pisano (2003), we consider efficiency and breadth of IT use. *Efficiency of IT use* primarily refers to the extent to which cost and productivity advantages accrue in the deployment of IT assets and capabilities.

Breadth of IT use reflects the extent to which IT assets and capabilities are used in supporting work processes across the organisation (Sambamurthy and Zmud 1992). Underlying the breadth in use are two distinct constructs: *breadth in current IT use*, and *breadth in potential IT use*. Here, the former breadth aspect reflects work processes currently being enabled/supported by IT while the latter reflects the recognition of work processes that, though not currently, should be enabled/supported by IT.

4.2 Data Sources

Transcriptions of the interviews were coded by three individuals (the author and two research assistants knowledgeable about IT but not otherwise involved in the study) using a coding scheme developed based on the priori specification of constructs[3]. The coding scheme captures the location of IT decisions, how senior management was involved in IT decision-making, the channels used to communicate IT policies, guidelines and procedures, and organisational success in IT use. Independent coding was first conducted, and the initial inter-rater reliability was 79%. Coding differences were then identified and reconciled through discussions among the three coders.

Interview comments from the CIOs were used to capture governance practices in each organisation as the CIOs were the informants possessing the most comprehensive understanding of their organisations' IT governance structures and processes, senior management involvement in IT-related decision processes, and the organisations' communication practices regarding IT governance policies, guidelines and procedures. Interview comments from the senior operating/functional managers were used to capture IT performance as these individuals possessed (collectively) the most realistic, unbiased views regarding the efficiency of IT use, where IT is currently deployed, and where IT should be (though not currently) deployed. To achieve a consistency in the cross-site analysis, analytic attention was limited to the "investment and prioritization" IT decision domain, the only IT decision domain for which all three organisations had established IT governance processes. Table 3 presents the operationalization of each construct.

5 Data Analysis

The search for patterns in the data was assisted by 1) understanding of the governance practices and IT success within each firm, and 2) comparing the differences in governance practices and IT success across three firms. Table 4 presents the primary coding results. Our discussion of data patterns draws from both the coding result and interview comments.

5.1 IT Success

The three organisations as a group performed best in terms of the efficiency in IT use, then current breadth in IT use and lastly potential breadth in IT use. Nevertheless, we observed differences in the nature of these organisations' success in deploying IT.

---

[3] The authors can provide coding rules upon requests.

Table 4. Coding Results

	HealthCare	Agriculture	Pharma
Decision Loci	Centralized Corporate Executives CIO	Centralized CIO	Centralized CIO
Senior Mgt Involvement: Formal Involvement	Corporate Executives CIO	No use of formal steering committees	CIO Divisional Executives
Senior Mgt Involvement: Informal Involvement	Corporate Executives	Divisional Executives	Divisional Executives
Number of Communication Channels	2 Email Word of Mouth	3 Paper Document Formal Meeting Word of Mouth	4 Intranet Paper Document Formal Meeting Word of Mouth
Primary Communication Channel	Email	Paper Document	Intranet
Efficiency of IT Use	3.2 (moderate)	3.3 (moderate)	4.3 (high)
Breadth of current IT Use	3 (moderate)	2 (limited)	5 (high)
Breadth of potential IT Use	3 (moderate)	1 (limited)	1 (limited)

Pharma performed best regarding both the efficiency of IT use and the breadth of current IT use, but was limited in its breadth of potential IT use. Healthcare performed moderately well in all three performance categories and was observed to be the best in the breadth of potential IT use. Agriculture was observed to have limited performance in both current and potential breadth of IT use but moderately well in efficiency in IT use.

5.2 IT Governance Structure

We observed from the data that each of the organisations applied a centralized IT governance structure. The comments given below illustrate that, in general, key IT decisions were the responsibility of the CIO alone at Agriculture and Pharma, and by the CxOs (including the CIO) at HealthCare.

Now as those things (building an infrastructure) have been put in place, and hopefully become reliable and functional, we've tried to turn towards what tools we need from a business perspective, and from an operational perspective. Those decisions in terms of what we need are ultimately mine. (CIO, Agriculture)

Work prioritization is a daily decision but is critical to customer service. We have global standards for many things, like Microsoft BackOffice, things like that. But there are many decisions that are made on how you are going to sit on infrastructure, what tools you are going to use, how tight do you need to be on security, where are you going to focus your energies, and how do you manage your money. For this site, it (the decision right) will be here (with me). (CIO, Pharma)

The IT steering committee is made up of the CEO, the COO, the CFO, and the CIO. We collectively make those decisions. (CIO, HealthCare)

5.3 Senior Management Involvement in IT Governance Processes

Interviewees indicated the involvement of senior management as either formal via IT governance bodies such as steering committees or informally via personal relationships driven by the CIO. More specifically, formal senior management involvement was observed at HealthCare and Pharma, whereas informal senior management involvement was observed at Agriculture.

Formal IT steering committees enable participating senior management to meet regularly to discuss, debate and contribute to IT decisions, thus providing a formal, recurring vehicle through which the CIO interacts with other senior managers. The IT steering committee at HealthCare consisted of the CxO officers including the CIO. Divisional/operating senior managers had limited, if any, direct involvement in IT-related decision processes:

We have a formal IT steering committee. The IT steering committee is made up of the CEO, the COO, the CFO, and the CIO. We collectively make IT decisions. (CIO, HealthCare)

An IT steering committee also existed at Pharma. Although decision rights were ultimately with the CIO, divisional/operational senior managers were directly engaged in IT decision processes through this committee. Unlike HealthCare, however, corporate senior managers had limited direct involvement in IT-related decision processes:

We do have a committee that when people look at different systems and prioritize overall IT resources, we have a committee made up of different functional areas. We do have limited resources, and everybody's priority is number one. But you only have so many resources. So we have a committee for that. The committee has somebody from manufacturing, quality, maintenance, IT, and accounting. The nature of that group is to look at the various demands on IT. IT creates this committee so that everybody would know what's going on, and everybody has input to what projects will be worked on, where we are going to spend our resources. (CIO, Pharma)

Not all SMEs, however, implement formal steering committees for IT decision making. Nevertheless, the CIO still needs to connect with business managers to ensure the alignment between business and IT (Reich and Benbasat 2000). Such connections are established through informal interactions amongst the CIO and other senior executives. At Agriculture, no formal IT steering committee existed; rather, the CIO interacted informally with operational/functional executives to gain their input into key IT decisions:

Those decisions in terms of what we need are ultimately mine. But they are certainly made based on interaction and collaboration with the division directors of the three divisions. So I'll meet with those guys, we'll in a very informal manner talk about their needs, their coming needs. (CIO, Agriculture)

5.4 IT Governance Communication Practices

As the organisational structures of SMEs tend to be flat and lacks standardization and formally-defined work processes, rich information networks amongst members serve as a primary vehicle for work direction and coordination (Ghobadian and Gallear 1996). Consistent with such an orientation, we found informal, interpersonal channels (e.g. word of mouth) being used in all three organisations to communicate IT governance policies and procedures. Still, we did find differences across the three case sites with regard to the communication of their IT governance policies, guidelines and practices.

Pharma indicated the use of four communication channels, i.e., an Intranet site, paper documents, formal meetings, and word of mouth:

The general policies, which are really a few formal policies of IT, there are some in the employee handbook that all employees are assigned, which is the Internet for appropriate use, your email can be reviewed, all the fundamental information confidential, all that is in the employee handbooks that every employee has been assigned. Other policies as we write them, will be published on the company Intranet...When a new employee comes in, there is employee orientation and the handbook. Typically when someone comes in, someone from IT spends a few minutes with them, how you do your mail, here's this, here's that. And then they are informed where these things are. (CIO, Pharma)

In contrast, HealthCare only used two channels (email and word of mouth), while Agriculture used three channels (document, formal meeting, word of mouth).

The communication of IT policies and procedures is informal, maybe just via email or word of mouth. We don't have a documented IT steering committee, the policies and procedures that the whole company knows about. It's just informal with senior management. (CIO, HealthCare)

We use standardized form, standard language, standard layout for presenting the information, what projects were approved, what projects were not approved, and why they weren't approved... Employees get oriented to the firm, and its general business practices. When they bring a software request forward, they'll find out from their peers, their division director that's something we do on a quarterly basis, and that's the process. (CIO, Agriculture)

6 Recommendations for SME Governance Practices

Consistent with the results of prior research on IT governance (Brown 2005; Sambamurthy and Zmud 1999; Weill and Ross 2004) with the earlier reported research stating relatively low levels of IT process maturity as well as low levels of IT capabilities across SME employees, the patterns we observed across the three case studies allowed us to draw inferences that centralized IT decision structures would be most prevalent within SMEs. In addition, given that centralized structures enable an enterprise-wide perspective that lead to efficient allocation of IT and business resources (Brown 1997), we further suggest that SMEs tend to focus on operational efficiency when they implement a centralized decision structure.

Despite the commonality of centralized IT decision structures, the success achieved by SMEs in their IT deployments was observed to vary. We drew general inferences that differential effects from IT use across the three cases were induced by variations observed in these firms regarding senior management involvement in their IT governance processes as well as their IT governance communication practices. Based on these inferences, we give recommendations for IT governance practices in SMEs.

6.1 Senior Management Involvement in IT Governance Processes

Referring back to Table 4, it can be observed that Pharma and Healthcare had implemented formal IT steering committees while Agriculture had not. In addition, Pharma and Healthcare generally outperformed Agriculture (though Agriculture and Healthcare were essentially comparable regarding efficiency in IT use). The picture that emerges from our data indicates the performance advantages of establishing a formal IT steering committee within SMEs. A network perspective can be used in understanding the influence of IT governance structures with successful IT use (Granovetter 1985).

Rooted in Granovetter's original conceptualization of embeddedness is the distinction between structural and relational embeddedness (Granovetter 1992). Structural embeddedness stresses the structural position in the network, whereas relational embeddedness emphasizes the characteristics of the relationships within the network (Gulati 1998). Both types of embeddedness are associated with the organisational governance mechanisms in that structural embeddedness is involved with the fashioning of norms and practices at institutional level, while relational embeddedness facilitates the building of trust at the dyadic level (Rowley et al. 2000).

Drawing upon the network perspective, we consider senior management involvement as a social component of IT governance, as the involvement of senior management enables shared behavior expectations, produces norms of appropriate IT behaviors (Lewis et al. 2003), and serves as part of the social control mechanism that governs employee behaviors (Rowley et al. 2000). Through the involvement of senior management in formal IT governance bodies, both structural and relational embeddedness are forged as formal authority is invested through an institutionalized network structure and dyadic relationships amongst network participants are enhanced. Through informal interactions in the process of considering and taking IT-related decisions, personal relations are developed and relational embeddedness is enhanced.

Based on the discussion above, we anticipate the establishment of both structural and relational embeddedness of IT decisions at Healthcare and Pharma where formal steering committees were implemented. However, structural embeddedness is likely to be absent at Agriculture, where there seems to be only relational embeddedness built through informal personal interactions between the CIO and the operational/functional executives.

When an organisation's senior managers are connected through either structural or relational embeddedness, a consistency in organisation-wide IT values is more likely to arise with IT-related strategies and tactics adjusted to coordinate the needs of individual units (Feldman 1981). The existence of this consistent enterprise perspective facilitates the communication and coordination of IT behaviours across organisation units. As a result, the efficiency of IT use is likely to be improved. Furthermore, the diffusion of expectations from senior managers enabled by structural and relational embeddedness implies the importance of IT and encourages extensive use of IT, leading to improved breadth of IT use as well. In addition, as enterprise norms are enabled by both structural embeddedness and relational embeddedness, norms that do exist are weakened if either structural or relational embeddedness is lacking (Jones et al. 1997; Kale et al. 2000), consequently challenging the consistent and active use of IT. Therefore, we suggest that IT performance will be most improved when *both* structural and relational embeddedness are present. Given that the formal involvement of senior management in governance procedures enriches both structural and relational embeddedness while informal involvement with the CIO enriches relational embeddedness alone, we anticipate that senior management involvement through formal steering committees will result in higher levels of efficiency and breadth of IT use than senior management involvement through informal personal relationships when only one of these is observed. Therefore, we recommend:

Recommendation 1: In order to enhance performance of IT use (as indicated by efficiency and breadth of IT use) in SMEs, senior management should be involved through joint formal and informal IT governance interactions.

The evidence from this study also points to the fact that persons involved with the formal and/or informal IT governance interactions are important in explaining

172 R. Huang, R.W. Zmud, and R.L. Price

variation in an organisation's success in using IT. As shown in Table 4, Pharma outperformed HealthCare with both the efficiency of IT use and the breadth of current IT use, but not for the breadth of potential IT use – where, HealthCare outperformed Pharma. Such a pattern points to the importance of the composition of the IT steering committee. At HealthCare, it was the corporate executives that participated in the IT steering committee, whereas at Pharma it was the operational/functional executives who participated.

The CIO's IT-related decision interactions can involve corporate executives, operational executives, or both. Corporate executives are more knowledgeable about the corporate-level issues, but may lack deep knowledge of how IT can be used locally in improving organisational performance (Hadjimanoulis 2000). The involvement of corporate executives in IT decisions is critical to longer-term enterprise planning issue associated with IT, which requires substantial executive involvement in order to establish an appropriate alignment between IT directions and business directions (Segars and Grover 1998). In other words, with the involvement of corporate executives, conversations and explorations of where and how IT should be applied in the future are more likely to occur. We thus recommend that in order to improve the breadth of potential IT use, corporate-level executives should be involved in IT decision-making processes.

Recommendation 2: In order to improve the breadth of potential IT use in SMEs, corporate executives should be involved in IT governance processes.

On the other hand, operational executives have a greater understanding of local issues (IT-related and otherwise), but may lack a broad understanding of IT use from an enterprise-wide perspective. Given that operational managers are typically focused on meeting operational and budget performance targets, it is expected their primary interests with IT-related decisions will correspondingly focus on how to use IT in enhancing current operations and driving down costs (Tallon et al. 2000). Therefore, we expect the involvement of operational managers in IT governance processes to improve the breadth of current use of IT. Therefore, we recommend:

Recommendation 3: In order to improve the breadth of current IT use in SMEs, operational executives should be involved in IT governance processes.

6.2 IT Governance Communication Practices

Lastly, the data implied that heightened performance at Pharma regarding both efficiency in IT use and the breadth of current IT use may have been attributed to both the greater number – and nature (discussed below) – of communication channels used (Table 4). Effective IT governance communication practices are likely to prove influential in establishing an awareness of and familiarity with enterprise-wide IT governance policies, guidelines and practices across an organisation's management team. Communication practices that apply a variety of communication alternatives are likely to prove more effective than communication practices that apply only a few alternatives as targeted organisational members are more likely to access and, hence, be exposed to sent messages (Lengel and Daft 1988; Schmitz and Fulk 1991;

Te'eni 2001). Therefore, when IT governance policies, guidelines and practices are communicated through more rather than fewer channels, organisational members are more likely to attend to these messages and, hence, be more aware of their organisation's IT-related strategies, actions and behaviors. Consequently, communicating IT policies, guidelines and procedures through more channels is more likely to improve the success which results from IT use:

Recommendation 4: In order to improve the performance of IT use (as indicated by efficiency and breadth of IT use) in SMEs, IT governance policies, guidelines and practices should be communicated through a number of channels.

On another note, it is interesting to observe that, while Agriculture used more channels to communicate IT policies, guidelines and practices than did HealthCare, Agriculture was found to exhibit lower performance than HealthCare regarding current and potential breadth of IT use. Agriculture did not utilize electronic channels, which were observed with both Healthcare (email) and Pharma (email and Intranet). Although we could not infer the direct link between communication channels and IT performance, we suspect that information accessibility enabled by electronic channels may have contributed to the difference in performance across three firms. We thus suggest that the greater accessibility (O'Reilly 1982) to information regarding IT governance policies, guidelines and practices afforded through electronic communication channels increased the likelihood that these policies, guidelines and practices would frame IT-related decisions and actions (Huber 1990) and improve organisational success with IT use. Therefore, we recommend:

Recommendation 5: In order to improve the performance of IT use (as indicated by efficiency and breadth of IT use) in SMEs, IT governance policies, guidelines and practices should be communicated through accessible channels.

7 Discussion

We began this paper with the question: How can SMEs optimize IT performance through governance practices? As expected, the examination of IT governance processes and IT use within three SMEs indicates that SMEs exhibit centralized governance structures, and this orientation toward centralized governance seemed most effective in promoting efficiency in IT use. Still, we also observed considerable variance in these three organisation's success in IT use. So, given their use of centralized IT governance structures, under which conditions will SMEs achieve both efficiency and breadth in IT use? Inferences from the patterns in data emerged from our analysis. Our recommendations focus on the effects on the manner in which senior executives in these organisations were involved with IT governance processes as well as their IT governance communication practices.

Regarding senior executive involvement in IT governance processes, we observed both the use of a formal IT steering committee and the organisational roles which involved senior executives to be influential in differentiating success in IT use. Consistent with previous research (e.g., McKeen and Guimaraes 1985; Ross et al.

1996), the employment of formal IT steering committees was associated with higher success in IT use, rather than sole dependance on CIO-led interactions with senior executives,. Drawing upon the network perspective, we believe that IT steering committees enrich both structural and relational embeddedness, whereas CIO-led interactions enrich only relational embeddedness. Therefore, we suggest that it is through both the structural and relational embeddedness that social control mechanisms are enforced.

In addition to the presence of IT steering committees, it was observed that the identity of the individuals involved, formally or informally, with IT governance was also important. Weill and Ross (2005) suggest that steering committees largely comprising of enterprise-level participants tend to emphasize standardization and efficiency, whereas steering committees largely composed of operational managers tend to focus on improving operating performance. In addition to the intended focus, we built a direct connection between performance outcome and the composition of the committee. When corporate-level executives were involved, better performance was observed with the breadth of potential IT use; when operational/functional executives were involved, better performance was observed with breadth of current IT use. In other words, the involvement of corporate-level executives may be beneficial to IT performance in the long-run, whereas the involvement of operational executives may bring immediate benefits to IT performance. As none of the case sites were characterized by governance processes involving *both* corporate-level and operational/functional-level executives, we could not assess the value of such heterogeneous involvement practices – but we conjecture that such practices would prove helpful in organisational efforts to appropriate best value from IT investments.

Based on the observation that the involvement of corporate executives or operational executives leads to different outcomes in terms of IT performance, we wonder whether it is best to have a single steering committee with both corporate executives and operational executives, or two steering committees with one for corporate executives and one for operational executives. With one steering committee consisting of executives from both corporate and operational levels, it will be easier to connect the strategic and operational aspects of IT. Nevertheless, with a greater diversity in represented vested interests, it will likely be more difficult for participants to reach consensus and implement IT decisions.

On the other hand, establishing two separate committees – one focused more on strategic concerns and the other on operating concerns – will most likely result in more smoothly functioning governance bodies. Yet, by separating these two governance bodies the likelihood increases that disjunctures will surface in the policies and decisions that emanate. Both options have advantages and disadvantages, and existing literature lacks an exploration of resolution tactics. Given the important role that IT steering committees play in IT governance, we encourage future research that explores this issue within SMEs and within larger enterprises.

Regarding IT governance communication practices, prior research suggests that the dissemination of enterprise policies and guidelines is beneficial for achieving enterprise-wide understanding of IT expectations (Lind and Zmud 1995). We noted that the ways through which IT policies and practices are disseminated also mattered. The use of a greater number of channels may have contributed to greater success in IT use. More importantly, we observed that the use of electronic communication channels may prove especially effective in disseminating proscribed IT policies, guidelines and practices across an organisation's senior managers. As indicated from the three cases, Pharma utilized Intranet as a communication channel of IT policies and procedures and it outperformed the other two firms in terms of IT efficiency and breadth in current IT use. Given that an archival, electronic repository is most accessible and available, we wonder how beneficial it would be for organisations to electronically store important IT policies, guidelines and practices. Yet, given the limitation of our data, we cannot generate definite answers about this question, and we thus leave it open for future research.

8 Conclusion

This study has provided a view of IT governance practices in three SMEs, resulting in both an improved appreciation of the nature of IT governance practices in SMEs and the surfacing of key insights regarding effective governance practice that should enrich IT governance research in general. A qualitative and inductive study of three firms led us to recommend that in order for an organisation to improve overall IT performance, senior management should be jointly (both formally and informally) involved with IT decision-making processes and IT governance policies, guidelines and practices should be communicated to organisational members through more accessible communication channels. Furthermore, we also recommend that the involvement of corporate executives in IT governance processes will be beneficial for the breadth of potential IT use, whereas the involvement of operational executives will help the efficiency and breadth of current IT use.

Given that this study involves a small number of organisations, we acknowledge some of our observations may be due to the intrinsic nature of the organisations studied. For example, Agriculture is a non-profit organisation, and may not have sufficient resources to implement electronic media for disseminating IT policies and practices. The lack of formal steering committees at Agriculture may also deal with their business nature. On the other hand, HealthCare is relatively smaller than the other two firms, and may not need to disseminate IT policies and practices in multiple ways, resulting in a smaller number of communication channels used. Although we believe that the recommendations from this study is most salient to SMEs, we recommend that additional studies involving larger samples be conducted to validate the generalizability of our implications about IT governance in SMEs.

We sincerely hope that these ideas prove to be of interest and use to scholars interested in better understanding the structures and processes deployed by organisations to ensure that IT-related decisions are aligned with current operational goals and future strategies.

References

Bianchi, C.: Introducing SD modeling into planning and control systems to management SME's growth: a learning-oriented perspective. Systems Dynamics Review 18(3), 403–429 (2002)

Blau, P.M., Schoenherr, R.A.: The Structure of Organisations. Basic Books, New York (1971)

Bourgeois, L.J., Eisenhardt, K.M.: Strategic Decision Processes in High Velocity Environments: Four Cases in the Mircrocomputer Industry. Management Science 34(7), 816–835 (1988)

Brown, A.E.: Framing the frameworks: A review of IT governance research. Communication of the Association for Information Systems 15, 696–712 (2005)

Brown, C.V.: Examining the Emergence of Hybrid IS Governance Solutions: Evidence from a Single Case Site. Information Systems Research 8(1), 69–94 (1997)

Brown, C.V., Magill, S.L.: Reconceptualizing the Context-Design Issue for the Information Systems Function. Organisation Science 9(2), 176–194 (1998)

Carlson, J.R., Zmud, R.W.: Channel Expansion Theory and the Experiential Nature of Media Richness Perceptions. Academy of Management Journal 42(2), 153–170 (1999)

Child, J.: Organisational Structure, Environment and Performance: The Role of Strategic Choice. Sociology 6(1), 1–22 (1972)

Cross, J., Earl, M.J., Sampler, J.L.: Transformation of the IT function at British Petroleum. MIS Quarterly 21(4), 401–424 (1997)

Daft, R.L., Lengel, R.H.: Organisational Information Requirements, Media Richness and Structural Design. Management Science 32(5), 554–571 (1986)

Doll, W.J.: Avenues for top management involvement in successful MIS development. MIS Quarterly 9(1), 17–35 (1985)

Doll, W.J., Torkzadeh, G.: The Relationship of MIS Steering Committeteo Size of Firm and Formalization of MIS Planning. Communications of the ACM 30(11), 7 (1987)

Dubé, L., Paré, G.: Rigor in Information Systems Positivist Case Research: Current Practices, Trends, and Recommendations. MIS Quarterly 27(4), 597–635 (2003)

Earl, M.J., Feeny, D.F.: Is Your CIO Adding Value. Sloan Management Review 35(3), 10 (1994)

Edmondson, A.C., Winslow, A.B., Bohmer, R.M., Pisano, G.P.: Learning How and Learning What: Effects of Tacit and Codified Knowledge on Performance Improvement Following Technology Adoption. Decision Science 34(2), 197–223 (2003)

Ein-Dor, P., Segev, E.: Organisational Context and MIS Structure: Some Empirical Evidence. MIS Quarterly 6(3), 55–68 (1982)

Eisenhardt, K.M.: Building Theories from Case Study Research. Academy of Management Review 14(4), 532–550 (1989)

Feldman, D.C.: The Multiple Socialization of Organisation Members. The Academy of Management Review 6(2), 309–318 (1981)

Foong, S.Y.: Effect of end user personal and systems attributes on computer based information system success in Malaysian SMEs. Journal of Small Business Management 37(3), 81–87 (1999)

Ghobadian, A., Gallear, D.N.: Total quality management in SMEs. Omega 24(1), 83–106 (1996)

Granovetter, M.: Economic Action and Social Structure: The Problem of Embeddedness. American Journal of Sociology 91, 481–510 (1985)

Granovetter, M.: Problems of explanation in economic sociology. In: Nohria, N., Eccles, R.G. (eds.) Networks and Organisations: Structure, Form, and Action, pp. 25–56. Harvard Business School Press, Boston (1992)

Gulati, R.: Alliances and networks. Strategic Management Journal 19(4), 293–317 (1998)

Hadjimanoulis, A.: A resource-based view of innovativeness in small firms. Technology Analysis and Strategic Management 12(2), 263–281 (2000)

Hagmann, C., McCahon, C.: Strategic information systems and competitiveness: are firms ready for an IST-driven competitive challenge? Information & Management 25, 183–192 (1993)

Hall, R.H.: Organisations, Structure and Process. Prentice-Hall, Englewood Cliffs (1972)

Hay, M., Kamshad, K.: Small firm growth: intentions, implementation and impediments. Business Strategy Review 5(3), 49–68 (1994)

Huber, G.P.: A Theory of the Effects of Advanced Information Technologies on Organisational Design, Intelligence, and Decision Making. Academy of Management Review 15(1), 47–71 (1990)

Jenkins, J.M., Santos, R.F.: Centralization vs. Decentralization of Data Processing Functions. In: Goldberg, R., Lorin, H. (eds.) The Economics of Information Processing, pp. 62–67. Whiley-Interscience, New York (1982)

Jones, C., Hesterly, W.S., Borgatti, S.P.: A General Theory of Network Governance: Exchange Conditions and Social Mechanisms. Academy of Management Review 22(4), 911–945 (1997)

Kale, P., Singh, H., Perlmutter, H.: Learning and Protection of Proprietary Assets in Strategic Alliances: Building Relational Capital. Strategic Management Journal 21, 217–237 (2000)

Kaplan, B., Maxwell, J.A.: Qualitative Research Methods for Evaluating Computer Information Systems. In: Anderson, J.G., Aydin, C.E. (eds.) Evaluating Health Care Information Systems: Methods and Applications, pp. 45–68. Sage, Thousand Oaks (1994)

Keasey, K., Watson, R.: Small firm management. Blackwell, Cambridge (1993)

Krishnan, M.S., Rai, A., Zmud, R.W.: Editorial Overview: The Digitally Enabled Extended Enterprise in a Global Economy. Information Systems Research 18(3), 233–236 (2007)

Lengel, R.H., Daft, R.L.: The selection of communication media as an executive skill. Academy of Management Executive 2, 225–232 (1988)

Levy, M., Powell, P.: Strategies for growth in SMEs. Elsevier, Burlington (2005)

Lewis, W., Agarwal, R., Sambamurthy, V.: Sources of Influence on Beliefs about Information Technology Use: An Empirical Study of Knowledge Workers. MIS Quarterly 27(4), 657–678 (2003)

Lind, M., Zmud, R.W.: Improving Interorganisational Effectiveness through Voice Mail Facilitation of Peer-to-Peer Relationships. Organisation Science 6(4), 445–461 (1995)

Lybaert, N.: The information use in a SME: its importance and some elements of influence. Small Business Economics 10, 171–191 (1998)

McKeen, J.D., Guimaraes, T.: Selecting MIS Projects by Steering Committee. Communications of the ACM (December 9, 1985)

Meyer, M.W.: Size and the Structure of Organisations: A Causal Model. American Sociological Review 37(4), 434–440 (1972)

O'Reilly, C.A.: Variations in Decision Makers' Use of Information Sources: The Impact of Quality and Accessibility of Information. Academy of Management Journal 25(4), 756–771 (1982)

Porter, M.E.: Competitive Advantage: Creating and Sustaining Superior Performance. Free Press, New York (1985)

Pugh, D.S., Hickson, D.J., Hinings, C.R., Turner, C.: Dimensions of Organisation Structure. Administrative Science Quarterly 13(1), 65–105 (1968)

Reich, B.H., Benbasat, I.: Factors That Influence the Social Dimension of Alignment between Business and Information Technology Objectives. MIS Quarterly 24(1), 81–113 (2000)

Ross, J.W., Beath, C.M., Goodhue, D.L.: Develop Long-Term Competitiveness through IT Assets. Sloan Management Review 11 (Fall 1996)

Rowley, T., Behrens, D., Krackhardt, D.: Redundant governance structures: an analysis of structural and relational embeddedness in the steel and semiconductor industries. Strategic Management Journal 21(3), 369–386 (2000)

Rumelt, R.P.: How Much Does Industry Matter? Strategic Management Journal 12(3), 167–185 (1991)

Sambamurthy, V., Bharadwaj, A., Grover, V.: Shaping Agility through Digital Options: Reconceptualizing the Role of Information Technology in Contemporary Firms. MIS Quarterly 27(2), 237–263 (2003)

Sambamurthy, V., Zmud, R.W.: Managing IT for success: The empowering business partnership. Financial Executive Research Foundation, New Jersey (1992)

Sambamurthy, V., Zmud, R.W.: Arrangements for Information Technology Governance: A Theory of Multiple Contingencies. MIS Quarterly 23(2), 261–290 (1999)

Schmitz, J., Fulk, J.: Organisational colleagues, media richness, and electronic mail: A test of the social influence model of technology use. Communication of the Association for Information Systems 18, 487–523 (1991)

Segars, A.H., Grover, V.: Strategic Information Systems Planning Success: An Investigation of the Construct and Its Measurement. MIS Quarterly 22(2), 139–163 (1998)

Starbuck, W.H.: Handbook of Organisations. Rand-McNally, Chicago (1965)

Storey, D.: Understanding the Small Business Sector. Routledge, London (1994)

Storey, D., Sykes, N.: Uncertainty, innovation and management. In: Burns, P., Dewhurst, J. (eds.) Small Business and Entrepreneurship, pp. 73–93. Macmillan, London (1996)

Street, C.T., Meister, D.B.: Small Business Growth and Internal Transparency: The Role of Information Systems. MIS Quarterly 28(3), 473–506 (2004)

Tallon, P.P., Kraemer, K.L., Gurbaxani, V.: Executives' Perceptions of the Business Value of Information Technology: A Process-Oriented Approach. Journal of Management Information Systems 16(4), 145–173 (2000)

Te'eni, D.: Review: A Cognitive-Affective Model of Organisational Communication for Designing IT. MIS Quarterly 25(2), 251–312 (2001)

Thong, J.Y.L.: Resource constraints and information systems implementation in Singaporean small businesses. Omega 29(2), 143–156 (2001)

Thong, Y.L.: An Integrated Model of Information Systems Adoption in Small Businesses. Journal of Management Information Systems 15(4), 187–214 (1999)

Torkzadeh, G., Xia, W.: Managing Telecommunications by Steering Committee. MIS Quarterly 16(2), 13 (1992)

Uzzi, B.: The Sources and Consequences of Embeddedness for the Economic Performance of Organisations: The Network Effect. American Sociological Review 61(4), 674–698 (1996)

Vadapalli, A., Mone, M.A.: Information technology project outcomes: user participation structures and the impact of organisation behavior and human resource management issue. Journal of Engineering and Technology Management 17(2), 25 (2000)

Walker, G., Kogut, B., Shan, W.: Social Capital, Structural Holes and the Formation of an Industry Network. Organisation Science 8(2), 109–125 (1997)

Weill, P.: Don't just lead, govern: How top-performing firms govern IT. MIS Quarterly Executive 3(1), 1–17 (2004)

Weill, P., Ross, J.W.: IT Governance: How Top Performers Manage IT Decision Rights for Superior Results. Harvard Business School Press, Boston (2004)

Weill, P., Ross, J.W.: A Matrixed Approach to Designing IT Governance. Sloan Management Review 46(2), 9 (2005)

Wilensky, H.: Hierarchical Control and Optimum Firm Size. Journal of Political Economy 75(2), 123–138 (1967)

Yin, R.: Case Study Research. Sage Publications, Beverly Hills (1984)

Zmud, R.W., Boynton, A.C., Jacobs, G.C.: The Information Economy: A New Perspective for Effective Information Systems Management. Data Base 18(1), 17–23 (1986)

Life Cycle Model for IT Performance Measurement: A Reference Model for Small and Medium Enterprises (SME)

Can Adam Albayrak[1], Andreas Gadatsch[2], and Dirk Olufs[3]

[1] Harz University of Applied Sciences
Friedrichstr. 57 – 59
38855 Wernigerode, Germany
[2] Bonn-Rhein-Sieg University of Applied Sciences
Grantham Allee 20
53757 Sankt Augustin, Germany
[3] DHL Express Europe
De Kleetlaan, 1
1831 Diegem, Belgium

Abstract. IT performance measurement is often associated by chief executive officers with IT cost cutting although IT protects business processes from increasing IT costs. IT cost cutting only endangers the company's efficiency. This opinion discriminates those who do IT performance measurement in companies as a bean-counter. The present paper describes an integrated reference model for IT performance measurement based on a life cycle model and a performance oriented framework. The presented model was created from a practical point of view. It is designed lank compared with other known concepts and is very appropriate for small and medium enterprises (SME).

Keywords: IT management, SME, small and medium enterprises, reference model, process model.

1 Introduction

In business and administration we have witnessed a permanent change away from a technical view to a business orientation. In the seventies and eighties the electronic data processing was dominated by a rule based batch processing and automatisation of mass data oriented business processes (e.g. book-keeping, warehousing and salary statement). IT supported only selected business functions which were not integrated. IT costs were only covered by a central IT cost centre. There were no further calculations of business cost centres which have used the IT output (e.g. computing time, data space). During this time the status of the IT department was very exclusive. Only IT managers had access to external suppliers of hardware and software or to consulting companies. Real time software (e.g. ERP-Systems like SAP® R/3®) increasingly changed the traditional batch processing software. During the nineties, there were a lot of business process reengineering projects undertaken to remove legacy software

G. Dhillon, B.C. Stahl, and R. Baskerville (Eds.): CreativeSME 2009, IFIP AICT 301, pp. 180–191, 2009.

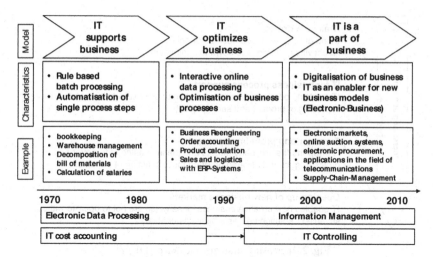

Fig. 1. From a technique to a business orientation

systems by changing business processes (Hammer and Champy 1994). The main aim in this age was to optimize the internal business processes by IT.

During the last decade, IT was identified as a weapon in competition and as an enabler for new business models. Electronic markets, online auction systems, electronic procurement, applications in the field of telecommunications or supply chain management were invented and further developed during this time.

As the latest information dating to the nineties indicates, *information management* has been used as a management tool to control the dominating technical oriented data processing. The head of information management is often called the head of IT but actually the chief information officer (CIO) is responsible for the fulfilment of the production factor *information*.

The acceptance of the production factor *information* can be seen by the grading of the CIO role inside of the companies. Often the CIO was a part of or has to report to the management board or was positioned a level below. A current overview of the personnel anchoring of the CIO role is described by Riedl et al. (2008).

Now, not only has the CIO role changed in companies, the role of the IT departments has also been changing dramatically. In former years, IT was classified as a cost factor only. In the current times, IT is more and more seen as a business partner and business enabler for generating strategic advantages (see fig. 2). This change of tenor has had repurcussions on the challenges and ranking of the IT performance measurement concept. However, business departments see the IT department not as an end in itself. They see it as a tool or service partner for business process support and to create added value for the company. Managers from business departments wield more influence to IT oriented decisions than in the seventies or in the eighties. IT is increasingly becoming an essential part of the business.

An extreme position while discussing the importance of IT was presented by Carr in his paper *IT Doesn't Matter* (Carr 2003) and later in more precise papers (Carr 2004). Carr states that IT has the similar significance like energy or other bulk goods. He doesn't see any strategic relevance. IT will be a commodity or a standardized bulk

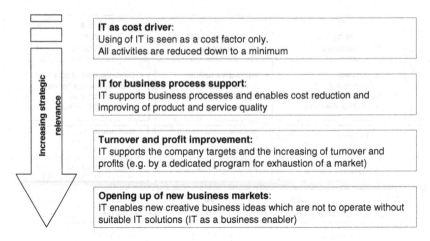

Fig. 2. Increasing strategic relevance of the IT

good like electric power from a socket. Examples show that this opinion is not generally accepted. A lot of examples of companies like Amazon, Google, Dell and so on show us that the the production factor information enables business which is not possible without this factor. The processing and delivering of information in large amounts and high speed would not be possible without using IT. However IT is a strategic factor. Zarnekow and colleagues along with many other authors, describe how to manage the production factor information along the information life cycle (Zarnekow et al. 2006).

2 IT Performance Measurement from a Current Perspective

The *term IT performance measurement* is sometimes called *IT controlling* is interpreted in various ways. We do not want to give a nomenclature to those who do IT performance measurement, because the task of IT performance measurement can be done in different roles, even if the task list of the IT performance measurement in companies varies very strongly. In the following section we describe the main tasks in a context of IT performance measurement as an enabler for the IT management and as a main part of IT governance.

2.1 IT Performance Measurement as an Enabler for the IT Management

A very narrow opinion describes IT performance measurement as a cost inspector of the IT department which is placed below the board of management or inside of the IT department. This view is a partial definition of the duties, because it covers only cost and technical aspects. Such definitions are misleading and not adequate. Newer definitions see IT performance measurement as a tool for decision support by using IT resources. Becker and Winkelmann (2004) define IT performance measurement as purchasing, preparation and analysing of data to prepare target oriented decisions for purchase, realise and run hardware and software. Those who do IT performance measurement act as a service partner interface between company performance measurement and/or company controlling and management. They bridge communications and cultural barriers between technical and economic perspectives, and they contribute towards a better understanding and an adequate culture when using IT resources (GI 2008).

Different experiences often falsify the scope of duties of IT performance measurement. Cautioned by the increaseing cost pressure, IT performance measurement often is mistaken for cost cutting in the IT arena. One reason for this is the strong penetration of business processes within IT and the increased IT cost share. A lack of transparency of this cost pool leads to an impression of a necessity of cost reduction by the IT management.

The individuals who do IT performance measurement are in danger of being degraded to a cost cutter. A performance oriented view recognises that using IT is connected with performance enhancement and efficiency improvement. It is being more and more accepted that the IT department is not a manual worker but a core element for ensuring the competitiveness of a company. IT performance measurement supports the ability to deliver IT in companies.

The IT performance measurement have to work on an operational and strategic level. Schauer enumerates as strategic tasks: fixing of the IT strategy, IT budgeting, management of the IT portfolio and performance measurement of the benefits (Schauer 2006). Kütz defines for operational task the plan/current comparison for key performance indicators, the analysis of variances and the launching of correction activities (Kütz 2007).

There are different tools available to meet the challenges of operational and strategic IT performance measurement. The usage of the balanced scorecard (Kaplan and Norton 2001), benchmarking and IT portfolio management are assigned to the strategic level. Cost accounting, process modelling and reporting are tools for the operational level. Applications of the balanced scorecard as an IT performance measurement instrument can be found e.g. in (Bernroider et al. 2003), (Martinsons et al. 1999), (Müller et al. 2002) and many other publications.

2.2 IT Performance Measurement as a Part of IT Governance

The *IT Governance Institute* is a non profit organisation that is developing international IT standards for the planning and control of internal information systems. They define *IT governance* as a main target to foster understanding of the strategic relevance of IT in optimiing the company's targets and strategies for future enhancement of business operations (IT Governance Institute 2008). Weill and Ross (2004) defines IT governance as "the decision rights and accountability framework for encouraging desirable behaviours in the use of IT". Meyer and his co-authors give an overview on IT governance in (Meyer et al. 2003). Van Grembergen and his co-authors (2004) consider IT governance more inside of the context of temporary orientation and business process orientation. According to their definition IT governance is more than IT management, which has a strong internal orientation to the entity. IT governance is more externally oriented and more strongly adjusted to the future but not as intense as a long term IT strategy.

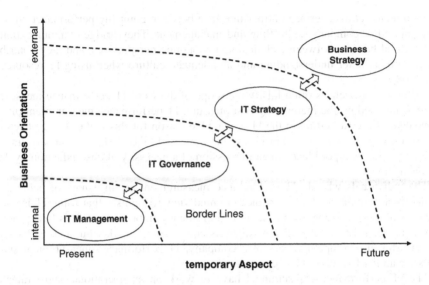

Fig. 3. Classification of IT management and IT governance, according to (van Grembergen et al. 2004)

The authors of this paper agree with CobiT (CobiT 2008) that IT governance is the management function of the IT department following the pretend framework. The target of IT governance is to align all activities of the IT department continuously to the company's targets and business processes (IT business alignment). IT governance has to follow the following restrictions: Sustainable and gentle usage of IT resources (resource management), minimizing IT risks (IT risk management) and following law, rules and IT standards (IT compliance). We consider IT performance measurement as both: as a part of IT management and as a part of IT governance.

3   Reference Model for IT Performance Measurement

In this chapter we first take a short look at known reference models. Then we present our new reference model for small and medium enterprises (SME).

3.1   Reference Models for IT-Performance Measurement

According our declarations in the chapter above, IT performance measurement supports IT management and the IT governance. Following this we divide these into known reference models for the IT management process and the IT governance process.

There are some standard reference models for IT governance. One of the most important standard models is CobiT (Control Objectives for Information and related Technologies) from the IT Governance Institute (ITGI). The ITGI emphasises that CobiT is a tool for the strategic reengineering process which is compatible with other standard process models.

CobiT keeps their main focus on the IT life cycle viewed by the process owner of the relevant IT processes. CobiT divides into control area, planning and organisation, procurement and implementation, running and operations and supervising of 34 IT processes. For every one of the 34 main processes, CobiT formulates specific control targets to ensure the support of the business processes. The central criteria are efficiency of quality, integrity, trust and availability of safety. The level of fulfilling the criteria is measured on a scale within 0, which means *not existing* and 5, which means *optimised* (Cobit 2008 and IT Governance Institute 2008).

Likewise, there are a lot of reference models for IT management processes. We only mention some examples. For IT service management ITIL is well known in practice as a commonly accepted best practice model. For maturity level in software engineering we recommend CMMI and for implementing and running of IT management systems, we mention the Standard Security Framework ISO 17799 (now ISO 27001). CobiT integrates ITIL and ISO 9000 for quality management, CMMI and ISO 17799 by compatibility of CobiT with these models.

3.2 IT Process Model for SME

Small and medium enterprises (SME) are characterized by simple structures, high flexibility and a high sensitivity in costs. The consequences are at a lower significance in IT management and very tall processes compared to bigger companies. A standard process model like CobiT with 34 main chapters is too complex for use in SME's.

Hence we present an IT process model for SME's first which is oriented as a life circle for IT investments. When we take a look at the processes planning, development and running of IT applications, we see the following sub processes as depicted in fig. 4.

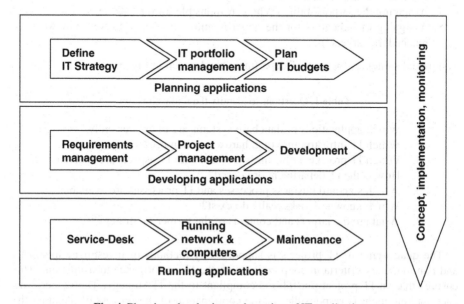

Fig. 4. Planning, developing and running of IT applications

The process of *developing applications* starts with the investigation of the requirements which have to be transformed into existing or new IT applications. The project manager ensures the smooth execution of the projects using dedicated methods for project management. The development of software or customization of standard software is supported by the IT department.

After the roll out of the software packages, the process *running applications* is following. First there are activities to build up the IT infrastructure e.g. data centre, network, desk top computers. Following this is the maintenance of applications. Requests of end users are supported by the service desk. All tasks are run through the phases of the life cycle concept, implementing and monitoring, where the IT performance management has to be involved. There is no clear dividing line between the strategic and operational IT performance measurement. Inside the process *planning applications,* a comprehensive IT strategy has to be designed. The IT strategy should cover the implementation and monitoring of IT oriented projects to reach the companies targets.

The main content of an IT strategy comprises:

1. Transparency of the starting point (Where are we now? See possible questions in table 1)
2. Defining the future situation (Where do we want to be?)
3. Describing the strategic gap (What do we have to do? Where are the weaknesses?)
4. Identifying of alternatives for actions? (Which choices do we have?)
5. Adjustment with business departments? (IT business alignment- Does everybody agree to our strategy?)
6. Setting of targets and defining of tasks (What has to be done concretely? Until when do we have to reach our targets?)
7. Arranging the responsibility (Who is responsible for the tasks?)
8. Assigning of indicators for the target monitoring (When do we know we have reached the targets?)

The partial strategies for each IT department can be seen in Fig. 5.

Table 1. Questions to identify the initial situation

1. Which applications or data base systems are in use currently?
2. Which IT infrastructure (e.g. hardware) is in use?
3. Which IT projects or business projects with IT aspects are enabled?
4. How is the IT department organised?
5. Which standard business processes and IT processes are available?
6. Which known IT risks really do exist?
7. What are the targets and contents of the former IT strategy?

The quantifying of IT projects is supported by methods of investment appraisals and non monetary criteria in cooperation with the IT performance measurement. This ensures that an IT project portfolio is compliant to the IT strategy. The IT performance measurement is responsible for the coordination of the process of planning the IT budgets.

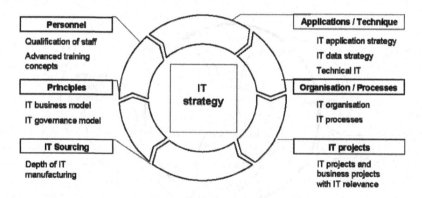

Fig. 5. Partial IT strategies

3.3 Life Cycle Model for SME

A life cycle model is necessary for planning, implementing, analysing and maintenance of IT services, IT processes, IT application systems and IT projects (Kütz
2007). We present a three step based life cycle model with networked elements for IT
performance measurement (compare fig. 6). The model is not derived from CobiT.

3.3.1 Cycle 1: Creating and Matching an IT Strategy

The first cycle ensures the creating and matching of the IT strategy with the business
strategy of a company. This step of matching is called IT business alignment. It assures that the results of the IT planning process (IT portfolio planning) only follows
targets which have a counterpart in the business strategy. The method of IT balanced
scorecard controls the compliance of key performance indicators and target values for
success control. The result of the first cycle is a package of arrangements having tasks
which are necessary for supporting the company's strategy.

3.3.2 Cycle 2: Selection, Development and Roll Out of IT Applications

After the constitution of the IT strategy and the IT portfolio, several IT projects can
be defined and started. Topic of this cycle is the business oriented problem analysis
and conceptual design, software development and the provision, testing and optimisation of information systems.

The challenge of IT performance measurement in this cycle is to support this process
with suitable tools. IT project controlling supports the compliance of time schedules, results and budgets. The IT investment appraisal ensures the profitability analysis. Outsourcing, offshoring or nearshoring concepts allow the transfer of software development
into more cost efficient countries. To minimize risks, IT performance measurement has
to be involved in these processes. IT standards (e.g. life cycle models for project management, templates for projects) help to limit the costs of IT development. IT performance measurement supports the IT project manager by enforcement of standards aimed
at increasing the welfare of the whole company.

The results of the second cycle are ready for running IT applications which are
compliant with the company's IT strategy. They can be practised and incorporated for
the daily use.

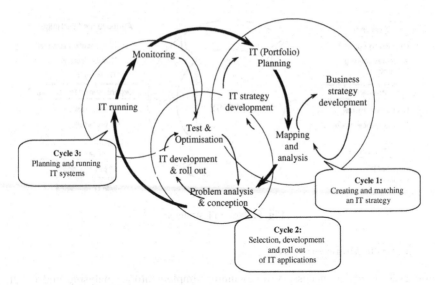

Fig. 6. Life cycle model for IT performance measurement

3.3.3 Cycle 3: Planning and Running IT Systems

The last cycle provides the IT infrastructure (e.g. hardware, network, ITstaff). Service level agreements help to ensure the compliance of contracts between the IT service partner (e.g. a data centre) and the IT customer (e.g. the end user). IT standards help to harmonise the IT service processes and to reduce the costs of IT ownership. Outsourcing concepts help to transfer the responsibility of IT delivery process onto the third party supplier. As a part of the monitoring, an analysis of targets and results is necessary. In case of noticeable variances, a change of the IT portfolio is necessary or a modification of the IT strategy.

4   Case Study

Here, we want to give a real world validation of our reference model for IT performance measurement. We describe the structure and the state of a case study, even if final results are not available yet.

4.1 The Company

Some people would be surprised if we take a look at the logistics company DHL for validating our SME reference model for IT performance measurement. But we will show that DHL is suitable for the validation.

DHL Express Europe operates in Europe within 31 countries generating revenue of 6.5b Euro in 2008. Half of the revenue is being generated by 7 large country-wide organisations with more than 500m Euro annual revenue, while the majority of the companies are medium and small and placed in small countries generating the other 50%. The business model used is more or less the same in each country organisation since DHL Express Europe is providing domestic and international shipping services through a harmonised product portfolio across Europe.

The IT cost as percentage of revenue in high revenue countries typically is lower than in small and medium sized countries. However, the IT complexity in high revenue countries is often higher due to a lower level of standardization driven through local system enhancements and unique customer requirements, and a higher volume of locally initiated projects. Smaller sized countries usually have a different IT profile since they are benefiting from a higher level of standardization supporting the business processes and a lower amount of local IT projects.

Central IT measures were in the past, often focussed on high revenue countries because their impact on the organisation is higher. These IT measures support transparency, planning of application roadmaps as well as infrastructure optimization strategies. However, these IT measures are too heavy to be implemented for smaller country organisations because the overhead with the implementation is in some case not affordable.

The IT Management of DHL Express Europe intends having IT measures in place both for larger and smaller countries. However, it appears that for smaller countries, a different approach has to be taken. Therefore, the IT management of DHL Express Europe seeks measures for smaller countries with its own set of IT measures and tools as well.

The IT organization and costs in smaller sized countries are comparable to the IT organization and costs in medium sized companies. The intent of this case study is to identify if the described approache for SME organizations can be applied in the context of smaller and medium sized organizations at DHL Express Europe and for supporting them in achieving their overall goals.

4.2 Questions of the Management

The IT management of DHL has raised the following questions:

1. Is the concept applicable in the context of smaller sized countries of DHL Express Europe?
2. Does the concept support achieving underlying business and IT goals (i.e. adapting the IT context in a challenging business context?)
3. Can the lifecycle drive efficiency within the IT organisation?
4. Does the concept support the IT management in their decision making process, locally as well as in the centre?
5. Does the concept increase the level of transparency?
6. Which are the possible implications for the business management?
7. Does the concept provide necessary information for IT management?
8. Which tools are necessary for the initial implementation of the cycles?

The case study has been established at the beginning of 2009 and final results are not available yet. However, the first intermediate results can be shared here:

- The transparency of the status of the local organization has been increased
- Tools are absolutely necessary to gain the full benefits and improve the ease of use
- Lack of common understanding for which detailed data was needed
- The process needs to be detailed in order to be spread across the organization

The study is still ongoing and will provide an insight into the questions raised above.

5 Summary and Outlook

Small and medium enterprises (SMEs) are characterised by simple structures, high flexibility and a high sensitivity in cost management. This is the reason why IT processes in SME are *lanker sized* than in bigger companies. We have presented a reference model for the processes of the whole IT area. Based on this, we presented a reference model for the whole IT process life cycle of IT performance measurement which is suitable for SME because of its lankiness.

References

Becker, J., Winkelmann, A.: IV-Performance measurement. Wirtschaftsinformatik 46(3), 213–221 (2004)

Bernroider, E.W.N., Hampel, A., Sumper, A.F.: An Application of the Balanced Scorecard as a Strategic IT-Performance measurement Instrument for E-Business Development. In: The Third International Conference on Electronic Business - Business Paradigms: Strategic Transformation and Partnership. Academic Publishers/World Publishing Corporation (2003)

Carr, N.G.: IT Doesn't Matter. Business Review (5), 41–49 (2003)

Carr, N.G.: Does IT Matter? Information Technology and the Corrosion of Competitive Advantage. Harvard Business School Publishing Corporation, Boston (2004)

CobiT. CobiT 4.1 Excerpt, IT Governance Institute (2008),
http://www.isaca.org/AMTemplate.cfm?Section=Downloads&Template=/ContentManagement/ContentDisplay.cfm&ContentID=34172
(accessed May 21, 2008)

Gadatsch, A.: Grundkurs Geschäftsprozess-Management, 5th edn. Vieweg, Wiesbaden (2008)

GI. Leitbild IT-Controller/IT-Controllerin. Fachgruppe IT-Performance measurement der Gesellschaft für Informatik (2008) (in preparation)

van Grembergen, W., de Habs, S., Guldentops, E.: Structures, Processes and Relational Mechanisms for IT Governance. In: van Grembergen, W. (ed.) Strategies for Information Technology Governance, pp. 1–36. Idea Group, London (2004)

Hammer, M., Chamby, J.: Business Reengineering. Die Radikalkur für das Unternehmen, 3rd edn. Campus, Frankfurt/New York (1994)

IT Governace Institute (2008), http://www.itgi.com (accessed May 21, 2008)

Kaplan, R.S., Norton, P.N.: Strategy Maps: Converting Intangible Assets into Tangible Outcomes. Harvard Business School Publishing Corporation, Boston (2001)

Kütz, M.: IT-Controlling für die Praxis. dpunkt, Heidelberg (2005)

Kütz, M.: Grundelemente des IT-Controllings. Praxis der Wirtschaftsinformatik, HMD 254, 6–15 (2007)

Martinsons, M., Davison, R., Tse, D.: The balanced scorecard: a foundation for the strategic management of information systems. Decision Support Systems 25(1), 71–88 (1999)

Müller, A., Thienen, L.v.: E-Business-Controlling mit der Balanced Scorecard. In: Blomer, R., Bernhard, M. (eds.) Balanced Scorecard in der IT, Praxisbeispiele - Methoden - Umsetzung, Symposion Publishing GmbH, Düsseldorf, pp. 183–209 (2002)

Meyer, M., Zarnekow, R., Kolbe, L.M.: IT-Governance Begriff, Status quo und Bedeutung. Wirtschaftsinformatik 45(4), 445–448 (2003)

Riedl, R., Kobler, M., Roithmayr, F.: Zur personellen Verankerung der IT-Funktion im Vorstand börsennotierter Unternehmen: Ergebnisse einer inhaltsanalytischen Betrachtung. Wirtschaftsinformatik 50(2), 111–128 (2008)

Schauer, H.: Vergleichende Buchbesprechung IT-Controlling. Wirtschafsinformatik 48(3), 212–218 (2006)

Weill, P., Ross, J.W.: IT Governance on One Page, Center for Information Systems Research Working Paper No. 349. MIT Sloan School of Management (2004)

Zarnekow, R., Brenner, W., Pilgram, U.: Integrated Information Management: Applying Successful Industrial Concepts in IT, pp. 39–60. Springer, Heidelberg (2006)

Knowledge Management in Small Firms

Jessada Panyasorn, Niki Panteli, and Philip Powell

University of Bath, UK

Abstract. This paper explores knowledge management in small and medium-sized firms (SMEs). It investigates the use of Lotus Notes in SMEs of a developing country as a counterpoint to the large firm, developed country emphasis of existing research. It develops taxonomy of Lotus Notes use within the context of different knowledge management processes; notably communicating, co-ordinating and collaborating. The study employs an interpretive approach using three case studies. The key findings suggest that publishing, searching, sharing and retrieving are the user modes for enabling sharing and storing information. Evidence of knowledge creation is found at the departmental level but not at the organizational level. Further, small firms may explore more groupware potential than large organizations and this reflects their different context. Finally, implications for further research are identified.

1 Introduction

Complex, competitive and dynamic business environments necessitate adaptive, flexible and responsive organizations. Accordingly, organizations are often compelled to invest in information technologies (IT) that enable access to a wider pool of resources and, in particular, knowledge sharing. A variety of information technologies have been designed and implemented to facilitate the management of knowledge including groupware (Arumn et al, 2008; Bellanger and Allport, 2008; Ciborra, 1996; Hayes, 2001) that supports communication, collaboration and co-ordination (Orlikowski, 1996). This paper investigates the use of Lotus Notes, a well-known groupware application. It advances the debate on the potential of groupware in knowledge management. It posits that although Lotus Notes is the focus of existing research, a paucity of studies exists about its use in relation to knowledge management in the context of small and medium-sized enterprises (SMEs) and none in developing countries.

The paper is structured as follows: first it reviews existing studies on Lotus Notes and identifies its uses for knowledge sharing. Then a framework of Lotus Notes use modes is developed which is examined within the context of specific organizations in Thailand.

2 Theoretical Foundations

The use of Lotus Notes for knowledge management activities has been studied in a variety of organizations. Lotus Notes, a combination of document creator and indexer,

G. Dhillon, B.C. Stahl, and R. Baskerville (Eds.): CreativeSME 2009, IFIP AICT 301, pp. 192–210, 2009.
© IFIP International Federation for Information Processing 2009

database generator and manager, and messaging platform (Vandenbosch and Ginzberg, 1996), allows information to be distributed between different users in a structured or semi-structured way (Brown, 2000). Drawing upon the existing literature, this section presents the main functions of Lotus Notes in knowledge management. Nine major case studies discussing the use of Lotus Notes and its potential to knowledge management are reviewed. The selection of these cases is based on the rich descriptions of how Lotus Notes is implemented and used for facilitating information and knowledge management. Table 1 provides a synopsis of these studies taking account of the research site, the functions of Lotus Notes used, methods for collecting data and length of the study.

Seven cases are studied in large organizations, whereas the other two cases (Robertson et al., 2001; Karsten and Jones, 1998) are SMEs. The sectors are diversified, however, the main sector is consulting (Robertson et al., 2001; Orlikowski, 1993; Karsten and Jones, 1998). In terms of research approach, these studies employ in-depth cases in which interviews are the main method of data collection. The main identified benefit of using Lotus Notes is that shared information and knowledge on Lotus Notes can be accessed and retrieved by users regardless of time and location. Most studies find that factors embedded in the organizational context have a major influence on the successful use of Lotus Notes: collaborative culture (Orlikowski, 1993), incentive structure (Robertson et al., 2001; Orlikowski, 1993), homogeneous group (Hayes, 2001), management style (Karsten and Jones, 1998) and organizational dispersion (Ciborra and Suetens, 1996).

First, Lotus Notes is used to publish information. Published information is disseminated in different forms and for different purposes. For example, an interactive newsletter was published to disseminate news within an international department of the French energy provider *EDF* (Ciborra and Suetens, 1996). Technical documents were published and disseminated outside the customer support department of *Zeta* (Orlikowski, 1996). Meeting minutes were published to inform those not present in *CCC* (Karsten and Jones, 1998).

The second use mode of Lotus Notes is searching. Lotus Notes comprises capabilities such as full-text search and document indexer for searching or acquiring information. In *Universal consulting* (Robertson et al., 2001), project leaders used the indexing and search facilities of Lotus Notes to acquire specific information found in email and discussion databases. In *Zeta* (Orlikowski, 1996), the provision of a powerful search capability within the Incident Tracking Support System (ITSS), an application on Lotus Notes, allowed specialists to search their database quickly and easily for well-documented incident histories. Searching ITSS provided potentially reusable problem resolutions as well as knowledge about problem-solving processes. Similarly, expertise in *Alpha* (Orlikowski, 1993) used Lotus Notes for organizational database browsing. Using Lotus Notes for searching information is also found in *EDF* (Ciborra and Suetens, 1996). Managers at *EDF* could search for others' experience of foreign cultures before they left for missions abroad.

The third use mode of Lotus Notes is retrieving. This mode focuses on using Lotus Notes to record and maintain a computer-based 'organizational memory' such as best practices, business process and frequently asked questions. For example, in *Compound UK* (Hayes, 2001), contact recording database enabled employees to record the views, interests and requirements of particular doctors that could be retrieved for future use.

Table 1. Summary of the previous studies of Lotus Notes use

Study	Site and size	Lotus Notes functions	Method	Length
Robertson, Sorensen and Swan (2001)	Universal consulting: Medium	Email Discussion databases	Interviews Non-participant observation Documentation	Over 2 years (1996-Spring 1998)
Vandenbosch and Ginzberg (1996)	American insurance firm: Large	Lotus Notes databases	Interviews Surveys	Ten months (began after decision to expand use of Lotus Notes from 200 users to whole firm)
Orlikowski (1993)	Alpha: Large consulting firm: competitive culture	Electronic mail, discussion database, some databases for browsing	Unstructured interviews Documentation Participant observation	Five months (began prior to Lotus Notes installation)
Hayes (2001)	Compound UK: Large multinational pharmaceutical	Email Strategic selling databases Discussion databases Contact recording databases	Semi-structured interviews Informal discussions and interactions	Two-and-a-half year period (18 months after first Lotus Notes implementation)
Brown (2000)	Narajo: Large oil firm	Public forum databases: firm notice board and 'challenge' database Workflow database Tracking database	Participant observation Interviews	3 months (began after Lotus Notes implementation)
Ciborra and Suetens (1996)	EDF: Large, an international distribution part of a French energy provider	Email Discussion forum and databases such as world culture, news forum, expert databases.	Interviews	Over a year and a half (began after Lotus Notes was implemented)

Table 1. (*continued*)

Ciborra (1996)	Roche: Large Diagnostic division of multinational pharmaceutical	Cosis applications: multidisciplinary knowledge base	Interviews	Over 2 years (began after Lotus Notes was implemented)
Orlikowski (1996)	Zeta: Large software firm	Incident Tracking Support System Training database six firm-wide bulletin boards with electronic mail	Unstructured and semi-structured interviews. Non-participant observation Documentation	6 months (began two years after the ITSS developed on Lotus Notes.)
Karsten and Jones (1998)	CCC: Small computer consulting firm	Discussion and news databases, project databases	Participant observation Interviews Documentation	3 years (began prior to Lotus Notes implementation)

A training database in *Zeta* (Orlikowski, 1996) maintained sample problems extracted from the ITSS database which new hires worked with to try and resolve problems. Quality project documentation, which is a valuable by-product of using Lotus Notes for discussion on project work across countries, is maintained on the Lotus Notes databases of *Universal Consulting* (Robertson et al., 2001).

The fourth use mode is sharing. With this mode, individuals and groups in the organization use Lotus Notes to discuss and share ideas, experience, information and knowledge with each other. This use mode exists in all the cases, as Lotus Notes provides several mechanisms including email, discussion databases and public fora. In *American Insurance Company* (Vandenbosch and Ginzberg, 1996), geographically dispersed people participated in discussions about process change aimed at standardising the company's key activities across its regional divisions. Similarly, a strategic selling database was created in *Compound UK* (Hayes, 2001) to enable employees in different functions to input views and information in a structured way with the aim of bringing together their shared knowledge to facilitate a successful sale.

The final use mode of Lotus Notes is creating. This mode uses Lotus Notes to understand and create individuals' and groups' tacit knowledge. This mode is different from the other modes in that individuals' tacit knowledge is made explicit on Lotus Notes shared database. Others can use the shared knowledge database, as the tacit knowledge within groups allows them to understand the subtleties that underlie the meaning expressed on the shared database (Hayes, 2001). Hence, tacit knowledge is created in individuals' mind. However, the creating mode of Lotus Notes is likely to depend on the organizational context. For instance, within the same functions in *Compound UK*, employees could draw on their shared tacit knowledge to interpret skilfully and make judgements concerning the views recorded on the shared databases by members of their own functions (Hayes, 2001). On the other hand, the attempt to create a common knowledge pool for the global organization of *EDF* was not satisfied due to their misalignment to the virtual organization context with a highly dispersed structure and based on the strong competence and autonomy of agents and experts. As a result, it is difficult to reconcile the style of working and knowing with prescriptions to share information (Ciborra and Suetens, 1996).

In summary, Lotus Notes has been developed and used in different ways for supporting knowledge management activities. Table 2 synthesises these different use modes.

Table 2. Summary of use modes of Lotus Notes

Use Mode	Use Description	Source
Publishing	publishing information (e.g. newsletter, technical documents, product catalogues, employee directories).	Orlikowski (1996), Ciborra and Suetens (1996), Karsten and Jones (1998)
Searching	searching for or acquiring organization information (e.g. full text search capabilities, document indexer).	Robertson et al. (2001), Orlikowski (1993, 1996), Ciborra and Suetens (1996)
Retrieving	recording and retrieving a computer-based 'organizational memory' (e.g. best practices, business process, frequently asked questions).	Robertson et al. (2001), Vandenbosch and Ginzberg (1996), Orlikowski (1993, 1996), Hayes (2001), Brown (2000), Ciborra and Suetens (1996), Ciborra (1996), Karsten and Jones (1998)
Sharing	discussing and sharing ideas, experience, information and knowledge with other individuals and groups in the organization (e.g. via Email, discussion databases, public fora).	Robertson et al. (2001), Vandenbosch and Ginzberg (1996), Orlikowski (1993), Hayes (2001), Brown (2000), Ciborra and Suetens (1996), Ciborra (1996), Karsten and Jones (1998)
Creating	understanding and creating individuals' and groups' tacit knowledge (e.g. shared databases within homogeneous group).	Hayes (2001)

3 Interaction Richness Model of Use Modes

This section develops the interaction richness model that taxonomises the use modes of Lotus Notes on two dimensions. The first dimension entails the types of interaction that may take place in a Lotus Notes environment, which may either be human-Notes interactions or human-human Notes-mediated interactions. The second dimension involves the types of knowledge management processes experienced in a Lotus Notes environment: coordination, communication and collaboration.

Coordination is regarded as the direction of individuals' efforts toward achieving common and explicitly recognised goals (Blau and Scott, 1963). The use modes that fall into the coordination category are 'searching' and 'publishing'. Searching leads to human-Notes interactive coordination process as people search for information and knowledge on databases in order to complete their individual tasks such as answering customers' enquiries. Publishing is concerned with human-human mediated interactive coordination since human uses Lotus Notes as an information sending channel to receivers, contributing to the exchange of knowledge.

The communication process emphasises the exchange of information between dispersed individuals and it mainly includes increasing connectivity, bandwidth and protocols for the exchange of many types of information such as text, graphics and voice (Ellis et al., 1991). 'Retrieving' and 'sharing' use modes can be put into this category. As the 'retrieving' use mode focuses on records of information and knowledge retrieved by users, databases act as agents that communicate the maintained information to individual receivers. Therefore, retrieving is regarded as the use mode stimulating human-Notes interactive communication process. On the other hand, the sharing mode emphasises the exchange of knowledge between individuals who are both senders and receivers, thus it is an exemplar of human-human mediated interactive communication process.

Finally, collaboration is a process of shared creation: two or more individuals with complementary skills interacting to create a shared understanding (Schrage, 1990). Thus, the fifth use mode of Lotus Notes, 'creating', belongs to the human-human mediated interactive collaboration process as it refers to understanding the shared knowledge database by drawing on individuals' shared tacit knowledge. From the existing literature, it is not possible to identify a use mode that belongs to the human-Notes interactive collaboration process. However, due to the interpretive flexibility embedded in information technology (Orlikowski, 1992) it is argued here that users

	Coordination	Communication	Collaboration
Human-Human mediated interaction	Publishing	Sharing	Creating
Human-Notes interaction	Searching	Retrieving	Exploring

Fig. 1. Interaction richness model of Lotus Notes use modes

will, over time, learn to explore further the potentials of Lotus Notes contributing to a collaboration between humans and technology where each benefits from the other. Thus, this study adds another use mode, 'exploring', wherein humans can consult and collaborate with Lotus Notes to enrich their knowledge.

4   Knowledge Management in SMEs

This study investigates how these use modes facilitate knowledge management in SMEs and whether and how the use modes relate to one another over time. Further, most studies on Lotus Notes focus on large organizations whereas the use of Lotus Notes in SMEs is neglected. This study, therefore, takes a step towards filling this void by focusing on the use of Lotus Notes as a knowledge management tool in the context of SMEs.

As with other aspects of business and management, the issue of knowledge management in SMEs may not be simply a scaled-down replica of large firm experiences (Sparrow, 2000). Some characteristics of SMEs lead to unique challenges in knowledge management. Within the constraints and opportunities afforded by their internal and external environment, SMEs need to develop knowledge management practices that address the knowledge needs of employees and organizational learning (Sparrow et al., 2000).

In addition, all the previous studies on Lotus Notes were carried out in developed countries. No study has examined the use of Lotus Notes or groupware in general within a developing country. As argued by Sahay and Avgerou (2002), the study of information systems in developing countries is important as it provides rich and meaningful problem domains resulting from the diversity in contexts, situations, work cultures and interests groups.

SMEs in developing countries need to respond effectively to customers' demands and keep up with the rapid changes occurring in the domestic and global markets in order to survive and compete with regional competitors (Abdullah, 2002; Brimble et al., 2002). This drives SMEs to manage their knowledge in order to improve their products and processes, provide customers with added value innovation and learning capabilities (Corso et al., 2001). As proposed by Sparrow (1999), SMEs with more advanced information systems such as Lotus Notes may be more committed to the principles of knowledge management and more willing to address knowledge management issues. As Lotus Notes enables employees to communicate, coordinate and collaborate within and across organizations, it may also provide opportunities to SMEs to manage their knowledge more effectively.

This research now investigates how Lotus Notes is used in supporting knowledge management activity within the context of a small firm in a developing country.

5   Research Method

The interpretive epistemological approach is dominant in the nine studies (Table 1). The need for detailed understandings of human actions and meanings within specific contexts is emphasised while an in-depth case study approach is adopted in all.

Accordingly, this study follows the interpretive approach (Walsham, 1993) as its focus lies on the subjective meanings that human actors ascribe to Lotus Notes technology in a specific context of SMEs located in a developing country.

The case method is the most appropriate approach here as it is a well-accepted approach to study the complex phenomena of technology implementation in an organizational setting (Alavi and Carlson, 1992). The specific research site and data collection methods adopted are discussed next.

6 Research Site and Data Collection

As the main aim is to explore the use of Lotus Notes in SMEs in a developing country, Thailand is chosen as the research site. Thai SMEs are defined by the Ministry of Thai Industry (www.industry.go.th) as firms with less than 200 employees and with fixed assets of less than 200 million Thai Baht (€3.8m).

For the purpose of this study, three cases are selected; they are all IT consultancy firms, described as knowledge-intensive because they employ highly qualified technologists and rely heavily on the integration and synthesis of their specialist knowledge to create novel products and processes in response to clients' problems (Robertson et al., 2001).

The data collection took place within the companies: ComNotes, Procom and Comtech (pseudonyms) and a variety of qualitative data collection methods were used: interviews, review of firm industry and project documentation, and non-participant observation. The fieldwork took seven months. In total, the study involved semi-structured interviews with 33 key people across different organizational layers, including the CEO, sales & marketing director, sales assistant manager, system administration supervisor, technical development supervisor, customer services manager and customer services supervisor from the three companies. Each interview lasted 45-60 minutes. Most of the interviews were recorded, transcribed and then translated into English. Manuals of Lotus Notes applications and marketing promotion materials such as brochures and posters were collected. Further, informal conversations and discussions with the interviewees and other staff members in the company were conducted during each visit in ComNotes. Observations of how members use Notes were made so as to provide further insights into the functions of Lotus Notes applications.

7 Company Background

7.1 ComNotes

ComNotes's aim is to assist the customers to improve their productivity, efficiency and organizational effectiveness through the use of productivity-driven applications e.g. Customer Relationship Management (CRM), Human Resources Management (HRM), call centre, e-procurement, and document management.

ComNotes structure involves three departments, including sales & marketing department, technical support department, and customer services department. The sales & marketing department is responsible for understanding customers' requirements and retrieving customers' satisfaction. The technical support department integrates two responsibilities - system administration and development. The role of system administration is to implement the system and settings for its customer at the first instance, while development is involved with application design and maintenance. The customer services department is responsible for after-sales services and receiving calls from customers.

7.2 Procom

Procom provides hardware, software and integration services for manufacturing, finance and securities trading, and education. Procom supports a wide range of software products to help customers implement IT infrastructure. It offers solutions such as Lotus Notes for communication and document management; Cognos for business intelligence solutions; and LANSA for application development. Procom's hardware and software offerings are complemented by a complete range of services. Services such as installation and setup of software and hardware, network cabling, and configuration are bolstered by a complete range of educational services for advanced systems.

Procom employs forty staff members. The company is divided into two main departments, Operations and Sales & Marketing. The Operations department comprises of Systems Engineering and Technical Support, Purchasing and Administration, Presale and Support and OA products. The Sales & Marketing department includes Presale and Support, hardware and software Sales and Administration. Responsibility of the Operations department is to implement solutions for customers and support customers after implementation, whereas the Sales & Marketing department promotes products and services and acquires customer requirements.

7.3 Comtech

Comtech is a software business set up to serve comprehensive infrastructure technology solutions for online businesses. For its consulting services, Comtech develops solutions for different industries and work processes. Its main clients range from small to large enterprises, and financial institutions. Comtech employs around fifty staff members performing three main functions: Sales & Marketing, Infrastructure and Developers. Infrastructure is responsible for network and anti-virus software. The Infrastructure team is divided into four sub-teams - Operating System (OS), Network, Application, and Support and Maintenance (Support & MA). The team of OS, Network and Application focus on implementation systems for customers, whereas Support & MA tracks and supports customers after implementation. The Developers team is responsible for developing Notes applications on and for other IBM products such as web portals. The Infrastructure and Developers teams also work as a support team including both pre-sale and after-sale services. The Sales & Marketing team is responsible for promoting products and services, and obtaining customers' requirements.

Lotus Notes has been implemented in all three cases. In general, users are authorised to access and shared the same resources in most of the databases. However, some applications were designed to meet the needs of different departments.

8 Findings

8.1 Uses of Lotus Notes

This section focuses on the concept of the six use modes identified in the interaction richness model and the case material in order to investigate how the use modes facilitate knowledge management in SMEs and how the use modes relate to one another over time. In particular, what follows explores the role of Lotus Notes applications used in the three case studies for coordination, communication and collaboration.

8.2 Coordination

Coordination appears to be the main knowledge management process in the three cases. With the email feature of Notes, all employees can add a document link to any database. With regards to the interaction richness model, this may be considered as publishing use mode as the senders would like someone to be informed or to be instructed to do something. As the director of ComNotes explained:

"...people live with their email...Lotus Notes is very good in that you can automatically generate documents that get emails to people and within those documents there are the links [that would enable them to access additional information]".

"...[for example] this email. It's an order required approval on 9th January. There is a doc link on that. I click on that and it opens up the e-procurement system. So, I can see all the information about this sale....That's everything I need to know so I'm happy with that. So, I click on approval. I can even enter any comments and now notification has been sent to the accounts department for them to issue the purchase order".

"There are few people who post knowledge to this database. So we should have read it. It has sometimes been sent to me by mail. When people post it to databases, there will be a message alert. We check emails everyday, so we should have come across this knowledge." (Software consultant, Procom)

In addition, the information on the customer contact database was made available to everyone in Comtech in order to contact customers:

"I mainly use Notes for customer databases. I always lose name cards of people so I post them on knowledge management database...It facilitates searching. When there are many people to be contacted, it is a single point for everyone to see. It helps everyone to find contact details of the customers." (Sale staff)

Searching is another use mode of the coordination process. Users can acquire important documents maintained in Notes by using the search function enabling access to a wide range of information posted by different people. The sales director explained:

"What we correspond everyday is a kind of knowledge. Knowledge is embedded in emails. It is being kept systematically. If we want to refer to what we have mentioned, we search for that email. This is a kind of searching for knowledge".

Moreover, the search facility is used for locating expertise:

"We have a human resource application to keep employee's profile and history. Lotus Notes is very good at searching. We use this function. For example, I want to search for a person good at technical skills and tennis. I can search on this application rather than looking it up from paper documents by myself. This is expertise location. It's also a type of knowledge management. So, we can put the right man on the right job in our company"

Similarly, members of Comtech also used an application to search for customers' contact details. Therefore, individuals used Notes to search for, and co-ordinate themselves with the right people they need to contact:

"...There is a record of customer list; company A,B,C... In company A,B,C record, it preserves the contacted person's name...What is his responsibility? Is he a decision maker or an IT manager? It's a database of our customers..." (sales staff)

It was noted that even if everyone knows each other due to the small size of the company, the dynamic and knowledge intensive nature of business, drives the company's need for such a tool. This is because different projects require different skills of people and it needs a record of profiles to refer to. Therefore, this facility is as important for small firms as it is for large ones.

In Procom, Notes was used as a search tool for solutions which were kept on the databases, i.e. to find out if the same problems had been faced before:

"...if the customers asked for problems that we experienced. For example, the server is down...the support people will open the database called knowledge management database...look up the software, hardware index which have been maintained. They will look up for the keyword..." (Software consultant manager)

9 Communication

Lotus Notes was utilised as the main mechanism for communication in ComNotes. As the system was widely employed throughout the company, it was particularly noted that: *"It is very convenient for human to human communication"* (technical development supervisor).

The 'sharing' use mode of communication process takes place when human uses Lotus Notes applications to correspond to each other and this was evident in the case studies. Discussion databases are used to share knowledge within the technical support department of ComNotes:

"When we receive calls from customers, we will keep it in call log (an application of Lotus Notes). It will identify different problems of the customers...I can choose whom I want to send the complaints to. When they receive my email, they will make comments and ...I can [then] send it to the customers for approval". (Customer services manager, ComNotes)

Similarly, in Procom, new information or solutions were shared on databases when the users could not find existing solutions to problems when searching:

"If they don't find the keyword, they will put a new topic. But they will ask others for solutions. If it is solved, the solution will be maintained. If not, the solution will be kept pending and asked for from the others later... If the solution has been kept, they can use it because mostly they will keep the solutions..." (Software consultant manager. Procom)

In Comtech, the information posted onto the KM database may have been found from external resources such as the Internet, which the person who found it deemed appropriate to share with others. As a result, several people can retrieve and use such information and knowledge:

"The documentation is useful for the next customers because when we get requirements from customers, there will be many systems. However, most systems are similar. We can see from the knowledge management database whether there has been a similar application so that we can modify it for another customer. Some codes can be applied to new applications." (Developer, Comtech)

However, the sharing mode is often bound within one department as the information may not be related to other departments and access to some databases is limited to the relevant department.

Further, the 'retrieving' use mode implies the use of Lotus Notes applications to retrieve information and knowledge from databases. Retrieving refers to the use mode that Notes is used to acquire a computer-based 'organizational memory' such as best practices, business processes and frequently asked questions where users can retrieve them. The Customer Services supervisor of ComNotes explained that:

"I keep my presentation file in the discussion database. Anyone can access it... and use at his disposal".

In Procom, the Notes databases were used as a shared space since they were used to maintain different information in different departments. This information was useful for colleagues to follow up work in progress, and to learn from others' experience:

"...if someone went to meet customers, it will appear in the service record. He will type in whether the problems have been solved or whether they continue. For

example, there is sales tracking in Marketing. This is to show who are our prospective customers. We can follow if the sale is successful or the potential to close the sale... We keep it, for the new salespersons to follow rather than start learning again" (Software consultant manager)

Furthermore, for the Developers team of Comtech, the KM database was used to retrieve technical knowledge such as programming codes:

"...I have found (programming) codes from somewhere, I can post on the databases in order to be used for the next time...No one can remember all the codes...we have to retrieve them from the previous codes..." (Developer)

10 Collaboration

Collaboration entails the process by which two or more individuals create a shared understanding of what has been maintained on databases. The 'creating' use mode is understood by drawing on individuals' shared tacit knowledge as was found in the case of ComNotes. Though, Lotus Notes was used for information sharing throughout ComNotes, shared understanding remained limited due to specific knowledge hold by individuals in different departments. For example, the technical support department has their own language to describe problems and solutions or technical language that can be created on Lotus Notes databases, whereas other departments used Lotus Notes to maintain information required for day-to-day operations. The customer services manager noted that:

"In the technical support department, they have their own knowledge because they have solutions which are linked to programming codes. In my department, we keep only requirements from customers. They're just information. It's required for our day-to-day work. Knowledge will be used to do that work. Knowledge is any 'how to' [For example] our knowledge would be how to write a report or how to respond to mail...We do not have online documents for this. We prefer face-to-face meetings to transfer this knowledge".

The KM database of Notes helped individual staff create their personal knowledge or skill in carrying out a task in Comtech:

"At least I know what we have to prepare. It's very useful for new-comers. When I was new, I didn't have to ask much from others. I can study from those files how to do this and that. How we should carry out ours" (Sales staff, Comtech)

However, knowledge creation was limited within this same department. Notes databases were particularly designed to support operations within the technical department:

"...Knowledge for support is more apparent because it can be shared and in the same department or across department the databases can be used to support or solve problems for customers..." (Software consultant manager, Procom)

"Everyone is allowed to read our knowledge base... However, if they're not involved in the job, they won't read it. There are thousands of records. No one will see all the department databases. So, we mainly use our own department's databases" (System administration supervisor, ComNotes).

This implies that though some knowledge is widely accessible, individuals may not make use of it.

In addition to the five use modes of Notes identified in the literature, a sixth use mode 'exploring' was identified. Exploring is the use mode of Lotus Notes that could develop further the collaboration between users and technology to the point where each benefits from the other. This means Lotus Notes may act as a consultant that helps users to achieve a common goal. There is evidence of this in ComNotes. The decision was taken to link a new communication tool, SameTime, to Notes to improve collaboration using synchronous communication across different departments and organizations in ComNotes. SameTime, an e-messaging application of IBM that enables synchronous communication another IBM product, was used to complement Lotus Notes and enable communication between company's employees in the Head office and a branch in Cambodia. Accordingly, SameTime in the case study was not merely a tool that enabled sharing of knowledge but also a tool that further explored the potentialities of Notes for efficient intra- and inter-organizational communication.

In addition, the web portal was linked to Notes databases and applications in order for travelling staff members to access their applications on Notes from other locations and retrieve the information on databases. The use of Notes, therefore, tended to be integrated with other systems that facilitated users in exploiting Notes features even if they worked remotely:

"SameTime is mostly utilised across departments. Within the department, we prefer face-to-face meetings as we are in the same place...We're sometimes at customer's site or abroad. Someone might ask us through SameTime about technical problems. So, we tell them the solutions or techniques through SameTime. We act as both inquirer and solving persons...We also keep the solutions on Notes databases". (Technical Development supervisor)

Comtech also planned to use a new system 'workplace' in the future instead of Notes. Workplace allows users to access the same application of Notes through the website:

"If we use 'workplace' application, we will access databases through website. There won't be license fees. The website could be used instead of Notes client." (Support & MA staff)

Hence, by integrating other systems in order to explore the further potential of Notes, it would provide better collaboration between users and IT for KM.

11 Discussion

This section discusses the use of Notes as a KM tool within the context of SMEs. It was found that even though the system was not implemented in the organizations studied as part of their strategy for KM, it provided facilitation for KM activities. The creation of new knowledge also occurred through accidental rather than planned combinations and exchanges, reflecting emergent patterns of accessibility to knowledge and knowledge processes (Nahapiet and Ghoshal, 1998). As explained by Grover and Davenport (2001) emergent KM processes are tied into the work processes themselves, which may not be visible to participants. In Procom where Notes was not recognized as a tool to support for KM, the findings show that, to some extent, Notes supports KM activities through human actions that the staff pursues on Notes. This is because Notes was implemented in these organizations in order to improve co-operation in their business processes, whilst the concept of intentionality (Giddens, 1984) is an influence on social action in which the staff acknowledges as possibilities that outcomes may turn out to be different from those anticipated. Similarly, Orlikowski (1996) contended that the use of Notes leads to changes that are enacted both intentionally and opportunistically and are accompanied by some unanticipated consequences. Deliberate KM processes (Grover and Davenport, 2001) occur in ComNotes and Procom since the organizations are better aware of KM initiatives than Comtech.

Having found that KM is either an emergent or deliberate outcome of Notes use, the discussions on the question as to whether knowledge is processed through Notes are in line with much literature which has argued that technology in itself lacks the capability of KM (e.g. Sherif et al., 2004; Galliers and Newell, 2003; McDermott, 1999; Walsham, 2001; Wilson, 2002). However, based on the existing literature on Notes, this study conceptualized the use modes of Notes explaining the relationship between the human interaction processes with IT and knowledge as a result of the interactions. The first four use modes of Notes, including publishing, searching, sharing and maintaining are not only used in order to manage information, they are also enablers to the creation of knowledge of organizational members and hence lead to the other two features of Notes, 'creating' and 'exploring' use modes. This is because information is important in providing a basis for action (Coleman, 1988).

Having said that knowledge is not an object which resides in such technology as Notes, this study contends that Notes supports human actions in relation to the KM activities where knowledge of individual can be exploited and knowing or know how emerges from human actions in a particular context (Sambamurthy and Subramani, 2005). The 'Creating' use mode was utilized by the staff to create their tacit knowledge in order to work for organizations. However, the attempt to utilize 'exploring' use mode was not sufficiently manifested in the case studies. This may be because the organizations studied still lack speciality in KM practice which they have to realize that "without the ability to seamlessly collect, index, store and distribute explicit knowledge electronically whenever and wherever needed, an organization will not fully exploit its capabilities and incentives" (Zack, 1999, p.55). Therefore, they might not put in much effort to explore and develop the use of Notes for KM. Next, the paper explores the SMEs context in which Notes was implemented and contrasts this to that of large organizations.

12   SMEs and Large Organizations

In comparing large and SME organizations, several factors deriving from the context of SMEs are found to influence the use of Notes for KM. First, Notes is more likely to be used as a tool to build relationship among the staff in large companies. In other words, Notes impacts the pre-existing formative context questioning the hierarchical structure and the functional division of labour (Ciborra and Patriotta, 1996). For example, the use of Notes in Compound UK (Hayes and Walsham, 2001a), Unilever (Ciborra and Patriotta, 1996), Roche (Ciborra, 1996) and Alpha (Orlikowski, 1993) facilitated work across boundaries which allowed staff an increased familiarity with individual personalities, as well as opening up a forum of discussion surrounding the assumptions and perspectives of experts from different functions (Hayes and Walsham, 2001a). In large organizations Notes may be used to bridge the gap of time and space in connecting several people together and this could lead to the obstacles in co-operation on Notes since the norms for co-operation are limited prior to the implementation of Notes. Similarly, Ciborra (1996) found that no one fully trusted the databases in a large pharmaceutical company which relates to the traditional problems that plague inter-functional, centralized databases in large, bureaucratic organizations.

Unlike large companies, this study found that, due to the close relationship in SMEs between the staff, such interpersonal relationships are likely to drive them to interact through Notes. Hence, the size of organizations in which Notes is implemented is found to have an influence on the use of Notes for KM. This may be because the smaller organizational context allows more opportunities for staff to collectively learn and foster joint understanding and expectations. As argued by Orlikowski (1993), since individuals are used to personal computing environments, shared technology use is difficult to grasp in large organizations. This could inhibit the learning on how to use Notes in large organizations which results in less co-operation on Notes than in a smaller firm context. In addition, in large organizations such as Compound UK, many employees were not confident that they could make their views on a particular issue clear on the databases, and feared offending others or writing something stupid or irrelevant to other employees (Hayes and Walsham, 2001a). In contrast, this is not an issue in the cases of SMEs here. This may be because the size of the organizations in which everyone knows each other engender a friendly environment for sharing ideas and opinions. Further, the relationships among the people in ComNotes and Comtech are likely to motivate the members to interact with each other through Notes. The organization size also helps in forming in-depth relationships between staff in different departments and functions. This happens through working together and other means such as meeting around break periods as the staff are all located in the same place.

However, not only does the size of organization enable the use of Notes for co-operation, but the use of Notes, on the other hand, is also found to enhance the co-operation among the staff in small organizations. This is because staff members are likely to be away from their office and Notes acts as a medium in their co-operation. As found by Karsten and Jones (1998), a small computer consultancy company employed Notes to increase co-operation among individual consultants which previously appeared to be decentralized, with each consultant pursuing their own approach. Similarly, staff in ComNotes, Procom and Comtech are likely to use Notes to increase participation on co-operation when they work remotely. It also enables a more centralized form of organizational structure where the top management can control their staff who are always away. Further, the findings of this study are consistent with Karsten and Jones (1998) in that Notes supports horizontal and vertical co-operation. For example, the staff can use Notes for horizontal co-operation for joint projects where different departments are needed. Notes is also used for vertical co-operation by providing a history of work that the staff can consult if a project had to be transferred to another consultant.

Notes appears to be an appropriate tool for KM in a developing country such as Thailand, since it uses email as the main mechanism in the various co-operation processes. Emails require less bandwidth per user, which is a welcome feature in developing countries where bandwidth is often limited (Wagner et al., 2003). Hence, staff members do not need to send large-size files, which contain enormous knowledge to others as they can be maintained in several forms such as pictures on the central server which is directed by emails. However, the inscriptions of Western values in technology may also negatively influence the adoption of IS in a developing country (Walsham and Sahay, 1999). This is because there is the gap between the assumptions inscribed in the technologies developed in the context of industrialized countries and the prevailing way and state of organizational life in the countries to which the technologies were being transferred (Sahay and Avgerou, 2002). Similar to the GIS technology studied by Walsham and Sahay (1999), Notes may embed the assumption of coordinated action in the developed country. For example, the workflow capability of Notes enables the user to co-ordinate with several departments throughout organizations. However, the findings of this study appeared that Notes is mostly utilized as a specific tool for each department. This may be because of the rigid functionality and uncoordinated action (Walsham and Sahay, 1999) that tend to occur in Thai organizations. Staff members do not use Notes to interact with people in other departments. Hence, the use of Notes to co-operate between different people in Thai organizations is limited.

13 Conclusions and Implications

This paper has investigated the potential of Lotus Notes as a knowledge management tool in three SMEs in Thailand. Its aim was to explore Notes use in a developing country SME as a counterpoint to the large firm, developed country emphasis of existing research. It has developed a taxonomy of Lotus Notes use within the context of different knowledge management processes using the cases of three IT consultancy firms.

Future studies of groupware use in other types of consultancy firms or knowledge intensive firms, which are situated in a SME in a developing country, are needed for a greater and deeper understanding of how Notes supports KM in this specific context. As this study was carried out in IT, it would set out the practical use of Notes in other industries. However, a detailed understanding of a specific organizational context cannot be neglected in order to bring a successful implementation of groupware for KM. Hence, another implication for further research is due to the limited degree of generalization. As the focus is the use of Notes in SMEs, researchers may conduct additional research in other industries apart from IT. Future research may also investigate other collaborative tools whether and to what extent it can be used to support KM in developing country SMEs. This would help to increase generalizability of the interaction richness model and to clarify more potentials of each use mode in relation to KM presented in this study. Research may compare the use of such collaborative tools or other groupware to Notes to see if it leads to more or less efficiency of KM in developing country SME contexts.

References

Abdullah, M.: An overview of the macroeconomic contribution of SMEs in Malaysia. In: Harvie, C., Lee, B.C. (eds.) The role of SMEs in national economies in East Asia. Studies of small and medium sized enterprises in East Asia, vol. II. Edward Elgar, Cheltenham (2002)

Aurum, A., Daneshgar, F., Ward, J.: Investigating knowledge Management practices in software development organisationas – An Australian Experience. Information and Software Technology 50(6), 511–533 (2008)

Alavi, M., Carlson, P.: A review of MIS research and disciplinary development. Journal of Management Information Systems 8(4), 45–62 (1992)

Belanger, F., Allport, C.D.: Collaborative Technologies in Knowledge telework: an exploratory study. Information Systems Journal 18(1), 101–121 (2008)

Blau, P., Scott, W.R.: Formal organizations: A comparative approach. Routledge & Kegan Paul Ltd., London (1963)

Brimble, P., Oldfield, D., Monsakul, M.: Policies for SME recovery in Thailand. In: Harvie, C., Lee, B.C. (eds.) The role of SMEs in national economies in East Asia. Studies of small and medium sized enterprises in East Asia Volume, vol. II. Edward Elgar, Cheltenham (2002)

Brown, B.: The artful of groupware: an ethnographic study of how Lotus Notes is used in practice. Behaviour & Information Technology 19(4), 263–273 (2000)

Ciborra, C.U.: Mission critical: Challenges for groupware in a pharmaceutical company. In: Ciborra, C.U. (ed.) Groupware and teamwork: Invisible aid or technical hindrance? John Wiley & Sons, Chichester (1996)

Ciborra, C.U., Patriotta, G.: Groupware and teamwork in new product development: The case of a consumer goods multinational. In: Ciborra, C.U. (ed.) Groupware and teamwork: Invisible aid or technical hindrance? John Wiley & Sons Ltd., Chichester (1996)

Ciborra, C.U., Suetens, N.T.: Groupware for an emerging virtual organization. In: Ciborra, C.U. (ed.) Groupware and teamwork: Invisible aid or technical hindrance? John Wiley & Sons, Chichester (1996)

Coleman, J.S.: Social capital in the creation of human capital. American Journal of Sociology 94, 95–120 (1988)

Corso, M., Martini, A., Paolucci, E., Pellegrini, L.: Information and communication technologies in product innovation within SMEs-The role of product complexity. Enterprise and Innovation Management Studies 2(1), 35–48 (2001)

Ellis, C.A., Gibbs, S.J., Rein, G.L.: Groupware: some issues and experiences. Communications of the ACM 34(1), 38–58 (1991)

Galliers, R.D., Newell, S.: Back to the future: from knowledge management to the management of information and data. Information Systems and e-Business Management 1, 1–9 (2003)

Giddens, A.: The constitution of society. Polity Press, Oxford (1984)

Grover, V., Davenport, T.H.: General perspectives on knowledge management: Fostering a research agenda. Journal of Management Information Systems 18(1), 5–21 (2001)

Hayes, N.: Boundless and bounded interactions in the knowledge work process: the role of groupware technologies. Information and Organization 11, 79–101 (2001)

Hayes, N., Walsham, G.: Participation in groupware-mediated communities of practise: a socio-political analysis of knowledge working. Information and Organization 11, 263–288 (2001)

Karsten, H., Jones, M.: The long and winding road: Collaborative IT and organisational change. In: Proceedings of the CSCW 1998, Seattle, USA (1998)

McDermott, R.: Why information technology inspired but cannot deliver knowledge management. California Management Review 41(4), 103–117 (1999)

Nahapiet, J., Ghoshal, S.: Social capital, intellectual capital, and the organizational advantage. Academy of Management Review 23(2), 242–266 (1998)

Orlikowski, W.J.: The duality of technology: rethinking the concept of technology in organizations. Organization Science 5(3), 398–427 (1992)

Orlikowski, W.J.: Learning from Notes: Organizational issues in groupware implementation. The Information Society 9(3), 237–250 (1993)

Orlikowski, W.J.: Evolving with Notes: Organizational change around groupware technology. In: Ciborra, C.U. (ed.) Groupware and teamwork: Invisible aid or technical hindrance? John Wiley & Sons, Chichester (1996)

Robertson, M., Sorensen, C., Swan, J.: Survival of the leanest: Intensive knowledge work and groupware adaptation. Information Technology & People 14(4), 334–353 (2001)

Sahay, S., Avgerou, C.: Introducing the special issue on information and communication technologies in developing countries. The Information Society 18, 73–76 (2002)

Sambamurthy, V., Subramani, M.: Special issue on information technologies and knowledge management. MIS Quarterly 29(1), 1–7 (2005)

Schrage, M.: Shared minds. Random House, New York (1990)

Sherif, K., Hoffman, J., Wetherbe, J.: Can technology build organizational social capital: The case of a global IT consulting firm. Paper presented at the tenth Americas Conference on Information Systems, New York (2004)

Sparrow, J.: Supporting knowledge management in small and medium sized enterprises. Knowledge Management Centre, Birmingham (1999)

Sparrow, J.: Knowledge features of small firms. Knowledge Management Centre, Birmingham (2000)

Sparrow, J., Matlay, H., Bushell, M.: Knowledge management: The challenge for small business support. Knowledge Management Centre, Birmingham (2000)

Vandenbosch, B., Ginzberg, M.J.: Lotus Notes and collaboration: Plus ca change. Journal of Management Information Systems 13(3), 65–81 (1996)

Wagner, C., Cheung, K., Lee, F., Ip, R.: Enhancing e-government in developing countries: Managing knowledge through virtual communities. The Electronic Journal on Information Systems in Developing Countries 14(4), 1–20 (2003)

Walsham, G.: Knowledge management: The benefits and limitations of computer systems. European Management Journal 19(6), 599–608 (2001)

Walsham, G., Sahay, S.: GIS for district-level administration in India: Problems and opportunities. MIS Quarterly 23(1), 39–66 (1999)

Wilson, T.D.: The nonsense of knowledge management. Information Research 8(1) (2002)

Zack, M.H.: Managing codified knowledge. Sloan Management Review 40(4), 45–58 (1999)

An Action Research on Open Knowledge and Technology Transfer

Isabel Ramos[1], Margarida Cardoso[1], João Vidal Carvalho[1], and José Ismael Graça[2]

[1] University of Minho, Portugal
[2] Município de Vila Verde, Portugal

Abstract. R&D has always been considered a strategic asset of companies. Traditionally, companies that have their own R&D function are better prepared to compete in the globalized economy because they are able to produce the knowledge and technology required to advance products and services. SMEs also need to become highly innovative and competitive in order to be successful. Nevertheless, their ability to have an internal R&D function that effectively meets their innovation needs is usually very weak. Open innovation provides access to a vast amount of new ideas and technologies at lower costs than closed innovation. This paper presents an action research study being carried out at University of Minho to develop a business model and technology platform for an innovation brokering service connecting ideas and technologies being developed at Universities with the specific innovation needs of SMEs. The expected contributions of the study include the empirical investigation of the effectiveness and risks of crowdsourcing innovation when applied in the socio-economic context of a European developing country where SMEs represent 99,6% of the businesses.

1 Introduction

R&D has always been considered a strategic asset of companies. Traditionally, companies that have their own R&D function are better prepared to compete in the globalized economy because they are able to produce the knowledge and technology required to advance products and services.

However, large companies are the best equipped to invest in the resources required to keep a R&D function that meets their innovation needs. In addition, a number of factors converge to make it difficult, even for large companies, to internally produce all the knowledge and technologies they need to innovate: the instability of the world economy, the fast pace of scientific knowledge being produced in all disciplines, the complexity of the multi-disciplinary knowledge required to support innovation, the rapid decrease of products and processes life cycles. Even in an economy that is no longer growing or is growing at a much slower rate than before, the pressure to innovate and to offer valuable products and services is strategic; due to decreasing investment and purchasing power, investors and consumers will probably become more selective and demanding.

G. Dhillon, B.C. Stahl, and R. Baskerville (Eds.): CreativeSME 2009, IFIP AICT 301, pp. 211–223, 2009.
© IFIP International Federation for Information Processing 2009

SMEs also need to become highly innovative and competitive in order to be successful. Nevertheless, their ability to have an internal R&D function that effectively meets their innovation needs is usually very weak. Often, these companies are dependent on their ability to rapidly detect and take advantage of opportunity windows. For this to happen, SMEs may require competencies and technologies that they do not possess internally.

In fact, SMEs have always been forced to use others' technologies due to their sparse internal resources which are devoted to innovation. Competitive advantage can be achieved if technology and ideas are available. Brokers can help SMEs to access the market of ideas and solutions, structured knowledge repositories and networking along the value chain.

Open Innovation (Chesbrough, 2003a) is a strategy that is emerging as highly promising in an unstable and uncertain world, where a global workforce of knowledge workers is eagerly seeking for work opportunities perceived as enriching and empowering. This strategy acknowledges the emergence of a market for ideas and emerging technologies supported by vast global offerings of complex knowledge and skills. In this paper we call this strategy 'crowdsourcing innovation'.

In a networked environment, where relations need to be established in a near real-time basis with a large base of potential customers, using the service of a crowdsourcing innovation broker can be the solution to counteract SME's scarce means and scalability difficulties.

Crowdsourcing innovation provides access to a vast amount of new ideas and technologies at lower costs than closed innovation. However, this innovation strategy, or any other open innovation strategy, should not completely replace internal R&D function. Internal R&D is still necessary to ensure the learning required for evaluating the relevance of external knowledge and technologies and to support the organizational and business changes that must be implemented to integrate them.

In the European Union, 99% of businesses are SMEs and they provide two-thirds of all private sector jobs (http://ec.europa.eu/enterprise/entrepreneurship/facts_figures.htm).

Given the key role played by SMEs in the European economy, it will come as no surprise if the open innovation strategy finds many adepts in EU. European managers are increasingly becoming interested in open innovation as a strategy to improve and extend the innovation capability of their companies. Nevertheless, this strategy is not yet fully developed as a new management practice and there are still many challenges to be overcome in the appropriate implementation of it which require further scientific research.

This paper presents an action research study being carried out at the University of Minho that aims at developing a business model and technology platform for an crowdsourcing innovation brokering service connecting ideas and technologies being developed at Universities with the specific needs of SMEs.

The paper starts by presenting the foundations of the planned research. The concepts of community and network are presented, followed by a brief discussion on their relevance in the context of crowdsourcing innovation.

The rationale underlying the study being carried out at the University of Minho is presented. The research planned for the next three years is explained and justified. Finally, the expected contributions, both for theory and practice, are put forward.

2 Open Innovation: Concept and Communities

Chesbrough and Schwartz (2007) define open innovation as the "(...) use of purposive inflows and outflows of knowledge to accelerate internal innovation, and expand the markets for external use of innovation, respectively", (Chesbrough and Schwartz, 2007: 55). More specifically, firms can include the following archetypes of core processes, when adhering to an open innovation process: outside-in or inside-out processes or a coupled one (Gassmann and Enkel, 2005).

The open innovation paradigm implies co-developmental partnerships, developing a mutual working relationship (versus the traditional defensive business strategy), and using external sources of knowledge. These partnerships might look for the delivery of a new product, technology, or service, to reduce R&D expenses (Chesbrough and Schwartz, 2007), to expand the innovation output and its impact, and even to open new markets which are otherwise inaccessible. Recent studies on innovation have stressed the growing relevance of external sources of knowledge and creativity (Perkmann and Walsh, 2007). These studies have showed that more than trusting their R&D labs, organizations should adopt the open innovation strategy (Chesbrough and Crowther, 2006). This means that innovation can be considered the result of knowledge networks connecting several organizations instead of a function within one organization (Coombs et al. 2003; Powell et al. 1996). In the same line of reasoning, the concept of interactive innovation was established to understand the non-linear, iterative and multi-agent nature of the innovation processes (Kline,1985; Lundvall, 1988; Von Hippel, 1988).

Collaboration with suppliers is already an important part of the innovation strategy of large organizations (Törrö, 2007). Simultaneously, the traditional outsourcing of innovation, in which the full responsibility for part of the innovation process is transferred to another organization, is growing in popularity. The trend is, however, to form extensive networks in order to reach external competencies.

The challenge is now to diversify the innovation sources by identifying and attracting individuals and organizations worldwide in order to gather ideas and solutions and to, eventually, choose the ones that can complement the internal innovation process (Bowonder et al., 2005; Moitra and Krishnamoorthy, 2004; Perrons and Platts, 2004; Fowles and Clark, 2005; Quinn, 2000; Chesbrough, 2003a).

Laursen and Salter (2006) have explored the relationship between the opening of the organization to its external environment and its innovation performance. They have concluded that organizations that are open to external sources of innovation, or that use external inquiry channels, have a higher level of innovation performance. By studying British industrial companies, the authors showed that these companies adopted systematic strategies to search various channels and in doing so they were able to get ideas and resources that enabled them to identify and explore opportunities for innovation. This study follows the work of Cohen and Leventhal (1990), who argue that the ability to explore external knowledge is a key element of the innovation performance.

The open innovation model lays emphasis in the knowledge flow through the organization boundaries (1) to enable the accelerated development of internal innovations (i.e., supported by the licensing of technologies developed by others), and (2) to expand the use of technologies internally developed that could become underused.

The main challenge in adopting the open innovation model is in finding the right people and in fostering the collaborative work with the aim of integrating scientific discoveries in an innovative way (Chesbrough et al., 2006).

2.1 Collaboration in the Context of Open Innovation

Collaborative networks are crucial for the overall open innovation concept. Some studies show their importance in the improvement of companies' innovation performance. Nieto and Santamaria (2007) research shows how different types of collaborative networks contribute to the upgrading and innovation of industrial products. Using longitudinal research data about Spanish industrial companies, results show that a collaborative network is of crucial importance to reach a higher degree of innovation in specific products. Collaboration with suppliers, customers and other firms has a positive impact in innovation, while the collaboration with competitors has a negative impact. This study also offers evidence that the main positive impact on innovation comes from collaborative networks holding different types of participants.

Perkmann and Walsh (2007) explore characteristics of collaborative relationships between universities and industry through an open innovation perspective. Authors present a model, distinguishing university-industry partnerships from other mechanisms such as technology transfer or just human mobility processes.

Crowdsourcing innovation, one of the several open innovation strategies, brings in the need for collaboration within and between two main groups: the seekers, individuals and organizations seeking intellectual assets; and the solvers, individuals and organizations willing to produce those assets. Whether these groups should be called knowledge communities or networks is still under discussion and in need of further research.

Though seen in conjunction many times, the concepts of community and network can be safely parted. Dal Fiore refers to the difference between the tension that occurs with-in a community, towards homogenization and conservation, as something that makes it a space of belonging; and the network implying a tension towards differentiation, creative communication and also a space for competing (Dal Fiore, 2007) or instead, being just a more adequate notion to larger scale social realities (Mitchell, 1974).

When analyzing internet commercial sites and associated knowledge built-up processes, Loong (2008) calls attention to the fact that the community concept is somewhat fluid but nevertheless contains significant association to the object of the author's analysis, increasing value through informal knowledge creation. The author says community stands for "local social arrangements beyond the private sphere of the home and family" (Loong, 2008, p.182) and this shows through the development of relationships in online communities. Authors like Gee-Woo et al. (2005) call our attention to the fact that motivational factors are important, referring to individual benefits, reciprocal and community interests' defense behaviors, and organizational benefits. The authors suggest at its importance to nurture knowledge sharing behaviors and also sustain active communities. As Magalhães says, "Through the sharing of knowledge, the commitment of the group's members is strengthened and as new knowledge is produced the group gradually develops its own identity." (Magalhães, 2004, p.95). On the other hand, community can be considered a distributed communication system or systems, considering distributed communities which account for dispersion and individualization (nodes), and also using the Internet as an enabler tool (Gochenour, 2006).

The network concept might have entered social sciences through urban complex grounds, opposing the previous notion of community inherent to anthropological original studies in small-scale societies (Mitchell, 1974). Attention is called to the fact that usually authors either choose a morphological approach or an interactional one. Morphology can include several aspects, considering connectedness, density, anchorage, accessibility. Interaction includes content, directedness, durability, intensity and frequency. Sometimes, too, authors mingle criteria to obtain specific and more expressive operational constructs. Mitchell gives particular attention to content, which includes communication contents, transaction (or exchange) and normative content (relational).

A social network is something that affects the flow and quality of information (Granovetter, 2005; Ahonen and Lietsala, 2007; Perkmann and Walsh, 2007), that means also the need for coordination mechanisms (Gassmann and Enkel, 2005). Sources of reward but also punishment (Granovetter, 2005; Ahonen and Lietsala, 2007), networks are based on social capital (Bourdieu, 2001; Lin, 2001), establishing layers of intellectual capital (Törrö, 2007) - somehow a parallel with the sociotechnical model of Bressand and Distler (1995), which includes a layer one, for infrastructure (physical support for communication); a layer two, for infostructure, formal symbolic communication rules; and finally a layer three, for infoculture, the background taken-for-granted knowledge (Lehaney et al., 2004). These networks integrate ideas, and one must consider that the acceptance of an idea is part of its comprehension (DiMaggio, 2007), and so being the comprehension of related knowledge and technology. Trust is an important factor (Granovet-ter, 2005; Ahonen and Lietsala, 2007), and most of all a network is embedded in an interconnection of networks. This means that an additional layer is built in the organization.

Gassmann and Enkel (2005) make an in-depth study of 230 networks to determine their management mechanisms: through this study they come to know that firms gain if they integrate networks' work in their R&D, because they are enabled to capture knowledge from the outside of the organization. The network might also facilitate a company's transition from a rigid structure to a flexible one (see Gass-mann and En-kel (2005), for a comprehensive enunciation of a network's structural elements). Networks can also be defined as social processes or configurations, as Perkmann and Walsh (2007) state.

2.2 Open Innovation Brokering

There is a growing interest in innovation brokering services (Arora et al., 2002; Chesbrough and Crowther, 2006). The number of companies that mediate the intellectual capital transactions and provide their clients with a new approach to implement inbound and outbound crowdsourcing innovation is growing.

Organizations must integrate a set of specific competencies and capabilities to efficiently manage ideas and suggestions. Brokering companies (brokers) have emerged to deal with a growing demand for creativity and solutions: the new market of ideas.

Brokers require a strong presence in the Web through intelligent platforms that facilitate the innovation management and implement security mechanisms that ensure the confidentiality of exchanged information and the anonymity of seekers and solvers. These companies act as intermediaries that make available a set of services supporting innovation for their company clients (seekers) (Chesbrough, 2003). These platforms are part of the Web 2.0 and are integrating concepts and technologies of the so called Web 3.0 (Lassila and Hendler, 2007).

Companies as Innocentive, yet2.com, Nine Sigma, IdeaWicket, IdeaConnection and YourEncore are well known examples of crowdsourcing innovation brokers. They help in creating a global market for scientific knowledge, where everyone can contribute with her/his ideas and own developed technology. These brokers have been studied and are key players in the crowdsourcing innovation brokering for medium and large companies. As far as the authors know, no such studies have been performed for brokers offering a specialized service for micro and small companies and cultural issues affecting open innovation brokering have not yet been studied.

3   Crowdsourcing Innovation at the University: An Action-Research Project

Portuguese SMEs are dominant in the Portuguese business-related structure, representing 99,6% of the businesses and being responsible for 75,2% of private jobs and generating more than ½ of the national wealth (IAPMEI Report for 2008 at http://www.iapmei.pt/resources/download/sobre_pme_2008.pdf). Micro and small firms assume a key role in Portuguese economy, representing 97,3% of all firms, offering 55,2% of the private jobs and 1/3 of the national turnover.

The stronger economic sectors in which SMEs operate are commerce and services (including tourism). Other important sectors are construction, manufacturing industry, and energy.

Traditionally, SMEs are located in North of Portugal and Lisbon (2/3), therefore 70% of the private jobs are in these two regions. These SMEs are responsible for more than 70% of the national turnover. The remaining 1/3 of the firms are located in the Center, South, Madeira and Azores.

The University of Minho is located in North of Portugal, in the Minho region. The University is renowned for the quality of its teaching and research. It holds strong links with the regional and national academic and business communities, consolidated through many teaching and project collaborations and multi-disciplinary projects. It has also a significant experience in international collaborations, both with universities and companies.

University of Minho has a student population of 16,000, 1,900 of them being postgraduate students. The University has 1,200 teaching staff and 600 administrative and technical staff.

Open Innovation is now capturing the attention of European managers. In Portugal, medium and large companies have already gathered important experience by collaborating with Universities in research projects that integrate the participation of PhD students. Some events supported by companies operating in the IT sector have launched events and challenges to post-graduate students in order to stimulate creativity and entrepreneurship. However, at present, there aren't brokering initiatives linking SMEs (seekers) to knowledge and technologies being developed in Universities by post-graduate students whose work is integrated in R&D academic projects.

Most Portuguese SMEs, especially micro and small companies cannot afford the costs of accessing the brokering services provided by Innocentive and other international brokers. Since many of the Portuguese Universities are public universities, it seems highly desirable that public budget that is made available to Universities should end up generating intellectual assets benefiting SMEs, the main producers of national wealth. The remainder of this paper describes a study designed to investigate the process of implementing an crowdsourcing innovation initiative along the lines just described, eliciting the practices, dynamics and risks of a broker operating in a developing country and focusing the socio-economic constraints affecting SMEs.

The study being carried out at the Department of Information Systems at University of Minho has as its main goals:

a. To define a contextualized business model for a Crowdsourcing Innovation Broker focused on facilitating SME's access to ideas and technologies being developed at Universities, and in providing consulting services to support their integration in the SME's business processes.

b. To develop a web platform prototype to support the broker's processes, community's interactions and access to knowledge assets, and to support the collective memory functions such as re-construction of past experience, identity reformulations, and spontaneous formation of free associations.

To achieve these goals, a research program was defined for the next three years, which started in 2008 with the integrated research work of three PhD students in the areas of (1) online communities and networks, (2) crowdsourcing innovation and supporting web platforms, (3) organizational memory.

The research method used to guide the study is action research that "is an interventionist approach to the acquisition of scientific knowledge" (Baskerville and Wood-Harper, 1996), that can be applied according the assumptions of post-positivist or interpretivist paradigms (Elden and Chisholm, 1993). Action research can also be considered as a kind of transformative methodology (Gobo, 2008), meaning a way of interfering with the state of the object, including manipulation of some of its states. Together with action research, Gobo presents a set of qualitative methodologies for social research such as interviews, surveys (qualitative), ethnography, documentary and other.

Action research can be compared, at least in terms of impact over the subject, to the ethnographic approach and case study. While the case study method allows a set of steps to gather and analyze information (Yin, 2003), the ethnographic method means immersion in the field; it requires observation skills and records to apply the method and offer testimonials of the context (Flick, 2005).

The choice of action research is based on the fact that it implies a certain degree of experimentation and production of technology which is scientifically grounded. The ethnographic methods don't imply this immediately, because of their immersive nature and because they do not include the experimental component.

Therefore, the study described in this paper applies the action research method according to the interpretivist assumptions about what constitutes 'valid' research and which research methods and techniques are appropriate.

The Fig. 1 shows the action research cycle, adapted to the study of the OI brokering service to SMEs.

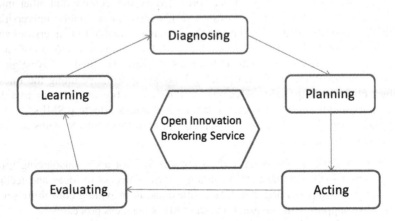

Fig. 1. The Action-Research Cycle applied for the study

The focus of the research is the definition and implementation of a brokering service for expanding the innovation capabilities of SMEs by employing the creativity and motivation of post-graduate students at public Universities to produce intellectual assets that can leverage the competitiveness and internationalization of Portuguese SMEs.

Diagnosing corresponds to understanding of the innovation benefits and constraints of the service. It also seeks to define the business and organizational models. Planning corresponds to defining the actions required to implement the defined models. The produced plan defines the target for change and the approach to change.

Acting corresponds to implementing the plan, requiring changes to be made. In the evaluating stage, the success of the actions carried out is evaluated against the expected outcomes, previously defined upon existing scientific studies on open innovation brokering services.

The experience gained within each action research cycle is consolidated in the learning stage, which is then used to start a new cycle that begins with a new "Diagnosing" activity.

Figure 2 shows the architecture of the service that we expect to develop by the end of our study.

We have planned three action-research cycles in the next three years. In each cycle, the service will be improved and deployed. The first cycle started in July 2008 with the first implementation of the brokering service. This implementation integrates small communities of seekers and solvers, but with strong ties with the service providers, the master programs management board. The main challenges of this initial stage are to ensure the quality of the service and its reputation beyond the present

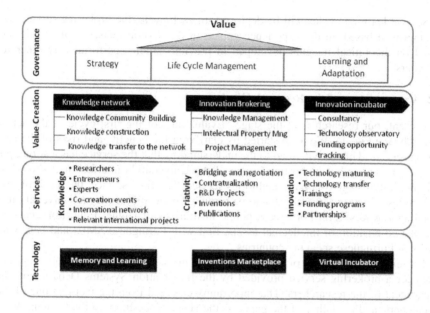

Fig. 2. The Architecture of the Service

communities involved in order to widen both communities. In preparation for the next action-research cycle, efforts are being made (1) to develop information services that can support creativity and project execution, and (2) to make available a knowledge network of national and international specialists in various scientific areas, willing to collaborate with the service to provide contents and knowledge transfer activities.

3.1 Research Design: Research Questions and a Plan for Action

At present, building the University crowdsourcing innovation's community (seekers and solvers) relies on a personal interaction and face-to-face communication, researchers' network and credibility, and the national reputation of its Information Systems master courses. SMEs are complying due to multiple and probably subjective factors. Nevertheless, as Foth (2006) stresses, "the majority of communication and interaction facilitated by global networks can be categorized as social and informal and takes place within the geographical vicinity of actors." (Foth, 2006, p.207).

The research questions that will be answered in the next three years are:

a. What are the key success factors of a crowdsourcing innovation brokering service focused on the specific innovation needs of SMEs?
b. What are the specific characteristics of the business model that ensures the sustainability of the service? What risks must be considered?
c. What are the functional components of a web platform that adequately supports the service?
d. What practices and technologies should be put in place to ensure a collective memory that adequately fosters creativity and knowledge co-construction among the members of both solver and seeker communities?

Several learning cycles will be deployed. In each cycle, the brokering service will be improved based on the experience gained in the several phases of the cycle and based on theoretical insights developed in previous studies performed by other researchers.

3.2 Present Stage of the Research Work

At present, our research is at the stage "Evaluating" of the first cycle of the action research (see Fig. 1). We have started by clarifying the benefits and risks of the brokering service. This activity lead to the understanding that the service has a strong potential for success but its hosting in one of the University's interface unit should be only the initial stage of a more ambitious service. The final service, the result of several cycles of action research, should be provided by a spin-off of the University that could aggregate several Portuguese public institutions of Higher Education and support the co-creation of intellectual assets, first with Portuguese SMEs and later with SMEs of Portuguese speaking countries.

To guide the first cycle of action-research, a mission, goals and strategy were defined for a brokering service provided by the Information Systems Department, the department of the researchers. The opportunity emerged from the fact that one of the researchers, and co-author of the paper, is the Head of the Information Systems Master programs. This fact facilitates the access to an initial community of solvers (the master students doing the dissertation) and a community of seekers (the companies that usually employ master students after they complete the program). In addition, Information Systems PhD students are also encouraged to solve innovation problems made available by the seeker companies.

Having identified both communities and having the process of Dissertation as the underlying structure for the service, plans were made to implement this first instantiation of the brokering service. The main concern was to define the steps to ensure reputation that will then support the success of next action research cycles in which more and more complex instantiations of the service will be deployed and studied. This reputation involves the delivery of valuable results to the SMEs and ensuring that students develop technical and soft skills required to their professional success. It also requires the adequate support to project management and the guarantee that the seeker and the solver commitments (financial prizes, available resources, effort, and others), defined at the initial stage of the project, are fulfilled.

The first activity taken was to host two creativity facilitating events called Knowledge Safari. In these events, companies were invited to share their innovation problems and goals with the researchers of the Information System Department. From these events, involving a modest number of 10 companies and 12 researchers representing all relevant research areas in the department, resulted 44 ideas for Dissertation projects. Most of these ideas were made available to master students.

While the paper is being written, students are choosing their dissertation process and defining their project's plan. We are evaluating the results we are obtaining and are already able to draw some insights:

  a. Given the initial phase of the initiative, the strong ties that the department holds with the participating companies as seekers were central to the success of the creativity fostering events. Participants in the events, both managers and researchers, positively responded to the sense of community and were motivated to share ideas and problems.

b.   The established reputation of the master programs was pivotal for the establishment of the initial reputation of the service.

c.   Some companies that collaborate with the Department in other educational programs, and that usually employ the graduates and post-graduates, decided to wait and watch before getting involved with the service.

d.   Even with this simple instantiation of the brokering service, it is clear that the huge amount of effort is required to manage interactions with both communities, to negotiate the different interests, to expand the communities, to manage the projects being carried out, and to facilitate the access to information and knowledge.

e.   In order to involve other departments of the University, with the aim of widening the community of solvers and also of encouraging multidisciplinary projects, the service must be hosted by an interface unit of the University. Being delivered by the Department of Information Systems places the service in the Information Systems and Technologies field and implies a secondary role for the other departments.

f.   Based on the insight in e), it is also evident that to leverage the service to a national and international level it cannot be hosted by the University of Minho but by an independent broker. This conclusion reinforces the initial assumption that in one of the next cycles, the creation of a University's spin-off company is required to enlarge its scope and quality.

These insights will be refined and extended in the near future. They will provide the ground for understanding the implementation of a crowdsourcing innovation brokering service in the academic context of a developing country where SMEs are responsible for the major part of its national turnover.

In order to prepare for the next action research cycle, a proposal for a funded project is being prepared to apply for the funding required to implement a service hosted by one of the interface units the University. This will attempt to define a business model that ensures the sustainability of the service as well as the required autonomy and flexibility needed to improve the service quality and widen its reach.

4 Conclusions

The paper presents an action research study being carried out at the University of Minho to develop a business model and the supporting web 3.0 platform for a brokering service focused on the innovation needs of SMEs.

The study is planned for three years and will integrate several action research cycles aimed at delivering increasingly sophisticated versions of the service.

The expected contributions of the study include the empirical investigation of the effectiveness and risks of crowdsourcing innovation strategy when applied in the socio-economic context of a European developing country where SMEs represent 99.6% of the businesses.

The study will result in the definition of a functional architecture of a web platform that takes advantage of the Web 3.0 technologies and supports the specific requirements of an innovation brokering service for SMEs, followed by the development of a prototype that implements that architecture.

Practitioners will benefit from the insights produced which will be integrated in a methodology for guiding the definition and implementation of a brokering service focused on the specific innovation needs of SME and in the architectural aspects of a web platform that adequately supports the service.

References

Ahonen, M., Lietsala, K.: Managing service ideas and suggestions - information systems in innovation brokering. In: Innovation in Services. Conference Proceedings. Tekes, Berkeley (2007)

Arora, A., Fosfuri, A., Gambardella, A.: Markets for Technology. The Economics of Innovation and Corporate Strategy. MIT Press, Cambridge (2002)

Baskerville, R.L., Wood-Harper, A.T.: A Critical Perspective on Action Research as a Method for Information Systems Research. Journal of Information Technology (11), 235–246 (1996)

Bourdieu, P.: Razões práticas: Sobre a teoria da acção. Celta Editora, Lisboa (2001)

Bowonder, B., Racherla, J.K., Mastakar, N.V., Krishan, S.: R&D spending patterns of global firms. Res. Technol. Manag. 48(5), 51–59 (2005)

Bressand, A., Distler, C.: La planète relationelle. Flamarion, Paris (1995)

Chesbrough, H.: The era of open innovation. MIT Sloan. Manag. Rev. 44(3), 35–41 (2003)

Chesbrough, H.: Open innovation: The New Imperative for Creating and Profiting from Technology. Harvard Business School Press, Boston (2003a)

Chesbrough, H., Crowther, A.K.: Beyond high tech: early adopters of open innovation in other industries. R&D Manag. 36(4), 229–236 (2006)

Chesbrough, H., Schwartz, K.: Innovating business models with co-development partner-ships. Res. Technol. Manag. 50(1), 55–59 (2007)

Chesbrough, H., Vanhaverbeke, W., West, J.: Open innovation: researching a new paradigm. Oxford University Press, Oxford (2006)

Cohen, W.M., Levinthal, D.A.: Absorptive capacity: A new perspective on learning and innovation. Adm. Sci. Q 35(1), 128–152 (1990)

Coombs, R., Harvey, M., Tether, B.S.: Analysing distributed processes of provision and innovation. Ind. Corp. Chang. 12, 1125–1155 (2003)

DiMaggio, P.: Culture and congnition. Annual Review of Sociology 23, 263–287 (1997)

Elden, M., Chisholm, R.F.: Emerging Varieties of Action Research: Introduction to the Special Issue. Human Relations 46(2), 121–142 (1993)

dal Fiore, F.: Communities versus networks: the implications on innovations of social change. American Behavioural Scientist 50, 857–866 (2007)

Flick, U.: Métodos qualitativos na investigação científica, Lisboa, Monitor (2005)

Foth, M.: Network action research. Action Research 4(2), 205–226 (2006),
http://arj.sagepub.com/cgi/reprint/4/2/205 (15.10.2008)

Fowles, S., Clark, W.: Innovation networks: good ideas from everywhere in the world. Strat. Leader 33(4), 46–50 (2005)

Gassmann, O., Enkel, E.: Management mechanisms of network layers in MNE. Presented at the European Academy of Management (EURAM) 2005 Conference, Munich (2005),
http://www.scientificcommons.org/836 (accessed April 26, 2008)

Gee-Woo, B., Zmud, R.W., Young-Gul, K., Jae-Nam, L.: Behavioural intention formation in knowledge sharing: examining the roles of extrinsic motivators, social-psychological forces and organizational climate. MIS Quarterly 29(1), 87–111 (2005)

Gobo, G.: Doing ethnography. Sage, Los Angeles (2008)

Granovetter, M.: The impact of social structure on economic outcomes. Journal of Economic Perspectives 19(1), 33–50 (2005),
http://www.stanford.edu/dept/soc/people/mgranovetter/ (21-09-2008)

Kline, S.J.: Innovation is not a linear process. Res. Manag. 28(4), 36–45 (1985)

Lassila, O., Hendler, J.: Embracing Web 3.0. IEEE Internet Computing 11(3), 90–93 (2007)

Laursen, K., Salter, A.: Open for innovation: The role of openness in explaining innovation performance among U.K. manufacturing firms. Strat. Manag. J. 27(2), 131–150 (2006)

Lehaney, B., Clarke, S., Coakes, E., Jack, G. (eds.): Beyond knowledge management. Idea Group Publishing, London (2004)

Loong, W.: Trust in e-commerce. Risk and trust building. In: Brennan, L.L., Johnson, V.E. (eds.) Computer-mediated relationships and trust. Managerial and organizational effects, pp. 176–193. Information Science Reference, Hershey (2008)

Lin, N.: Social capital: a theory of social structure and action. Cambridge University Press, Cambridge (2001)

Lundvall, B.: Innovation as an interactive process: from user–producer interaction to the national system of innovation. In: Dosi, G., Freeman, C., Silverberg, G., Soete, L. (eds.) Technical Change and Economic Theory. Pinter, London (1988)

Magalhães, R.: Organizational knowledge and technology. An action-oriented perspective on organization and information systems. Edward Elgar, Northampton (2004)

Mitchell, J.C.: Social Networks. Annual Review of Anthropology 3, 279–299 (1974)

Moitra, D., Krishnamoorthy, M.B.: Global innovation exchange. Res. Technol. Manag. 47(4), 32–38 (2004)

Nieto, M.J., Santamaría, L.: The importance of diverse collaborative networks for the novelty of product innovation. Technovation 27, 367–377 (2007),
http://www.elsevier.com/locate/technovation (accessed January 24, 2008)

Perkmann, M., Walsh, K.: University-industry relationships and open innovation: towards a research agenda. International Journal of Management Reviews 9(4), 259–280 (2007)

Perrons, R., Platts, K.: The role of clockspeed in outsourcing decisions for new technologies: insights from the prisoner's dilemma. Ind. Manag. + Data Sys. 104(7), 624–632 (2004)

Powell, W.W., Koput, K.W., Smith-Doerr, L.: Interorganizational collaboration and the locus of innovation: networks of learning in biotechnology. Adm. Sci. Q 41(1), 116–145 (1996)

Quinn, J.B.: Outsourcing innovation: The new engine of growth. Sloan Manag. Rev. 41(4), 13–28 (2000)

Törrö, M.: Global intellectual capital brokering. In: Facilitating the emergence of innovations through network mediation, Espoo 2007. VTT Publications (2007)

von Hippel, E.: The Sources of Innovation. Oxford University Press, New York (1988)

Wellman, B.: Little boxes, glocalization, and networked individualism, Center for Urban & Community Studies. University of Toronto (2002),
http://www.chass.utoronto.ca/~wellman/publications/ [25-04-2008]

Yin, R.K.: Case study research. Design and methods, 3rd edn. Sage, Thousand Oaks (2003)

Services Supporting Knowledge Maturing in Small and Medium-Sized Enterprises

Ronald Maier

School of Management, Information Systems
University of Innsbruck, Austria

Abstract. The hype around Web 2.0 has again sparked tremendous interest in IT-supported knowledge management and technology-enhanced learning in organizations. Although there has been abundant evidence of how to benefit from Web 2.0 technologies, information on how to go about deploying these in small and medium-sized enterprises in a coordinated manner are scarce. Based on the findings of an empirical study and an ethnographically informed study on knowledge maturing, this paper suggests a set of knowledge services to support a series of knowledge actions chained with the help of the knowledge maturing model. This set of services can be used by small and medium-sized enterprises for analyzing IT tools and systems which currently support their employees' knowledge maturing activities, to foster knowledge cooperation with customers, suppliers and partners in their business environment and to find gaps which can be filled particularly by consuming services over the Web.

1 Introduction

Work in organizations is increasingly information- and knowledge-intensive and the share of knowledge work has risen continuously during the last decades (Wolff, 2005). Since the late 90s, organizations have been faced with the transformation to knowledge-intensive organizations in order to significantly increase speed of innovation and improve productivity of knowledge work (Drucker, 1994). Knowledge-intensive organizations represent a substantial share of small and medium-sized enterprises (SMEs) which are considered the backbone of innovation in the European economy. Knowledge intensity refers to, among other things, a high share of highly skilled and/or creative employees, operations that aim at providing knowledge-intensive products and services, high importance of experiences, high degree of innovations, in some industry sectors this results in a high number of patents, central importance of customer knowledge, high need for communication and a high degree of information needs (Starbuck 1992, Alvesson 2004). However, compared to more traditional, predominantly manual, data- or service-oriented work, the unstructured, creative and expertise-driven knowledge work cannot be designed with standardized management approaches and cannot be easily supported by information and communication technologies (ICT), e.g., workflows or single application systems.

Resorting to Knowledge management (KM) has been suggested to help solve these issues. During the last twenty years, businesses have faced four distinctive phases of

G. Dhillon, B.C. Stahl, and R. Baskerville (Eds.): CreativeSME 2009, IFIP AICT 301, pp. 224–238, 2009.

KM. The first phase could be termed human-oriented KM. Organizations realized the value of their "human capital" and bundled a number of instruments aiming at the individual knowledge worker and her productivity. The next phase was backed by tremendously increased opportunities offered by ICTs and could be called technology-oriented KM. Organizations were eagerly experimenting with new ICTs in attempts to benefit from the promised changes that would come about by implementing KM tools and systems. In a third phase which primarily was fueled by the emphasis on business processes typical for German-speaking countries, KM methods, tools and instruments were repositioned as knowledge processes and linked to knowledge-intensive business processes. Thus, KM initiatives could be designed with the same language as was used in organizational design and ICT support of business activities in general, the language of business processes. After human-oriented, technology-oriented and process-oriented KM, recently a fourth KM phase has reached businesses backed by the hype keywords Web 2.0 and social software: collaborative KM. While in many organizations knowledge workers are busy trying out new alternatives for production of contents, for networking and for self-directed learning, questions arise how these activities can be coordinated or guided so that they are in line with organizational goals.

As a result, an enormous number of fragmented KM measures, procedures, instruments and tools have been proposed which claim to solve particular knowledge-related problems, but are not connected or integrated. Even though many authors have studied the strategic perspective of KM, e.g., (April, 2002; Hansen et al. 1999; Ordóñez de Pablos, 2002; Zack, 1999), process-oriented KM strategies in particular (Davenport et al. 1996), in order to integrate KM initiatives and guide their organization-wide implementation, these considerations still remain on an abstract level. Particularly actors designing KM initiatives for SMEs are overwhelmed by the number of measures, procedures, instruments and tools proposed in the literature and thus require guidance in selecting and composing services to support those knowledge activities that are deemed most valuable in their business context.

This paper argues that composition or integration of knowledge services in organizations requires their alignment with the help of the knowledge maturing model (Maier & Schmidt 2007) that connects them according to a set of knowledge activities. Section 2 briefly introduces the concept of knowledge service. Section 3 describes the knowledge maturing model. Section 4 presents a list of knowledge services supporting the activities defined in the knowledge maturing model. Section 5 finally discusses application of the model in KM initiatives for SMEs and concludes the paper.

2 Knowledge Services

Since software engineering was founded as a discipline in the 70s, computer scientists have searched for ways to describe basic or advanced building blocks out of which software systems can be composed. The main advantages are reduced cost and time as well as improved quality through modularization, reusability, stability and interoperability of the resulting software systems. There are a number of different terms for building blocks, e.g., functions, procedures, modules, classes or components. Recently, service has been the central concept for a redefinition of the technical and conceptual foundation for these main building blocks from a more business-oriented perspective. A service consists of contract, interface and implementation. It has distinctive functional meaning typically reflecting a high-level business concept covering data and business logic (Krafzig et al. 2005). A service is an abstract resource that represents a capability of performing tasks that form a coherent functionality from the point of view of the providers entities and requesters entities (W3C 2004). Service descriptions provide information about:

- service capability: conceptual purpose and expected result,
- service interface: the service's signature, i.e. input, output, error parameters and message types,
- service behavior: a detailed workflow invoking other services,
- quality of service: functional and non-functional quality attributes, e.g., service metering, costs, performance metrics and security attributes.

The service concept has gained popularity with the advent of a set of standards (i.e. URI, XML, UDDI, SOAP and WSDL) for open interaction between software applications using Web services. Web services are one way of implementing business and technical services in a service-oriented architecture (SOA). A SOA comprises application frontend, services, service repository and service bus which make functions available so that they can be accessed without any information about their implementation. SOAs promise more flexibility and adaptability In the context of SOA, services have to be interoperable in terms of platform independence, own a network addressable interface and be dynamically discovered and accessed. "SOA-enabled" organizations are called agile, on-demand or service-oriented enterprises. These metaphors attempt to carry over SOA semantics to organizational design. This has connotations for changes in ICT's general role in business (transforming business models), value creation (value networks), business processes (dynamically designed, net-like with emphasis on parallel processing) as well as organizational structure (service consumer-provider relationship complementing or even replacing traditional hierarchies). Whereas the technical definition of services is supported by a set of standards, it is the conceptual part (i.e. defining types of services that are useful) that is currently lacking.

Knowledge services are a subset of services whose functionality supports high-level KM instruments as part of on-demand KM initiatives, e.g., find expert, submit experience, publish skill profile, revisit learning resource or join community-of-interest. For example, a knowledge service "search for experts" might be composed of the basic services (1) expert search, (2) keyword search, (3) author search, (4) employee search and (5) check availability. The (1) expert search service delivers a list of IDs, e.g., personnel numbers, for experts matching the input parameter of an area of expertise. The (3) author search service requires a list of keywords describing the area of expertise provided by a (2) keyword search service. Keywords are assigned to areas of expertise in a database solution or in a more advanced semantic integration system based on ontology. With the help of an inference engine, these relationships, together with rules in the ontology, can be used to determine a list of keywords. The (3) author search service then returns a list of IDs of matching authors or active contributors to the CMS. An (4) employee search service takes the personnel numbers found in expert and author search and returns contact details, e.g., telephone number, email address, instant messaging address. Finally, the (5) check availability service delivers the current status of the experts and a decision on their availability. Knowledge services describe a set of services provided by heterogeneous application systems that can be arranged to support activities of knowledge maturing.

However, SOA and services are concepts that so far mostly impact large organizations, because creating a SOA is a costly and complex undertaking. Furthermore, it remains difficult to show that the value of KM initiatives exceeds corresponding efforts. Also, KM tools often need a "critical mass" of contributors which is much easier to achieve in large organizations than in SMEs. Therefore, many KM projects, particularly in SMEs, have been abandoned leaving knowledge workers with the insight that KM is important, yet left unsupported. The developments termed as Web 2.0 provide the "raw material" for a solution to these challenges as they offer cheap, easy-to-use technologies that are used by a broad range of people from which SMEs can profit. As Web 2.0 is a hype term rarely defined, in the following lines, some characteristics differentiating Web 2.0 from its predecessor are discussed from the perspective of how they can be beneficial for SMEs (after O'Reilly 2005).

Web as platform: Software is developed not to work in the environment of a single vendor's operating system, but on the Web tied together by a set of open interaction standards that are the result of agreements between major players in Web development and usage. This gives rise to benefits for SMEs as they can avoid vendor lock-in effects as well as profit from the benefits of combining Web services offered by different sites to present them to employees.

Network effects: Harnessing collective intelligence means services get more value with every increase of the number of people using it. Important phenomena typically related to goods and services that follow a pattern of network effects are start-up problems, switching costs and lock-in effects. The start-up problem describes the effect related to the low benefits of the service right after its start with nobody (yet) using it, it is difficult to promote a new service. Switching costs mean the effect that switching would require all knots with which one is connected to also switch to a new service thus creating lock-in effects. Due to small numbers of active participants in SMEs, these effects are of particular importance as they might prevent application of potentially useful tools. This calls for providing user-generated content and services in a form that allows remixing by others in the business ecosystem of the SME or even beyond and thus sparks an "architecture of participation" crossing organizational boundaries.

Value of data: User-generated content is the single most important asset in typical Web 2.0 applications. Several start-up companies have quickly made a fortune by attracting large numbers of users to provide content. Some Web 2.0 applications also consume and remix data from multiple sources. Strictly speaking, a plethora of data without users coming back to the site is worth nothing. So, it is data plus (returning) people that drive a Web site. SMEs can profit on the one hand from the plethora of data that can be remixed and consumed by them and on the other hand open up portions of their data to have other people help check it and improve its quality.

Webtop instead of Desktop: Interaction with the Web used to be strongly limited when compared to a Desktop application. With the advent of XHTML, CSS, DOM, XMLHttpRequest and Javascript, bundled under the term of AJAX, it has become possible to create Web sites that allow for rich user experiences, i.e. a look-and-feel similar to Desktop applications. Thus, Web 2.0 applications are sufficiently user friendly to be applied even by those SME employees who are not very technology-savvy.

End of the software release cycle: Software in the Web 2.0 is continuously developed and consequently in a permanent Beta status. Software is therefore delivered as a continually-updated service with no versioning or releases. SMEs can benefit by allowing them to realize quick wins even before large investments need to be taken and have services co-tested and developed by people within and outside the SME so that they gradually and quickly get better.

Software above the level of a single device: Many people do not only have a PC at their disposal, but also other information devices e.g., laptops, personal digital assistants or smartphones which share the ability to connect to the Web. One aspect of Web 2.0 is also accessibility of contents and services from varying types of devices. The single most important factor is that many people tend to have mobile devices with them almost all of the time, which gives rise to benefits also in those SMEs in which most employees do not continuously work on a PC.

Lightweight models: Web 2.0 stands for the opposite of heavyweight programming models typically used for application design in intra-organizational settings of large organizations. Web 2.0 applications are loosely coupled systems, that are designed for re-mixability and their innovation is in assembly, not in creating new entire systems in an isolated way. SMEs with their often higher flexibility compared to large organizations can potentially quickly move to these models and profit from first-mover advantages.

To sum up, with more light-weight Web 2.0 technologies such as tagging, RSS and mash-ups and the corresponding network effects created by numerous people using contents and services offered partly freely over the Web, also individuals with their personal knowledge environments and consequently SMEs comprising individuals with their personal work environments can benefit from arranging services flexibly to help them fulfill their knowledge needs. The personal, collaborative KM initiatives, often associated with haphazard, trial-and-error, grass-roots level approaches, need to be guided without losing the momentum created in KM activities by individuals. This is the main goal of the knowledge maturing model presented in the following section.

3 Knowledge Maturing

As described above, numerous systems aim at improving knowledge and learning processes which are typically designed and managed according to the specific needs of the respective organization. Employees thus use a fragmented systems landscape in which each system supports a certain part of knowledge and learning processes. Specific to knowledge-intensive SMEs is the fact that often many knowledge processes cross organizational boundaries, and employees use a considerable number of tools and systems provided by other institutions, mostly over the Web. There are substantial conceptual challenges of designing learning and knowledge processes that bring together the separated organizational support infrastructures fostered by different organizations. Organizations and corresponding application systems typically target knowledge of different degrees of maturity.

Pruning the tree of types of knowledge elements and guiding employees on how to use the channels of knowledge transfer is a pivotal task in any KM initiative. In the following paras, the knowledge maturing process is described in order to provide a framework for designing and integrating types of knowledge elements, processes and channels in KM. In a first step of structuring this process, Figure 1 shows the five phases that have been identified after analyzing several practical cases in applied research projects (Schmidt 2005), on the basis of a large empirical study (Maier 2007) as well as an ethnographically informed study on individual knowledge maturing routines (Maier & Thalmann 2008). Figure 1 lists a number of key concepts that explain the individual steps of the knowledge maturing model. The steps are further differentiated with the help of:

- Drives: Evolution theory postulates that during evolution humans have developed a set of innate psychological mechanisms that drive their behavior: acquire, defend, bond, comprehend (after Watson 2008) and pass-on.
- Motives: There are numerous motivation theories explaining human behavior as an aim to satisfy a set of motives (many of which build on Maslow 1943). Motives that drive the knowledge maturing process are social belonging, power, status, curiosity and self-realization.
- Actions: The steps typically involve many (knowledge) actions, e.g., access, collect, converge, coordinate, create, discuss, distribute, evaluate, identify, inquire, network, prepare, request and review (Hädrich 2008). However, there is a set of distinguished actions which describe the core of the step, i.e. the main activities that persons engage in when pursuing a certain step.
- Informing practices: Finally, the steps can be characterized with the help of the primarily targeted informing practice: expressing, monitoring, translating, networking (Schultze 2000) and personalization, i.e. marking a knowledge element as one's own so that one can trace back future developments towards an individual's creation in order to have the individual benefit from it.
- Knowledge elements: Organizations typically handle large number of knowledge elements for a variety of reasons. Some of them can be classified into types of knowledge elements that are typical for individual steps of the knowledge maturing process.

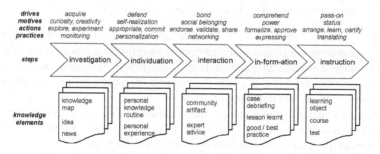

Fig. 1. Knowledge maturing model (based on Maier & Schmidt 2007)

The individual phases are described in the following points.

- Investigation: New ideas are developed by individuals either in highly informal discussions or by browsing the knowledge spaces available inside the organization and, with respect to SMEs, particularly beyond- e.g. in the Web. This step is driven by curiosity and creativity. The knowledge is subjective and deeply embedded in the context of the originator. The vocabulary used for communication is vague and often restricted to the person expressing the idea.
- Individuation: New ideas or results found in the investigation phase that have been enriched, refined or otherwise contextualized with respect to their use are now appropriated by the individual. This means that the individual marks his contributions so that he can benefit from its future (re-)use. The experience is thus personalized.
- Interaction: This step is driven by social motives and the benefits that individuals typically attribute to sharing knowledge. These are, among others, belonging to a preferred social group, thus increasing probability of getting back knowledge from the community when one needs it. From the perspective of semantics, this accomplishes an important maturing step, i.e. the development of common terminology shared among community members, e.g., in discussion forum entries or Blog postings.
- In-form-ation: Artifacts created in the preceding two steps are often inherently unstructured and still highly subjective and embedded in the context of the community. In this phase, purpose-driven structured documents are created, e.g., project reports or design documents or with a stronger knowledge connotation, rich case descriptions, lessons learnt or good practices, in which knowledge is de-subjectified and the context is made explicit.
- Instruction: Documents produced in the preceding step are typically not well suited as learning materials because no didactical considerations were taken into account. Now the topic is refined to improve comprehensibility in order to ease its consumption or re-use. The material is ideally prepared in a pedagogically sound way, enabling broader dissemination. Individual learning objects are arranged to cover a broader subject area and thus are composed into courses. Tests and certificates confirm that participants of formal trainings have achieved a certain degree of proficiency.

Knowledge thus can be classified according to its level of maturity. The class then suggests the appropriate form of learning and technical support. The following criteria have been identified as useful to define classes of knowledge:

- Validity: Certainly, the most obvious categorization refers to a validation process and could distinguish in as a first step between unproven and proven knowledge. In a more refined version that considers the specifics of organizational knowledge, validation could take into account the number of successful uses of knowledge, systematic tests or, (mathematical) proves.
- Hardness: In analogy to mineralogy, this criterion describes the (alleged) reliability of information or knowledge. According to Watson (2005), a possible scale runs from unidentified sources of rumors up to stock exchange data.
- Context: With deepened understanding, connections to other topics become visible which play an important role in learning (Siemens 2005). This must not be confused with inherent contextualization of knowledge which decreases in the knowledge

maturing process and refers to the degree of implicit linkage to the creation context, so that it cannot be used outside the original context. Inherent contextualization and inter-connectedness are inverse properties.

- Commitment/legitimation: Knowledge can be structured according to the amount of support it gets. Support can be in the form of commitment by members of groups, teams or communities within SMEs or in their business environment. Another form of support can be authorization to use knowledge by supervisors, executives or committees as well as legalization and standardization, i.e. forms of legitimation.
- Form of learning: As knowledge maturing is basically interconnecting individual learning processes in which knowledge is taught and learnt, an important criterion is teachability. Whereas immature knowledge is hard to teach, even to experts, formal training by definition allows for wide-range dissemination.

4 Knowledge Maturing Services

Knowledge maturing is used as concept to structure the core knowledge maturing services in an enterprise knowledge infrastructure that helps SMEs to streamline the IT services offered by internal or external IT service providers. This layer of core services builds upon infrastructure and integration services. The Intranet infrastructure provides basic functionality for storage, processing, synchronous and asynchronous communication, sharing of data and documents as well as management of electronic assets in general and of Web content in particular. Sources for structured and semi-structured data can be classified into organization-internal and organization-external sources. In case of SMEs, organization-external sources play a particularly important role due to the fact that typically a large portion of required knowledge cannot be built and maintained without customer, supplier and partner organizations. An ontology helps to meaningfully organize and link knowledge elements that come from a variety of sources and are used to analyze the semantics of the organizational knowledge base. Integration services are needed to manage meta-data about knowledge elements and the users that work within the system. Synchronization services export a portion of the knowledge workspace for work offline and (re-)integrate the results of work on knowledge elements that has been done offline. In case of SMEs, tagging and light-weight ontologies that are developed collaboratively, such as folksonomies, are seen as a promising solution for the challenge of integrating knowledge elements from diverse sources (e.g., Braun et al. 2008, Zacharias et al. 2009).

In the following section, services to support the steps of the knowledge maturing model are briefly described.

4.1 Investigation

Investigation services help to identify relevant knowledge in various forms and formats, particularly documented knowledge represented by various types of information resources. This relates to information retrieval, business intelligence, data mining and visualization for exploring structured data, enhanced visualization techniques for browsing knowledge resources and functions for monitoring knowledge sources. Figure 2 presents four groups of investigation services structured by means of a cycle.

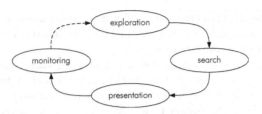

Fig. 2. Investigation services

The first two types of services are based on a distinction between two general search modes. Exploration supports a process of retrieving information whose main objectives are not clearly defined in the beginning and whose purpose might change during the interaction with a system, i.e. if users lack knowledge about the domain or if they cannot express it precisely. Important ways of support are knowledge visualizations, e.g., representations of sources of knowledge as well as their relationships. Search in contrast relates to a focused mode where a user needs to be able to describe a problem at least to some degree, e.g., by formulating a search query consisting of a number of keywords. Presentation deals with representing search results which particularly concerns ranking, visualization of relevant information as well as the obtainment of user feedback. Monitoring services support continuous non-focused scanning of the environment and gathering of useful "just in case" information.

The general sequence of these services as shown in the figure indicates that an explorative mode of search can be seen as the first step for investigating information resources. The more knowledge is acquired about a topic, the more specific becomes the information need and the required results can be formulated. Consequently, exploration is followed by a more focused search as well as by presentation of potentially relevant results. Monitoring is positioned as the last step within the cycle as it is concerned with relatively specific topics whose development is observed over different resources. The dashed line between monitoring and exploration means that monitoring may trigger further investigation cycles when it yields new fields of knowledge that should be investigated. However, the sequence of services shown in the figure only should be taken as a general ordering. Principally, investigation services can be accessed in any order. The same is true for the cycles described in the next sections.

4.2 Individuation

The concept of individuation so far has been neglected in many initiatives to create knowledge infrastructures. This means that many services in this category are quite rudimentary, because the other services have been deployed systematically for a much longer period of time. Many efforts have focused on transparency of knowledge and on supporting knowledge workers in sharing knowledge or even detaching knowledge from humans as "media" of knowledge. However, at least in a more individualistic culture stressing diversity, the individual knowledge worker also requires support concerning appropriation of knowledge.

Figure 3 gives an overview of four classes of services helpful for individuation including (1) reflection of individual experiences, (2) expression of ideas and proposals in a way that makes sense for the individual, (3) building competence and managing one's individual career and (4) achieving the final step of individual professional development, i.e. expert status in a certain knowledge domain.

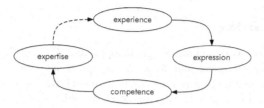

Fig. 3. Individuation services

The concept of individuation is widely used in a number of scientific disciplines, most notably psychology and philosophy. Its origin can be traced back to the Latin adjective "individuus" which means indivisible, inseparable or undivided. It describes processes in which the undifferentiated becomes individual, or processes in which separable components become an indivisible whole. When translating this rather abstract definition to knowledge infrastructures, it comprises four steps in the maturing of knowledge that can be supported by services.

- Experience: First, knowledge workers have to make sense of a vast and chaotic amount of material, e.g., the material available on a company Intranet or the Web. Thus, they shift their focus or awareness to knowledge elements which they differentiate out of the mass of material and connect to them. This might mean reading and understanding a resource on the Web and then tagging or bookmarking it in order to connect to it.
- Expression: Second, the knowledge worker then needs to make sense out of the separate knowledge elements that she has connected to in order to learn and, in subsequent steps, to build competence and expertise which means the encapsulation of knowledge elements into an inadvisable whole. This might mean connecting contents from diverse sources in order to express what the knowledge worker knows about a certain knowledge domain. It might also mean that the knowledge worker expresses some personal idea or proposal that is at first unconnected to the rest of the accessible knowledge elements.
- Competence: Competence reflects the relationship between an individual's skills and the requirements of the work to be completed by the individual. Competence services aim at supporting individual knowledge workers to develop their own knowledge and skills in a self-guided way. This includes reflecting on and making sense out of the development of individual competencies in the pursuit of a sequence of tasks.
- Expertise: While competence reflects on the fact that an individual's skills are sufficient to complete work in a certain domain, expertise reflects on an individual knowledge worker's long-standing experience in a domain of knowledge which differentiates her perception and acting inside the domain, from non-experts. Some authors extend the hierarchical model of data, information and knowledge by competence and further on by expertise which should reflect the increasing abstraction

from the concrete happenings, but also the increasing integration of separate individual experiences into a coherent whole - an expert's profound knowledge that
marks the highest (supportable) step of individuation with respect to knowledge
workers' professional development.

4.3 Interaction Services

Understanding group work and the design of supportive ICT tools has been researched
for over two decades under the topic of computer-supported cooperative work
(CSCW). It is an interdisciplinary research field and was started as an effort by
technologists to learn from members of other disciplines, e.g., economists, social
psychologists, organizational theorists and educators (Grudin 1994, 19f). Technical
support may focus on various aspects of interaction in group work as exchange of
knowledge in shared workspaces, provision of communication media, structuring
cooperative work processes and guidance of decision processes.

Figure 4 shows classes of interaction services. Every communicative relationship
at some point is initiated. Initiation services thus target establishing links between
people. Networking services target deepening, renewal and care-taking for these links.
Communication services focus on exchanging knowledge between people and offer
various channels to enable or enhance this. Finally, community services target supporting groups characterized by long-term, social relationships with many rather weak
links between their members. Consequently, these services form a cycle of increasingly closer forms of interaction as outlined above. Not every relationship evolves
through all of these stages. The dashed line between community and initiation indicates that every community may be reenergised by developing links to new people.

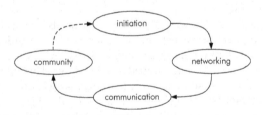

Fig. 4. Interaction services

4.4 In-Form-Ation Services

In-form-ation services bring knowledge into a form so that it can be easily distributed
and reused. This process can be labeled as "formalization" since knowledge is expressed by means of, e.g., written language, graphical representations and formulas
which involve a more or less strong formalization process in order to emphasize that
individual knowledge is transformed to contextualized information instead of knowledge as soon as it is expressed and incorporated by any type of information resource.

Figure 5 displays four general groups of in-form-ation services. Capturing refers to the process of making potentially large amounts of information resources electronically available in the required format and quality. This comprises scanning of paper-based information resources and further processes such as visual post-processing and optical character recognition. It may also include conversion and loading of legacy data in various electronic formats. Manipulation services support coordination and management of changes on information resources. Translation services concern transforming information resources into different structures and formats. They serve the important task of publishing information on the Intranet or the Web. Archiving services help managing retention periods of information resources, storing them in a secure and cost-effective manner and ultimately assist their deletion. They are relevant because legal regulations oblige organizations to keep information resources for defined periods of time and to be able to provide them as pieces of evidence.

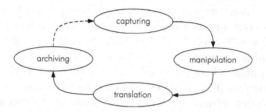

Fig. 5. In-form-ation services

4.5 Instruction Services

Instruction services target turning material provided in the former steps of the maturity model, particularly formal documents from the in-form-ation step, but also individual contributions from the interaction step, into resources that can be used for self-guided learning or formal instruction. Ultimate aim is to didactically refine material in order to help knowledge workers in building individual and team knowledge. Although instruction services generally can be applied for all types of knowledge, they are primarily instruments to facilitate communication and to transfer implicit, personal knowledge. Figure 6 shows four main categories used to subdivide instruction services.

Contents produced in the preceding steps of the maturing model are typically not well-suited for supporting self-guided learning or formal training. Enrichment services help knowledge workers to refine material deemed suitable for learning with the help of pedagogical and didactical approaches. Composition services use prepared learning material or learning objects as input for creating courses, i.e. arrangements of related learning material or objects. Consumption marks the transition between design time of learning resources and run-time. It primarily consists of using courses delivered to learners by a run-time environment such as a learning management system which needs to be administered. Finally, assignment services describe test and examination instruments that can be used in order to evaluate what has been learned.

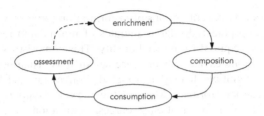

Fig. 6. Instruction services

5 Discussion and Conclusion

Generally, SMEs are on the one hand in a relatively good position with respect to handling of knowledge compared to large organization because of factors like a lower level of knowledge fragmentation and spreading across geographical entities, low degree of formalization and specialization, strong ties between members of the organization, direct access to "knowers", hardly restricted access to documented knowledge, stronger identification of employees with the organization and an often tighter network of informal contacts between employees. On the other hand, it is less likely to find required expertise within the organizational boundaries resulting in a higher need to cooperate, it is often difficult to recruit talent, there are no specific roles that support or guide knowledge activities and, last, but not least, there are little financial resources or time to be allocated to KM initiatives.

This results in a situation in many SMEs that introducing centralized KM systems is seen as not feasible and consequently many employees rely on their own arrangement of ICT services to support their knowledge activities. This calls for flexible ways of arranging services supporting knowledge activities when and by whom they are needed. As one cannot expect large amounts of time and resources for guidance, pragmatic models that allow for a quick analysis of the services that are currently supporting employees in their knowledge activities are needed.

This is what the knowledge maturing model and the corresponding services as described above are intended for. With their help, one could analyze local "good practices" of individual employees (investigation, individuation), informal collections of employees, also called communities (individuation, interaction), teams and work groups (interaction, in-form-ation), the formal handling of documented knowledge (in-form-ation) as well as apprenticeship, mentor-mentee and other relationships with a teaching part (instruction). Specific to SMEs could be an endeavor to extend the scope of analysis to business partners, particularly "good practices" found in supplier, customer and cooperation partner organizations due to close relationships that have to be built with them in order to foster knowledge cooperation.

Moreover, as argued in the section "knowledge services", SMEs can potentially benefit substantially from contents and services offered in a Web 2.0 manner over the Internet. Consequently, "good practices" supposedly include an increasing portion of Web 2.0 contents and services. The knowledge maturing model can be applied to govern the use of such contents and services. For example, services supporting each phase that have been initiated by individual employees can be selected to be shared, described, recommended or even composed into the SME's ICT infrastructure using mashup or SOA technology so that compliance can be assured with respect to the regulations applicable to the organization. A next step could be the analysis of gaps between the services applied to support the individual steps in the knowledge maturing model. Finally, arrangements of services targeting individual steps as well as the connections between them could be suggested as a flexibly configurable knowledge infrastructure.

In summary, this paper presented the knowledge maturing model together with a structured list of knowledge services and discussed their potential support from the perspective of SMEs. The paper gave several examples of how this model could be used as a pragmatic instrument to help SMEs in exploiting the promised benefits of Web 2.0 services and deploying a KM approach that can be characterized as "lightweight", "on-demand" and "just-in-time" (Davenport & Glaser, 2002; Tsui, 2005) as opposed to the often far-reaching, resource-intensive and centralized KM approaches suggested for large organizations.

Acknowledgement

This work was partly funded by the European Commission under the Information and Communication Technologies (ICT) theme of the 7th Framework Programme (FP7) within the Integrating Project MATURE (contract no. 216356).

References

Alonso, G., Casati, F., Kuno, H., Machiraju, V.: Web services. Concepts, architectures and applications, Berlin (2004)

April, K.A.: Guidelines for developing a k-strategy. Journal of Knowledge Management 6(5), 445–456 (2002)

Alvesson, M.: Knowledge work and knowledge-intensive firms, Oxford (2004)

Braun, S., Schmidt, A., Walter, A., Zacharias, V.: The Ontology Maturing Approach to Collaborative and Work-Integrated Ontology Development: Evaluation Results and Future Directions. In: International Workshop on Emergent Semantics and Ontology Evolution (ESOE), ISWC 2007, Busan/Korea (2007)

Davenport, T.H., Glaser, J.: Just-in-time delivery comes to knowledge management. Harvard Business Review, 5–9 (July 2002)

Davenport, T.H., Jarvenpaa, S.L., Beers, M.C.: Improving knowledge work processes. Sloan Management Review 37(4), 53–65 (1996)

Drucker, P.F.: The age of social transformation. The Atlantic Monthly 274(5), 53–80 (1994)

Grudin, J.: Computer-Supported Cooperative Work: History and focus. IEEE Computer 5(27), 19–26 (1994)

Hädrich, T.: Situation-oriented Provision of Knowledge Services. PhD Thesis, Martin-Luther-University of Halle-Wittenberg 2008 (2008)

Hansen, M.T., Nohria, N., Tierney, T.: What's your strategy for managing knowledge. Harvard Business Review, 680–689 (March-April 1999)

Krafzig, D., Banke, K., Slama, D.: Enterprise SOA: Service-oriented architecture best practices, Upper Saddle River (2005)

Maier, R.: Knowledge management systems. Information and communication technologies for knowledge management, 3rd edn., Berlin (2007)

Maier, R., Hädrich, T., Peinl, R.: Enterprise knowledge infrastructures, 2nd edn., Berlin (2009)

Maier, R., Schmidt, A.: Characterizing Knowledge Maturing. A Conceptual Process Model for Integrating E-Learning and Knowledge Management. In: Proceedings of WM 2007 - 4th Conference on Professional Knowledge Management. Experiences and Visions, Potsdam 2007, pp. 325–333 (2007)

Maier, R., Thalmann, S.: Institutionalised collaborative tagging as an instrument for managing maturing learning and knowledge resources. International Journal of Technology Enhanced Learning (IJTEL) 1(1), 70–84 (2008)

Maslow, A.H.: A Theory of Human Motivation. Psychological Review 50, 370–396 (1943)

Ordóñez de Pablos, P.: Knowledge management and organizational learning: Typologies of knowledge strategies in the spanish manufacturing industry from 1995 to 1999. Journal of Knowledge Management 6(1), 52–62 (2002)

O'Reilly, T.: What Is Web 2.0. Design Patterns and Business Models for the Next Generation of Software (2005),
http://www.oreillynet.com/pub/a/oreilly/tim/news/2005/09/30/what-is-web-20.html (30.9.2005)

Schmidt, A.: Knowledge Maturing and the Continuity of Context as a Unifying Concept for Integrating Knowledge Management and E-Learning. In: Proceedings of I-KNOW Conference 2005, Graz (2005)

Schultze, U.: A Confessional Account of an Ethnography about Knowledge Work. Management Information Systems Quarterly 1(24), 1–39 (2000)

Siemens, G.: Connectivism: Learning as Network Creation, elearnspace (2005),
http://www.elearnspace.org/Articles/networks.htm
(last access: 2008/12/12)

Starbuck, W.H.: Learning by Knowledge-Intensive Firms. Journal of Management Studies 29(6), 713–740 (1992)

Tsui, E.: The role of IT in KM: Where are we now and where are we heading? Journal of Knowledge Management 9(1), 3–6 (2005)

Watson, R.T.: Data Management. Data Bases & Organizations, 5th edn., New York (2005)

Watson, R.T.: Evolutionary Information Systems. Presentation at the University of Innsbruck (2008)

W3C. Web services glossary (2004),
http://www.w3.org/TR/2004/NOTE-ws-gloss-20040211/
(last access: 2008/12/12)

Wolff, E.N.: The growth of information workers. Communications of the ACM 48(10), 37–42 (2005)

Zacharias, V., Braun, S., Schmidt, A.: Social Semantic Bookmarking with SOBOLEO. In: Murugesan, S. (ed.) Handbook of Research on Web 2.0, 3.0 and X.0: Technologies, Business, and Social Applications (2009)

Zack, M.H.: Developing a knowledge strategy. California Management Review 41(3), 125–145 (1999)

The Emergence of 'Power with': The Case of a Born Global Organization

Lin Yan[1] and Niki Panteli[2]

[1] University Of Greenwich, Uk
[2] University Of Bath, Uk

1 Introduction

Thanks to the advancement of Information and Communications Technologies, the past decade has seen the rise of Born Global organizations (Rennie, 1993; Oviatt and McDougall, 1994; Karra and Philips, 2004; Zahra, 2005). Broadly defined as 'business organizations that, right from inception, seek to derive significant competitive advantages from the use of resources and the sales of outputs in multiple countries' (Oviatt and McDougall, 1994: 49), Born Global organizations are small, young, and internationally dispersed. While sharing the characteristics of 'smallness' and 'newness' of Small- and Medium-sized Enterprises (SMEs), Born Global organizations also bear 'foreignness', similar to that of Multinational Corporations (Zahra, 2005). Born Globals therefore need to strike a balance between 'global reach' and 'local touch' as in Multinational Corporations (Bartlett and Ghoshal, 1989); yet they have to do so with scare resources and organizational uncertainty similar to SMEs, and with 'lean' and 'mean' communications afforded by ICT (e.g. Sproull and Kiesler, 1986). This study is an initial attempt to untangle the combined challenges in Born Globals' innovative way of management. Through a longitudinal case study, we aim to explore the issue of power in a Born Global's endeavour to manage its global knowledge via technology mediation.

In this study, our aim is to address the following questions: 1). "How is power articulated and negotiated in Born Global organizations? and 2). "What is distinctive about power in Born Global organizations when compared to traditional SMEs?" To this end, we first introduce the concept of 'Born Global' and provide an overall perspective of the innovative management often found in Born Globals. We then focus on the relevant literature on power in 'traditional' organizational setting. Following this, we present an empirical case study to illustrate how power was articulated and negotiated in a Born Global organization. Based on the findings, we conclude the paper by analysing the implications and limitations of the study and call for further research.

2 Born Global Organizations

Over a decade ago, Rennie (1993) surveyed 310 firms in Australia and identified 'a new breed of Australian firms' that accounted for almost 20 percent of the country's high-value-added manufacturing exports. Contrary to other firms in the survey,

G. Dhillon, B.C. Stahl, and R. Baskerville (Eds.): CreativeSME 2009, IFIP AICT 301, pp. 239–256, 2009.
© IFIP International Federation for Information Processing 2009

which started exporting after about 27 years after establishment, this 'new breed' exported at an average age of two years. They were also different from 'the traditional idea of exporting firms' (ibid: 45) in that they were expanding to and indeed winning in the international market without a prior base with 'strong skills, solid financial capability, and a sound product portfolio' at home. What was striking was the co-existence of small size, young age and their 'ability to compete globally' (ibid: 48). Their emergence, according to Rennie (1993), signalled a new direction of growth for SMEs. 'Contrary to popular wisdom', summarised Rennie (1993: 45), 'they were born global'.

As a new form of SME in the international era, cases of Born Global organizatons have been reported in many major countries in the world, constituting a significant proportion of national economies, and inspiring an expanding and dynamic field of research (e.g. McDougall and Oviatt, 2003, Zahra, 2005). In addition to the liabilities of 'newness' and 'smallness' often found in traditional SMEs, what is unique about Born Globals is the 'liability of foreignness' (Zahra, 2005), a 'trait' mostly confined to large, multinational organizations. The interplay between its 'newness', 'smallness', and 'foreignness' demands Born Globals to adapt innovative ways of management, more complex than the management of traditional SMEs.

Oviatt and McDougall (1994), in one of the earliest studies of Born Global organizations, termed this innovative management as the 'alternative governance structure'. Due to the lack of resources and market experience on the one hand, and the demand for international operations on the other, Born Globals do not, and indeed cannot, own all the resources they need. While ownership is the conventional means of governing resources, Born Globals are often found to rely on 'alternative' structures. For Born Globals, it is their 'resourcefulness'– not the amount or even types of resources they own – that matters (Zahra, 2005: 21).

Like domestic SMEs, the most typical alternative governance structure in Born Globals is social network, connecting Born Globals with other organizations through personal or professional relations (e.g. Oviatt and McDougall, 1994; Bell, 1995; Servias and Rasmussen, 2000; Sharma and Blomstermo, 2003; Zahra 2005). Unlike domestic SMEs, however, the network in and around Born Globals is international, geographically dispersed, and often involving people from diverse professional, social, and cultural backgrounds. This 'distributed' feature of Born Globals makes them an interesting venue to explore innovative management in SMEs. In this paper, we report a case study that unveils how management power is articulated and negotiated via the use of Information and Communication Technologies (ICTs) in a Born Global organization.

3 Power

This study was largely exploratory and grounded in nature. The issue of power was not what we looked for initially. With the progress of data collection and analysis, however, the power issue became more and more salient. We now briefly review the literature on resource and identity-based powers. We found these two themes to be particularly pertinent to our data, in order to assist readers in understanding our later analysis of power. While earlier studies maintain that power derives from the procession and mobilization of scarce resources (e.g. Blau 1964; Dahl 1957), later studies emphasize shared identity as the basis of power (Clegg et al., 2006).

The earlier approach defines power around resource-dependency. Power derives from one party (an individual or group) having (or being perceived to have) the ability to impose its will on another by virtue of the resources at its disposal (e.g. Blau, 1964; Dahl, 1957; Kaplan, 1964; Webber, 1947). The procession and mobilization of scarce resources enable one party to have power over others through withdrawing or withholding resources (Allen, Colligan, Finnie and Kern, 2000; Rassingham 2000). When one party controls scarce resources, it has power. Lukes (1974) later presented a more eclectic conceptualization of power, known as the 'three dimensions' of power. In the first dimension, power is directly associated with scarce resources, while the second and third dimensions link power to the manipulation of 'meanings', through the control of either process or content, so that the 'real interest' of those under power is overlooked, or at least undermined, by the construction and articulation of social meanings. This approach emphasizes the notion of 'power over'. Power was thus mainly seen as prohibitive, preventing those under power from behaving in certain ways.

An underlying assumption of such prohibitive power is the notion of conflict. It was assumed that the fundamental relation between those in power and those under power was the continuous competition to possess scarce resources. As Clegg et al (2006: 191) noted:

> Conflict was seen as the basis of organizational life. The resolution of one conflict would become the foundation for the next. Social change was seen as ubiquitous, rather than unusual, and conflict was normally one of its major mechanisms. Order emerges because some members of society are able to constrain others. Their acts of containment are episodes of power, usually accompanied by conflict.

This assumption of conflict was often challenged in the later theorizations of power (Bloomfield and Coombs, 1992). Simon and Oakes (2006), for instance, rejected the view that social power is essentially conflict-ridden and quite ugly; Brocklehurst (2001) contended that power is not necessarily a zero-sum game due to struggles between conflicting interests. Instead, *shared* meanings between those exercising power and those being managed, based on shared social identities, was introduced. Simon and Oakes (2006), for instance, depicted 'four faces of power', with the fourth 'face' dedicated to the production of shared identity. 'Rather than the violent, coercive dictators', Simon and Oakes (2006: 119) argued that 'entrepreneurs of identity' are likely to become 'the most powerful social actors' through recruiting others under a shared identity. This notion of power based on shared identities is labelled as 'power *to*' (Clegg et al., 2006). Different from the conflict-based and constraining notion in 'power over', 'power to' is both prohibitive and enabling.

In Born Global organizations, where power is mostly exercised over distance via technology mediation, where direct control by owner or entrepreneur seems an unlikely option, how is power articulated? How is it negotiated by those under or receiving power? These are the questions we aimed to explore at a research site in a Born Global organization.

4 Research Methods

Beta Ltd. (a pseudonym) was chosen as the research site due to its small size, rapid international expansion, geographically dispersion, multiple layers of membership, and concentration in the 'knowledge-intensive' sector – some of the major characteristics of Born Globals.

Beta specializes in management consulting. Established in 1999, Beta soon developed into a global organization with offices, associates and affiliates in 18 countries, including the Netherlands, Italy, Germany, Lithuania, Canada, China, the US, and UK, boasting itself as 'a global network of top consultants'. Beta saw that its competitive advantage lay precisely in the small size and global reach. To utilize these, it had a multiple layers of membership, namely a core team of members and a network of associates. They addressed themselves as the 'Beta Network', with 16 'core' members, 15 'associate' members, and 22 'affiliates'. 'Core' members were those who are officially on Beta's payroll, 'associates' were regular contractors and 'affiliates' were more *ad hoc* participants of Beta's international projects. Instead of having a 'pyramid', hierarchical, structure, Beta's organizational structure was flat, with most employees at the senior levels as 'partners', 'senior consultants', or 'consultant'. This reflected the experiences and prestige of the members, as most were regarded as experts in their individual fields.

The fieldwork was conducted during May 2003 and July 2004. Data collection started with participant observation. We gained access to Beta's 'Centre' in London as a consultant who helped with Beta's IT systems. We later had the opportunity to conduct an organization-wide survey on the use of the Intranet, and thus began our direct contact with the dispersed members of the organization. As rapport built up, we then had the opportunity to directly participate in the organization's international projects and work closely with some of the international members of the organization. Along with this increasing involvement in the field, the scope of data collection gradually expanded beyond the use of IT to generic management issues, and the methods of data collection included document analysis and semi- and unstructured interviews, in addition to participant observation. Overall, broad access was obtained in the organization, including their Intranet, conference calls, meeting minutes, internal training sessions, meetings with clients and suppliers, newsletters, group emails, and on some occasions, emails that were exchanged between the individual members.

The participant observation focused on the conducts of the head of the Centre in London and her comments about managing a Born Global organization. Two rounds of semi-structured interviews were conducted with all 'core' members of the organization, usually lasting 45 minutes to one hour. The first round was conducted after my survey of IT use in Beta. These interviews usually started with follow-up questions from the survey, and aimed at exploring the management issues behind the use of IT and introducing myself to the individuals outside London. Questions such as 'You mentioned in the survey that you don't really use the Intranet, would you tell me why?' and 'You commented that international conference calls were not helpful, what are the key areas to be improved in your view?' were asked. The responses to such questions allowed further exploration of the management issues at Beta, issues that were later picked up in unstructured interviews when we had the opportunity to work with several consultants on their international projects. These un-structured interviews were carried out mostly during discussions on work progress, and mainly aimed at exploring issues that seemed most pertinent in their relationships with London. The impressions, hints and hunches from these 'casual talks' enabled me to carry out a second round of semi-structured interviews towards the end of the fieldwork. Substantiated by the conduct and comments from the consultants obtained from observation and unstructured interviews, this round of semi-structured interviews focused on the consultants' responses to the key 'management measures' that London put in place.

The data analysis was broadly guided by Grounded Theory (Glasser and Strauss, 1967). These field notes, interview transcripts, company documents, meeting/conference call/conference minutes, newsletters, contents of the Intranets, and emails, were manually coded. While acknowledging the limitation of manual coding (e.g. slow speed, lack of quantitative accuracy, and being 'subjective'), we nonetheless found manual coding a helpful process in eliciting the key themes from the data, with the particular advantage of the researcher's constant closeness to data. The data on how London manages the dispersed consultants was coded along the four major actions of the London office, namely the initiation of the Intranet, organization of conference calls, distribution of newsletters, and project management. The data on the consultants' responses to London was coded along the degree of compliance in their comments and conducts. While some showed clear compliance with London's requests, others negotiated or even resisted. The code of 'power', as a second-order code, did not emerge till the late stage of data analysis. In my searching for an overarching concept that captured the interactions between London and the consultants, 'power' came to be a notion that linked it all. There were, of course, alternative concepts, but they either seemed partial (such as 'control' or 'impression management') or did not address the fundamental social relations in this organization (such as 'structural misfit' or 'conflict'). This is not to say that power was the only force in play. Indeed, most of the concepts mentioned above bear close connections to power. The limitation of adopting this concept is acknowledged, and will be elaborated later, but given the centrality of power in organizations in general (Clegg et al., 2006), and the common theme from the data, we focused on power. In what follows, we report the data on London's assertion of power, and the consultants' compliance, negotiation, and resistance of power.

5 Results

London was Beta's 'Centre', or 'Central Office', purposely set up to manage the dispersed consultants and to bridge the difference between consulting practices as practised in the US and the EU, two of Beta's largest markets. The 'Centre' was headed by Melanie and had two other staff, Holly for finance/accounting and Valentina for marketing. Beyond London, all the heads of local offices were also virtual members of the 'Centre'. While Melanie was responsible for the Centre's day-to-day operations, 'strategic issues', such as negotiating partnership contracts and developing new services and markets, were often involved and decided by the virtual members.

In theory, London controlled some of the key assets of the organization – finance, accounting records, marketing materials, project supervision, and personnel management. No project at Beta were seen as 'official' until it had been registered with London, at which point, Melanie became the project manager overseeing the progress. It was also within Melanie's remits to add, withdraw, or transfer consultants in her role of the Project Manager. This power, however, was rarely exercised (not once during my fieldwork). In practice, London was seen as fairly powerless, both by the consultants and Melanie herself. London's involvement in international projects seemed to be confined to documentation, book-keeping, and 'information processing'. Much of the work was organized in 'gangs', or sub-groups. There did not seem to be any fast rules about how and why these 'gangs' were formed. Furthermore, they were not consistent and stable over time. 'Personal connections' and 'previous projects' were the common reasons the consultants cited, while professional background, geographic location, or social/cultural background did not seem salient in the forming and re-forming of the 'gangs'. Overall, this Born Global's management seemed to be a struggle between the structured and formalized approach taken by Melanie and the fairly autonomous 'rebellious' attitude adopted by the consultants.

5.1 Asserting Power

London attempted to assert its power as the 'Centre'. This was done by initiating and managing Beta's Intranet, requesting the members' presence at global conference calls and newsletters, and regulating virtual presence in project management.

First, Melanie stressed the importance of having a 'managed' Intranet for information storage and retrieval. During the planning phase of the Intranet, Melanie surveyed all members about their needs and requirements for the Intranet. This was quickly followed by an invitation to all members to submit documents and 'any relevant materials' to London. Melanie then 'polished' and 're-wrote' some of these, mainly changing styles and formats, before loading them onto the Intranet. Once the Intranet went live, Melanie considered London as having the 'ownership responsibility' for it. She requested active participation from the members, and highlighted the importance of comprehensive information and timely updating. To be present on the Intranet, to Melanie, should not only be part of the members' everyday tasks, but also part of their identity as a consultant.

> "Well, the Intranet is about what we do, or rather, what we are. We are consultants, we need to persuade clients that we have tried and tested tools to solve problems. At the central office, we provide these tools, the weapons to fight, on the Intranet, so that everyone can learn from here and draw out whatever he needs. It's absolutely central."

Melanie put great emphasis on updating 'cases'. Once a project concluded, each consultant was requested to write a report to be uploaded onto the Intranet. Melanie was not particular about the format of these reports. As she commented, only the consultants knew what is important; but she was adamant that this should be done, and as promptly as possible. What was valuable to Melanie was the consultants' participation and involvement in the Intranet. However, in actual practice, Melanie had some concerns. While fragmented information concerning past projects were often quickly circulated among the consultants, few summative reports were submitted to London. Most completed projects were not reported. At London, Melanie reluctantly closed the files of these cases after several reminders, knowing that little information could be added to the Intranet except the basic information such as client names, services provided, revenue generated and the duration of the project. The lack of 'reflection' and 'forward thinking' frustrated Melanie, as did the lack of recognition of London as the 'information centre' of the organization.

To catch up with fragmented information, Melanie initiated a second measure – global conference calls – to facilitate 'continuous communications'. Lasting for an hour or so, these calls were organised once a month. Although it was not a formal obligation for the consultants to take part, Melanie repeatedly emphasized the benefits of timely information-sharing. Initially, London was only responsible for the organization of the calls, such as issuing passwords and providing technical support. The contents were decided by the dispersed partners; and a partner located in Italy was appointed as the chair. But seeing the calls gradually 'drifting', as in becoming irregular, and also lacking clear agenda, Melanie decided to take further action. She started by requesting all members to participate in the forthcoming call; then chaired the call herself by having a 'round-the-table' report from each participant; this was later followed by emails detailing to-do lists, such as this one:

We agreed to concentrate on Companies ranking between 201 and 300 and first that piece will be circulated from London with a chance for everyone to give the following input:

1. *Have you worked for any of them?*
2. *Do you know any of them or do you have contacts in them (contact name)?*
3. *Do you know what issues any of them are currently facing?*
4. *Choose 15 each that you'd like to follow-up.*

At the next conference, we will assign the companies and the team (2 people) who will follow it up.

Third, Melanie distributed newsletters, and paid particular attention to the broad representation of consultants in the newsletters. Unlike the Intranet and the conference calls, however, Melanie did not actively edit the contents of the newsletters. An email was usually sent out a week before the issue date, inviting contribution. Melanie was only to copy and paste the information she received. For Melanie, the newsletters were 'for fun', aimed at establishing a sense of community rather than business building, but she was careful to ensure that all offices had fairly even coverage in the newsletters, and there was some coverage of the London office in each issue.

Finally, in addition to managing these everyday communications, Melanie also gave great importance to playing an active role in project management. Beta operated a 'twin leaders' system on international projects – one 'project owner' who provided professional expertise to the participating consultants, and one 'project manager' who oversaw its progress, undertaking tasks such as filing documentation and managing deadlines. Melanie was the 'default' project manager in most cases given her role as the head of the 'Centre'. Due to the twin leader system, project communications were supposed to follow a 'matrix', with both the owner and manager fully informed of new progress. But in practice, Melanie often felt left out. Given the lack of comprehensive IT communication systems (as are often the case in SMEs), Melanie relied on being copied in emails to keep pace with project development. This proved to be unsatisfactory. Although Melanie was able to get a rough idea of project progress, she was concerned with both the contents and frequency of the emails she received. She felt she was being overloaded with information *and* left out of key developments. In her words, the emails updates were not used 'properly':

> *"Because we're in so many countries, we use emails a lot. But I find them a bit difficult...for example, I find myself being copied in a lot of emails; some of them, perhaps 50%, don't have much to do with us in London. But on the other hand, I do miss out some important updates; somehow they don't come to me. I suspect it's not very different for others. So I thought we should have a (sort of) standard of using emails, especially for ongoing projects, as part of project management."*

Melanie eventually failed to develop the 'standard of using emails'. Till the end of the fieldwork, she continued to receive, and being frustrated, by the volumes of emails that were 'not particularly useful'.

In summary, despite possessing some key resources, London failed to exercise its full power as the 'Centre'. It 'managed' the consultants mainly in fairly 'under-handed' and indirect ways, through formalization and requesting of virtual participation. These attempts largely failed, as the consultants offered diverse responses to the formalization and participation requests from London; some complied, some negotiated, while others resisted.

5.2 Complying with Power

The Canadian office was a 'one-woman band'. As one of the newest offices, it was 'headed' by Susan, an experience consultant. Compared to the bulk of work in Europe and the US, the Canadian market was seen as strategically less important by many consultants in the organization, including Susan herself. Its main function was as a satellite of the US office – carry out work for the US office during busy times, and carry out 'experimental' services which were offered provided in Europe in Canada before they were rolled out to the US. Susan took a 'pro-active' approach in her communications. Not only was she an active user of the Intranet, she was also a regular participant in global conference calls (14 times out of 14 during the fieldwork period). Unlike most of her colleagues, Susan was prompt in updating case studies on the Intranet (usually on the next working day after the conclusion day of the project), contributed to each edition of the newsletters, and tended to be the first one to reply to group emails sent from London before her colleagues who were located in the same or similar time zone as London. Furthermore, Susan was also 'active' in communicating project progress with London. She copied a large number of emails to Melanie. During an interview, she revealed that the aim was to be 'visible' to Melanie, to remedy the 'damage' of being a less significant, emergent, and 'remote' office. To Susan, the 'Centre' needed to be impressed:

> "I copy London in, most of my project emails. I think it's good to let them know what I'm doing. Here in Canada, we are not very big, not always on international assignments. So I want London and the partners to know that we're working."

5.3 Discounting Power

Susan's compliance with London was the exception rather than the rule. For others, London was to be 'listened to, sometimes'. Most of the consultants complied with London's requests selectively and tactfully negotiated their relations with the 'Centre'. Most of them had moderate usage of the Intranet; occasionally participated in the conference calls, and found the newsletters helpful in that they provided a channel to scoop recent news without much commitment. In addition, they used project-related emails to manoeuvre their social distance from London.

My data on this aspect started with the use of the Intranet. Most consultants commented that the Intranet lacked rich content and timely information. According to my survey, the most accessed part of the Intranet was the personal profiles. Yet even this confined use was found to be unsatisfactory among most consultants. A Dutch associate, for instance, commented:

> "The content is very limited. I think the Intranet should be a content site. It's OK that now if I want to talk to someone, I'll just look at the Intranet and find their phone number. But that is information, that's not what I call content."

The profiles on the Intranet were managed by Melanie but contributed by the individual consultants. As with their reluctance in reporting recent projects, they were also less committed to updating personal profiles. Some profiles ran no more than a couple of key words on specialisation and the contact information. This, according to some consultants, explained why they were not keen to use the Intranet. For instance, one remarked:

> "The problem with the information on my colleagues is that it needs to be updated. The Intranet is a database, it gives you something you're looking for, but we would need a phone call to assure that. In the database, it's general information. You would need more, more information, for example, the industry might be completely different, we need to be more customer-focused, we need to be more precise on the Intranet."

Some remedied this 'lack of information' on the Intranet with social contacts:

> "The disadvantage of the Intranet is that you have to use it...creatively. I mean, when someone has done a project, it's very likely that it's not there. But still, you know someone must have done this sort of thing

> *before. Then, I'll tap into my relations, and ask one or more people I know, not using the Intranet."*

For others, this profile information was largely redundant; they had better means of securing timely and accurate information:

> *"Oh, yes, I use the Intranet for profiles, but to be honest, when you know the people, you know who to ask. The initiation of these dialogues is very classic - emails. I don't use the Intranet very much, though it could be a 'knowledge platform', it's not there yet."*

The consultants' involvement with the Intranet seemed to be trapped in the circle of 'not-using and not participating'. It was similar with the use of conference calls – most of them attended the calls half-heartedly, as one comment suggested:

> *"These conference calls last an hour or so. Normally the chair is giving some introduction and information, and then every company, each has something to say, the French, the German, the Italian, and everybody. I don't really have the incentive to listen to them all. Do you think anyone is seriously listening to the whole call? I don't know."*

Some were concerned with the lack of in-depth information at the calls:

> *"The calls have (a) limited value in sharing information; every country can tell what they have done, what problems they have. If that's the quality of the conference call, it's ok. But you want to know more about it. You call them afterwards, but that's my approach."*

Some complained about the passivity present in the calls:

> *"Getting together on the phone and have nothing in common to say is not value for time. There's too much, passiveness (sic) in the telephone conferences."*

While according to others, conference calls should not take this 'blanket-bombing' approach, but should be organised only within project teams:

> *"I don't phone in for the conference calls. No, I don't take part. I interact with a selective group of people in the network, When we had projects, we used to talk on a regular basis... (Interviewer: ... that is, outside the monthly conference calls?) Yes, it's for the project. As we currently don't have an ongoing project, I don't phone in on the conferences."*

As regards copying Melanie in project emails, it seemed that the consultants not only selected the contents to be seen by London, but also carefully crafted the timing. Some used this to manage the expectations of London. For instance, one commented:

> *"Umm, we usually have deadlines, several deadlines on one project. I will copy emails to Melanie, a couple of days before the deadline?*

> *Yeah, a couple of days before; and she knows that when the deadline comes, I'll perhaps have done this, or more...(Interviewer: Why don't you copy Melanie in at other time?) Hmm, it's just small things, not worth mentioning."*

Others timed this as a 'warm-up' for their forthcoming face-to-face meetings at London:

> *"[e]very now and then, I will copy Maria in the emails, especially when I'm scheduling some meetings in Europe, so that in Maria's head, I'm around, not just a castaway."*

In summary, most people's connection with London seemed to be some sort of detached attachment – complying with some requests by London yet attempting to retain a sense of autonomy.

5.4   Resisting Power

As with the case with Susan, another extreme case was with Katherine, a senior consultant and the only consultant based in London. Despite sharing an office with the 'Centre', Katherine mostly worked off site, either with clients or from home. Like other consultants of the organization, most interactions between Katherine and the 'central office' were via ICT. As a founding member of the organization, Katherine saw herself 'very much as a freelance working with great friends'. On several occasions, she commented that it was the identity of 'being a consultant', rather than a Beta member, that directed her work and interaction with the 'Centre'. Beta's advantage, in Katherine's view, is precisely in its lack of 'bureaucracy':

> *"The way Beta works is to get rid of the 'backpackers', I mean, admin (administration) and the junior consultants, in large consulting companies. Beta consultants work at the senior level only. In exceptional cases, when I need support, my colleagues abroad are always very helpful."*

It was perhaps not surprising that Katherine was not keen on using and updating the Intranet. During an interview, she commented about updating case studies:

> *"I'm not very good at doing the case studies, (laugh) I know that. At the moment, all my incentive is that Vale (Valentina, Melanie's assistant) makes me a nice cup of tea, and keeps staring at me every five minutes. (laugh) ...Suggestions for that? Well, have something simple, tick boxes, what I call 'one, two, three, and done' sort of thing."*

Katherine did not participate in the monthly conference calls organized by Melanie, but when the need arose, she organized 'project calls'.

In contrast, the newsletters were the best way of communication for Katherine, for the relative lack of interference from the 'Central Office':

> *"With all respect to the conference calls, and the Intranet, I'd say the news mails are the most efficient thing to keep us connected....the good thing is that you can control the output. If something isn't relevant to you, skip it, so you have your own version of the news, so to speak. I think that's hugely beneficial, in that, you can identify your own 'gang', but also keep your ears open for something else."*

Instead of relying on Melanie for key resources, such as financing or project assignment, Katherine was self-sufficient in initiating and managing international projects, thanks to her extensive contact network in- and out-side the organization.

> *"I would say that nine times out of ten, I got involved in international projects through Rob. But often I know where these all comes from before Rob emails me, I mean, I usually know who's doing what...Yes, from Melanie and Vale as well, but as I say, if there's something I'm interested in, I would have contacted the local consultants well before any, third party, so to speak, tells me about it...I do this by talking to my 'gang' once in a while, catch up...yes, sometimes I don't wait for the newsletters or the conference calls, I'm in touch with my own little network, so to speak."*

On Melanie's project management, she remarked:

> *"Generally we're on track, without much pushing and whistling ... It could be, demoralising, if I'm rushing to a deadline, and all of a sudden receive an email from the project leader, saying that I should have done this and that, by tomorrow. We're consultants, deep at heart, we're rebels (laugh) – we have to work creatively, and we're usually very driven. Deadline management is important, but I just think it's essential to draw a line between attentiveness and pressure."*

Katherine did not copy her project emails to Melanie unless it was 'absolutely necessary' to do so:

> *"Oh yes, I left a lot of things that I don't copy Melanie in. Well, if everyone copies everything to Melanie, how on earth could she cope?*
>
> *Well, the purpose of copying Melanie in my emails to other colleagues, is to give Melanie some flavour of the progress of the project, as this is important for her, central co-ordination. But unless it's about the critical timeline of those large-scale, critical projects, I think we generally rely on our own discretion."*

From Melanie's assertion of power, to the compliance, negotiation, and resistance from the consultants, Beta displayed a variety of power relations. Table 1. is a brief summary of the data.

Table 1. Types of Power in the Case

What?	Who?	Where?	How?
Assertion	Melanie	At the 'Centre'	Establishing 'infrastructure': - Intranet - Conference calls - Newsletters - Project management
Compliance	Susan	Canada office (small, new, and 'remote')	Copying May in all of her emails; To say 'we are working'
Discounting	Most members	At dispersed local offices	Use the Intranet 'creatively'; Passivity in participating conference calls; Selective report of information; Punctuated presence to London
Resistance	Katherine	London office (as a founding member of the organization)	Self-sufficient in initiating new projects; Organize own conference calls in her 'gangs'; Found using Intranet over-complicated; Found May's request for emails a pressure; Leave May out of most emails unless they concerned critical deadlines.

6 Discussion

Born Global organizations would not have emerged without the advancement of ICT. In this case, we saw a typical Born Global that adhered to the common realities found in small businesses. How has this facilitated or hindered their management? Regarding Born Globals in particular, how did they untangle the challenge of 'smallness', 'newness', and 'foreignness' in their daily operation via ICT? As a grounded study, the initial aim of the fieldwork was not to explore power, but to understand the innovative management often found in Born Global organizations. With the progress of fieldwork, however, more and more data illuminate the power relations between Melanie and her dispersed colleagues. The concept of 'power' seemed to be particularly helpful in making sense of the data. But why power? Are there not any concepts and theories that 'captured' the spirit of the data? What does 'power' tell us about managing Born Global organizations? In what follows, we will first report my thinking in ruling out alternative theories, then elaborate on power in this case.

6.1 Why Power?

Several alternatives came to mind when analyzing the data, including Impression Management (Goffman, 1959), Leadership, task and structural mismatch, and boundaries such as location, time zone, cultural diversity, and professional background. None of these, it seems, fully corresponded with the data. Impression Management and Leadership seemed to help illuminate part of the data. The consultants' tactful use of ICTs may be seen as attempts to establish and maintain impressions that are congruent with the perceptions that they wanted to convey to their 'Centre' in London, or acts of 'impression management'. Yet this concept alone failed to account for the actions of their perceived audience – Melanie – and her efforts in deliberately shaping and developing the 'drama'. In contrast, Leadership, broadly defined as 'influence exerted...over other people to guide, structure, and facilitate relationships in a group' (Yukl, 1998: 3), seemed to keep too much focus on Melanie at the expense of accounting for how the consultants' actions influenced her 'leadership' style. Furthermore, none of the consultants referred to Melanie as their 'leader'. It seemed overstretching if we, the researchers, make unfounded judgment on whether Melanie could count as a 'leader'. Either 'impression management' or 'leadership' would tell only half of the story. A third 'rival hypothesis' was the mismatch between the 'natural' work process which was implicitly accepted in the organization and the communication structure imposed by Melanie. This notion of 'structural misfit', though found in the data, was not central. The consultants readily acknowledged that the structure Melanie introduced was necessary. It was in the implementation that consultants found it important to negotiate their power relationship with the 'Centre'. In addition, the structure Melanie introduced was not uncommon. Similar mechanisms were found in other cases of Born Global organizations. It would be difficult to conceive an international organization, small though it is, surviving without any centralization and formalization. Even in temporary, largely self-governed project teams, 'it would be prudent to have regular and structured project status and performance reviews' (Lee-Kelley, 2006: 242), as

Melanie was trying to do. It is not our intention to justify the structure Melanie put in place. Rather, the point is that focusing on the structural mismatch would lead to a 'non-through road', where the only solution is to go back and try another way. Finally, could the interactions in the case be attributed to the dispersion of the consultants, the lack of frequent face-to-face interactions with London, and/or the diversity in their social, cultural, and professional backgrounds? Setting aside the fallacy that individuals are 'representatives' of their society, culture, or profession, the small number of individuals in this case made it necessary to explore relations between individuals, rather than between sub-groups. The spatial and temporal distances and the problems arising from 'lean' communications (e.g. DeSanctis & Monge, 1999; Cramton, 2001; Kiesler and Cummings, 2002; Gibson and Cohen, 2003, Sproull and Kiesler, 1986) were not salient in the data.

Ruling out alternative concepts, we came to focus on the notion of 'power', which seemed to capsulate the interactions between Melanie and her colleagues, underlying both issues of impression management and leadership, and having the potential to shed light on understanding the 'alternative governance structure' of Born Global organizations.

6.2 Power in the Case

In this case, Melanie's **assertion** of power was met with **compliance, negotiation,** and **resistance.** How is this power distinctive from that in traditional organizational settings? In what follows, we will focus on two aspects of power in the case – its articulation and negotiation.

First, power in the case was articulated in a rather 'under-handed' way, in both 'power over' and 'power to'. Melanie did not assert her power by upholding or withdrawing key resources such as finance or manpower, neither did she directly attempt to define or promote a shared identity across the organization. Instead, Melanie's actions revolved around setting up procedures, behavioral norms, and regulations via ICTs and requesting virtual presence from the consultants. Her power soon seemed to come to its limit when the consultants overlooked the procedures and negotiated their virtual presence. For the consultants, the articulation of their powers was also subtle. None of them withdrew scarce resources, notably, their knowledge and expertise, nor did most of them (except Kathleen) mention any alternative identity that intervened with their identification with the 'Centre' in London. Like Melanie, they mainly articulated their power through virtual presence and absence.

Similarly, virtual presence and absence were central in the negotiation of power. Some used virtual presence to enhance their link with London, some punctuated their presence, while others minimized their presence to indicate social distance from London. The virtual presence in relation to Melanie may be seen as less about exchange of information and knowledge than the manipulation of social relations. In other words, the contents of the emails were less important than their frequency and timing. Like the articulation of power, no direct reference was made to the scarce resources they held, notably their knowledge and expertise. Neither did the consultants cite any lack of shared identity as an explanation of their negotiation of power with Melanie. The exception was Katherine, who mentioned her professional identity as a reason for rejecting Melanie's requests. This, however, does not support the notion of 'power to' as conceptualized in the literature. It has been suggested that individuals often have several congruent or competing identities (e.g. Alvesson and Willmott, 2002). While Kathleen asserted her identity as a 'rebel', this does not indicate that the power relations surrounded identity management at the collective level.

The power in this case, mediated by ICT, seemed to reflect neither 'power over' nor 'power to'. Then how to conceptualize power in this Born Global organization? We readily acknowledge that any theorization based on one case study has its limitations (this will be further elaborated later), but this case was nonetheless helpful in shedding light on power relations in an emergent and innovative form of small organization that needs to balance smallness, newness and foreignness simultaneously. Power in the case did not seem to be based on possession and access to scarce resource, as in 'power over'. Indeed, it was difficult to identify what constituted scarce resources. Did these include finance, manpower, and project knowledge possessed by Melanie, or knowledge and expertise possessed by the consultants? Indeed, all these may count as scarce resources in my view. As with the geographic dispersion of the organization, its scarce resources were distributed across the locations and resided with individual members as well as the 'Centre'.

In terms of 'power to', it is clear that there was no attempt from the 'Centre' to establish and maintain a shared identity. From the only comment on identity made by Katherine, it may also be inferred that there was probably a lack of organizational identity in Beta, let alone power relations based on identity management. Instead of 'power over' and 'power to', we would like to coin the term 'power with' to illustrate the power relations in the case. Unlike 'power over' and 'power to', 'power with' assumes a network relation among individuals, where there is no salient distinction between 'centre' and 'peripheries'. Power is not based around possession of scarce resources, nor definition and management of shared organizational identity. Instead, 'power with' is distributed among individuals, not necessarily evenly, and subject to ongoing negotiations between them, as we have seen from the Beta case. Much remains to be explored about the notion of 'power with', as will be elaborated below. Bur for now, it is important to conceptualize power as 'power with' to capture the negotiated and distributed nature of power that resides in neither scarce resources nor identity management as found in this case.

7 Conclusions, Limitations, and Further Research

Based on an emergent and innovative form of small business, this study was an initial step in exploring power relationships which were primarily exercised via ICT. Drawing upon the traditional concepts of 'power over' and 'power to', it suggested a new concept of 'power with' to capsulate the subtle, negotiated, and distributed power relations found in this case study. There are several limitations in this study. First, it was a single case study that involved a small number of individuals. Data from this site might appear 'simple' compared with fieldwork that involved multiple cases and large number of participants. The conclusion from the study is necessarily limited in scope and further investigations are needed to enrich our understanding of 'power with'. But as a 'typical' Born Global organization, Beta has provided an interesting site to unveil the power relations in a new form of small business, enabled and facilitated by ICT. Second, there are many other concepts closely linked with power, such as 'control', 'coordination', 'collaboration', just to name a few. This paper focused on power as it underlies the other concepts and constitutes a fundamental social relation (Clegg et al., 2006). But it was also found that 'power' was an overarching, and indeed broad, concept. With the notion of 'power with', further studies on the related 'sub-concepts' of power, would be useful in enriching our understanding of how technology transforms social relations in Small and Medium-sized Enterprises.

The contribution of our study is mainly three-fold. First, it investigated a new form of small organization in the 'Internet Era', the Born Globals. Given its smallness, newness and globalness, Born Globals pose new management challenges not faced by large organizations, nor traditional domestic small businesses. While much research is currently focusing on the internationalization process of Born Globals, in the study, the 'black box' of its organization and internal social relations were explored. Second, thanks to the small size of the organization, this study explored power relations at the micro – individual – level. This complements current studies on power that are mostly at organizational, group, or national levels (Clegg *et al.*, 2006). Finally, we proposed the notion of 'power with'. Although this was only an initial study of its kind on power relations in a new organizational setting, we hope this notion of 'power with' will facilitate our quest to understand power, particularly in new and emergent organizational forms. Much remains to be explored on how information technology shapes and re-shapes SMEs. Putting Born Global organizations directly in the spot light, this paper hopefully takes an initial step in untangling the interplay between power, ICT, and innovative management in emergent organization forms.

References

Allen, D., Colligan, D., Finnie, A., Kern, T.: Trust, Power and Inter-Organizational Information Systems: the Case of the Electronic Trading Community TransLease. Information Systems Journal (10), 21–40 (2000)

Alvesson, M., Willmott, H.: Identity Regulation as Organizational Control: Producing the Appropriate Individual. Journal of Management Studies 39(5), 619–644 (2002)

Bartlett, C., Ghoshal, S.: Managing across Borders: The Transnational Solution, 2nd edn. Harvard Business School Press, Boston (1989)

Bell, J.: The Internationalization of Small Computer Software Firms: A Further Challenge to 'Stage' Theories. European Journal of Marketing 29(8), 60–75 (1995)

Blau, P.: Exchange and Power in Social Life. Wiley, New York (1964)

Bloomfield, B.P., Coombs, R.: Information Technology, Control and Power: The Centralization and Decentralization Debate Revisited. Journal of Management Studies 29(4), 459–484 (1992)

Brocklehurst, M.: Power, Identity and New Technology Homework: Implications for 'New Forms' of Organizing. Organization Studies 22(3), 445–466 (2001)

Clegg, S.R., Courpasson, D., Phillips, N.: Power and Organization. SAGE, London (2006)

Cramton, C.: The Mutual Knowledge Problem and its Consequences for Dispersed Collaboration. Organization Science 12(3), 346–371 (2001)

Dahl, R.A.: The Concept of Power. Behavioral Science (2), 201–216 (1957)

DeSanctis, G., Monge, P.: Introduction to the Special Issue: Communication Processes for Virtual Organization. Organization Science 10, 693–703 (1999)

Gibson, C., Cohen, S.: Virtual Teams that Work: Creating Conditions for Virtual Team Effectiveness. Jossey-Bass, San Francisco (2003)

Glaser, B., Strauss, A.: The Discovery of Grounded Theory. Aldine, Chicago (1967)

Goffman, E.: The Presentation of Self in Everyday Life. Doubleday (1959)

Kaplan, A.: Power in Perspective. In: Kahn, R.L., Boulding, E. (eds.) Power and conflict in organizations. Tavistock, London (1964)

Karra, N., Philips, N.: Entrepreneurship Goes Global. Ivey Business Journal 69(2), 1–6 (2004)

Kiesler, S., Cummings, J.N.: What do We Know about Proximity and Distance in Work Groups? A Legacy of Research. In: Hinds, P.J., Kiesler, S. (eds.) Distributed Work. MIT Press, Cambridge (2002)

Lee-Kelley, L.: Locus of Control and Attitudes to Working in Virtual Teams. International Journal of Project Management 24(4), 234–243 (2006)

Lukes, S.: Power: A Radical View. Macmillan, London (1974)

McDougall, P., Oviatt, B.: Some Fundamental Issues in International Entrepreneurship (2003), http://www.usasbe.org/knowledge/whitepapers/mcdougall2003.pdf (accessed October 15, 2008)

Oviatt, B., McDougall, P.: Toward a Theory of International New Ventures. Journal of International Business Studies 25(1), 45–64 (1994)

Rassingham, P.: Risks in Low Trust among Trading Partners in Electronic Commerce. Internet Research: Electronic Networking Applications and Policy 10(1), 56–62 (1999)

Rennie, M.: Global Competitiveness: Born Global. The McKinsey Quarterly 4, 45–52 (1993)

Servais, P., Rasmussen, E.S.: Different Types of International New Ventures. In: Academy of International Business Annual Meeting, Phoenix, AZ, USA (2000)

Sharma, D., Blomstermo, A.: The Internationalisation Process of Born Globals: A Network View. International Business Review 12, 739–753 (2003)

Simon, B., Oakes, P.: Beyond Dependence: An Identity Approach to Social Power and Domination. Human Relations 59(1), 105–139 (2006)

Sproull, L., Kiesler, S.: Reducing Social Context Cues: Electronic Mail in Organizational Communication. Management Science 32(11), 1492–1512 (1986)

Webber, M.: The Theory of Social and Economic Organization. Free Press, New York (1947)

Yukl, G.: Managerial Leadership: A Review of Theory and Research. Journal of Leadership and Organizational Studies 4(3), 110–125 (1998)

Zahra, S.: A Theory of International New Ventures: A Decade of Research. Journal of International Business Studies 36, 20–28 (2005)

The Chiasmus of Design: Paradoxical Outcomes in the e-Government Reform of UK Children's Services

David Wastell[1], Sue White[2], and Karen Broadhurst[2]

[1] Nottingham University Business School, UK
[2] Department of Applied Social Science,
University of Lancaster, UK

Abstract. This paper describes a detailed ethnographic study of the design problems of a major national IT system in the UK- The Integrated Children's System (ICS). The implementation of the ICS has disrupted social work practice and engendered growing professional resistance, prompting a fundamental review of its design. Marshall McLuhan's concept of chiasmus is a central feature of our analysis of the vicissitudes of ICS. Chiasmus refers to the tendency of any system, when pushed too far, to produce unintended contradictory effects, and is an intrinsic feature of the behaviour of complex, socio-technical systems. The dysfunctions of the ICS provide a pertinent, large-scale example. The ICS constitutes an attempt, via technological means, to re-organize child welfare services in the UK. Whilst aimed at improving child safety, the ICS has had the opposite effect of increasing the potential for error. This chiasmus has been exposed through the multi-site ethnography reported here, which shows how rigidly designed processes, enforced by IT systems, force social work professionals into unsafe investigative and recording practices which increase the risk of errors. The paper ends by proposing an alternative approach to design, based on socio-technical precepts, emphasizing the principles of minimum critical specification, user-centeredness and local autonomy.

1 Introduction

UNISON wishes to draw attention to the seriousness of the problems being experienced by social work staff with the Integrated Children's System. The problems appear to be fundamental, widespread and consistent enough to call into question whether the ICS is fit for purpose.... we have reports of a number of industrial disputes or collective grievances brewing or underway and in many more cases staff are voting with their feet and not using the system when they can get away with it (Unison, 2008).

The above quotation is taken from the submission of the UNISON trade union (to which many UK social workers belong) to the independent enquiry recently set in train by the Secretary of State for Children, Schools and Families, Ed Balls, in response to the tragic and brutal death of a 17 month old child ("Baby P") in the London Borough of Haringey in August 2007. The trial of the child's mother,

G. Dhillon, B.C. Stahl, and R. Baskerville (Eds.): CreativeSME 2009, IFIP AICT 301, pp. 257–272, 2009.
© IFIP International Federation for Information Processing 2009

boyfriend and another man, which concluded in November 2008, was widely reported in the British press and caused considerable moral outrage. Significant short-comings in the child protection services in the Borough were brought to light. As well as the enquiry, a national "Social Work Task Force" was also set up, charged with a fundamental review of all aspects of front-line social work practice. Press reports of the case drew attention to the deficiencies of a national IT system designed for children's services, and the role that this was playing in undermining safe professional practice. This is the Integrated Children's System (ICS) referred to in our epigraph. An article in the Guardian newspaper of 19th November (p. 7) is typical of the coverage: entitled "Child protection stifled by £30m computer system", the article highlighted the vast amount of time taken "filling out forms" on ICS and the pressures created by the system's deadlines, together acting to "restrict the time available for family visits". The urgent need to review the design of ICS is one of the priority areas for the above-mentioned Task Force[1].

The failure of IT projects is by no means a new phenomenon (Beynon-Davies, 2009), with a research literature reaching back to the classic papers of the discipline (e.g. Markus, 1983) over twenty five years ago. In this article, we shall focus our analysis on the failings of the ICS, attempting to tease out the fatal flaws responsible for the paradox of a system designed to enhance child safety seemingly having the contrary effect. As a major national initiative directly aimed at transforming social work practice, ICS is worthy of investigation in its own right. With a total professional workforce of around 20,000 social workers and care managers, and an annual budget for children's social services of over £5 billion per annum, it is vital to understand its defects in order to devise appropriate and efficacious remedies. We also believe that the problems inherent in ICS are by no means unique, and that there are lessons to be learned for the design of IT systems in general. These lessons are especially relevant in the context of public sector reform where technology features so centrally as the instrument of "modernization", with e-Government now embedded as a global phenomenon (Wastell, 2006).

Marshall McLuhan's concept of *chiasmus* plays a central role in our analysis. In typically gnomic style, McLuhan defines chiasmus as "the reversal of process caused by increasing its speed, scope or size - every process pushed far enough tends to reverse or flip suddenly" (McLuhan and Carson, 2003, p. 222). Chiasmus emphasizes the indeterminacy of design, especially in the context of complex systems (where the presence of multiple, interacting variables means that outcomes are inherently unpredictable) and is a much-needed antidote to simplistic cause-effect thinking. In the case of ICS, the "process pushed too far" is regulation; through an excess of formalisation and control, aimed an enhancing professional performance. ICS instead disrupts that practice and engenders widespread resistance from its users, as exemplified in the opening quotation. The dangers of over-specification and the need to find the golden mean, the right balance of structure and discretion, are central in designing any system and are well-known in organisational theory. As Argyris (1999) put it "All organisations are designs… managers specify ahead of time the jobs and roles of the players as completely as possible without the specifications being so complex that they immobilise performance". The socio-technical theorists propound

---

[1] As a result of the research reported here, one of the authors (SW) is a member the Task Force.

the same wisdom: "details of a work system should not be overspecified in advance. Sociotechnical analysis proceeds by specifying ... only those things that must be defined: the *minimum critical specification*" (Pava, 1983). Sadly, this core precept of design seems not to have been known to the architects of the ICS.

In the next section, we will briefly set out the main theoretical ideas which our analysis will draw on, namely the systems approach to error management, and the work of James Reason in particular (Reason, 1997; 2000). We then introduce the organisational context for our research, the referral and assessment process for children's services. We will contend that the analysis of errors in organizational settings should focus on *systemic* weaknesses, in particular the "latent conditions" for error (Reason, 1997; 2000) which generally increase the risk of failure. We then present our empirical findings in detail, describing the results of our multi-site ethnographic investigation of the impact of ICS on child welfare practices, presenting evidence that policy initiatives to enhance child safety have had the contrary effect. These paradoxical outcomes are subtle though, only to be teased out by careful, ethnographic analysis of the local adaptations of practice arising from the user/technology interaction[2]. Our conclusions will, *inter alia*, reiterate the imperative for a thorough understanding of the needs of users and their working practices in system design.

2 The Systems Approach to Error Management in the Context of "Modernised" Children's Services

There is a substantive body of work that argues for such a systems approach to error management (Reason, 1997; Munro, 2005a; Bostock et al., 2005). Reason (1997; 2000), perhaps the most well known exponent of this standpoint, argues that errors in human systems have their origins "not so much in the perversity of human nature as in upstream, systemic factors" (p768, 2000). Coining the notion of "latent conditions for error", he argues that the analysis of errors in organizational settings should focus on general *systemic* weaknesses, rather than mistakes made by particular individuals on particular occassions. Such latent conditions refer to generalised, immanent characteristics of a designed system (typically non-obvious and unintended) that increase the risk of errors occurring in the operational situation.   In aviation, for instance, efforts to automate pilot functions were based on the premise that this would improve safety (Norman, 1990). However, by displacing the pilot from the "control loop", his/her grasp of what was currently going on in relation to the the status of aeroplane, was necessarily eroded. Such reduction of "situational awareness" provides an example of a latent condition of error, a direct paradoxical consequence of infelicitous design. When the pilot was obliged to take over control in exceptional conditions, the likelihood of mistakes was increased and indeed several serious accidents were attributed to such a causal pattern (Norman, 1990).

---

[2] We use "technology" in its widest sense to encompass formally-defined procedures and methods (administrative technology) as well as physical machinery, such as the ubiquitous personal computer.

An extensive quotation from Reason (2000, p.769) provides a useful summary of the main features of the concept. Designating latent conditions as the inevitable "resident pathogens" within the system, he goes on:

They arise from decisions made by designers, builders, procedure writers, and top level management.... All such strategic decisions have the potential for introducing pathogens into the system. Latent conditions have two kinds of adverse effect: they can translate into error provoking conditions within the local workplace (for example, time pressure, understaffing, inadequate equipment, fatigue, and inexperience) and they can create long-lasting holes or weaknesses in the defences (untrustworthy alarms and indicators, unworkable procedures, design and construction deficiencies, etc). Latent conditions—as the term suggests— may lie dormant within the system for many years before they combine with active failures and local triggers to create an accident opportunity.

From a systems perspective, approaches to error management that focus on individual breaches of procedure or unwanted aberrations of human conduct will inevitably be limited to delivering safer worker practices. Individuals are fallible and will always err, the trick is to design safe systems that minimise the likelihood and the consequentiality of such inevitable failures. A systems perspective requires that more attention be focused on minimizing "the number of latent conditions in the system that can contribute to user error" (Lowe, p.2, 2006).

The main interest of our ethnographic field work has centred on the interface (the "front door") between social services departments and other agencies (e.g. police, health services) and with the general public. Whilst the ICS covers all aspects of social work with children, from referral and assessment through to the provision of family support, the enactment of child protection procedures (including the potential removal of children into local authority care), it is the early assessment stages that have been particularly subject to "re-engineering", aimed at improving their safety and efficiency. In 2000, *The Framework for the Assessment of Children in Need and their Families* was introduced (Cleaver and Walker, 2004) which clearly defined the initial statutory response as a distinct stage in the assessment process (Horwath, 2002). Since its advent, the importance of initial assessment practices has been further reinforced by the public inquiry into the death of Victoria Climbie (Laming, 2003) which heavily criticised the social services department involved (Haringey was again involved) for failings in their referral and assessment processes.

Initial assessment (IA) emphasizes the importance of the initial professional response, especially the need to see the child at the earliest point. The Integrated Children's System (ICS) has accordingly been designed to ensure that workers follow the various steps specified in a formally defined "model" of the assessment process, creating a indelible, auditable trace of day-to-day practices. A standardised IA form prompts workers to collect information in a systematic way, with the expectation that the data so-garnered will contribute usefully to further assessment. Consistent with the universal application of Performance Management throughout the UK public sector (Bevan and Hood, 2006), a burgeoning range of targets and timescales have been stipulated. Within 1 day of a referral being received, social service departments are mandated to make and log a decision about the requisite response. When an initial assessment is deemed necessary, this must be completed within 7 days, including the requirement to see the child.

In this heavily regulated regime, latent conditions for error are all too readily found. Work volumes create severe pressures in most settings. It is estimated that, on average, some 300 referrals must be processed every month by the typical social services department[3], although precise measures are difficult, given definitional issues and local practice adaptations. Teams are legally bound to respond to referrals; they receive no extra compensation or flexibility regarding staff sickness levels, rather targets must be met whatever the particulars of local context or case. Pressures are further compounded by the widespread problem of recruiting and retaining experienced staff (Audit Commission, 2002). Where referral rates are high and resources are constrained, trade offs are inevitable between urgent child-protection work and assessments leading to more generalised forms of family support. Our work draws attention to the short-cuts that the IA process necessitates, given the immutable timescales and excessive audit requirements it imposes. Imperatives to safeguard children and support families appeared at odds with, rather than enhanced by, new modes of e-governance and associated performance targets. In particular the procrustean timescales set for the completion of the initial assessment inevitably pushed workers to make precipitous categorisations based on, at best, one home visit. Equally, the standardised but tortuous assessment forms appeared to invite a range of problematic recording practices. The general aim of this paper is to draw attention to the unsafe practices that the ICS appeared to necessitate in its demand for rapid case disposals, and the latent error conditions that this ineluctably creates.

3 The Field-Work and Findings

The project comprised a multi-site ethnographic study, based in five local authorities in England and Wales and drawing data from 15 social work "initial assessment" teams. The five local authority areas comprise: a London borough (Metroville); a county council (Shire); a metropolitan borough in the North of England (Westford); a unitary authority (Seaton); a Welsh rural authority (Valleytown). The field-work began in 2007 and is still underway. Informed by appropriate standards for ethical research, the ethnographies have involved various levels of engagement across the sites. Everyday interactions between team leaders and social workers, middle and senior managers have been observed as well as more formal meetings. In total, we estimate that this has amounted to around 240 days of observation and analysis of everyday practice, including worker interactions and meetings, supplemented by the inspection of key documents and case files. In addition, a total of 10 focus groups and 60 formal interviews have also been conducted. Transcripts and fieldnotes were uploaded to a dedicated project web-site to allow the research team to share and discuss the data. Regular meetings were held to examine and validate emergent themes, supported by group email exchange and discussion. Through these means, we

---

[3] National performance statistics for England show an average monthly referral rate of 306 for 2006/07.

have ensured that the pattern of findings reported below provides an accurate representation of the situation across the five sites.

Each of the five initial assessment teams is tasked to respond to initial contacts and referrals that come by way of telephone calls, faxes, emails, multi-agency assessment forms etc. These various external contacts cover the range from reports of serious injuries to children, more uncertain concerns about children's welfare, right through to simple requests for information and advice. In all sites, there is increasingly little opportunity for a "customer" to walk in and directly request help, rather all approaches are mediated through some form of "front of house" customer service interface, either centralised or within the team. Whilst practices varied across our sites, we found a number of distinct commonalities reflecting the influence of the performance management elements of ICS and the concomitant preoccupation of staff with maintaining "workflow". Workers consistently claimed that it was easy to lose sight of the primary activities of supporting families and safeguarding children, to the second order activities of performance and audit. In the rest of this Section, we will focus on the latent conditions for error created by this administrative regime embodied within the ICS. We illustrate these risky adaptations in the sub-sections that follow, limiting our report to three discrete aspects of the initial assessment process, (i) accepting a contact/referral (ii) making further enquiries and seeing the child and (iii) the completion of the IA record.

3.1 Accepting a Contact/Referral

Our assessment teams reported variable referral rates, ranging from 80 to figures significantly higher than 300 per month. In all but one site, far more contacts/referrals were received than could be managed. The requirment for an initial decision within 24 hours necessitates a rapid but not necessarily reliable response, and where workloads are high, the potential for error is clear:

> *Admin worker: The phone will be ringing continuously, you put the phone down and it rings straight away...one comes and another one comes... and your mind just gets frazzled, I might have writtten 5 or 6 pages of A4 paper ...and when I come back to reading them, it's all looking a bit messy...I can't quite make out what I've got down...*

Such pressures created significant anxieties for experienced staff workers, who understood that the pace of work created less than ideal conditions for practice, but there was also evidence of 'speed-practices' becoming habituated and normalised, especially in newer staff. For staff higher up the hierarchy, it was critical that only a manageable number of referrals were actually allocated for initial assessment. In the extract below, taken from one of our busiest teams, the team leader makes clear her reasons for clearing contacts by the end of the day, in anticipation of tomorrow's influx. The practical mandate for her actions is directly related to the exigencies of managing work-flow dictated by performance timescales.

> *Team leader: 'There are 50 contacts in your inbox... you are under pressure because you have to clear them by the end of the day ...and the question of whether you are more likely to close them in these*

circumstances? Well yeah.. so, really we are looking to <u>close</u> cases not open them... that's why we work to the highest thresholds'

The IT systems maintained the pace of work, typically by providing digital reminders of deadlines and timescales. In one site, we found an 'e-tracking device' in the form of traffic lights, which informed workers about how much time was left before the specific episode was deemed out of timescale. In another site, 'higher management' were planning to print out weekly graphs of levels of attainment in meeting targets, alongside tables exposing individual failures.

In order to manage the volume of referrals, we consistently observed that the teams had well established 'general deflection strategies' that included: *strategic deferment*, i.e. sending the referral back to the referrer to ask for more information; and *signposting*, deflecting the case to a more 'appropriate' agency. Whilst such adaptations are sensible if proportionate, the inherent risks are also clear. Where insufficient time precluded the pursuit of more detailed information from a referrer, other decision-making heuristics came into play. These included the routine categorisation of anonymous referrals as malicious (indeed referrrals from neighbours and family members were also often treated as suspect). We were told that children aged over 13 were routinely 'NFA-ed' (an outcome of no further action was recorded) on the basis that these children and young people *'must have lived with these concerns for a long time and be quite resilient'*. Similarly we found questionable methods for dealing with domestic violence notifications often on the basis of scant information. For example, in one site, first and second notifications were responded to automatically by a letter to parents; upon receipt of a third notification a visit would be made. We found that well-intentioned, but very busy workers, became habituated to these methods of rationing, with little time to reflect on, or question, such rationales and the risks they entailed.

In the following extract, the worker indicates how the imperative to prioritise a case already categorised as child protection (S47, i.e. section 47, Children Act 1989) required that she give less priority to an incoming referral, which also sounded malicious. Although she acknowledges her lack of knowledge, she justified her decision as follows:

> **Social worker:** *'I've got this S47 and actually this family are in crisis and I want to put support in for them, before I worry about this other family that don't even know I'm coming, because it's an anonymous referral from a neighbour ... and you think, well OK, I don't know if there's a real risk or not, but from reading it it sounds a bit malicious, well this family, actually are about to fall apart if you don't put something in'*

In order to manage workflow, we also observed some 'safer' locally-improvised methods for meeting timescales, that generally amounted to holding a case open for 'review', but logging the IA as complete on the system so as to meet the target. In cases where the seven days has not provided sufficient time to establish confidence about the child's welfare, this 'review space' could enable further information to be gathered. However, such workarounds, even when they are constructive, by their very nature can only survive while they remain undetected by inspecting agencies and their technological proxies.

3.2 Making Further Enquiries and Seeing the Child

A number of cases will get through the first layer of filtering and be allocated to a social worker for initial assessment, which will include making further enquiries and seeing the child. At this second stage, we also found short-cuts in operation. There was a tendency to abort an assessment whenever the 'opportunity' arose. In the case of the referral from a grandmother below, the routine treatment of referrals from family members as potentially suspicious, and that the health visitor had seen the child, together enabled swift disposal of the case.

> *Team leader: Being a bit cheeky...we contacted the health visitor and said when did you last see the visitor and <u>lucky enough</u> the health visitor had seen the baby recently and it wasn't as bad as the grandmother had alleged..so we didn't take it any further, no further action*

Workers widely reported that the timescales created undue pressure. One senior practitioner observed: "I personally worry about sometimes the time scales that you've, you've got to do it in ...I've been sort of worrying about work for, for a while really".   The tempo and volume of work, together with the 7-day target for IA completion, were widely reported as making cases at this second stage equally susceptible to partial analysis and rapid disposal.

> *Social worker: If it's not looking that serious...sometimes you don't get all the information and the temptation is then to take a short-cut and maybe not contact the school, or because the school are on holidays you say I think I've got sufficient information to make a decision- NFA*

Needless to say, school holidays are not factored into the 7 day timescale! Neither are parents and children who are not at home, nor health visitors who are on sick leave and so forth. These factors necessarily interrupt the expeditiousness of the assessment process, but the system offers no accommodation for the individual tasked with the work. Thus, timescales can create *perverse incentives* to dispose early on the basis of incomplete information. Whilst in many cases, an "NFA" decision may be quite appropriate, our file analysis of open cases did find a common pattern of repeated initial assessments of escalating severity, before the case eventually found its way through the front-door.

Front-line team managers played a key role in the operation of ICS. In some teams, acutely aware of the possibility of error, managers worked closely alongside new recruits to defuse their inevitable frustrations and induct them into 'local methods' which would enable them to get them to the best out of ICS. Managers could play a key role in mitigating the potential for errors in ICS, via detailed supervision of worker's practices, as the following extract indicates:

> *Team Manager: I <u>always</u> look at what the referrals were saying what the concerns were at that particular time and then I look at the initial assessment to see if they have covered the history and whether they have identified repeated patterns of concern*

However, we also found some tension between workers and their managers regarding the primacy of meeting targets. For example, in a particularly pressurised team, managers described their frustrations with workers spending too much time 'social chatting' or needing lessons in 'diary management'; such critical attitudes would seem likely only to exacerbate work that was already stressful enough. Invoking 'safeguarding' could buy a worker more time, but only in cases where there was a clear moral mandate to set aside the all-important target. The degree of assertiveness required to challenge the performance system could also lead to overt conflict:

> **Social worker:** *My manager said to me "why haven't you finished that yet?"… and I said "well the health visitor hasn't called me back"… and they said, "well no, if you've decided that it's family support, then the outcome won't change, whatever they say". I said "I disagree" and of course that information informs my assessment, I'm not putting my name to that.*

Where workers were juggling the completion of IAs with serious cases needing pending to progress and further investigation, 'NFA' was described as a welcome relief. Again, we see the latent potential for errors in this expediency; in the busiest of teams and in spite of the good intentions of workers, time precludes, for example, getting back to the referrer to inform him/her of a decision, which closes down any immediate challenge to the categorisation. Seeing 'the child' is a central and critical part of initial assessment. However, even in relation to this imperative, we found worrying short-cuts, as the following extract illustrates:

> **Social worker:** *'My new manager…she comes back and says, it [the IA] doesn't say have <u>you</u> seen the child, it says "has the child been seen?", you can put "yes" and then make it clear that the teacher has seen the child. I thought hmm, I bet the teacher saw Victoria Climbie as well, you know, what's the point me even doing an assessment if I haven't seen the children'*

Children are not easy to 'see' under the conditions of initial assessment, for a variety of reasons. First, there is a requirement to see all children irrespective of ages, but older children can be difficult to track down. Second, 'seeing' should involve talking to the child alone to make an assessment of the child's development and needs, but this is hard to achieve within 7 days in a single visit. With initial response to telephone calls increasingly mediated by administrative staff and home visits curtailed to a single visit, the space between help-seeker and help-provider is steadily widening. Skilled workers might attempt to reduce this space, but for many, in the absence of knowledge derived from face-to-face work with families, they fall back on readily auditable, bureaucratic justifications, often offered by fellow professionals, which invoke missed health appointments, school attendance problems and the like.

3.3 Completing the Record

A standardised assessment record invites workers to comment on a range of factors relating to the child, his/her parents or carers and the presenting concerns. A general observation across our sites was the paucity of information recorded on the actual initial assessment document. In one site, we examined 65 records of individual children; the scantness of the information, compounded by the difficulties of piecing together fragments of narrative scattered across multiple boxes[4], made it very difficult for the reader to glean a holistic picture of the child and his/her family. The IA record presents as a rather badly designed tool, requiring copious information that is difficult to glean from one home visit and from other professionals; it thus invites workers to discard the majority of its sections as irrelevant. With not unsurprising consistency, we found an expedient method of 'front and back-ing' (or 'back-to-back-ing') had spontaneously sprung up across all our sites, wherein middle sections of the document were omitted altogether:

> *Researcher:* '*So what about the middle of the document, because everyone seems to miss this out?*
> *Social worker: What middle document?*
> *Researcher: You know, practitioners are concerned with the referral and the outcome on the back, but what about all those pages in between about the child?*
> *Social worker: (laughing) To me well... yes, there is a page about the child, I would always put in something, depending on what the child is like...I would always put something in, but in IA you wouldn't...this is initial assessment*'

It was clear that workers were trying to make the form fit their work, rather than *vice versa*, as illustrated by the telling statement that '*this is initial assessment*'. Whilst most practitioners welcomed the general principle of electronic recording, the Initial Assessment Record was not only overly long, but the standardised questions and sub-headings were not easily adapted for this or that case (c.f. White et al. 2008), so workers went straight to '*analysis*' of '*that dreadful form*', putting '*nothing-in-between*'. Scrolling through the pages of the record ourselves, we found it difficult to distinguish between the material typed by workers and material already on the form, i.e. the numerous sub-headings and explanatory notes provided. Workers have become experts with the copy-and-paste function, as material is regularly and mechanistically repeated. In addition, the principle that for every family, a record of each child was required, tended to encourage practitioners to produce a general homogenising account that 'fitted' all the children.

> *Social worker: 'If I know that the IA is more than likely going to turn into no further action, and I know that after I've had my conversation with the*

---

[4] The initial assessment form is typically 10 pages in length. Apart from the usual administrative fields for structured data, there are well over twenty free text fields addressing the developmental status of the child and relevant environmental factors: including the child's 'social presentation' or 'self-care skills', the 'family's social integration' etc.

family, then I will massage the information on each of the children and talk in plural "the children presented" '.

Whilst workers were clearly attempting to work-around the excessive audit demands of ICS, to salvage some time to spend with families, even the most perfunctory response to audit left too little time for the real work of face-to-face comunication (Peckover et al. 2008; White et al. 2008). The speed with which workers attempted to complete the IA record also meant that errors of recording were common. In the busiest teams, such errors were compounded when 'students' (for example) were asked to catch up with recording cases they knew nothing about! Whilst workers were aware of these errors, they also reported that it was difficult to make corrections as material was 'locked down' in the system after 24 hours. After that period, a worker would have to seek special permission to undertake corrections. Very obvious errors, such as putting a case note in the wrong file might prompt such requests, but simply improving wording was just too much trouble, though vital to comprehensibility.

We have particularly highlighted aspects of risky practice in teams that were under pressure, to demonstrate the latent conditions for error. It was clear that teams with lower referral rates and better resources could manage the tensions better, without the same ingrained recourse to risky short-cuts. However, even here the demands of timescales and performance management appeared to dominate and were not always seen as conducive to good practice with families:

> *Social Worker: we're told by supervisors to work towards the timescales 'cos it's their indicators isn't it, then they go off to the Department of Health, so you're trying to think of the best outcomes for the family and for the child but ... you're trying to get things done in timescales and cases moved on, they don't want to hold cases in a duty and assessment team so it's moving them on, which is not, it's not always probably in their best interests.*

4 Discussion

> *The Platonic approach can be described as Utopian engineering, as opposed to ... piecemeal engineering. The Utopian approach is the more dangerous... the Utopian engineer will claim that mechanical engineers plan even very complicated machinery as a whole and that their blueprints cover not only a certain kind of machinery, but even the whole factory.... (Karl Popper, The Open Society and its Enemies, 1999)*

Since the Laming report (2003) there has been a very significant reconfiguration of children's statutory services in the UK. Rigorous information recording and performance management are the mantras of this brave new world; however it is important that the tools we provide for our workers are fit for purpose (Munro, 2005b). We would argue, however, that the increased audit demands of ICS, together with on-going resource constraints, have served to increase the burden on front-line workers (Peckover et al., 2008; Bell et al. 2007). From our analysis, it is clear that the design of the modernised initial assessment system of children's statutory services, as embodied within the ICS, is not only flawed, but that its dysfunctions provide the latent conditions for error. In response to the intractability of the IA process, the workers in our study had devised a range of artful "work-arounds". However, errors are inevitable in the context of such expediencies, which have been extemporized simply to maintain an overly rigid workflow. An excessive zeal for structure and standardisation has thus engendered a reversal of the intended outcome; rather than improving safety, the latent conditions for failure have been exacerbated. The principle of chiasmus is the antithesis of simple, deterministic models of change; its precautionary wisdom is writ large here.

The short-cuts that have been fashioned in the "electronic cage" of the ICS typically take the form of early categorisations based on incomplete information, or the fudging of details of a 'home-visit', and so on. As illustrated in our ethnography, it is preferable to dispose of a seemingly nebulous referral in the face of the more immediate performance demands of the ICS. But it is often just those kinds of referrals that appear to be irrelevant, or somebody else's business, that can provide the warning signs of a more serious malaise[5]. Scarcity of resources will inevitably mean that giving priority to one part of the system, the most immediate, will result in cuts in another. (Rustin, 2004). It is no surprise to have found that workers continue to pursue opportunities to deflect incoming work, and dispose of cases on the basis of superficial analysis, or to fall back on fallible heuristics such as "it's *probably* malicious". Although Clarke (2007) argues that decision-making in public services takes place in less than theoretically optimum conditions, with workers responding to the immediate "exigencies of the here and now", he argues that we should nonetheless aim to "identify the ideal mode of decision-making" (pp. 68-69). In social services, priority needs to be given to reduce the distance between workers, family and community which many studies have cited (by both service users and front-line workers) as central to good practice (Pithouse and Holland 1999; Gray, 2002; Ruch, 2005). We have seen that the performance-driven ICS only detaches the professional further and further from the possibility of meaningful engagement with service users, offering instead a scientistic veneer of codes, risk scores and metrics.

Lipsky's concept of the "street level bureaucrat" (Lipsky, 1980) emphasizes the importance of professional discretion in effective front-line practice in the public services. Lipsky saw such discretion as essential in order to get the job done: "the situations they face are too complex to reduce to prescribed responses". In terms of systems theory, this is simply a reflection of the ineluctable writ of the Law of Requisite variety; discretion is not some incidental feature, it is fundamental to the operation of any "viable system"[6]. Pithily, the Law thus proclaims "Only variety

---

[5] The Laming report (2003) identified that everyday biases contributing to errors of judgement in Ealing and Brent social services included the treatment of anonymous calls as *a priori* malicious. Victoria was referred twice by Ms Akhet a family friend who asked to remain anonymous.

[6] The Law was coined by the British psychiatrist W. Ross Ashby, one of the founding fathers of the systems movement in his Introduction to Cybernetics (1956). Imagine a system (e.g. a family) to be "controlled" in the sense that we seek certain desirable outcomes (e.g. children do not suffer harm and achieve their full potential). Variety simply denotes the number of different "states" that the system can be in, which in the case of a human system (e.g. a family) is both large and dynamic. All families are different and the variety of the social care system must therefore possess a comparable degree of variety (repertoire of responses) in order to deal effectively with this variety.

absorbs variety". This, of course, is the exact opposite of the principle of standardisation, which in the limiting case provides for the same response whatever the input. Rules, policies and procedures are all abstractions and intrinsically lack variety; intelligent human agents provide the necessary "variety amplifiers" (Beer, 1994) which enable bureaucratic systems to work effectively. In a different context, Bourdieu (2003) makes the same point in defining the ability to improvise, to adjust responses to local, situated contingencies, as being the hallmark of competent practice.

The findings we present are controversial and are presented in a designedly polemical tone. We draw attention to the multiple opportunities for errors on the part of front-line social work professionals that are exacerbated given the current configuration of inital assessment process and its technological embodiment in the ICS. Performance management is designed to enhance rather than inhibit quality performance, yet our study has found this regime paradoxially worsens the latent conditions for errors. Whilst it is tempting to berate the maverick professional who subverts correct procedure, it is important to remember that there are "good" organisational reasons for such behaviours, i.e. they are an attempt to reconcile the competing elements of the ICS with imperatives to safeguard children and to support families. The latter role, however prominent in current welfare policy, is particularly vulnerable. Perhaps the real tragedy of ICS is that in busy teams, inevitably demands to *support* families will be routinely subordinated to pressures to maintain workflow.

Although this paper challenges the huge investment in systems of performance management and IT, we are not arguing for a wholesale Luddite abandonment of new modes of governance and new technology. The remedy, we believe, lies elsewhere, in a radically different approach to design, an approach which draws on core socio-technical precepts of user participation, minimum critical specification and the optimisation of local autonomy (Pava, 1983; Mumford, 2003). Above all, it is essential to found the design of systems on the needs of users and a thorough understanding of their working practices. This insight applies to the design of any artefact, be it a form, a process or a database. The case for user-centred design (UCD) has been cogently made in many design disciplines, including information systems and human-computer interaction (Norman, 1998). The arguments are both ethical and technical. Technically, UCD is essential in order to gain reliable knowledge for designing new tools and processes. Failure to involve users in the development of new systems inevitably engenders alienation, and there were unmistakable signs of practitioner disquiet (complaints of additional workload and excessive "bureaucratization") in pilot studies of the ICS (Cleaver and Walker, 2004; Cleaver et al., 2008; Bell et al., 2007). It is regrettable that such early warning signals apparently went unheeded, written off as "implementation issues" rather than more fundamental problems of design dogma. As a result, the strictures of the work regime imposed by ICS have not only produced unsafe practices but are now provoking overt resistance from an increasingly frustrated and mutinous workforce, as we saw in our opening quote.

We believe that new systems and technologies can be developed which both assist the users in their daily work and achieve desired organisational goals, but without an ethnographically-informed understanding of human practice (such as this paper provides), this virtuous circle will not be achieved. Ethnographic studies have shown time and again that even work which seems highly routine is a skilled accomplishment

(Gasser, 1986); its orderliness is a product of the artful worker, not determined by the imposition of a formal rule-base. It is noteworthy that some design methods explicitly call for ethnographic engagement in order to develop a valid evidence base for design, e.g. the SPRINT methodology which has been specifically developed for the public sector (Wastell et al., 2007). There is no final guarantee against chiasmus, but the deployment of such user-centred approaches certainly offers a less hubristic way forward.

We argued that our findings have relevance beyond the domain of children's services. Certainly, there appear to be parallel examples of similar problems in other large scale IT-enabled modernisation projects, such as the gargantuan National Programme for Information Technology (NPfIT) in the UK health service. Eason (2007, p. 258) argues that NPfIT has generally followed a "push strategy, thrusting new technology into the healthcare practices of the NHS", leaving little room for local design. Eason finds strikingly similar local adaptations (workarounds etc.) to those we have unveiled here, as well equally concerning symptoms of stress and mis-use. He goes on to argue a similar case for a flexible socio-technical approach fostering local diversity and based squarely on user needs. The command-and-control, performance management regime (combining "targets and terror") which we have seen in children's services is also pervasive across all UK public services, producing a common pattern of dysfunctional effects (Bevan and Hood, 2006). It is surely time to move away from such crude managerialism. Rather than pressing ever more urgently the cause of bureaucracy over professionalism, salvation may lie in reversing the direction of travel, of relaxing rather than tightening control. Indeed, this the direction suggested by the research evidence. Whilst setting targets and goals can improve performance, doing so in a participative way is known to be more effective that imposing them by fiat, especially for complex, uncertain tasks that cannot readily be routinized (Lock and Latham, 2002). It would seem perverse to continue to ignore such evidence.

Acknowledgements

This research was funded by the ESRC Public Services Programme: Quality, Performance and Delivery, grant number Res-166-25-0048.

References

Argyris, C.: On organizational learning. Blackwell, Malden (1999)
Ashby, W.R.: An Introduction to Cybernetics. Chapman and Hall, Boca Raton (1956)
Audit Commission, Recruitment and Retention: A Public Service Workforce for the 21st Century, London, The Stationery Office (2002)
Beer, S.: The Heart of Enterprise. Wiley, Chichester (1994)
Bell, M., Shaw, I., Sinclair, I., Sloper, P., Rafferty, J.: The Integrated Children's System: An Evaluation of the Practice, Process and Consequences of the ICS in Councils with Social Services Responsibilities. A report to the DfES and the Welsh Assembly, University of York and University of Southampton (2007)

Bevan, Hood, C.: What get's measured is what matters: targets and gaming in the English public health care system. Public Administration 84(3), 517–538 (2006)

Beynon-Davies, P.: Business Information Systems. Palgrave-Macmillan, Basingstoke (2009)

Bostock, L., Bairstow, S., Fish, S., Macleod, F.: Managing risk and minimizing mistakes in services to children and families. Report 6, London, The Social Care Institute for Excellence (2005)

Bourdieu, P.: Outline of a theory of practice. Cambridge University Press, Cambridge (2003)

Clarke, C.: Professional Responsibility, Misconduct and Practical Reason. Ethics and Social Welfare 1(1), 56–75 (2007)

Cleaver, H., Walker, S.: From policy to practice: the implementation of a new framework for social work assessments of children and families. Child and Family Social Work 9, 81–90 (2004)

Cleaver, H., Walker, S., Scott, S., Cleaver, D., Rose, W., Ward, H., Pithouse, A.: The Integrated Children's System: enhancing social work and inter-agency practice. Jessica Kingsley Publishers, London (2008)

Department for Education and Skills, Every Child Matters, London, The Stationery Office (2003)

Eason, K.: Local socio-technical development in the National Programme for Information Technology. Journal of Information Technology 22, 257–264 (2007)

Gasser, L.: The integration of computing and routine work. ACM Transactions on Office Information Systems 4, 205–225 (1986)

Gray: Emotional labour and befriending in family support and child protection in Tower Hamlets. Child and Family Social Work 7, 13–22 (2002)

Horwath, J.: Maintaining a focus on the Child? Child Abuse Review 11, 195–213 (2002)

Laming, H.: The Victoria Climbie Inquiry: Report of an Inquiry by Lord Laming, Command 5730, Norwich, Stationery Office (2003)

Edwin, A., Locke, E.A.: University of Maryland

Locke, E.A., Latham, G.P.: Building a Practically Useful Theory of Goal Setting and Task Motivation: a 35-Year Odyssey. American Psychologist 57(9), 705–717 (2002)

Lowe, C.M.: Accidents waiting to happen: the contribution of latent conditions to patient safety. Quality and Safety in Health Care 15(suppl. 1), 172–175 (2006)

Lipsky, M.: Street-level Bureaucracy; Dilemmas of the Individual in Public Services. Russell Sage Foundation, New York (1980)

Markus, M.L.: Power, politics and MIS implementation. Communications of the ACM 26(6), 430–444 (1983)

McLuhan, M., Carson, D.: The book of probes. Ginkgo Press (2003)

Mumford, E.: Redesigning human systems. Information Science Publishing (2003)

Munro, E.: What tools do we need to improve identification of child abuse? Child Abuse Review 14(6), 374–388 (2005a)

Munro, E.: A systems approach to investigating child abuse deaths. British Journal of Social Work 25, 531–546 (2005b)

Norman, D.A.: The 'problem' with automation: inappropriate feedback and interaction, not 'over-automation'. Philosophical Transactions of the Royal Society B327, 585–593 (1990)

Norman, D.A.: The design of everyday things. MIT Press, Cambridge (1998)

Pava, C.H.P.: Managing new office technology; an organizational strategy. The Free Press (1983)

Peckover, S., White, S., Hall, C.: Making and managing Electronic Children: e-assessment in child welfare. Information Communication and Society 11(3), 375–394 (2008)

Pithouse, A., Holland, S.: Open access family centres and their users: positive results, some doubts and new departures. Children and Society 13, 167–178 (1999)

Reason, J.: Managing the risks of organizational accidents. Aldershot, Ashgate (1997)

Reason, J.: Human Error: models and management. British Medical Journal 320, 768–770 (2000)

Ruch, G.: Relationship-based practice and reflective practice, holistic approaches to contemporary child care social work. Child and Family Social Work 10, 111–123 (2005)

Rustin, M.: Learning from the Victoria Climbie Inquiry. Journal of Social Work Practice 18(1), 9–18 (2004)

Unison. Unison memorandum to Lord Laming: Progress report on safeguarding (December 2008)

Wastell, D.G.: Information systems and evidence-based policy in multi-agency networks: the micro-politics of situated innovation. Journal of Strategic Information Systems 1, 77–98 (2006)

Wastell, D.G., McMaster, T., Kawalek, P.: The rise of the Phoenix: methodological innovation as a discourse of renewal. Journal of Information Technology 22, 59–68 (2007)

White, S., Hall, C., Peckover, S.: The descriptive tyranny of the common assessment framework: technologies of categorisation and professional practice in child welfare. British Journal of Social Work, 1–21 (April 2008)

How and Why Do IT Entrepreneurs Leave Their Salaried Employment to Start a SME? A Mixed Methods Research Design

Gaëtan Mourmant[1,2]

[1] CREPA, Centre de Recherche en Management & Organisation,
Dauphine Recherches en Management, CNRS UMR7088,
Université Paris Dauphine
Place du Maréchal de Lattre de Tassigny, 75116 Paris, France
[2] Robinson College of Business, Georgia State University, Atlanta, GA

Abstract. This method paper addresses an untapped but important type of IT turnover: IT entrepreneurship. We seek to develop a mixed methods research (MMR) design to understand the factors and processes that influence turnover behavior of prospective (nascent) IT entrepreneurs. To do this, we review two prior streams of research: the entrepreneurship literature and IT employee turnover. We incorporate the results of this literature review into a conceptual framework describing how the relevant factors leading to entrepreneurial and turnover behavior change over time, either gradually or suddenly, in response to specific events. In addition, we also contribute to the research by arguing that mixed methods research (MMR) is appropriate to bridge the gap between entrepreneurial literature and the IT turnover literature. A third important contribution is the design of the MMR, combining a longitudinal approach with a retrospective approach; a qualitative with a quantitative approach and, the exploratory design with the triangulation design [1]. Finally, we discuss practical implications for IT managers and IT entrepreneurs.

1 Introduction

Is your CIO quitting your company to create a SME in direct competition with you?

A major issue faced by companies is IT turnover; however, this issue becomes even more important when the IT professional launches his/her SME in competition with his/her former employer; thereby posing a threat to the IT capabilities of the employer's firm, [2]. Even though IT turnover represents a large body of research, to our knowledge, no studies specifically address the turnover of future IT entrepreneurs starting their own SMEs. Moreover, the entrepreneurship literature, while discussing the career reasons of entrepreneurs as well as the difference between entrepreneurs and non-entrepreneurs, does not consider the population of IT entrepreneurs. Therefore, there is a need to (1) bridge the gap between the two bodies of literature and (2) extend IT turnover research to the population of IT entrepreneurs starting their own SMEs.

Regarding the literature on IT personnel turnover, Joseph et al. identified a total of 43 constructs related to IT turnover intentions [3]. They classified these constructs into

G. Dhillon, B.C. Stahl, and R. Baskerville (Eds.): CreativeSME 2009, IFIP AICT 301, pp. 273–286, 2009.
© IFIP International Federation for Information Processing 2009

the following groups: desire to move, ease of movement, job search, individual attributes, job related factors and perceived organizational factors. Moreover, Joseph et al. insist on the necessity of studying those constructs within the context of environmental and organizational factors [3]. Finally, they also recommend considering new models such as the unfolding model of voluntary turnover, [4] and job embeddedness theory, [5] to address the weak relationship between intention and actual behavior. In his review of the entrepreneurship literature, Davidsson [6, p.6-9] identified more than 25 constructs related to entrepreneurial behavior. He classified them in the following categories: human capital (e.g. level of education), social capital (e.g. having parents or friends who are self-employed), financial capital (e.g. income), motivations and perceptions (e.g. self-efficacy). In addition to Davidsson's review, other theories which are worth noting are: *entrepreneurial self-efficacy,* [7], the work on *successful intelligence,* [8]; and the jack-of-all-trades theory, [9, 10], [11].

Our review of these two areas of literature shows a lack of specific studies on the actual turnover of IT entrepreneurs. This gap motivates our research as new constructs are very likely to emerge from any qualitative studies on this topic. In addition, it is well documented that both employee turnover and the creation of new ventures can be analysed using process models – the turnover process, [3] and the entrepreneurial process, [12], [13], respectively. Consequently, we seek to acquire in-depth knowledge of the IT entrepreneur's perspective using grounded theory methods (e.g. using the method of narrative analysis of life histories) to explain this process and identify new constructs (qualitative exploration). We also seek to conduct a quantitative study to identify trends and to generalize the findings from patterns of IT entrepreneurs to the IT personnel turnover and entrepreneurship literature [1 - p.33].

In sum, we consider the gap in both the IT turnover literature and in the entrepreneurship literature regarding IT entrepreneurs' turnover to be an important topic to address – which generates both practical and research implications. Because this topic requires both qualitative and quantitative approaches, we suggest using a mixed methods design (MMR), [1 – p. 34]. Therefore, we explore the following research question; "How and why do IT entrepreneurs leave their salaried employment to start a SME?" In addition, to answering this research question, we seek to explain the underlying process, by drawing from both elements of turnover process models and entrepreneurial process models. Also note that the dependent variable is two-fold. First, there is the decision to leave salaried employment and second, the decision to start a SME. Therefore, for purposes of theory building, we assume that the IT professionals quitting their jobs will start their SMEs as they leave paid employment (very shortly before or thereafter).

The rest of the paper is structured as follows: First, we briefly review the two streams of literature and present the conceptual framework of this research. We then discuss the MMR design. Finally, we discuss the contribution of this paper, its practical and research implications and its limitations.

2 IT Turnover Literature Review

Here, we briefly review the first literature stream: specific features of the IT industry that influence IT employees' turnover, including the individual, organization, and environmental levels, as suggested by [3].

A large body of research has identified individual level factors that influence IT personnel turnover. Among them, [14], [15], [16], [17], [18]. In their narrative review of the literature, Joseph et al. summarized 43 antecedents to IT turnover intention [3]. Among them, some were positively linked to turnover intention, such as *role ambiguity, role conflict* (with the exception of one study), *threat of professional obsolescence,* and *work exhaustion;* other constructs were negatively linked to IT employees' turnover intention (e.g., *boundary spanning activities, job autonomy, satisfaction with pay, promotability,* and *fairness of rewards*). Other factors yielded inconsistent results in explaining turnover intention, such as *age, education, IT job tenure* and *organization tenure.*

Joseph et al. noted the omission of IT industry's contextual factors in studies of IT personnel turnover [3]. In studying nascent IT entrepreneurs (NE)[1], it is even more critical to include IT industry factors, as entrepreneurs seek business opportunities specifically within the IT industry. Based on Ang and Slaughter's work, attributes of the IT context can be divided into two subsets: the internal organizational context and the external environment context [19]. The former includes factors specific to a given firm, including its IT strategy, its organizational structure, size, organization lifecycle, and finally, the IT work process. The external context includes general technology trends, IT labour markets, legal concerns, effects of national culture, and the growing influence of globalisation in the IT industry. For example, the current robustness of the labour market is a key contextual factor, as highlighted by Panko (2008), who states that the perceived or real health of the IT industry should be regarded as an important factor at the environmental level. Indeed, he states that "post bubble job losses and unemployment growth was very short lived and was not as bad as many people believed" [20, p.194].

3   Entrepreneurship Literature

There exists a large and growing body of theory and data on entrepreneurs – one that is rarely cited or acknowledged in the IS literature. Here, we briefly review specific portions of this literature that we consider directly relevant for purposes of theory building specific to IT professionals. Three different types of entrepreneurs are generally identified in the entrepreneurship literature (e.g. nascent, new or established). Since the first of these, nascent entrepreneurs (NE) is most relevant to our work, we focus on them, [21, p.44]. Within the entrepreneurship literature, one stream of research compares the individual attributes of NE with non-entrepreneurs. In order to summarize the differences identified in such studies, we use Davidsson's classification scheme, [6], first considering *human* and *social* attributes of entrepreneurs, followed by *perceptual factors.* We also review a second stream of research that focuses on factors that trigger the decision to start a SME.

---

[1] The definition of nascent entrepreneurs according to Reynolds et al. is the following : "An individual may be considered a "nascent entrepreneur" given three conditions: first, if *she/he* has done something — taken some action — to create a new business within the past year; second, if *she/he* expects to share ownership of the new firm; and, third, if the firm has not paid wages or salaries for more than three months".

A first large and growing body of literature has focused on the question of how NE differ from non-entrepreneurs. By comparing NE to non-entrepreneurs, researchers have identified similarities and differences, thereby revealing indicators of subsequent venture creation.

Human capital. The individual's *level of education* is related to entrepreneurship; however, the type of relationship is complex. Specifically, Wagner suggests an inversed U-shaped curve between education level and entrepreneurial behavior, with low propensity to become a NE at the extreme levels of education (both those who did not complete secondary school and those who completed a graduate degree) and much higher propensity to become an entrepreneur for those with moderate levels of education (i.e., secondary school and university graduates) [22].

More complex theoretical developments help to clarify the role of *education* and *prior experience* as they relate to propensity to start a business. E.g., Lazear and others ([9, 10], [11] support a "jack-of-all-trades" view of entrepreneurship where *breadth of education*, the *balance of skills*, and the *number of roles* served in prior job positions are better predictors of entrepreneurial behaviour than specialization or years of experience. The importance of varied or balanced prior experience is further clarified in recent psychological studies [8] focusing on *successful intelligence*. Indeed, according to Sternberg, an entrepreneur will be successful if three types of intelligence (analytical, practical and creative) are combined in a balanced set. Sternberg also insists that practical intelligence is developed through a process that he calls *learning from experience*, i.e. "some people can be in a job for years and know less than someone who has been in the job for months" (p.195).

In addition, *need for achievement*, is consistently shown to be a key predictor of entrepreneurial behavior [23]. Although conflicting conclusions have been reached by other authors (due, in part, to the fact that managers share the same trait of high need for achievement as entrepreneurs), nonetheless, high need to achieve is important to recognize [24]. Lastly, *self-efficacy*, *innovativeness*, and *risk-taking* are other important attributes. Arenius and Minniti found a strong role for confidence in one's skills as a factor distinguishing entrepreneurs from non-entrepreneurs [25] – a result confirmed by others [26], [27], [28]. Chen et al further specified entrepreneurial self-efficacy (ESE) into five sub-factors: marketing, innovation, management, risk-taking and financial control or self-efficacy [7]. Their study found that entrepreneurs are more likely to be innovative and risk-taking, compared to managers – but there were no significant difference for the other self-efficacy factors (marketing, management, and financial control self-efficacy).

Social capital. The second dimension of Davidsson's framework is *social capital* [6]. Wagner reports that the probability of becoming a NE is "more than twice as high for those who know an entrepreneur" compared to those who do not [22, p.8], a finding that is confirmed by [28].

Perceptual factors. In addition to self-efficacy, other perceptual factors increase the propensity of becoming a NE. Wagner reports that the proportion of NE is "twice as high among those who consider *fear of failure* not a problem, compared to those who do" [22, p.8]. Another perceptual factor, *overconfidence* in one's ability to succeed, also plays a role in several studies, [28], [29]. Indeed, Koellinger et al., suggest that overconfidence generates a perceptual bias – one that is "common among individuals in general [...] and [...] entrepreneurs in particular", [28, p. 520] – which affects the *"perceived chances of outcomes* and *risks"* of starting a business [28]. Another important construct is *perception of business opportunities*, often labelled *alertness to opportunities* [25], which is, in turn, shaped by overconfidence. Of course overconfidence influences an individual's propensity to start a business [28] [25]. For instance, Wagner reported that 14.5% of NE's perceive good opportunities for venture creation compared to 4.3% of non-entrepreneurs [22].

Some limitations regarding the research on NEs have been addressed by Davidsson [6]. Davidsson acknowledges that the basic logic underlying cross-sectional comparisons of NE to non entrepreneurs seeks to answer the wrong question, "How does involvement in a start-up process affect the person?" rather than the true question: "What attributes of [individuals] cause them to enter a start-up process?" This means that issues of causality must be seriously scrutinized in cross-sectional research on entrepreneurs [6, p.10]. Davidsson reminds us that it is the *venture* which is nascent (i.e., about to begin), rather than the person[2] [6].

In sum, although we acknowledge some weaknesses that have been identified in the entrepreneurship literature comparing NE and non-entrepreneurs, we do not share the sceptics "limited enthusiasm" for this stream of research [6, p.10]. The theoretical importance of constructs such as balanced skill sets, diverse work experience (i.e., the "jack-of-all-trades"), entrepreneurial self-efficacy, and overconfidence are useful constructs that have emerged from this line of work. These constructs help contribute to a deeper understanding of entrepreneurs. Next, we address the career reasons that underlie entrepreneurs' start-up behaviour.

A second, key stream of entrepreneurship literature focuses on the factors that trigger employees to leave their existing jobs to start a new venture. One primary reason why people become entrepreneurs is because they "could find no other suitable work" (e.g. they are unemployed) [30, p.6]. Of course, this is not the only reason. Indeed, one landmark study of career factors underlying entrepreneurial behaviour was conducted by Carter et al. (2003). The authors deepen our understanding of career-related factors leading to entrepreneurship by offering a prospective comparison of factors among NE's and non-entrepreneurs. They identified six career attributes among NEs that explain 68% of the variance in outcomes (i.e., becoming an entrepreneur or not). Among their six factors, four did *not* differ significantly between the two groups, while just two factors were different – and surprisingly, entrepreneurs scored *lower* on these two constructs: these were *recognition* and *roles* [31].

As Davidsson suggested, these results may support a 'rebel' theory of entrepreneurship [6]. Moreover, we would have expected that *roles* (e.g. *continue a family tradition, follow the example of a person that they admire*) and *recognition* would rate higher in importance for entrepreneurs. The four attributes that did not differ between NE and non-entrepreneurs were *self-realization, financial success, innovation* and *independence*.

Recent results from the *Panel Study of Entrepreneurial Dynamics* (PSED) by Schjoedt and Shaver also show that pre-entrepreneurial job satisfaction tends to be

---

[2] A NE is not necessarily a novice entrepreneur who is starting his/her first business. A NE is simply a person in the early stages of starting a business.

higher for NE's compared to non-entrepreneurs. Apparently, those who become entrepreneurs are not forced to leave their firms due to low job satisfaction [32]. Schjoedt and Shaver partly attribute this finding to the possibility that "entrepreneurs may simply be more optimistic and positive people" [32, p.747]. Hence, their level of job satisfaction is merely a reflection of their general personality type, rather than serving as the motive for leaving their existing job.

4 Conceptual Framework

Next, we present the conceptual framework (Fig. 1) underlying the research. We introduce a process model of IT entrepreneurial turnover embedded within a set of contextual factors [19], [3]. This framework also considers the evolution of the relevant attributes during this process. Drawing from Lee and Mitchell's definition, a shock is "a particular jarring event that initiates the psychological analyses involved in quitting a job"[3] [33]. In the IT turnover literature, Niederman et al. [34] report that 66% of the leavers (IT professionals) experienced a shock, revealing the importance of this construct. Consequently, the evolution of the relevant attributes can be the direct result of one or several shocks that cause an IT employee to reconsider his job (e.g. a success in the implementation of an ERP can generate a sudden increase of the IT self-efficacy of the IT professional, and then produce thoughts of quitting and starting his/her SME), [4], [35] or simply the normal evolution over time of several attributes (e.g. the same boring maintenance of software application can generate an overall boredom). Then, at some point, the individual may consider that everything is in place for her/his departure, and then she/he may leave and start her/his SME.

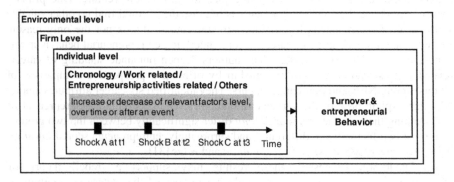

Fig. 1. Conceptual Framework

5 Methods

This section explains the MMR approach that we follow. Because we seek to answer a "how and why" question, regarding a phenomenon (i.e., where its boundaries with

---

[3] In addition, this "shock to the system" can be internal or external to the individual, positive or negative, job-related or non-job-related, and expected (a pregnancy) or unexpected.

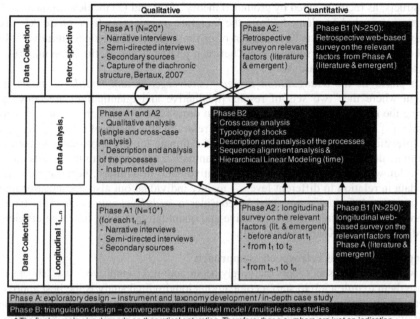

Fig. 2. Mixed Methods Design

the context, organization and environment are not clear), a multiple case-study appears to be the most appropriate approach, [36]. Moreover, we also collect additional quantitative data on other IT entrepreneurs via surveys, so that additional statistical methods can lead to further insights when merging the results of the qualitative and quantitative data, [1]. Our MMR design is summarized in Fig. 2 and could be defined as follows.

As a method, MMR "focuses on collecting, analyzing, and mixing both quantitative and qualitative data in a single study or series of studies. Its central premise is that the use of quantitative and qualitative approaches in combination provides a better understanding of research problems than either approach can alone" [1 – p.5]. We address our research questions using two broad phases.

Phase A follows an *exploratory design – instrument and taxonomy development*. Although we generally follow the premise of [1 – p. 58-88], this is not the only available framework for MMR [37]. This design consists of two distinct phases: qualitative (A1) followed by quantitative (A2), [1 – p.5]. In this design, the constructs to be included in the survey are based on literature, and also on the qualitative data collection and analysis. For these reasons, we propose completing phase A1 prior to phase A2.[4] Then, we intertwine these two types of data, following grounded theory recommendations, [38]. The rationale for this approach is that the qualitative data and analysis provide an in-depth understanding, leading to (1) the emergence of new

---

[4] It is unlikely that phase A1 and A2 will overlap or that phase A2 will happen before phase A1, however, there could be exceptions (e.g. confirming or classifying a result).

constructs, as recommended by grounded theory[5], [39] and (2) the development of the instrument, including elements from the literature or emerging from phase A1. Such an exploratory design has been used in prior research on IT personnel turnover, [40]. Although there may be some overlap between phases A and B, the large majority of phase B occurs after phase A.

In phase B, the *triangulation design – convergence and multilevel model* is a design where the "two sets of results [qualitative and quantitative] are converged during the interpretation, and the intent is to draw valid conclusions about a research problem" [1 – p.84]. The multilevel aspect refers to "the intent of forming an overall interpretation of the system", [1 – p.84]. The rationale for this approach is to combine and mutually enrich the results from the quantitative approach with the results and in-depth knowledge acquired from the qualitative data. In addition, because we collect the data in relation to different levels – mainly individual but also organizational and environmental factors – we need to consider a *multilevel approach*. This type of approach, merging multilevel qualitative and quantitative results, has been efficiently used by Reich and Kaarst-Brown [40].

Longitudinal versus retrospective approach
As we regard shocks as events that rarely occur among IT employees (i.e., shocks that cause them to quit a job to start a company), a longitudinal study is the best approach, given an ideal setting and timing. Unfortunately, this method is clearly not sufficient as it may result in a very small number of suitable cases. This is, in part, because most IT employees do not quit their jobs. Moreover, due to difficulties in terms of timing (e.g. doing the interview close to the occurrence of a shock that triggers employee departures), confidentiality issue (e.g. the IT entrepreneur may not want to share information regarding his/her future plans) and feasibility (e.g. there may be no interesting behaviour for long periods of time). Therefore, in addition to the longitudinal approach, we consider a retrospective method, which presents the advantage that the IT entrepreneur can see "the whole leaving process in a relatively holistic and measured way", [35]. Moreover, leaving and starting a company is an important and emotion-arousing event, which improves the likelihood of respondents remembering these events clearly, [35], which thus reduces the problem of bias in retrospective recall. For all those reasons, we heed the recommendation from Leonard-Barton, who argues that researchers should use both longitudinal and retrospective case studies at the same time, allowing them to achieve benefits of each method, while minimising their respective weaknesses [41]. Next, we describe the data collection process in detail.

Sample selection and sample size
During phase A, the subjects are selected following the principle of theoretical sampling and the sample size is linked to saturation. Those terms are from grounded theory and have been defined as follows: [38, p.143]

---

[5] As we reviewed the literature before collecting the data, we describe our approach as following the Straussian version of grounded theory. In this approach, it is required to do a search of the literature before and during data collection. In our case, this is justified as an important body of research related to IT turnover and entrepreneurship already exists. Therefore, we are expecting the emergence of new concepts at (1) the intersection of the two streams of research as well as (2) related to the conceptual framework of analysis we suggest.

"Theoretical sampling: A method of data collection based on concepts/themes derived from data. The purpose of theoretical sampling is to collect data from places, people and events that will maximize opportunities to develop concepts in terms of their properties and dimensions, uncovers variations and identify relationship between concepts". For example, we may seek to collect data from young entrepreneurs and senior entrepreneurs, so that concepts may emerge from the experience of the latter (e.g. recognition of overconfidence or naïve perceptions at the time of the decision). In addition, as the concepts emerge during the literature review, as well as the data collection/analysis, it is impossible to precisely and exhaustively predict the criteria for theoretical sampling in advance. That said, at this stage of the research, we have already established several criteria such as experience (as explained before), gender, type of company (service vs products) or growth expectations.

"Saturation: Saturation is usually explained in terms of "when no new data [is] emerging". But saturation is more than a matter of lack of new data. It also denotes the development of categories in terms of their properties and dimensions, including variation, and if theory building, the delineating of relationships between concepts." For example, if after 4 or 5 new cases, no new concept/relationship emerged, we could conclude that saturation has been reached. Because of that, the final sample size is unknown. However, we anticipate collecting 10 longitudinal case studies and 20 retrospective case studies. These numbers are partly linked to time constraints.

Data collection and analysis, phase A

For the most part – this data collection broadly follows the two sub-phases (A1 and A2) discussed above. Phase A1 consists of a life story approach, [42], [43], [44], and collection of secondary sources. Indeed, the "life story" approach is a form of collecting data according to "oral, autobiographical narratives", [42]) and one of its main tools is the narrative interview. In this specific type of interview, the researcher asks the interviewee to "tell all or part of his experience"[6], [43 – p.11]. In addition to this approach, we also use semi-structured interviews and secondary sources to complement and triangulate the narrative interviews. Phase A1 is divided between a retrospective and longitudinal data collection exercise. The former emphasizes the use of life story, whereas the latter captures the current situation, favouring semi-structured interviews and secondary sources. Then, we conduct qualitative analysis of the data which leads to the emergence of additional factors, [39]. Following a Straussian grounded theory approach; we intertwine the data, its analysis and the literature (the loop in Fig. 2).

---

[6] Bertaux (2007, p.63-66) suggests to keep in mind those three phases of the interview. First, start the interview, by posing a "social context", reaffirm the goal of the interview and ask a question (use the word "tell"). Secondly, follow the narrator, by acknowledging and letting him tell the story, with a minimum of interruptions. He also suggests exploring the other trajectories the narrator could have followed and why he eventually didn't. Third, Bertaux recommends that the interviewer manages the unexpected by acknowledging without hesitation his/her emotions or the narrator's emotions. Finally, he recommends ending the interview with a positive question (e.g. the narrator's greatest success) and, once the tape recorder is off to stay attentive, as some key elements can be revealed at this moment precisely because this will be off the record.

Due to space constraints, we omit additional details of our proposed analysis. We rely on the primary references for analyzing qualitative data [45], [36], [46]. However, we detail the life story approach, which complements this analysis with specific tools, such as the research of the diachronic structure (i.e. the succession of remarkable events, linked with 'before/after" type of relationships) and the sequential causality, [43 – p.74]. Based on the results of this analysis and the literature, we adapt the instrument and collect (phase A2) retrospective and longitudinal quantitative data. We collect the relevant information before and after the shocks in order to report their influences, but also at regular intervals during the period of the narrative review, to capture a gradual evolution of the relevant dimensions.

Data collection and analysis, phase B

During Phase B1, we administer a modified (web-based) version of the retrospective and longitudinal questionnaire (taking into consideration the literature and the emergent constructs) to a much larger sample of IT entrepreneurs[7], so that we achieve a sufficient sample size (N>250). In this modified version, we address the existence of shocks, filter the relevant factors and finally, capture data regarding several constructs at different points in time (before and after the shock, but also at regular interval as illustrated in Fig. 1). This questionnaire is interactive, so that we can reduce the overall number of questions to only focus on the relevant factors. We administer the specific questionnaire through a web-based survey. The choice of items is customized to the individual respondent, depending on the number of shocks that occurred and the relevant time intervals. This level of interactivity in the survey is needed to minimize the large number of survey items that might otherwise be required[8].

The quantitative analysis requires further investigation. Our goal is to explore the process patterns which help an IT professional become an IT entrepreneur. The final quantitative dataset is composed of three types of categories: the shocks, the dates and the relevant factors influencing the decision to quit and start a business. In addition to the analysis of the processes and shocks, we also consider two statistical methods. The first method, multiple sequence alignment uses the Clustal program. Although originally designed to compare and align the protein sequences; thanks to the molecular biologists who combined their effort with computer scientists, several improvement have been made to this method. In IS, this method has been used [47] to assess IS development. Although this method is about events, it is possible to assess different dimensions of one event, for instance, the activity, its location and who else was present [48]. The second statistical model refers to Hierarchical Linear Models (HLM), [49] which allows "multilevel model for change", exploring longitudinal change over time [50, chapter 3 and 6].

---

[7] We use a newsletter addressed to 10 000 individuals, among them a large number of (future) IT entrepreneurs.

[8] Based on the chronology above (Figure 3), we would need to consider an estimated potential of 2 520 (70 factors (IT turnover + entrepreneurial + emerging) x 9 time period x 4 items/factor) items which is of course impossible. Thus, by selecting only the relevant dimensions and weighing the options in term of measurement, we greatly reduce the overall number of questions.

6 Discussion

Next, we discuss the contributions of this paper. First, we suggest a conceptual framework to address the gap between IT turnover and entrepreneurship research, i.e. the IT entrepreneur's turnover. Although this framework is in the process of being validated and enriched, it constitutes a sound basis for future research, and we believe that seeking to understand IT entrepreneurs' actual turnover behaviour increases our knowledge of IT turnover. Secondly, we argue that MMR is appropriate to bridge the entrepreneurial literature with the IT turnover literature. Third, another important contribution is the design of the MMR (Fig. 2), combining a longitudinal and retrospective approach, [41]; a qualitative with quantitative approach (data collection and analysis) and, finally, the *exploratory design – instrument and taxonomy development* with the *triangulation design – convergence and multilevel model*. Although Creswell and Plano Clark strongly recommend the use of "a single design that best matches the research problem", [1 – p. 79] we believe that our research question does not allow us to follow only one design. Moreover, Petter and Gallivan [37] found that this combination is frequently used in IS studies involving MMR. Finally, the use of MMR responds to several calls to go beyond the dominance of positivist, quantitative research, [37], [51].

7 Practical Implications, Limitations and Future Research

The implications can be discussed at two levels; for IT managers and IT entrepreneurs. The benefits to IT managers lie in generating a better understanding of IT entrepreneurs' turnover, in order to potentially change the levels of IT employee rewards, challenge, or other job attributes, so as to prevent turnover among prospective entrepreneurs – or to allow the employee to leave in a "kinder and gentler" way. For example, Schjoedt and Shaver show that pre-entrepreneurial job satisfaction tends to be higher for (NE) compared to non-entrepreneurs. Apparently, those who become entrepreneurs do not leave their firms due to low job satisfaction [32]. Such a result (which contradicts the general IT turnover literature), if replicated with IT entrepreneurs, has some practical implication for IT managers. Moreover, by recognizing that events at work – and elsewhere – can influence the gradual evolution of various factors leading to turnover/entrepreneurial behaviour, IT managers (i.e., those who supervise IT workers who are "at risk" of becoming entrepreneurs) may be able to predict future evolution and future turnover.

For IT entrepreneurs, our model may offer a road map for the journey that leads to their ultimate objective: creation of their business enterprise. For example, research found that the construct of a shock, [4, p.451] is necessary for certain paths leading to IT personnel turnover, [34]; if this finding is replicated with IT entrepreneurs, this knowledge may lead IT entrepreneurs to (intentionally) provoke such a shock to occur. Moreover, by identifying trends in the evolution of their relevant factors, future IT entrepreneurs may be able to more clearly identify the subsequent steps which lead to actual turnover.

Several limitations can be addressed. First the data collection/analysis of this research is not presented here. Although we are currently working on 13 different case studies, our goal is to validate the overall research design before going too far into the data collection/analysis. Second, we recognize several challenges in this research design. Some are linked to the longitudinal aspects of the data collection (as previously discussed), others to the size of this project. To address the latter, a careful evaluation of the needed resources (e.g. funds, researchers, web designers) is necessary. Finally, following Mingers, we are conscious of the limitations of the MMR, regarding philosophical, cultural, psychological and practical feasibility [51], however, despite the large amount of required resources, we are confident, based on the currently on-going data collection and data analysis, that those limitations are not insurmountable. Even though this paper contributes to the literature by providing two frameworks, one to analyse IT entrepreneur's turnover and the other to conduct a mixed methods research combining exploratory and triangulation design, future research will seek to apply and test those frameworks and generate interesting findings.

References

1. Creswell, J.W., Plano Clark, V.L.: Designing and Conducting Mixed Methods Research. Sage, Thousand Oaks (2007)
2. Bharadwaj, A.S.: A Resource-Based Perspective on Information Technology Capability and Firm Performance: an Empirical Investigation. MIS Q 24(1), 169 (2000)
3. Joseph, D., Kok-Yee, N., Koh, C., Soon, A.: Turnover of information technology professionals: a narrative rev., meta-analytic structural equation modeling, and model development. MIS Q 31(3), 547–577 (2007)
4. Lee, T.W., Mitchell, T.R., Holtom, B.C., McDaniel, L.S., Hill, J.W.: The unfolding model of voluntary turnover: a replication and extension. Academy of Management J. 42(4), 450–462 (1999)
5. Mitchell, T.R.: Why People Stay: Using Job Embeddedness to Predict Voluntary Turnover. Academy of Management J. 44(6), 1102 (2001)
6. Davidsson, P.: Nascent Entrepreneurship: Empirical Studies and Developments. Foundations and Trands in Enterpreneurship. Now publishers Inc. (2006)
7. Chen, C.C., Greene, P.G., Crick, A.: Does entrepreneurial self-efficacy distinguish entrepreneurs from managers? J. of Bus. Venturing 13(4), 295–316 (1998)
8. Sternberg, R.J.: Successful intelligence as a basis for entrepreneurship. J. of Bus. Venturing 19(2), 189–201 (2004)
9. Lazear, E.P.: Entrepreneurship. Working Paper 9109. National Bureau of Economic Res. (2002)
10. Lazear, E.P.: Balanced skills and entrepreneurship. American Economic Rev. 94(2), 208–211 (2004)
11. Wagner, J.: Are nascent entrepreneurs 'Jacks-of-all-trades'? A test of Lazear's theory of entrepreneurship with German data. Appl. Economics 38(20), 2415–2419 (2006)
12. Bygrave, W.: The entrepreneurial process. The Portable MBA in Entrepreneurship. John Wiley and Sons, Chichester (1994)
13. Carter, N.M., Gartner, W.B., Reynolds, P.D.: Exploring start-up event sequences. J. of Bus. Venturing 11(3), 151–166 (1996)
14. Igbaria, M., Greenhaus, J.H.: Career orientations of MIS employees: An empirical analysis. MIS Q 15(2), 151 (1991)

15. Igbaria, M., Parasuraman, S.: Work experiences, job involvement, and quality of work life among information systems personnel. MIS Q 18(2), 175 (1994)
16. Moore, J.E.: One road to turnover: an examination of work exhaustion in technology professionals. MIS Q 24(1), 141–168 (2000)
17. Ferratt, T.W., Agarwal, R., Brown, C.V., Moore, J.E.: IT Human Resource Management Configurations and IT Turnover: Theoretical Synthesis and Empirical Analysis. Inf. Syst. Res. 16(3), 237–255 (2005)
18. Agarwal, R., Ferratt, T.W., De, P.: An experimental investigation of turnover intentions among new entrants in it. The DATA BASE for Advances in Inf. Syst. 38(1), 8–28 (2007)
19. Ang, S., Slaughter, S.: The missing context of information technology personnel: a rev. and future directions for research. In: Zmud, R.W. (ed.) Framing the Domains of IT Management: Projecting the Future through the Past, pp. 305–327. Pinnaflex Educational Resources, Cincinnati (2000)
20. Panko, R.R.: IT employment prospects: beyond the dotcom bubble. European J. of Inf. Syst. 17(3), 182 (2008)
21. Reynolds, P.D., Bygrave, W.D., Autio, E., Hay, M.: GEM Global Entrepreneurship Report, Summary Report: Babson, Wellesley, MA and London Bus. School, London, 47 (2002)
22. Wagner, J.: Nascent entrepreneurs. In: Forschungsinstitut zur Zukunft der Arbeit, Bonn, Germany (2004)
23. Shaver, K.G., Scott, L.R.: Person, process, choice; The psychology of new venture creation. Entrepreneurship: Theory & Practice 16(2), 23 (1991)
24. Wagner, K., Andreas, Z.: The nascent entrepreneur at the crossroads: entrepreneurial motives as determinants for different types of entrepreneurs. In: Discussion Papers on Entrepreneurship and Innovation. Swiss Institute for Entrepreneurship, Chur (2008)
25. Arenius, P., Minniti, M.: Perceptual variables and nascent entrepreneurship. Small Bus. Economics 24(3), 233–247 (2005)
26. Boyd, N.G., Vozikis, G.S.: The influence of self-efficacy on the development of entrepreneurial intentions and actions. Entrepreneurship: Theory & Practice 18(4), 63–77 (1994)
27. Zhao, H.H., Seibert, S.E., Hills, G.E.: The mediating role of self-efficacy in the development of entrepreneurial intentions. Journal of applied psychology 90(6), 1265–1272 (2005)
28. Koellinger, P., Minniti, M., Schade, C.: "I think I can, I think I can": Overconfidence and entrepreneurial behavior. Journal of Economic Psychology 28(4), 502–527 (2007)
29. Forbes, D.P.: Are some entrepreneurs more overconfident than others? Journal of Business Venturing 20(5), 623–640 (2005)
30. Reynolds, P.D., Bygrave, W.D., Autio, E., Cox, L.W., Hay, M.: GEM Global Entrepreneurship Report, 2002 Executive Report: Babson, Wellesley, MA and London Business School, London, 47 (2002)
31. Carter, N.M., Gartner, W.B., Shaver, K.G., Gatewood, E.J.: The career reasons of nascent entrepreneurs. Journal of Business Venturing 18(1), 13–39 (2003)
32. Schjoedt, L., Shaver, K.G.: Deciding on an entrepreneurial career: a test of the pull and push hypotheses using the panel study of entrepreneurial dynamics data. Entrepreneurship: Theory & Practice 31(5), 733–752 (2007)
33. Lee, T.W., Mitchell, T.R.: An alternative approach: the unfolding model of voluntary employee turnover. The Academy of Management Review 19(1), 51–89 (1994)

34. Niederman, F., Sumner, M., Maertz, C.: Testing and extending the unfolding model of voluntary turnover to it professionals. Human Resource Management Journal 46(3), 331–347 (2007)
35. Morrell, K., Loan-Clarke, J., Arnold, J., Wilkinson, A.: Mapping the decision to quit: a refinement and test of the unfolding model of voluntary turnover. Applied Psychology 57(1), 128–150 (2008)
36. Yin, R.K.: Case Study Research: Design and Methods. SAGE Publications, Thousand Oaks (1981)
37. Petter, S.C., Gallivan, M.J.: Toward a framework for classifying and guiding mixed methods research in information systems. In: Proceedings of the 37th Annual Hawaii International Conference on System Sciences, Waikaloa, HI (2004)
38. Corbin, J., Strauss, A.L.: Basics of qualitative research. Sage, Thousand Oaks (2008)
39. Strauss, A.L., Corbin, J.: Grounded Theory in Practice (1997)
40. Reich, B.H., Kaarst-Brown, M.L.: 'Seeding the Line': Understanding the Transition From IT to Non-IT Careers. MIS Quarterly 23(3), 337 (1999)
41. Leonard-Barton, D.: A dual methodology for case studies: synergistic use of a longitudinal single site with replicated multiple sites. Organization science 1(3), 248 (1990)
42. Bertaux, D., Kohli, M.: The Life Story Approach: A Continental View. Annual Review of Sociology 10, 215–237 (1984)
43. Bertaux, D.: Le récit de vie. Armand Colin, p. 126 (2005)
44. Bertaux, D.: Life Story, p. 160. Sage Publications, Thousand Oaks (2008)
45. Glaser, B., Strauss, A.L.: The Discovery of Grounded Theory: Strategies for Qualitative Research: Aldine Transaction (1967)
46. Miles, M.B., Huberman, A.M.: Qualitative Data Analysis, 2nd edn. SAGE, Thousand Oaks (1994)
47. Sabherwal, R., Robey, D.: An Empirical Taxonomy of Implementation Processes Based on Sequences of Events in Information System Development. Organization Science 4(4), 548–576 (1993)
48. Wilson, C., Harvey, A., Thompson, J.: ClustalG: Software for analysis of activities and sequential events. In: Workshop on Sequence Alignment Methods, Halifax (2005)
49. Raudenbrush, S.W., Bryk, A.S.: Hierarchical Linear Models. Advanced Quantitative Techniques (2002)
50. Singer, J.D.: Applied Longitudinal Data Analysis: Modeling Change and Event Occurrence (2003)
51. Mingers, J.: Combining IS Research Methods: Towards a Pluralist Methodology. Information systems research 12(3), 240 (2001)

Towards a Model of Technology Adoption: A Conceptual Model Proposition

Pat Costello and Rob Moreton

School of Computing and IT,
University of Wolverhampton,
Wolverhampton, U.K.

Abstract. A conceptual model for Information Communication Technology (ICT) adoption by Small Medium Enterprises (SMEs) is proposed. The research uses several ICT adoption models as its basis with theoretical underpinning provided by the Diffusion of Innovation theory and the Technology Acceptance Model (TAM). Taking an exploratory research approach the model was investigated amongst 200 SMEs whose core business is ICT. Evidence from this study demonstrates that these SMEs face the same issues as all other industry sectors. This work points out weaknesses in SMEs environments regarding ICT adoption and suggests what they may need to do to increase the success rate of any proposed adoption. The methodology for development of the framework is described and recommendations made for improved Government-led ICT adoption initiatives. Application of the general methodology has resulted in new opportunities to embed the ethos and culture surrounding the issues into the framework of new projects developed as a result of Government intervention. A conceptual model is proposed that may lead to a deeper understanding of the issues under consideration.

1 Introduction

For many SMEs innovation is not about 'blue-sky' research and leading edge technology but about the adoption of technology that will allow new processes to be employed by the company that are innovative for them (Mehrten, 2001). The decision to adopt technology brings into play a myriad of both business and technology issues that can be overwhelming for an SME. Many models have examined Electronic Data Interchange (EDI) adoption (Jackson and Sloane, 2007) and the transferability of these models from EDI to Internet but the testing of the model's adoption into all technologies has been less well examined. Academicians and governments have attempted for many years to address the issue of increasing efficient adoption of ICT and this quest has been gathering pace in recent years, fuelled by work such as that of Sheppard et al.(2007). Sheppard determined a link between efficient and effective technology adoption and increases in productivity. This paper attempts to take this work a step further by developing a model for adoption based on earlier models devised by other researchers in this area. The research study developed to address the question: Is it possible to develop an overarching model of ICT adoption using current models which can be applied whatever the technology?

G. Dhillon, B.C. Stahl, and R. Baskerville (Eds.): CreativeSME 2009, IFIP AICT 301, pp. 287–305, 2009.

In spite of many years of research in the area of ICT adoption, progress is slow mainly due to the myriad of complexities in the subject area. Investment by the United Kingdom (UK) Government continues, albeit regionally and not on a national scale. Where there is investment, it focuses on a single technology and does not address the concerns surrounding the environment within which SMEs operate. There is a need to embed the culture and skills required within SMEs and raise awareness regarding ICTs potential which may aid any future adoption of technology. SME engagement is crucial as they form an important part of the business community and have the ability to impact in a major way on customers and suppliers. Large organisations that have turned to electronic means of communication, for example, will often find that the 'bottleneck' in the supply chain will be an SME who is an immature technology user (Costello et al., 2006).

Poon and Huang (in Ai-Qirim, 2003) describe the need for a more integrated approach to ICT adoption research stating that a continuation of the single approach in studies leaves the field with yet more disparate conclusions. The inherent problem with the multi-faceted approach called for by Poon and Huang is the depth of the study which if broad in approach can be shallow in content. However, they then call for the need for triangulation in 'method, theory, measures or observers'. The research approach recommended by Poon and Huang was integrated into the research reported here.

2 Government Intervention in the Adoption Process

Academics and governments have previously attempted to address the issue of increasing efficient adoption of ICT and this issue is gathering pace in the West Mildlands (WM) UK fuelled by the work of Sheppard et al., (2007). This determines a strong causal link between efficient and effective technology adoption and increases in GVA[1]. However, in spite of many years of work in the field of ICT adoption by scholars, progress is slow, as complexities inherent in this area make it a difficult research topic. Investment by Government also continues in an attempt to increase the adoption of ICT by SMEs as this has been shown to be a very effective way of increasing GVA. However, much of the work supported by Government involves a single technology and does not address the concerns surrounding the environment within which SMEs operate which may have an adverse effect on the success of adoption and also limits future take up.

In spite of attempts by the Government, the small business sector still has problems and is often suspicious of those that work to help them (Bennett and Robson, 1998). There is now a plethora of government funded support services available for SMEs and this in itself can be confusing for owner-managers. Support to adopt ICT is often superficial, aimed at end users and of limited use to companies whose core business is ICT. Policy makers need to address the benefits for SMEs, rather than the need to hit government targets (Culkin and Smith, 2000) and indeed be concerned with the SMEs need and not with personal career development (Mercer, 1996). It has been suggested

---

[1] Gross Value Added (GVA) measures contribution to the economy of each individual producer, industry or sector in the United Kingdom. GVA + taxes on products - subsidies on products = GDP http://www.statistics.gov.uk/cci/nugget.asp?ID=254 accessed 11/10/2007.

that many intervention projects address the needs of the policy makers' career rather than the intervention itself (Culkin and Smith, 2000); although that is an understandable concern given the often transient nature of job roles in this area.

The way Government initiative targets are set and defined point towards a 'generalist' view of SMEs (Martin & Matlay, 2001). In work done by MacGregor and Vrazalic (2005) eBusiness was recognised as a major source of competitive advantage and they state that this now means that Governments worldwide have recognised this and are creating funding schemes and initiatives to facilitate e-Commerce adoption in small businesses. There have also been many attempts by authors to categorise barriers and enablers in this major area of concern. The Department for Trade and Industry (DTI) a United Kingdom (UK) central government department who recently changed its' name to the Department for Business, Enterprise and Regulatory Reform (BERR) published the governments 'adoption ladder' for their UK online initiative. The model underpins much of the understanding around the area of ICT adoption in SMEs (Sergeant 2000 cited in Martin and Matlay, 2001). Unfortunately, the only flexibility built into the model is to imply that not all businesses will start at stage one. However there is no flexibility for significant differences in size, sector, ethnicity, gender, human resources, financial resources, level of internationalisation. Neither is there a place for the entrepreneurial or innovative skills of owner-managers in this model. Martin & Matlay (2001) claim there is a lack of 'empirically rigorous data and focused research' on the topic of ICT adoption by small companies. Stating that the DTI literature claims that the adoption of new technologies is essential to survival and growth is based upon sweeping generalisations.

There is much evidence to suggest that linear models of development and adoption are inappropriate for SMEs and tend to oversimplify complex issues (Kai-Uwe Brook, 2000). Kai-Uwe (2000) refer to a paucity of academic research in this area and claim that further research is necessary in order to develop 'real understanding' of ICT adoption by SMEs. These findings are an echo of earlier research work by Lauder and Westhall (1997), Iacovou et al. (1995) and Blackburn and Athayde (2000). It is a concern that a blanket approach to investment of this kind informs government in this area as it may be inappropriate given that SMEs are created and 'die' in vast quantities every year. Many organisations involved in projects which attract Government funding to help establish their ICT, are not necessarily still 'established' a few years later. This creates the impression that the money has not been of any long term help. Although without statistics to show how many SMEs who take part in a particular project are still in business a number of years later, no assumptions can be made. Neither can it be established if the ICT project itself was a contributor to this failure. There is a strong need for impartial advice independent from vendors. Many need practical help in the form of trusted ICT Consultancy (Harindranath et al., 2007, Costello et al., 2008) as well as grants or loans.

Since the demise of the UK Online initiative, a government funded project to encourage businesses to use the Internet, the only government entity playing a national role in the ICT policy arena is e-skills UK. Its aim is to work with businesses to improve competitiveness and productivity by bringing together employers, educators and government, uniting them for a common, employer-led agenda for action on skills. In spite of the evidence of GVA increases there is currently no national level strategy to increase adoption of ICT by SMEs.

3   EDI, eBusiness and Internet Adoption Models

The theoretical underpinning of much of the work in this field is based on work by Rogers (1965 in Rogers, 2003) in his book Diffusion of Innovation which sets the scene and provides much of the basis upon which work regarding technology acceptance is grounded. Rogers' (1965) work categorised adopters of new innovations as innovators (2.5%), early adopters (13.5%), early majority (34%), late majority (34%) and laggards (16%) based on a bell curve. The study discussed the conviction that an innovation decision was based on a cost-benefit analysis and that people would adopt if they believed that the innovation could produce some relative advantage to the idea it replaced. Critics have remarked that it attempts to explain a very complex reality in too simplified a fashion. Nonetheless; this theory has remained as a starting point upon which much IS research in this area is based. Since this early work, research has consistently found that relative advantage (perceived need) is an important issue in the adoption decision (Bradford and Florin, 2003).

Fishbein and Ajzen's (1975) theory of reasoned action provided insight into the reasoning behind the behaviour of individuals and posited that a person's attitude towards behaviour (attitudes) and how they think others will view that behaviour (subjective norm) forms the basis upon which they intend to behave (behavioural intention). It was this work that formed the basis for the Technology Acceptance Model (TAM) developed by Davis et.al. (1989) and Bagozzi et al. (1992). Their work replaced the two attitude measures with two technology acceptance measures; *ease of use* and *usefulness*. Both models assume that an individual is free to act as they wish once they form the intent to act. In the real world this is not always the case as there are often numerous constraints. Work on the diffusion of innovation has also taken into account *perceived ease of use*. Tornatzky and Klein (1982) looked at the relationship between compatibility, relative advantage and complexity and found that these had the most significant link to adoption. Much work has centred on testing these models over the last few decades including looking at the validity of research instruments used in the original work. Venkatesh and Davis (2000) developed the work to include perceived usefulness and usage intentions; this model was referred to as TAM2. However, critics of TAM conclude that a limitation of the model is that it excludes influences on personal behaviour, economic factors and outside influences (Van Akkeren and Cavaye, 1999). TAM was subsequently developed into the Unified Theory of Acceptance and Use of Technology (UTAUT) (Venkatesh et.al., 2003).

Many ICT adoption models have been tested in large companies only (Chwelos et al., 2001, Jackson and Sloane, 2005, Levy and Powell, 2005, Lefebvre and Lefebvre, 1996) and many revolve around adoption of EDI, Internet and eBusiness. The main problem identified from the literature is defining the factors that impact the successful adoption of ICT. Many researchers have found that these models are transferable in the realm of communication technologies. There are, however, difficulties with transferring the models from large companies to SMEs as decision-making structures are incomparable. Neither have these models been tested and applied to successful adoption of *all* ICT infrastructures rather than just a specific technology.

However, the advent of the Internet era has allowed small companies to employ communication on a par with EDI for a fraction of the cost. Hence many models have been developed for the adoption of Internet and eBusiness. Sarosa and Zowghi

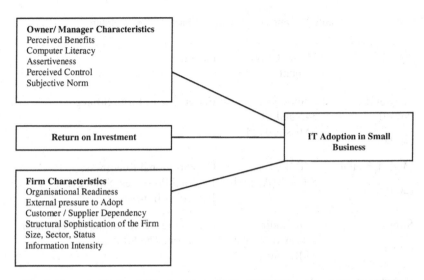

Fig. 1. Factors affecting ICT adoption in SMEs (Van Akkeren and Cavaye 1999)

(2003) state that research to date has concentrated on identifying drivers and barriers to adoption of ICT and there is still a lack of frameworks or models that actually guide SMEs in the adoption process. The most frequently asked question by any SME is how to adopt successfully. There is a very small body of academics examining adoption models at this time (Levy et.al., 2005b, Van Akkeren and Cavaye, 1999) especially in the area of SMEs. The fact that many factors are similar in so many models may indicate that the technology to be adopted is irrelevant. Levy (2005a) also indicated that industry sector is irrelevant although research for this paper examined one specific sector (ICT) which may be assumed to be more capable than other sectors and proficient at supporting others.

Van Akkaren et.al. (1999) study of the literature supports the conviction that in SMEs, issues around adoption can be divided into factors regarding the owner-manager characteristics, firm characteristics and other factors, including the need for an owner-manager to realise a return on investment (ROI). Fig. 1 shows the factors identified by that study as affecting adoption in small businesses. The study also claims that there are probably more factors than this as yet to be uncovered by future research and that current models do not include ROI. Research carried out by Jackson and Sloane (2007) shows that more subtle issues such as organisation culture and human resources have a major impact on the adoption of new systems and are therefore included in their model for e-Commerce. There is often an underlying assumption by SMEs that simply adopting new technology will automatically produce benefits for the company (Costello et al., 1999). In particular, SMEs tend to believe that the technology itself will improve business processes and do not always address the process improvements, trying instead to automate existing ones (Husein et al., 1999).

Mehrten et al. (2001) demonstrated that the CEO has a significant role in ICT adoption in SMEs, especially if the CEO is innovative and knowledgeable about ICT. This model was again developed from existing studies and had as its grounding the

Table 1. Summary of Adoption Factors from literature

Source	Model Development	Factors
Levy and Powell (2005)	2 Surveys : 343 and 21 SMEs in WM	Entrepreneur, Firm, Strategy
Merheten et al. (2001)	7 SMEs Case Studies (Australia)	Organisational Readiness, External Pressures, Strategy, Perceived Benefits.
Storey (1994)	Longitudinal survey on broad SME issues	Starting resources of the entrepreneur, The Firm, The Strategy.
Grandon et al. (2004)	9 Literature sources, 100 email surveys	Organisational Readiness, External Pressure, Perceived Usefulness + Perceived Ease of Use
Van Akkeren and Cavaye (1999)	6 Literature sources – no survey	Owner manager characteristics, Firm Characteristics.
Rashid and Al-Qirim (2001)	3 Literature sources – no survey (New Zealand)	Individual factors, Organisational factors, Environmental factors, Technological factors.
King-Turner and Bonnett (2005)	60 SMEs surveyed in WM	Personal factors, Economic Factors (cost and resource), Environmental factors, Relevant solution.

work of Lefebvre and Lefebvre (1996) and Thong and Yap (1995). Merhten's belief was previously identified in the work of Van Akkeren and Cavaye (1999) above. The research uncovered 3 issues that are prevalent in EDI adoption research: perceived benefits, organisational readiness and external pressures. These elements are then used to test ICT adoption issues. It was also revealed in this study that there is a need to have the skills in house as this supports the users during implementation. Merhten claims that further research could determine if the model was transferable to other technologies.

Storey's (1994) study over a three-year period between 1989 and 1992, completed work that helped form the basis of much of today's work with SMEs. His work spanned 10,000 SMEs in the UK and had a significant influence on much of the decade's policy making. The model developed which is of interest to this study, included factors influencing growth in small firms (Storey, 1994). In this model each of the three factors of the entrepreneur, the firm and the strategy are defined by a number of issues, the most significant of these were incorporated into the research for this paper.

Levy et al.(2005a) model was adapted from Storey's (1994) and a development of this model was applied to West Midlands (WM) UK SMEs. Their work on Internet adoption determined that business growth is a key driver in Internet adoption and therefore is a sound basis on which to develop a model. They also describe the SME market as investing in information systems at start up and then no further development until the business outgrows its first purchase. Levy et al. (2005b) claim that many of the drivers can be described as perceived benefits and many of the inhibitors are recognized as being due to management limitations.

Grandon and Pearson (2004) analysed ten ICT adoption models to determine the main ICT adoption factors and found that many of the same issues recurred throughout the literature. They summarised these factors into organisational readiness, external pressure, perceived ease of use and perceived usefulness. They determined a causal link between perceived strategic value of e-business and e-business adoption. The collated factors from the research from other authors represented the output from more than 1,700 small companies. The factors were amalgamated into a model which was tested via survey on a further 100 companies. The survey found that a positive change in attitude towards adoption of the technology based on the 'impression' of its strategic value to the firm was necessary to successful adoption.

Rashid and Al-Qirim (2001) considered the specific difficulties of SMEs and produced a considerably simplified model for these, by building on previous work by Thong and Yap (1995) and Premkuma and Roberts (1999). They concluded that issues such as the individual characteristics of the owner manager are essential in successful adoption of e-Commerce in SMEs and that competition also significantly influences adoption. Their findings also highlighted that often it is lack of knowledge of the technology that is the main barrier to adoption and the acknowledgement of the strategic importance of the technology usually came from the larger companies in the sample.

A subsequent model was developed and applied to 60 SMEs in the WM UK (King-Turner and Bonnett, 2005). The survey was conducted to determine factors in adopters and non-adopters of Open Source Software (OSS). The model developed was based on the work of Rashid and Al-Qirim (2001) but added other factors that had been evident during the course of regional work with SMEs. The main reasons given by the companies in their survey for adoption were Economic Factors, both the cost and the resources, which underpins the research indicated by Locke (2004) who found that hardware was considered to be the most significant cost and consideration by SMEs.

A summary of the models discussed here is provided in table 1, these were used to underpin the new model based on Van Akkeren and Cavaye (1999) framework which is proposed for the adoption of technology infrastructure in this study.

4 Methodology and Development of a New Model

A model was developed from those in table 1 above and explored amongst the SME sector in the WM, UK to ascertain if the factors could be applied to any technology.

Especially as many adoption models overlap or complement each other (Van Akkeren and Cavaye, 1999) and most involve at least some factors that are directly comparable. This research further explores the factors around ICT infrastructure adoption; looking at all technology purchases by SMEs by examining the last significant purchase the company made, with the significance being defined by the owner-manager. Table 2 shows a summary of the elements from the models used in the study. This was verified and supplemented by factors from the extensive literature review.

Table 2. Summary of Factors involved in ICT adoption for SMEs

Category Source:	Personal Factors	The Firm	Organisational readiness	External Pressures	Perceived Value	Strategy
National B2B (2005)	Personal factors		Economic Factors (cost and resource)	Environmental factors		Relevant solution
Rashid and Al-Qirim (2001)	Individual factors		Organisational factors	Environmental factors	Technological (innovation) factors	
Levy and Powell (2005)	Entrepreneur	Firm				Strategy
Merhetens et al. (2001)			Organisational Readiness	External Pressures	Perceived Benefits	
Storey (1994)	Entrepreneur	Firm				Strategy
Grandon et al. (2004)			Organisational Readiness	External Pressure	Perceived Usefulness + Perceived Ease of Use	
Van Akkeren and Cavaye (1999)	Owner manager characteristics	Firm Characteristics	Firm Characteristics	Firm Characteristics	Owner Manager Characteristics	Firm Characteristics

It was ascertained that firm characteristics can include, organisational readiness, external pressure to adopt, customer/supplier dependency, structural sophistication of the firm, sector and status (Grandon et.al., 2004, Levy et al., 2005, Van Akkeren and Cavaye, 1999, Thong and Yap, 1995, Rashid et al., 2001, Mehrten et al., 2001,

Storey, 1994). In this study, the sector is not considered as the survey was completed in one sector; although there are indications from Sheppard (2007) that the ICT sector is important and that this sector may embrace ICT more readily than others. However, this study looks at whether the ICT sector is in fact embracing technology for use within the business in a sophisticated way or if they do not 'practice what they preach'. The structural sophistication of the firm is not measured, instead the evidence from the literature review shows that companies become more structurally complex as they grow and that the larger the organisation the more likely they are to consider strategy, hence this element is captured via strategy. External pressures are examined and the pressure of customer and/or supplier noted. Organisational readiness examines the technology already in place within an organisation and their readiness to adopt. The factors which represent the firm's characteristics are encapsulated into Strategy, organisational readiness, the firm and external pressures.

The owner-manager characteristics can include perceived benefits, computer literacy, assertiveness, perceived control and subjective norm (Grandon et.al., 2004, Levy et al., 2005, Van Akkeren and Cavaye, 1999, Thong and Yap, 1995, Iacovou, 1995, Rashid et al., 2001, Mehrtens et al., 2001, Storey, 1994). These are seen in perceived value and personal factors within the model developed here. Given that the majority (69%) of the companies are micro (less than 10 employees), computer literacy is collated through the presence of a skilled ICT professional within the company and the owner-manager themselves as a technology champion within an ICT company. It is also considered within the implementation issues explored since skills levels may account for adoption problems experienced post adoption. Assertiveness, perceived control and subjective norm are not explored in any detail in this study as these were seen to be part of the sociological and psychological aspects and thus need further research outside of the scope. Although this split of owner-manager characteristics and firm characteristics is demarcated in the work of many researchers, it is often not as easy to clearly differentiate between these areas. For example the SME sophistication may be due to the owner-manager or the level of technology within the firm. The organisational readiness can be as much linked to the strategy or lack of strategy in the company as it can be to the owner-manager attitude to adoption.

Following an extensive literature survey, three pilot case studies were conducted at the start of the research to gain an understanding of the factors important to small companies when adopting ICT. This was followed by a sample survey of eight companies to further refine the model and also the survey instrument. This evidence was translated into the model which formed the basis of a survey of 206 SMEs in the ICT sector.

The approach to the survey was predominately qualitative and a questionnaire was designed that collected a limited amount of quantitative data. The questions were split into 4 sections: Company Background, Current ICT infrastructure, ICT Investment and Impact on Business Performance. The questionnaire was delivered in a semi-structured interview approach with 83% conducted by face-to-face interviews and 17% by telephone interview. The large number (200) of respondents was a challenge and the subsequent data was read several times and then categorised and encoded. Two techniques were involved in sampling the target population; the first was probabilistic in that companies attending ICT events throughout the local region were approached during the events and asked to take part in the research. This then led to snowball sampling as having gained the trust of the owner-manager of one company; they would often give details of associates, partners or collaborators who would also be willing to participate. From the 206 companies only 6% of responses were 'spoiled'; this left 69% micro companies (less than 10 employees), 17% small companies (less than 50 employees) and 8% medium companies (less than 250 employees).

Table 3. Individual elements in the new model development

Category	No of models the issue appears in:	Elements
Personal Factors	4	Educational experience, knowledge of IT
The Firm	3	Age, size, sector.
Organisational readiness	4	Advice sought, Internal pressures, Specialist skills in company, implementation issues (often linked to skills).
Perceived Value	5	Advantage over traditional methods, Measures of success, evaluation, perception of success.
External Pressures	5	Identification of external pressures in the decision making process, influences on the purchase.
Strategy	4	The level of decision making undertaken, reason for purchase, significance of purchase.

The categories and elements derived from this study are shown in table 3. The new model (table 3) encompasses 'measures of success' or return on investment (ROI) within the perceived value section. This element in an SME environment could be seen as the single most important factor and has been absent from prior models (Van Akkeren and Cavaye, 1999). It was encompassed in this way to include a pre-evaluation check (perceived benefits from previous models) and a post evaluation element not seen before. SME owner-managers have significant influence on ICT adoption and success rates; it is their 'perception' of the value to the company that is often either the inhibitor or the driver for the adoption. Previous models have looked at 'perceived usefulness' and 'perceived ease of use' of a specific technology investment. 'Perceived benefits' has been used more recently in surveys (Harindranath, 2007) and in this context this research attempts to broaden the concept to 'perceived value' to give a broader perspective and attempt to capture more than just the one aspect from the company.

5 Survey Findings and Discussion

The categories in the final model were adjusted according to the findings of the survey and some elements were merged to take account of the responses. The educational

Table 4. Summary of qualitative findings

Category	Elements	Findings
Personal Factors	Educational experience	This factor was a major influence in all other research areas related to SME growth and successful adoption and is again found to be a major influence within this research. The presence of an ICT professional through experience (self-taught) or through formal education was influential in success and also impacted the next factor of knowledge of IT.
	Knowledge of IT	Although knowledge of ICT is an important issue for all companies, if that knowledge of ICT has been gained through the educational experience of the owner-manager within ICT companies that was found to have an impact on both the company turnover and successful adoption. If an owner-manager considered themselves to be an ICT professional this also had an impact on both turnover and perceived success.
The Firm	Age, size, turnover.	These three factors were analysed together and it was found that there is sporadic growth and no guarantee of increased turnover as a company grows in terms of number of employees or years of operation. Neither was there any link between these factors and adoption. Companies were not more successful as they grew in experience.

Table 4. (*continued*)

	Turnover	Turnover was also examined alone and supports the fact that owner-managers who are degree holders have an increased turnover in comparison with non-degree holders. The discipline was irrelevant.
Organisational readiness	Advice sought	The advice sought is a major influence on the success of the adoption and in subsequent implementation problems. This study has again confirmed that most SMEs seek advice from the circle of known contacts.
	Specialist skills in company	The specialist skills examined here were the education of the owner-manager and whether that was formal or not and in ICT or not. This appears to have a major influence on adoption success as it impacts on both strategy and perceived value, may be indicating the presence of an ICT 'champion'.
	Implementation issues	The main implementation issues measured here were supplemented by asking what support the companies required. These companies have major implementation issues and concerns regarding support and the availability of consultancy support that can be trusted.
	Internal pressures	Very few companies recognised internal pressures although this has been identified as a barrier / enabler by other researchers. This could indicate that these companies are very reactive and do not attempt to drive forward the adoption agenda in their own company.

Table 4. (*continued*)

External Pressures	Influences on the purchase.	Main influences were seen as customers and upgrades and most upgrades were for customers. Demonstrating a very reactionary approach.
	Identification of external pressures in the decision making process	Most do not recognise external influences and when they do it is predominately customers or technology as above.
Strategy	Reason for purchase.	The main reasons for the purchase are those cited as influences under External Pressures. This demonstrates that micro companies' strategy is based on a reaction to either customers or technology and their reasoning does not extend beyond this.
	Significance of purchase	Most companies recognised the significance of technology being able to have an impact on the way the business was run. This may indicate that whilst they may not 'do' strategy there is willingness there and an understanding of the importance of technologies in their business which may require some awareness raising.
Perceived Value	Measures of success	Most measures of success were qualitative e.g. more profit or more customers. No companies use quantitative measures.
	Perception of success.	Seen predominately as efficiency or productivity gains. However as no econometric measures were used at all, this is mainly based on instinct.

attainment of the owner-manager still remains the most direct influence on an SME, although increasingly in ICT, SMEs having an educated ICT Professional in the company also cast a major influence on the success of adoption of the company as a whole. Levels of decision making became of lesser importance within the model as the majority of owner-managers in the sample had made the decision themselves. 'Advantage over traditional methods' was cited as an influence on investments along with other issues, it is therefore now incorporated as influences on the purchase rather than as a separate element.

Overall the issues arising would indicate a need to address the education of the owner-managers in the need to ensure that ICT purchases are aligned with their business needs. However as most micro SMEs see their strategy as being the next sale or the next customer this poses a particularly difficult field and business support actions are required for the ICT sector. The findings from the qualitative analysis are summarised in table 4. Those elements that companies did not consider to be a major influence have been removed from the model developed from the literature in table 3. In conclusion a number of points were highlighted by this research:

The owner-manager's knowledge and education was highlighted as essential in successful adoption. The findings indicated that it in order to be successful in this sector, a high level of education may be necessary, with over 50% holding a first degree and 20% holding post graduate qualifications. It is suggested that high technological competence and understanding of advances in this area may be necessary, especially as 24% of the respondents had an IT related degree and overall 70% considered them selves to be an IT Professional. The companies who had an owner-manager formally educated in ICT also reported feeling less need to use technology to attract new customers as only 2% felt this need, and less internal pressure stemming from the need to enhance performance with only 14% reporting this. Although other variables may affect this process, a thorough grounding in ICT will help with evaluation of technology as a means to enhance business growth. Companies were often focused on one set of customers and tried to make technology investments 'fit' their business needs and their customer's needs.

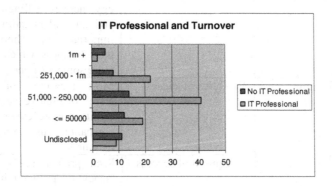

Fig. 2. IT professional vs Turnover for SMEs

Companies who had ICT professional skills in house had a higher turnover than those companies who did not. Also, those with no ICT Professional generally had a lower turnover (see Fig. 2). Previous research (Grandon et.al., 2004, Levy et al., 2005b, Van Akkeren and Cavaye, 1999, Thong and Yap, 1995, Iacovou, 1995, Rashid et al., 2001, Merhten et al., 2001, Storey, 1994) indicated that the presence of in-house skills is imperative in the successful adoption of technology. It would now appear that this also affects the growth in terms of turnover for ICT companies. It is believed that the sporadic rise and fall in turnover over time displayed by these companies may indicate how competitive the business environment is for ICT companies.

This research has again shown that most SMEs take their advice from friends and relatives (10%), ICT store representatives (12%), the Internet (24%), etc. In all cases companies indicated that they used the source they felt was the most reliable although this was not always seen as trustworthy. However, 54% stated they did not need advice, concerning the number of implementation problems encountered. This may mean that implementation problems could be exacerbated by the source of advice given prior to a decision to invest in new technologies that did not align well with the business model.

49% of implementation problems were due to lack of appropriate skills; in particular, technological know-how (10%) and third-party support (4%) were a problem. This is a major anxiety and may indicate these companies' inability to support other sectors. There is a need for policy makers to address how these companies can be supported to enhance their support of other sectors. Of more concern is the fact that these ICT companies did not recognise their own problems in this area, with many companies claiming they would not require any advice on what to purchase. The same companies later in the survey explained the implementation problems encountered and their support needs. Many do not recognise that making recommendations to customers and selecting ICT for their own business infrastructure which align to the business model require a very different skill set.

The majority of companies do not evaluate purchases (35%) or measure the success of those purchases (45%), using 'gut instinct' to make a decision as to the success of an adoption. Where a measure was used it was a single factor, usually described as 'efficiency' and none used an econometric measure. Companies stated such measures as more profit, no complaints from the customers, more customers, efficiency and simply 'It Works'. This may indicate that many SMEs simply do not understand the importance of measuring success in order to guide future investment.

Business impact was cited most often (54%) as the major impact afforded by adoption; this indicated that many found the adoption to have a major impact of how they conducted business. Many used ICT to develop their business and cited changes such as better communication, better customer demonstration facilities, a wider range of services, speedier software production etc. Again the indication from the findings is that the owner-manager education is imperative when recognising the significance of an adoption to the business, where significance indicates the subsequent impact of a purchase, with those formally educated in ICT indicating a more balanced approach to the drivers.

53% of the companies did not acknowledge any external pressures in their purchasing decisions. As many companies are reactive rather than proactive it could mean that they are simply unaware of the need to be vigilant of the macro environment, merely reacting instead to the need to respond to customers, implement new legislation, etc. 39% of companies cited keeping up with technology advances by upgrading the software or hardware and this was seen as the main influence on investment. The reasons for upgrades were cited as increasing speed, improving efficiency, increasing reliability, expanding storage, network security, running more sophisticated software environments, adding wireless and broadband technologies. These upgrades were viewed as necessary as the SMEs were often catching-up with new technologies.

Very few SMEs recognised the need to grow their business using new technological advances (1%) which may mean they are unaware of technological advances outside their field of expertise.

Perceived value to most companies (39%) is seen as being able to be more efficient. This was also cited as one of the main influences on the purchase, demonstrating that such companies can be very single-minded in their strategy with most still trying to increase efficiency and rarely focusing on innovative use or strategy. This leaves a very precarious situation for most companies as the perceived value of a purchase is explained in terms of its ability to increase efficiency. Yet, they do not subsequently measure that efficiency, citing instead the fact that they have had no complaints. The entire perception of success of an adoption, therefore, rests on the ability of the owner-manager to judge the successful increase in efficiency in a subjective manner. A number of issues are inherent in this and the need to increase the awareness of owner-managers about the importance of doing more than merely looking for the next sale will be a major hurdle to overcome.

Most companies also used a single 'perceived' measurement of success post-implementation. 39% viewed the fact that they had achieved the implementation and that it was working as the measure. For 32% if profit or customers had increased also, then this was considered a success. However, they had rarely actually measured the increase in profit or the increase in customer numbers. This often led to the attitude that technology was merely a cost and something that needed to be implemented in order to 'stay in business'. This past experience with adoption leads to a less than positive approach to subsequent adoptions. This can lead to a cycle of adoption only when necessary as the perception is not supported by historical data.

6 Conclusion and Conceptual Model Proposition

The factors evaluated through this qualitative research are shown in a conceptual model (Fig. 3) which is based on the Van Akkeren and Cavaye (1999) model. This new model demonstrates the impact of the owner-managers perception on the ICT adoption process. The owner-manager makes ICT investment decisions by using their own perception of the value of the purchase as the main criteria in the pre-evaluation stage. Post-adoption the owner-manager uses either the 'perception' of increased productivity, increased market share, or simply that 'it works' as a measure. This latter element has been missing from models published to date and forms the thrust of this conclusion. The suggestion is that the lack of historical data to feed into the next adoption situation means that the same mistakes are repeated, hence the feedback loop.

In this model the constraint variables are suggested as being those that impact the company in terms of size, sector, status and age, although those constraints are not directly tested through this research which concentrates on the ICT sector, this will prove to be constraints for further testing in other sectors. The moderator in this situation is seen as Government Intervention which has an opportunity to alter the course of adoption via funded initiatives and is also a factor which should be explored further, particularly in the wake of recent calls for closer collaboration between Government Department, Academics and Industry. The model is offered as a conceptual one that requires further evaluation to confirm or refute.

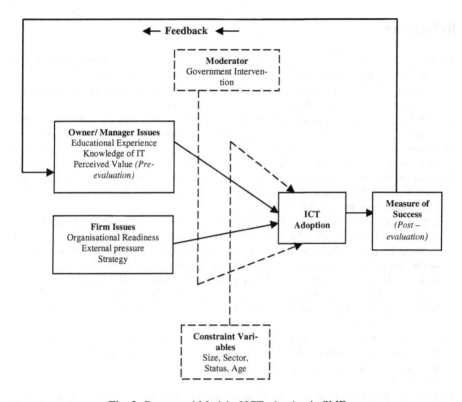

Fig. 3. Conceptual Model of ICT adoption in SMEs

Many past UK Government intervention initiatives concentrated on business support through Business Link, the Learning and Skills Council (LSC) and eSkills UK and e-business adoption initiatives. Most of this support is misguided and at the wrong level for these companies (Graham, 2007, Martin and Matlay, 2001), who not only need specific initiatives aimed at the technology related to the market they are in, but more basic support to help with implementation and adoption of IT. Currently they rely on instinct and/or customer-pressure which forces a situation which they then find costly and resource-intensive. They also need help in developing a feeling of trust, skills initiatives designed to improve their business and help with particular technological advances; including measures for evaluating technology more strategically.

The challenge therefore is two-fold. For Government initiatives, it is about recognising their role in the adoption process and that the main objective should be raising of awareness and embedding of appropriate skills within companies to endow them the ability to adopt successfully in the future. For academicians, overcoming the industry/academia divide and continuing this important quest should be prioritised. Especially as many academicians in this field have moved into other areas or, recognising that the issues are both complex and multi-layered have moved their work into the micro issues, leaving companies with no answers to their quandary.

References

Ai-Qirim, N.A.Y. (ed.): Electronic commerce in small and medium-sized enterprises: frameworks, issues, and implications. Idea Group Publishing, Melbourne (2003)

Bagozzi, R.P., Davis, F.D., Warshaw, P.R.: Development and test of a theory of technological learning and usage. Human Relations 45(7), 660–686 (1992)

Bennett, R.J., Robson, P.: The market for external business advice services in Britain. In: Proceedings: 21st ISBA Conference Celebrating the Small Business, pp. 770–790 (1998)

Blackburn, R., Athayde, R.: Making the Connection, the Effectiveness of Internet Training in Small Businesses. Education and Training 42(4) (2000)

Bradford, M., Florin, J.: Examining the Role of Innovation Diffusion Factors on the Implementation Success of Enterprise Resource Planning systems. International Journal of Accounting Information Systems 4(3), 205–225 (2003)

Costello, P., Garner, S., Homer, G., Thompson, D.: Can the Internet Provide the West Midlands Automotive Industry with the Ultimate Lean Production Tool?-A Case Study of the Autolean Project. In: Proceedings: 2nd International SMESME Conference: Manufacturing and Business Systems Group University of Plymouth, March 29-31 (1999)

Costello, P., Moreton, R., Sloane, A.: IT Evaluation Frameworks – Do they make a valuable contribution? A critique of some of the classic models for use by SMEs. In: Proceedings of ECITE 2006: 13th European Conference on IT Evaluation University of Genova, Italy, September 28-29 (2006)

Costello, P., Chibelushi, C., Sloane, A.: ICT Adoption by ICT SMEs in the West Midlands – the forgotten ICT Adopters. In: Proceedings of the 2nd European Conference on Information Management and Evaluation, Royal Holloway, University of London, UK, September 11-12 (2008)

Chwelos, P., Benbasat, I., Dexter, A.: Research Report: Empirical Test of an EDI Adoption Model. Information Systems Research 12(3), 304–321 (2001)

Culkin, N., Smith, D.: An Emotional Business: A Guide to Understanding the Motivations of Small Business Decision Makers. Qualitative Market Research: An International Journal 3(3), 145–157 (2000)

Davis, D., Bagozzi, R., Warshaw, P.: User acceptance of computer technology: a comparison of two theoretical models. Management Science 35(8), 982–1003 (1989)

Fishbein, M., Ajzen, I.: Belief, attitude, intention, and behavior: An introduction to theory and research. Addison-Wesley, Reading (1975),
http://www.people.umass.edu/aizen/f&a1975.html
(Date accessed: 15/07/2007)

Grandon, E., Pearson, J.M.: Electronic Commerce Adoption: An Empirical Study of Small and Medium US Business. Information & Management 42, 197–216 (2004)

Graham, F.: The Skills Survey 2007: A report into Skills for Enterprise and Growth for the ICT Cluster by Red Box Research (June 2007)

Harindranath, G., Barnes, D., Dyerson, R.: ICT Adoption and use in UK SMEs. In: Proceedings: The European Conference on Information Management and Evaluation, University of Montpellier 1, Montpellier, France, September 20-21 (2007)

Husein, T., Moreton, R., Sloane, A.: Electronic Commerce: A consideration of implementation for SMEs. Journal of Management Studies 5(1), 77–83 (1996)

Iacovou, A.L., Benbara, I., Dexter, A.S.: Electronic data Interchange, Small Organisations; Adoption and Impact of Technology. MIS Quarterly 19(4), 465–485 (1995)

Jackson, M., Sloane, A.: A Model for analysing the success of adopting new technologies focusing on electronic commerce. Business Process Management Journal 13(1), 121–138 (2007)

Kai-Uwe Brock, J.: Information and Technology in the Small Firm. Prentice Hall/Pearson Education, Englewood Cliffs (2000)

King-Turner, M., Bonnett, M.: Adoption of Open Source in SMEs: Lessons from the Front Line. Session in O'Reilly European Open Source Convention, Amsterdam (October 19, 2005)

Lauder, G., Westhall, A.: Small Firms Online. Commision on Public Policy in British Business, 6 (1997)

Lefebvre, E., Lefebvre, L.: Information and Communication Technologies: The Impact of Their Adoption on Small and Medium-sized Enterprises. IDRC Booktique ORDI (1996)

Levy, M., Powell, P.: Strategies for Growth in SMEs. The Role of Information and Information Systems. Elsevier Butterworth Heinmann, Oxford (2005a)

Levy, M., Powell, P., Worrall, L.: Strategic Intent and E-business in SMEs: Enablers and Inhibitors. Information Resources Management Journal 18(4), 1–20 (2005b)

Macgregor, R.C., Vrazalic, L.: A Basic Model of Electronic Commerce Adoption Barriers, A study of regional small businesses in Sweden and Australia. Journal of Small Business and Enterprise Development 12(4), 510–527 (2005)

Martin, L., Matlay, H.: Blanket approaches to promoting ICT in small firms: some lessons from the DTI ladder adoption model in the UK. Internet Research: Electronic Networking Applications and Policy 11(5), 399–410 (2001), http://www.emerald-library.com/ft (Date accessed: 2/03/2002)

Mehrtens, J., Cragg, P., Mills, A.: A model of internet adoption by SMEs. Information & management 39(3), 165–176 (2001)

Mercer, D.: Industry Scenarios: short-termism revealed. Industrial Management & Data Systems 96(8), 23–27 (1996)

Nathalie, N.M., Marsh, A.: Small Business and Information Technology: Risk, Planning and Change. Journal of Business and Enterprise Development 5(3), 228–245 (1998)

Premkumar, G., Roberts, M.: Adoption of new information technologies (1999); Rashid, M.A., Al-Qirim, N.A.: E-Commerce Technology Adoption Framework by New Zealand Small to Medium Enterprises. Research Letters in the Information and Mathematical Sciences 2(1), 63–70 (2001)

Rogers, E.M.: Diffusion of Innovations, 5th edn. Free Press, New York (2003)

Sarosa, S., Zowghi, D.: Strategy for adopting information technology for SMEs: Experience in adopting email within an Indonesian furniture company. Electronic Journal of Information Systems Evaluation 6(2), 165–176 (2003)

Sheppard, S., Hooton, S.: Regional Economic Impact of ICTs and the Role of RDAs/DAs. A White Paper: Informing the Policy Debate. Adroit Economics Ltd. (2007)

Thong, J.Y.L., Yap, C.S.: An information technology adoption model for small businesses. In: Proceedings: IFIP WG8.6 Working Conference on Diffusion and Adoption of Information Technology, Leangkollen, Oslo, Norway, October 14-17, 1995, pp. 429–442 (1995)

Storey, D.: Understanding the Small Business Sector. Thomson Business Press, London (1994)

Tornatzky, L.G., Klein, K.J.: Innovation characteristics and innovation adoption implementation: a meta-analysis of findings. IEEE Transactions on Engineering Management 29(1), 28–45 (1982)

Van Akkeren, J., Cavaye, A.: Factors Affecting Entry-Level Internet Technology Adoption by Small Business in Australia: An Empirical Study. In: Proceedings: 10th Australasian Conference on Information Systems, pp. 1716–1728. Victoria University of Wellington, New Zealand (1999)

Venkatesh, V., Davis, F.D.: A theoretical extension of the technology acceptance model: Four longitudinal field studies. Management Science 46(2), 186–204 (2000)

Venkatesh, V., Morris, M., Davis, G., Davies, F.: User Acceptance of Information Technology: Toward a Unified View. MIS Quarterly 27(3), 425–478 (2003)

Author Index